Behind the Curve

Can Manufacturing Still Provide Inclusive Growth?

Behind the Curve

Can Manufacturing Still Provide Inclusive Growth?

Robert Z. Lawrence

PETERSON INSTITUTE FOR INTERNATIONAL ECONOMICS

Washington, DC
September 2024

Robert Z. Lawrence, nonresident senior fellow at the Peterson Institute for International Economics, is the Albert L. Williams Professor of Trade and Investment at the John F. Kennedy School of Government at Harvard University, a Research Associate at the National Bureau of Economic Research and a Global Fellow at the MasterCard Center for Inclusive Growth. He was appointed by President Clinton to serve as a member of his Council of Economic Advisers in 1999. He held the New Century Chair as a nonresident senior fellow at the Brookings Institution and founded and edited the *Brookings Trade Forum*. Lawrence has been a senior fellow in the Economic Studies Program at Brookings (1983–91) and a professorial lecturer at the Johns Hopkins School of Advanced International Studies and Yale University.

PETERSON INSTITUTE FOR INTERNATIONAL ECONOMICS

1750 Massachusetts Avenue, NW, Washington, DC 20036-1903
(202) 328-9000   www.piie.com

Adam S. Posen, President
Steven R. Weisman, Vice President for Publications

For reprints/permission to use please contact the APS customer service department at:

Copyright Clearance Center, Inc.,
222 Rosewood Drive, Danvers, MA 01923;
or email requests to: info@copyright.com

Library of Congress Cataloging-in-Publication
Paperback ISBN 9780881327472
Ebook ISBN 9780881327489

Cover Design: Richard Fletcher
Cover Photo: ©tolgart/iStock/

This publication has been subjected to a prepublication peer review intended to ensure analytical quality. The views expressed are those of the author. This publication is part of the overall program of the Peterson Institute for International Economics, as endorsed by its Board of Directors, but it does not necessarily reflect the views of individual members of the Board or of the Institute's staff or management.

The Peterson Institute for International Economics is a private nonpartisan, nonprofit institution for rigorous, intellectually open, and indepth study and discussion of international economic policy. Its purpose is to identify and analyze important issues to make globalization beneficial and sustainable for the people of the United States and the world, and then to develop and communicate practical new approaches for dealing with them. Its work is funded by a highly diverse group of philanthropic foundations, private corporations, and interested individuals, as well as income on its capital fund. About 12 percent of the Institute's resources in 2023 were provided by contributors from outside the United States.

I dedicate this book to my wonderful family with love.

*I am deeply grateful to my wife, Nicole,
my daughters, Alex and Tasha, and their husbands, Dan and Daniel,
for the support and encouragement they gave me as I wrote this book.
I am eagerly looking forward to spending more time with
my grandchildren, Baila, Simeon, and Lev, now that it is done.*

Contents

Online Data Replication Package and Chapter Appendices
The data replication package for this book and appendices to chapters 1, 2, and 4 are available online at https://www.piie.com/bookstore/behind-curve-can-manufacturing-still-provide-inclusive-growth.

Preface

Manufacturing has been central to policy debates concerning material growth and progress for over two centuries, for economic as well as political reasons. Most economies that have surpassed middle-income status, apparently did so by working their way up the manufacturing export ladder. Growth in manufacturing employment provided high-earning work opportunities for less educated workers from the mid-19th through the mid-20th centuries, though the significance of this channel to the overall rise of the middle class is exaggerated in the public imagination. Manufacturing displays the most easily measurable forms of productivity growth to statisticians, the most discernible advances in technology to visual media, and the most intuitive evidence of economic competitiveness to the general public. Accordingly, government and popular support for manufacturing—whether through subsidies, training, public investment, or trade protection and negotiations—is evident in economies at every stage of development.

Unsurprisingly, rises and falls in manufacturing trade between economies have therefore been a recurrent source of conflict in the international economy. Many in the United States have blamed flawed trade and industrial policies, thought to be inadequate to international competition with China and others since 2000 (or with Germany and Japan in the 1980s and 1990s), for a sustained decline in the manufacturing share of the nation's workforce. Advocates of various stripes, including senior officials of both the Trump and Biden administrations, contend that these policy lapses have deprived workers and communities of potential opportunities to enjoy middle class lives. Beyond laying blame, they claim that different policies can restore manufacturing to its previous role in bringing prosperity to less educated workers and the towns they live in.

Robert Z. Lawrence challenges these views head-on with his research in this study, *Behind the Curve: Can Manufacturing Still Provide Inclusive Growth?* He develops a general theory of economic development that integrates the effects of trade, technological change, and spending patterns on a national economy. Lawrence clearly demonstrates that, while national policies and characteristics play a role, ongoing manufacturing employment share declines are widespread, seen even in trade surplus economies like China and Germany. These long-term trends result primarily from deeply rooted structural forces that are common to all countries. These forces lead a nation's share of manufacturing employment to follow an inverted U-shaped curve as countries develop, regardless of whether they run trade deficits or surpluses. He amasses compelling evidence that all advanced economies, including those with longstanding manufacturing trade surpluses such as Germany and Japan, and even many emerging-market economies with manufacturing surpluses such as China, Singapore, and Korea are now moving along the downward slope of the curve.

Lawrence's analytic framework for the determinants of manufacturing employment is then used to understand why the observed as predicted U-shaped curve has shifted downwards over time. In other words, manufacturing employment for any given economy peaks at a lower level than in the past. This has meant that countries that have emerged more recently will be unable to reach the manufacturing employment shares attained by those that developed earlier. As a result, they will experience difficulties in providing sufficient opportunities for workers leaving the rural and informal sectors. As with employment share declines seen in the already industrialized economies, the factors driving these trends are unlikely to change, even in the face of activist policy prescriptions.

The book then offers a more granular study of US manufacturing employment over the postwar-to-present period that applies the theory of the inverted U-shaped curve. It shows the important role played by manufacturing in US growth, income distribution, and regional convergence in the immediate postwar era. It then considers how after the 1970s changes in production technology, trade, and the response of spending on industrial goods to demand reduced the share of the employment in US manufacturing overall, especially for non-college-educated workers. This contributed to the reduced inclusivity of US growth in numerous dimensions, including growing inequality of wages along the lines of skill; declining shares of income that accrue to labor; exclusion of male workers without a college education from most of the fruits of US growth in recent decades; and the divergence of income among US regions.

That said, the US debate over declining manufacturing especially after 2000 is mistakenly centered on whether it was trade or technology—was it China or robots?—that took the jobs. Lawrence's analysis establishes that a slowdown in demand associated with two severe recessions between 2000 and 2010 played as major a role as trade or technology. While trade competition had detrimental effects on some specific US workers and local communities, the national multiyear impact of trade explains only a small part of the overall declines in manufacturing employment.

Behind the Curve's final section argues that industrial policy measures proposed or adopted in many countries will not increase the share of manufacturing employment, either sustainably or substantially. Policy measures that emphasize increased self-sufficiency, green growth, and development of digital technologies are likely to continue the trend toward less inclusive growth. In particular, while the programs of the Biden administration may succeed in boosting local manufacturing employment in a few US states, they will not generate a broad renaissance in US manufacturing. Accordingly, such measures will do little to improve the opportunities for most US workers without college degrees and most ex-urban communities that have stagnated. To revitalize the American middle class, increasing economic inclusivity requires measures beyond manufacturing-focused policies that promote a more equitable sharing of the fruits of technological advancement between people, places, and countries.

Both Lawrence and the Peterson Institute for International Economics (PIIE) have worked for decades at the nexus of economic development, labor economics, and international trade and investment. These studies have repeatedly uncovered evidence that economic nationalism is unlikely to result in either rising manufacturing employment or broader economic inclusion, and such policies will often result in the opposite. This is because openness, unfair trading practices, and trade deficits are not a major source of declines in manufacturing employment. Lawrence's past contributions on this set of issues include *Rising Tide: Is Growth in Emerging Economies Good for the United States?*; *Single World, Divided Nations? International Trade and the OECD Labor Markets*; and *Can America Compete?*. Previous PIIE studies of manufacturing trade and industrial policy include Marcus Noland and Howard Pack's *Industrial Policy in an Era of Globalization: Lessons from Asia*; Gary Hufbauer and Euijin Jung's *Scoring 50 Years of US Industrial Policy, 1970–2020*; Laura d'Andrea Tyson's *Who's Bashing Whom? Trade Conflict in High-Technology Industries*; a series of studies of Biden administration initiatives by Chad P. Bown; Arvind Subramanian's *Manufacturing or Services? An Indian Illustration of a Development Dilemma*; and my own *The Price of Nostalgia: America's Self-Defeating Economic Retreat*. We are proud to publish Lawrence's

Behind the Curve as a fresh and significant advancement of research on this economically and politically salient policy issue.

* * *

The Peterson Institute for International Economics is a private nonpartisan, nonprofit institution for rigorous, intellectually open, and indepth study and discussion of international economic policy. Its purpose is to identify and analyze important issues to making globalization beneficial and sustainable for the people of the United States and the world and then to develop and communicate practical new approaches for dealing with them.

The Institute's work is funded by a highly diverse group of philanthropic foundations, private corporations, and interested individuals, as well as income on its capital fund. About 12 percent of the Institute's resources in 2023 were provided by contributors from outside the United States. A list of all our financial supporters is posted at https://piie.com/sites/default/files/supporters.pdf.

The Executive Committee of the Institute's Board of Directors bears overall Responsibility for the Institute's direction, gives general guidance and approval to its research program, and evaluates its performance in pursuit of its mission. The Institute's President is responsible for the identification of topics that are likely to become important over the medium term (one to three years) that should be addressed by Institute scholars. This rolling agenda is set in close consultation with the Institute's research staff, taking input from its distinguished Board of Directors and other stakeholders.

The President makes the final decision to publish any individual Institute study, following independent internal and external review of the work. Interested readers may access the data and computations underlying Institute publications for research and replication by searching titles at www.piie.com.

The Institute hopes that its research and other activities will contribute to building a stronger foundation for international economic policy around the world. We invite readers of these publications to let us know how they think we can best accomplish this objective.

ADAM S. POSEN
President
Peterson Institute for International Economics

Acknowledgments

I am grateful to the Peterson Institute for International Economics (PIIE) and to the MasterCard Center for Inclusive Growth for financial support. I also thank participants in seminars at Harvard University, Harvard Kennedy School, PIIE, and Cape Town University. I thank Martin Baily, Olivier Blanchard, Robert Feenstra, Gordon Hanson, Brad Jensen, Marcus Noland, Steve Weisman, and Kei-Mu Yi for comments. I am also deeply thankful to Joao Alcantara, Aden Barton, Jacob Bicknell, Galit Eizman, Jack Fetsch, Austin Lensch, Yan Liu, M. D. Mangini, Rundong Ji, and Wei Meng for research assistance; Madi Sarsenbayev, Egor Gornostay, and Julieta Contreras for their excellent help on data accuracy; Madona Devasahayam, Barbara Karni, and Susann Luetjen for superb editorial and production assistance; and Daniel Lashkari, Yan Liu, and Lawrence Edwards for their coauthorship on parts of this study.

Introduction

Manufacturing jobs, once the backbone of economically advanced countries, have declined as a share of employment in recent decades, darkening opportunities for middle-class improvement. To reverse this phenomenon, many governments have erected new import barriers and adopted industrial policies that provide public support for domestic industries, especially those considered strategically important.

For the most part, these approaches have failed to arrest the trends. They have failed because the structural forces that led to the decline in the share of manufacturing jobs—trade, technological change, and changes in consumer spending patterns—are not likely to be reversed. Government-directed policies will not return manufacturing employment shares to the levels of the past.

Manufacturing played a historic role in growth and income distribution in the United States (and elsewhere), and manufacturing employment can still provide important benefits. But the evidence shows that in all advanced economies and many higher-income emerging-market economies, the manufacturing sector is following the earlier historic path of agriculture, marked by declining output, spending, and employment shares.

The challenge facing leaders throughout the world is daunting. The decline in the manufacturing employment share has made economic growth less inclusive, dimming the prospects of workers without college education and increasing the regional polarization of economic growth within countries. In the United States in just the decade after 2000, almost 6 million manufacturing jobs were lost. In many other industrial econo-

mies manufacturing employment shares have fallen. In developing economies, manufacturing no longer provides employment opportunities at the
rates it once did.

This book examines the causes and consequences of these developments, in order to help policymakers develop policies that could help ease
the pain of these declines and address real rather than imaginary causes.
The focus is on the United States, although relevant developments elsewhere are included to convince policymakers in the United States and elsewhere that their experiences are shared and often not evidence of unique
national attributes or policies.

The research presented provides overwhelming evidence that as countries develop, the share of manufacturing employment tends to move along
an inverted U path, rising as economic development takes off and then
falling as growth matures. The hump-shaped path that the manufacturing
employment share (MES) follows as countries grow is evident in almost
every country. In the United States, the pattern is evident in employment
share data over 200 years. The curve is also evident when the trend in the
MES is plotted against per capita income in a sample that pools data from
42 countries over five decades, and it is found when these countries are
grouped by level of development and by region.[1]

Regression analysis indicates that once unique country characteristics
are controlled for, the impact of rising per capita incomes almost always
produces a hump-shaped MES curve. And strikingly, the decline is also
evident in the very countries associated with manufacturing prowess, such
as Japan, South Korea, Singapore, Germany, and China, all of which are
now on the downward-sloping part of the curve.[2]

This book offers a general theory that explains this evidence by
accounting for the typical evolution of employment shares in agriculture, manufacturing, and services as economies develop. In the theory the
demand for labor in each sector responds to three drivers of structural
change: sector productivity growth, aggregate income growth, and trade,
producing the same hump-shaped path that evolves with economic development.

Despite the power of the theory and the overwhelming evidence of this
phenomenon, the public remains unconvinced. Just as the declining role of
agriculture was resisted more than two centuries ago by many who believed

---

1. Dani Rodrik (2016, 7) finds similar curves for manufacturing real output and nominal
shares in income, though the output shares tend to peak later.

2. In China, which had enjoyed manufacturing-led growth between 2013 and 2018,
manufacturing employment fell by 15.4.million. See Conference Board International Labor
Comparisons, https://www.conference-board.org/ilcprogram.

that land alone could provide real wealth, a widespread view persists that policies aimed at revitalizing domestic manufacturing production can reverse the declining MES trends, spur growth, and enhance opportunity for large numbers of less educated workers. Part of the reason for public doubts is the attraction of nostalgia and a failure to appreciate the fundamental forces driving change. It is also much easier to blame the erosion of the MES on flawed policies at home or unfair trade practices abroad than to accept the role of powerful universal forces that are unlikely to be reversed.

The Biden administration's aim to "Build Back Better" from the COVID-19 pandemic may provide some people with benefits from government spending and spur manufacturing employment in some states, but the manufacturing employment share is now so low that it is unlikely to do much to bring about more inclusion for most workers without college degrees or to help most stagnating local economies. Many other countries are also implementing new industrial policies to promote their domestic manufacturing, sometimes at the expense of their trading partners. They also claim these policies will enhance domestic technological capacity, bolster national security, improve supply chain resilience, and decarbonize the economy while providing well-paying jobs for workers without college degrees, especially in certain localities. Proponents of these initiatives sometimes invoke a narrative that blames the problems of the working classes on neoliberal policies that have promoted globalization and the interests of capital at the expense of workers and see greater government intervention and protectionism as the solution to worker misfortunes. While some of these new policies could temporarily boost domestic manufacturing employment, their aggregate labor market impacts are likely to be small. They could even be counterproductive, strengthening the very trends they are trying to reverse.

Manufacturing still contributes to national prosperity. Even as the manufacturing employment share has fallen because of the higher productivity growth in the sector, especially in the high-tech industries, manufacturing output continues to grow, although as with employment, as a share of GDP manufacturing output also generally follows a hump-shaped profile with development. Manufacturing accounts for most spending on research and development, paving the way for innovation and improved living standards. Semiconductors play a key role in national security, artificial intelligence, and the Internet of Things. Computers, cellphones, servers, and satellites provide the hardware that drive the digital economy; solar panels, wind turbines, electric vehicles, power grids, and heat pumps are needed to address climate change; medical equipment such as centrifuges and sequencers plays a key role in cell and gene therapy; and electron microscopes are crucial for nanotechnology. Manufacturing also still provides relatively high-paying jobs for the workers, predominantly men, who are lucky enough to obtain them.[3] But manufacturing's role in generating inclusive growth has declined. The manufacturing jobs of the future will require more training and education, leaving certain workers and places behind, and government support of the sector that encourages it to be more technologically advanced may actually hasten the problem of lost jobs for workers with low levels of education.

Manufacturing's Historic Role

The past was different. By allowing workers to move from jobs in agriculture, where their productivity was low, to jobs in factories, where they were more productive, manufacturing offered the chance for unskilled and less educated workers, especially men, to work in midlevel occupations, where they could earn middle-class incomes. Manufacturing employment growth encouraged the formation of unions and political parties that represented labor and often improved the wages, benefits, working conditions, and legal rights of all members of the lower and middle classes. Manufacturing plants also served as the economic and social focal points of many communities, creating common identities and cultures, emblematic in the nicknames of US cities such as Detroit (the Motor City), Pittsburgh (the Steel City), Grand Rapids (the Furniture City), and Akron (the Rubber Capital of the World). As production technologies evolved, they became standardized and more mobile, allowing poorer communities, especially in the south of the United States, to attract investment and converge toward the income levels of richer communities.

Manufacturing also increased the inclusion of many developed and developing economies in global growth. It enabled countries to become richer by escaping the limitations of their low domestic demand by exporting. Relatively small countries such as Belgium, the Netherlands, Sweden, and Switzerland became wealthy by exporting manufactured goods. Asian economies—some poorly endowed with natural resources, such as Japan, South Korea, Hong Kong, Singapore, Taiwan, and China—also developed through manufacturing export-led growth. Poor countries also attracted foreign firms and obtained access to advanced technology to produce intermediate inputs at low cost.

---

3. In the United States, for example, taking education, gender, race, and ages into account, the sector pays premium wages at all skill levels. See Langdon and Lehrman (2012) and Mishel (2018).

Changes in Manufacturing: Technologies, Places, and Politics

The digital revolution fundamentally changed manufacturing technologies, reducing the relative demand for workers without college degrees, a development known as skill-biased technological change. As automation proceeded, and technologies evolved, the once relatively large share of labor income in manufacturing fell in both the United States and Europe.[4] Today's automobiles are effectively computers with wheels. Manufacturing's fixed capital increasingly consists of intangible intellectual property assets, such as software, databases, patents, organizational capital, and branding, in which workers with college degrees play more important roles than workers with less education.

Manufactured products are now "made in the world," with inputs produced in many economies linked in global value chains (as people all over the world learned when the COVID-19 pandemic hit). This offshoring sometimes occurs within multinational firms and sometimes at arm's length, through networks centered on assembly hubs in places such as China, Mexico, and Central Europe. Generally, labor-intensive tasks such as assembly are performed where labor is cheap, and tasks involving innovation, design, and marketing are performed where educated labor is abundant. Although less significant than commonly believed, offshoring has hurt some less-educated midlevel workers in advanced economies, whose jobs can be routinized and performed abroad.

Another major factor in the decline of manufacturing employment is often overlooked. As incomes have risen, the share of spending on manufactured goods in all advanced economies has steadily declined, while spending on services has increased (see figure 1.2 in chapter 1).

All these factors have reduced the relative demand for lower-skilled workers, reducing the relative wages of workers without college degrees throughout the US economy (see figure 5.4 in chapter 5). These developments in manufacturing reinforced the broader national economic trends of noninclusive and unequal growth that occurred after 1980, ushering in a period in which US income growth slowed for all but the top 1 percent of households and income inequality increased.

Regional effects have had a major impact on how Americans perceive these trends. Since the 1980s, manufacturing plants in many towns and cities in the US Rust Belt have closed, because of technological change. At the

---

4. For the United States, see Robert Z. Lawrence, Labor's Waning Share in Manufacturing, PIIE Chart, February 27, 2015, https://www.piie.com/research/piie-charts/piie-chart-labors-waning-share-manufacturing. For Europe, see Dimova (2019).

same time, "superstar" cities—cities such as New York, Boston, Washington, San Francisco, and Seattle—thrived. Some people in these cities worked in high-tech manufacturing but most worked in services, information technology, media, finance, and government—and increasingly in jobs that required college degrees. Similar geographic developments were evident in Europe, as the locus of manufacturing moved eastward toward Central Europe, leaving behind stagnating regions whose experiences resemble those in the US Rust Belt.[5]

The political impacts of these developments for people and places have been seismic. Slowing economic growth in some parts of the world and cutbacks in social welfare spending have widened political polarization. This has led to the rise of "outsiders" like former President Donald Trump in the United States and right-wing parties in Europe, as populist and nationalist movements have become much stronger.[6] Places like Wales, the Midlands, and Northern England voted for Brexit as much out of despair as conviction.[7]

Premature Deindustrialization

Advanced economies are not alone in experiencing changes in the role of manufacturing. The inverted U curve relating the MES to income has been continuously shifting downward and peaking at lower income levels in many countries. This problem is especially pressing in Central America, sub-Saharan Africa, South Asia, and the Middle East, where the share of the population under 30 seeking work has experienced explosive growth and youth unemployment remains high. It is not surprising that the borders and shores of rich countries are increasingly filled with desperate immigrants seeking better opportunities—another trend igniting populist political responses.

In principle, developing economies could offset these domestic pressures by increasing their manufacturing exports. But the competitive environment has become more difficult than it was. To improve their export

---

5. Rosés and Wolf (2018) label as "industrial losers" European regions such as Hainut and the rest of Wallonia in Belgium, Wales in the United Kingdom, Haute-Normandie and Nord-Pas-de Calais in Northern France, and the Saxon regions in Eastern Germany.

6. For evidence that globalization and manufacturing have played an important role in populism see Helen Milner, "Globalization, Populism and the Decline of the Welfare State," International Institute for Strategic Studies blog, February 14, 2019, https://www.iiss.org/blogs/survival-blog/2019/02/globalisation-populism-and-the-decline-of-the-welfare-state.

7. For evidence of the role of trade in increasing support for the radical right in Europe and Brexit, see Colantone and Stanig (2018).

opportunities, many countries reduced their trade barriers and attracted foreign investment in order to join global supply chains. After 2012, however, the growth in global goods trade slowed down, as countries such as China added more value at home. Trade frictions increased as a result of US policies under the Trump administration, most of them kept on the books by President Joseph R. Biden Jr. The COVID-19 pandemic led many countries to question their reliance on international markets for global supplies of key inputs such as medicines, minerals, and semiconductors. In 2022, the war in Ukraine caused additional disruptions to global commodity markets, raising more questions about foreign dependence.

Nonetheless the outlook for trade is not entirely bleak. Amid all of these setbacks, digital e-commerce has flourished, new multicountry trade deals have been signed in Asia and Africa; and several developing economies, including Vietnam, Cambodia, and Mexico, have been able to partially replace China in global supply chains.

Dim Outlook for Less Educated Workers

The shift toward increased demand for skills in manufacturing seems set to continue. Promoting advanced manufacturing technologies is now a central objective of industrial policies in both advanced and developing economies. Increasingly, countries seek mastery of labor-saving technologies (such as robotics and 3D printing) and skill-intensive technologies (such as nanotechnology and advanced materials). Some are designing and building equipment for the Internet of Things and 5G and 6G telecommunications. Some are developing sophisticated green technologies such as renewable energy and electric vehicles. These new technologies will displace many workers who earn high wages in fossil fuel–based industries, including the production of vehicles based on internal combustion engines. The shift to autonomous vehicles could also lead to significant labor displacement (Groshen et al. 2019). The use of artificial intelligence (AI) is growing by leaps and bounds.

These efforts may spur growth. But most of these innovations are likely to further increase the relative demand for more skilled and educated workers (although the net skill bias of AI is as yet unknown). Given these fundamental changes in production technologies and products in advanced economies, many of the workers who once worked in manufacturing are no longer employable in that sector. And despite efforts to achieve "climate justice" and "leave no one behind" in climate change policies, the activities stimulated by the new policies are more likely to take place in cities centered on digital technologies and populated with college-educated workers with superior technological capabilities than in the former manufacturing hubs, which are populated by less educated workers, and in locations endowed with sun and wind rather than fossil fuels.

People with less education will have jobs installing these technologies and building the infrastructure they require; the construction industry will provide workers without college degrees with more opportunities. But once the investment in the plants using these technologies is completed, the opportunities that construction and maintenance provide to the less skilled are unlikely to make up for those that are lost.

Organization of This Volume

This book analyzes the causes of the changed role of manufacturing in providing employment opportunities and its consequences. It is divided into three parts.

Part I uses theory and international data to explore the evolution of manufacturing employment as countries develop. It presents a simplified general theory of structural change in an economy with three sectors (agriculture, manufacturing, and services) to show how the interaction of technological change, income growth, and trade determine the hump-shaped MES curve that countries have followed as they develop. It shows that, regardless of whether countries run trade deficits or surpluses in manufactured goods, once their manufacturing employment share peaks, countries tend to experience declining manufacturing employment shares. It also finds that higher productivity in manufacturing at each level of development and declining shares of investment are the causes most closely associated with lower manufacturing employment peaks reached by countries that develop later.

Part II uses the United States as a case study of the historical relationship between manufacturing and inclusive growth for people and places. It shows how, in the first three postwar decades, manufacturing helped the United States provide opportunities for non-college-educated workers to earn middle-class wages and poorer US states to grow more rapidly than richer states by attracting manufacturing investment and workers. By contrast, technological changes due especially to the digital revolution, changes in patterns of demand due to higher incomes, and, to a lesser degree, international trade reduced the manufacturing employment share and transformed its production processes to require more educated workers. Together these changes adversely impacted the sector's role in providing opportunities for less skilled workers and poorer places.

Part III considers the impacts of new industrial and trade policies on manufacturing's economic role. It describes efforts by the United States, the European Union, Japan, and China to enhance digital technologies, build more resilient global supply chains, and invest in renewable energy to decarbonize growth, through policies that promote domestic manufacturing, sometimes at the expense of products made by trading partners. The analysis shows that such policies are inadequate to restore the inclusivity of growth and thus offers proposals to improve the welfare of more people and places.

The three parts of the study reinforce one another, and challenge widely held views about the reasons the MES has declined and the potential for reversing it. The theory of and evidence on the MES curve expose widely held misconceptions about the causes of the declines in the MES in many countries and the inadequacies of the emphasis placed on manufacturing, in recent industrial policy initiatives, for generating truly inclusive growth. The declines in the MES are not basically the result of recent trade agreements, and although in some countries trade has played a role, in general, trade accounts for a relatively small share of deindustrialization.

In particular, the diminishing importance of manufacturing employment has been a feature of structural change in the United States since the 1950s, long before trade became a significant factor in the postwar American economy. The MES has declined in both economies adopting relatively free market policies (Hong Kong, the United States, the United Kingdom, Germany) and economies with highly interventionist industrial policies (Japan, South Korea, China), calling into question claims that neoliberal policies are the major reasons for the declines in some countries.

Given the diminished role of manufacturing in generating employment and growth, the Biden administration's industrial policies may be effective in strengthening supply chains, enhancing US technological capabilities, and advancing the green transition and may also boost manufacturing employment in some states. But claims of a broadly based industrial renaissance in the United States are oversold; the impact of the policies on the overall US labor force (and the Rust Belt in particular) will be very small. To make US growth more inclusive, policies that promote growth and inclusion beyond manufacturing are needed. First and foremost is the need to maintain high levels of employment without inflation, because a high-pressure economy is an especially powerful driver of opportunities for low-wage workers. In addition, specific measures should include spending on labor-intensive infrastructure; more progressive taxes and transfers; child allowances; adjustment and job placement assistance; wage-loss insurance for workers who are dislocated, regardless of whether their job loss is caused by trade or other reasons beyond their control; and grants for skills training and apprenticeship programs for workers without college degrees to equip them and help them find jobs that give them access to career ladders that lead to middle-class incomes. Structural policies should be expanded and become more focused on communities and places rather than only on people.

I

EXPLAINING THE MANUFACTURING EMPLOYMENT SHARE

This part of the book presents overwhelming empirical evidence that the manufacturing employment share (MES) tends to rise in the initial stages of development and then decline. Once the peak has been passed, the decline is continuous, regardless of whether countries run trade deficits or surpluses in manufacturing.

Chapters 1 and 2 develop a simple model with three sectors that illustrates this behavior. Chapter 3 uses the theory to explore whether after the MES peaks, countries continue to experience declining MES regardless of their trade balances in manufacturing. Chapter 4 explores premature deindustrialization. It uses the theoretical framework developed in chapters 1 and 2 to provide three possible explanations for why the curve shifts downward and inward over time. It then explores evidence in support of each explanation and finds important roles for relatively more rapid productivity growth in manufacturing and investment, with trade playing a more idiosyncratic role.

1

Economic Development and Structural Change

An early debate among the founders of the United States has long been cast as a disagreement between Thomas Jefferson, who saw agriculture as the backbone of the economy, and Alexander Hamilton, the champion of a future dominated by manufacturing. Hamilton would no doubt be astounded that by 2020, just 8 percent of US employment was in manufacturing—only 3 percentage points higher than it was in 1815 (figure 1.1). And Jefferson would be surprised that less than 2 percent of American workers remained in agriculture. Instead, the US economy is now dominated by services—a vast array of productive activities that includes diverse sectors such as wholesale and retail trade, education, financial and business services, health care, hospitality (restaurants and hotels), and technology and government services (Jorgenson and Timmer 2011).

This chapter explores the evolution of structural change as the core activity shifts from mainly agriculture to mainly services, with emphasis on what this evolution entails for the manufacturing employment share (MES). The first section presents empirical evidence of employment patterns using over 200 years of US data and data from a diverse sample of economies for 1960–2011. It shows that the MES follows a hump-shaped path as incomes grow, rising in the initial phases of development and then steadily declining as workers move from manufacturing to services. This shape captures behavior in almost all developed and many developing economies, suggesting that structural change is driven by forces that are common and pervasive. The data indicate that almost all developed, and many developing, economies have passed their peaks and are now on the

Figure 1.1
Sectoral employment shares in the United States, 1810–2020

percent of total employment

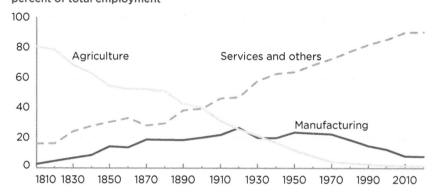

Note: The category "Services and others" includes nonagricultural and nonmanufacturing activities such as construction, mining, transportation, and trade.

Sources: Lebergott (1966); updated using US Bureau of Labor Statistics data from the Federal Reserve Bank of St. Louis, Federal Reserve Economic Data, https://fred.stlouisfed.org.

downward slope of the curve. There is also evidence that the share of manufacturing in real output follows a similar but more muted pattern.

The second section explains the humped employment path using a simple model that initially highlights the roles played by technological change and income growth. (The detailed model is in appendix 1A in the online data package for this volume posted on the PIIE website.)[1] It replicates the key structural characteristics of economies as they develop by assuming that productivity growth rates and income elasticities vary by sector and that demand in all sectors is price inelastic. (In order to focus on the role of productivity and income growth, this chapter assumes the economy is closed. Chapter 2 extends analysis to include the roles of trade and capital flows.)

The model is a simplification. In reality, countries have different factor endowments and technologies. Trade, productivity, and income all influence one another;[2] sector productivity growth rates vary over time; and

---

1. The The appendices are available in the online data package for this volume at https://www.piie.com/bookstore/behind-curve-can-manufacturing-still-provide-inclusive-growth.

2. In this study, trade, technology, and demand are treated as independent variables. In reality, they influence one another. Technology can cause trade. Indeed, classical theories of trade, such as the one developed by David Ricardo, explain patterns of trade specialization based on technological differences. Trade can cause technological change. Firms respond

sectors include many industries that differ with respect to their productivity growth, comparative advantage, and income elasticities.[3] The goal of the parsimonious analysis is to show that the basic patterns of structural change exert a powerful impact regardless of national differences in policies, institutions, and endowments. The model seeks to capture why in almost all countries the share of manufacturing employment follows a hump shape as they develop and why many countries are past that curve's peak.

The third section of the chapter examines whether the economic literature on structural change provides support for parameters assumed in the model. The fourth section explores the implications of how the structural change predicted by the model explains why emerging economies initially grow very rapidly before their growth rates moderate.

Typical Pattern of Structural Change

Sectoral employment shares in the United States have followed a distinctive pattern (figure 1.1).[4] Over time, the share of agricultural employment declined, and the share of other sectors (mainly services) rose. The manufacturing share has a humped shape, rising fairly steadily through the 19th and early 20th centuries, falling before the Depression of the 1930s, recovering and then leveling off until the mid-1960s, and steadily declining thereafter.

Two other features of the data are noteworthy. First, the common description of development as a three-phase process that moves from agriculture to manufacturing to services is not accurate. Throughout the 210-year period, employment growth was faster and larger in services than in manufacturing; even during the period in which the share of employment in manufacturing was growing—the period of so-called industrializa-

---

to international competitive pressures by innovating and introducing new technologies (Fort, Pierce, and Schott 2018). In addition, demand can affect technological change. Technological innovation is driven partly by both domestic and international demand (Matsuyama 2019). For example, the supply of new COVID vaccines was a response to the demand created by the outbreak of the disease. Inventors will be influenced by the availability of both domestic and international markets as incomes rise. Thus, although it often helps analytically to assume that these forces are independent to understand their effects in theory, making precise attributions of causation in practice can be problematic.

3. For an exploration of the diverse behavior of service industries with respect to employment and productivity trends, see Jorgenson and Timmer (2011).

4. David Andolfatto, of the Federal Reserve Bank of St. Louis, kindly provided these data. The historical data are from Lebergott (1966) and the Federal Reserve Bank of St. Louis, Federal Reserve Economic Data, https://fred.stlouisfed.org/.

tion—the employment share of services was larger and grew at a faster rate.[5] Second, since the 1960s, the major feature of structural change has been the shift from manufacturing to services (Edwards and Lawrence 2013).

Figure 1.2 reveals the relationship between sectoral employment shares and per capita incomes for a sample of 42 economies from the Groningen Growth and Development Centre database.[6] The structural change the United States experienced is typical, although in economies that have developed more recently, growth has been faster and the entire process more rapid.

The resemblance to the US data is clear. At low levels of development, the agricultural sector accounts for a large share of employment, and services and manufacturing account for small shares. As per capita income increases, the employment shares in agriculture and services move monotonically, with the share of agriculture declining and the share of services rising. The share of manufacturing behaves differently. At low levels of income, growth in per capita income is associated with a rising MES. At some point the share reaches a peak, after which the MES declines.

The dominance of services over manufacturing in the share of employment throughout the development process is perhaps surprising. Economic development is traditionally described as industrialization; the conventional version of economic development is the sequential movement of workers from agriculture to manufacturing (industry) to services (Dabla-Norris et al. 2013).

This characterization is not quite right, as the US figure shows. It is more accurate to describe economic growth as occurring in two phases (Bah 2011). In the first phase, the reallocation of employment is from agri-

---

5. Between 1810 and 1920, the share of US services employment increased by 30.9 percentage points and the share of manufacturing employment increased by 24.1 percentage points. Similar patterns are evident between 1800 and 2000 in other industrial countries (Herrendorf, Rogerson, and Valentinyi 2014). Maddison (1980) finds a shallow bell shape for manufacturing employment in all 16 of the Organization for Economic Cooperation and Development (OECD) countries he studied.

6. Purchasing power parity measures of per capita income for the Maddison data supplied by the Groningen Growth and Development Centre (https://www.rug.nl/ggdc/ historicaldevelopment) are in constant 2011 US dollars. The "agricultural" sector is the primary commodity sector and includes mining. The services sector incudes all other sectors. The economies in the sample include the following: sub-Saharan Africa: Botswana, Ethiopia, Ghana, Kenya, Malawi, Mauritius, Nigeria, Senegal, South Africa, Tanzania, and Zambia; Middle East and North Africa: Egypt and Morocco; Asia: China, Hong Kong (China), India, Indonesia, Japan, South Korea, Malaysia, the Philippines, Singapore, Taiwan, and Thailand; Latin America: Argentina, Bolivia, Brazil, Chile, Colombia, Costa Rica, Mexico, Peru, Venezuela; North America: United States; Europe: Denmark, France, Germany, Italy, the Netherlands, Spain, Sweden, and the United Kingdom. The sample covers 1950–2011. For sources and methods, see Timmer, de Vries, and de Vries (2015).

Figure 1.2

Sectoral employment shares in a sample of 42 economies, 1960–2011

share of employment (percent)

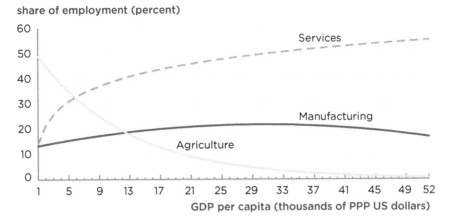

Note: GDP data per capita is measured in constant 2011 purchasing power parity (PPP) dollars.

Source: GDP data are from the Groningen Growth and Development Centre (GGDC) Maddison Project, https://www.rug.nl/ggdc/historicaldevelopment/maddison/releases/maddison-project-database-2020. Employment shares are from the GGDC database, https://www.rug.nl/ggdc/structuralchange/previous-sector-database/10-sector-2014.

culture to both manufacturing and services; in the second phase, although there is still some reallocation from agriculture to services, most of the movement is from manufacturing to services. Although the first stage of development is usually called industrialization, even during it the employment share in services is typically larger and growing more rapidly than the share in manufacturing.

At a minimum, a three-sector model is required to understand structural change, because developments in productivity growth and employment in agriculture play a key role in both stimulating demand for manufactured goods and services and providing workers to these sectors, particularly when the MES is rising (Święcki 2017). In the second phase of growth, when the agricultural employment share becomes so small that its impact on employment is relatively unimportant, structural change is mainly about the manufacturing sector supplying workers to services.

The inverted-*U* relationship between the MES and GDP per capita is evident globally, in both developed- and developing-economy aggregates, and in four major regions (figure 1.3). The developed economies are concentrated on the right-hand (downward-sloping) part of the curve; on the left-hand (upward-sloping) part of the figure are far more developing

Figure 1.3

Relationship between manufacturing employment share and per capita GDP, globally, by level of development, and by region

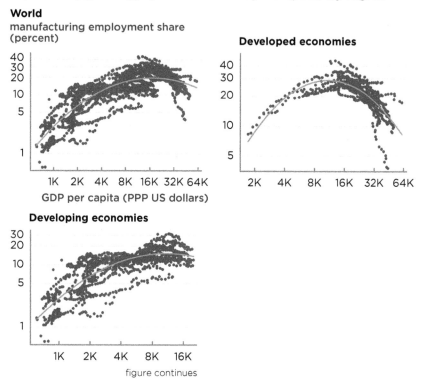

World
manufacturing employment share (percent)

Developed economies

GDP per capita (PPP US dollars)

Developing economies

figure continues

economies. Europe includes many economies that have passed their peaks; most of its economies are on the right-hand side. Africa and Latin America have peaks that are low and occurred at low-income levels. The Asian peaks are conspicuously higher than the peaks of other regions. (The chapters that follow explore some of the reasons for these differences.) A similar relationship, although tending to peak at higher levels of real income, can be found in curves fitted to the real share of manufacturing output in GDP (figure 1.4).

Table 1.1 reports regressions based on 42 economies, grouped by level of development and region, from 1960 to 2011. They reveal the pervasive nature of the relationship between economic growth and sectoral employment, which can be fitted by a quadratic equation. The MES is explained by per capita GDP and per capita GDP squared, population, and population squared; economy dummies are used as additional controls to capture unique national characteristics. The coefficients on GDP per capita are

Figure 1.3 continued

Relationship between manufacturing employment share and per capita GDP, globally, by level of development, and by region

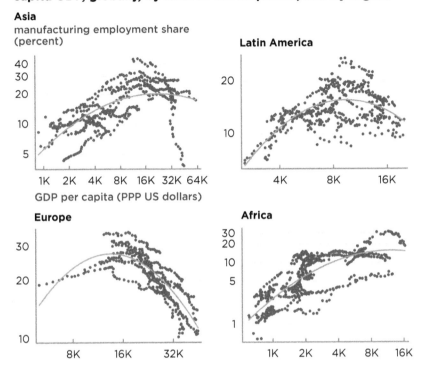

Asia
manufacturing employment share
(percent)

Latin America

Europe

Africa

GDP per capita (PPP US dollars)

Sources: Data from the Groningen Growth and Development (GGDC) database (https://www.rug.nl/ggdc/structuralchange/previous-sector-database/10-sector-2014?lang = en) and the Maddison Project Database, version 2020 from GGDC.

positive; the coefficients of GDP per capita squared are negative.[7] The dependent variable traces out a curve that peaks in 2011 at $9,210 (1990 dollars) in the global sample.[8]

These equations capture the humped curve with statistically significant coefficients on the logs of GDP and GDP squared (note the negative coefficient on the squared term) for both the full global sample (regression 1) for developed economies, developing economies, and all four

---

7. Similar regressions for real output can be found in appendix 4A.

8. The regression output for the global sample in table 1.1 is ln_share_mfg_emp = 1.11 * lngdppc –0.25* + 0.36 * lnpop – 0.06 * ln – 3.35. Taking the derivative with respect to LnGDPPC, one can solve for the maximum in logs by setting the derivative equal to zero (1.11/0.5 = 2.22). Taking the exponent of the logs indicates that per capita GDP at the global sample peaks at $9,210 (1990 dollars).

Figure 1.4

Relationship between the manufacturing real output share in GDP and per capita GDP, globally, by level of development, and by region

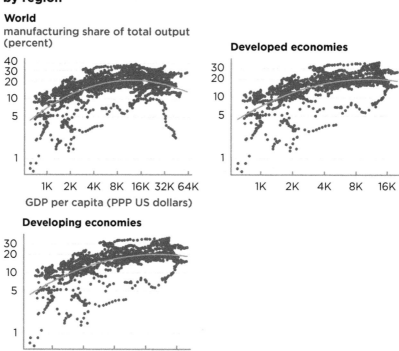

World
manufacturing share of total output (percent)

Developed economies

Developing economies

figure continues

regions (the squared term is less significant and smaller for Africa). These results establish that once idiosyncratic national features are controlled for, *a single profile underlies structural change globally and in economies in every region.*

Explaining the Hump in a Closed Economy

The humped shape of the MES results from a distinct set of mathematical properties. For the MES to rise, it must grow more rapidly than the combined employment share of the rest of the economy (agriculture and services).[9] Formally, $\%\Delta M$ is > $\%\Delta (A + S)$, where $\%\Delta$ is the percentage change and M, A, and S are the employment shares for manufacturing, agricul-

---

9. For this discussion, mining is included in the agricultural sector and construction and utilities are included in services.

Figure 1.4 continued

Relationship between the manufacturing real output share in GDP and per capita GDP, globally, by level of development, and by region

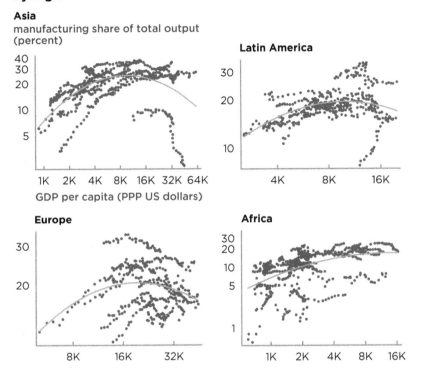

Asia
manufacturing share of total output (percent)

Latin America

GDP per capita (PPP US dollars)

Europe

Africa

Sources: Data from the Groningen Growth and Development (GGDC) database (https://www.rug.nl/ggdc/structuralchange/previous-sector-database/10-sector-2014?lang = en) and the Maddison Project Database, version 2020 from GGDC.

ture, and services, respectively. Even if employment in services grows more rapidly than employment in manufacturing (as is generally the case), a decline in the employment share of the agricultural sector could reduce the sum of $A + S$ sufficiently that in the denominator $A + S$ will grow more slowly than M. This pattern of growth is likely to occur in the initial phase of development, when agricultural employment, which is relatively large, is declining rapidly. Eventually, however, as the size of the agricultural sector shrinks, the role of the declining share in agriculture in the denominator becomes smaller and the role of the rising share of services in the denominator becomes larger. Once the change in $A + S$ exceeds the change in M, the MES will decline.

Table 1.1

Regression results on the relationship between manufacturing employment share and economic growth, 1960–2011

Variable	(1) Global	(2) Africa	(3) Asia	(4) Latin America	(5) Europe	(6) Developed economies	(7) Developing economies
Log GDP per capita	1.108*** (0.157)	0.440*** (0.139)	1.795*** (0.369)	2.539*** (0.466)	2.927*** (0.504)	2.071*** (0.320)	0.849*** (0.153)
Log GDP per capita squared	-0.251*** (0.0325)	-0.0998* (0.0461)	-0.352*** (0.0793)	-0.587*** (0.105)	-0.531*** (0.0953)	-0.404*** (0.0480)	-0.176*** (0.0523)
Log population	0.355*** (0.119)	0.888** (0.302)	0.468 (0.522)	0.107 (0.131)	-0.450 (1.801)	-0.224 (1.342)	0.400*** (0.129)
Log population squared	-0.0642*** (0.0227)	-0.113* (0.0543)	-0.135*** (0.0383)	-0.0559* (0.0297)	-0.135 (0.197)	-0.0505 (0.108)	-0.0644** (0.0240)
Constant	-3.352*** (0.270)	-4.414*** (0.443)	-2.929* (1.349)	-4.331*** (0.465)	-2.398 (3.798)	-2.603 (2.712)	-3.558*** (0.312)
Observations	2,043	627	503	466	396	676	1,367
R-squared	0.423	0.413	0.529	0.456	0.862	0.642	0.365
Number of economies	42	13	11	9	8	14	28

Note: North America is not included in the regional groupings. Robust standard errors are in parentheses.
*** $p < 0.01$, ** $p < 0.05$, * $p < 0.1$.

Sources: Data from the Groningen Growth and Development (GGDC) database (https://www.rug.nl/ggdc/structuralchange/previous-sector-database/10-sector-2014?lang = en) and the Maddison Project Database, version 2020.

Income Effects

Several models explain structural change. They generally stress the role of either income or price changes; some, including the model presented in appendix 1A in the online data package, combine these effects. Some models that emphasize differences in the growth of sector demand as income increases assume that sector income elasticities change as incomes rise (i.e., technically they are nonhomethetic). Others assume constant but different rankings of sector income elasticities.

The classic version of varying income elasticity is that of Ernst Engel (1895), who posited that the income elasticity of demand for agriculture (food) declines with income growth.[10] Colin Clark (1957) argues that the share of demand for manufactured goods in income is large at low levels of development and declines as income rises and demand shifts from goods toward services—a pattern that is evident in figure 1.5. These changing income elasticities can help explain the hump even in models in which productivity growth across sectors is the same and relative output prices do not change.

The hump can also be obtained by assuming a particular sector ranking of different constant income elasticities (i.e., that manufacturing has a lower income elasticity than services but a higher income elasticity than agriculture) (Comin, Lashkari, and Mestieri 2021). In this case, a larger share of the income generated by the common sector productivity growth rate will be spent on manufacturing than on agriculture and an even larger share will be spent on services.

Initially, if the income elasticity of demand for agriculture is very low but most income growth originates from agriculture, the share of spending on manufactures could exceed the combined growth in the shares of spending on agriculture and services as income increases, implying a rising MES. Once the share of spending on agriculture declines sufficiently, the share of demand will shift increasingly toward services. If the growth in services spending is larger than the growth in manufacturing spending, the MES will fall.[11]

---

10. A common utility function that is nonhomothetic is the Stone-Geary function, which includes a basic minimum subsistence requirement. This formulation is problematic for long-run extrapolations, because the role of basic requirements tends to disappear over time, as Comin, Lashkari, and Mestieri (2021) note.

11. In the model developed by Kongsamut, Rebelo, and Xie (2001), income elasticities are constant. As a result, the MES remains constant rather than following a hump-shaped pattern. By allowing for different income elasticities for new and old manufactured goods, Foellmi and Zweimüller (2008) obtain a nonlinear relationship between manufacturing growth and income. They assume that the most urgent desires are satisfied by agricultural goods, less urgent desires are satisfied by manufactures, and the least urgent desires are

Figure 1.5

Spending on goods as share of total consumption in the United States, by consumption quintile, 1986–2011

share of total consumption (percent)

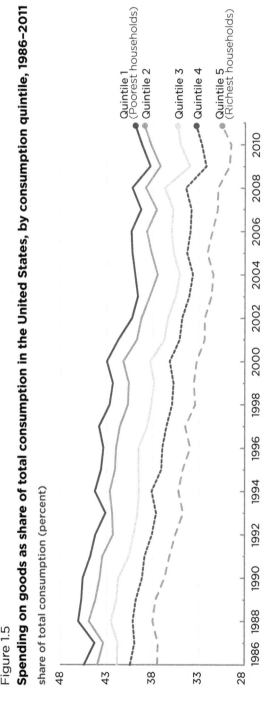

Source: Boppart (2014).

Price Effects

Some models emphasize the systematic differences in the evolution of sector product prices as income grows. The classic version of this price approach is by William Baumol (1967), who assumes that price changes in a sector reflect its productivity growth. Productivity growth is strong in the "progressive" sector (usually taken to mean manufacturing) and sluggish in the "stagnant" sector (identified as services). This phenomenon is sometimes called Baumol's disease, because the shares of spending and employment become increasingly concentrated in the stagnant sector as its relative price rises (Nordhaus 2008). It also explains why sectors with slow productivity growth (such as education, health, and public services) have become increasingly expensive over time.

The key feature in models such as Baumol's, in which price changes generate structural change and the economy ends up dominated by employment in the stagnant sector, is that at the sector level, demand is price inelastic (Baumol, Blackman, and Wolff 1985). Typically, demand is elastic when there are many substitution possibilities and producers have small market shares. The substitution elasticity of fruit and meat is lower than that of apples and pears but higher than that of food and clothes. It should not therefore be surprising that demand elasticity is typically low in response to changes in the relative prices of a large aggregate such as "all manufactured products," "all services," or "all agricultural products." Faster productivity in a large sector generally reduces employment: when productivity is rapid in a sector, relative prices of output in that sector will fall. Nominal spending on sector output will also fall, because the increased quantity demanded will not make up for the drop in inputs required for each unit of production. Thus, with higher productivity growth, fewer workers (and other inputs) will be demanded. If productivity growth in services tends to grow more slowly than in other sectors, services will become more expensive over time (Baumol and Bowen 1965, Baumol 1967). In this case, unresponsive (inelastic) demand will mean that the dollar share of spending devoted to services will rise, because the quantity of services purchased will not fall by much when its price rises.

The effects of demand will be felt not only in the sector experiencing technological change but in other sectors as well, as a result of spillovers. These spillovers will be positive when the demand for the sector with falling prices is inelastic and its share in spending declines, making sectors experiencing productivity growth and sectors experiencing positive demand

---

satisfied by services. This assumption yields a hump-shaped profile for the MES as the economy develops.

spillovers complements. When spending on manufactured goods declines because the relative prices of manufactured goods falls, for example, buyers will use the money they save on goods to buy more services. Paradoxically, therefore, because of this feature of demand, an important driver of the shift toward an economy with growing shares of spending on services is productivity growth in manufacturing. Similarly, productivity growth in agriculture will stimulate spending on manufacturing and services. This spillover is an important driver of the expansion of manufacturing employment, especially during the early stages of development.

In the Baumol model, relative price declines that reflect faster productivity growth in agriculture and manufacturing (the "dynamic sectors") and increase spending on services. The relative price of services rises, and, because demand is inelastic, the share of nominal spending on services and the share of employment increases. In this framework, the dynamic sectors are demand makers and the static sector (services) is a demand taker.[12]

What Explains the Hump?

The hump-shaped profile for manufacturing employment can be explained most simply in a pure price model if the sectors are assumed to have different productivity growth rates and the structural impacts of income growth are suppressed because income elasticities are assumed to be unity. In this case, the key to generating the hump-shaped evolution of the MES in a closed economy is that manufacturing productivity growth lies between the productivity growth rates of agriculture and services. If productivity growth is fastest in agriculture, the prices of agricultural goods fall relative to the prices of manufactures and services; if labor is the only factor of production and demand is inelastic, the increased demand for agricultural products will be insufficient to offset the decline in labor required to produce it, so employment in agriculture will fall. As productivity growth in services is slowest, the price of services relative to both agricultural goods and manufactures rises, and demand for services—and thus the service sector's share of employment—rises.

---

12. Characterizing a sector as large as services is as static involves a clear oversimplification. This description may apply to nonmarket services, such as education and healthcare, in which productivity may be slow but poorly measured, and to sectors such as personal finance and business services, which also have low productivity growth rates and increasing employment shares; it does not apply to distribution services and information and communications technology services. Using data for 1980–2005, Jorgenson and Timmer (2011, 26) find that productivity growth in market services exceeded productivity growth in goods production in Japan and the United States but not in Europe.

In a poor economy, the initial share of employment in agriculture is large, implying that %ΔM > %Δ (A+S), because manufacturing productivity growth will be slower than the weighted average of productivity growth in agriculture and services. (Recall that productivity and employment growth are inversely related.) As employment in agriculture declines and employment in services grows, manufacturing will eventually enjoy faster productivity growth than the combined productivity growth in agriculture and services, and the MES will decline (%ΔM < %Δ (A + S)).

Combining Price and Income Effects

The model—formally developed in appendix 1A and also used in chapter 4—combines demand and supply forces and structural change that is driven by both differences in productivity growth and sector demand elasticities (for simplicity, both sector income elasticities and productivity growth rates are assumed to be constant). The economy has only one factor of production (labor), the supply of which is fixed. Each sector has a constant but different income elasticity. An example with specific assumed parameters would be if all sectors had the same substitution elasticity (0.7). On the demand side, the income elasticity is assumed to be 1.5 for services, 1.4 for manufacturing, and 0.8 for agriculture. On the supply side, the rate of technological change is assumed to be 8 percent in agriculture, 2 percent in manufacturing, and 0 in services (table 1.2).

Figure 1.6 depicts the results of simulating the model with the parameters shown in table 1.2. It captures the way the interaction of productivity growth with demand generates structural change over time as the economy grows and a hump-shaped profile of the MES emerges as the demand for labor in manufacturing responds to changes in incomes and prices.

Two positive forces increase the MES: Cheaper agricultural products shift the share of spending toward manufactured goods, and income growth shifts spending shares toward manufacturing and services and away from agriculture (as the income elasticity of demand for agricultural goods is lower than the income elasticity of demand for manufactured goods or services).

Two negative forces reduce the MES. First, faster productivity growth in manufacturing reduces the price of manufacturing relative to the price of services; consumers react by allocating more of their spending to services and less on manufactures. Second, because the income elasticity of demand for services is greater than the income elasticity of demand for manufactures, a larger share of the increased income generated by faster manufacturing productivity growth is allocated to services than to manufactures or agriculture.

Table 1.2
Parameters of the model

Variable	Value
Elasticity of substitution (σ)	*0.7*
Income elasticity for agricultural goods (ε_a)	0.8
Income elasticity for manufactured goods (ε_m)	1.4
Income elasticity for services (ε_s)	1.5
Initial employment share in agriculture (l_{a0}) (percent)	80
Initial manufacturing employment share (l_{m0}) (percent)	9
Initial employment share in services (l_{s0}) (percent)	11
Initial GDP per capita (y_0) (2015 dollars)	*1,000*
Productivity growth rate in agriculture (τ_a) (percent)	8
Productivity growth rate in manufacturing (τ_m) (percent)	2
Productivity growth rate in services (τ_s) (percent)	0

Figure 1.6
Changes in the sectoral shares of employment in a closed economy (simulation results)

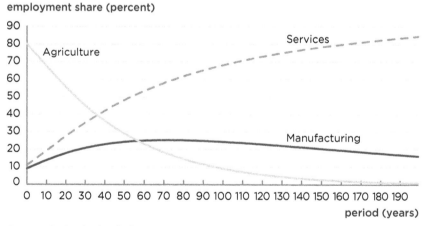

employment share (percent)

Source: Author's simulations.

In the early stages of development, when agriculture accounts for a large share of income, the two positive forces are greater than the two negative forces. Over time, as the share of the agricultural sector shrinks, the effects of positive forces from agricultural productivity and income growth originating in agriculture on manufacturing employment decline and the negative forces that reduce the MES prevail, causing the MES to decline.

The model yields an important lesson that is often ignored. To understand the behavior of employment in a sector, it is important to consider not only the supply of and demand for the products of that sector alone but also to take account of spillovers in both the supply of and demand from other sectors. Productivity growth in agriculture can be a major driver of employment growth in manufacturing. If a policy goal is to increase manufacturing employment, measures to improve agricultural productivity could therefore be just as important as policies that focus directly on manufacturing.

Much of the discussion about the negative effects of automation focuses on employment in the sectors that increase their use of robots or computers. But higher productivity in manufacturing from automation could raise income and increase spending on services (Autor and Dorn 2013; Gregory, Salamons, and Zierahn 2019). Displaced manufacturing workers who once performed routine tasks could thus not only be reemployed in services but also earn higher wages than before the robots that displaced them were introduced.[13]

Empirical Support for the Model

This model of structural change makes assumptions about sectoral income, price elasticities, and rates of productivity growth. To explore whether they are plausible, it is necessary first to specify what exactly is meant by a sector.

There are two methods of categorizing sectors and thus two different ways they can enter into demand: as different categories of final expenditure and as different categories of value added (Herrendorf, Rogerson, and Valentinyi 2013). The first method corresponds directly to categories of final demand (spending on food, other goods, and services). The second corresponds to industries that add value in producing final goods and services. From the standpoint of final demand, food in a restaurant might be classified as demand for agriculture. From the standpoint of value added, food in a restaurant reflects a combination of value added

---

13. These workers earn higher wages when the elasticity of substitution in production between robots and routine labor is higher than the elasticity of substitution in consumption between goods and services (Autor and Dorn 2013).

from the agricultural sector (the produce and meat); the services sector (the activities of the chefs and waiters); and the manufacturing sector (cutlery, cash registers, stoves, tables). In the 2018 US national income accounts, for example, goods (almost all of which were manufactured at some stage) accounted for 29.3 percent of GDP output, but manufacturing industries accounted for just 11.3 percent of value added.[14]

As this study focuses on employment in the manufacturing sector, the concern is primarily on value added. The relevant income and price elasticities are therefore for the value added by industries, not the income and price elasticities in final demand. Many studies of structural change ignore this distinction and use data on final demand. These studies classify as manufacturing the final output of nonfood (and nonfiber) goods, even though such output contains value added not only from the manufacturing industry but also from services, such as transportation, distribution, and wholesale and retail trade.

Francisco Buera and Joseph Kaboski (2009) and Bethold Herrendorf, Richard Rogerson, and Ákos Valentinyi (2013) find that substitution elasticities for value added at the sectoral level are very low, confirming the validity of the assumption of inelastic demand in the model. Indeed, they find that so-called augmented Leontief preferences (based on zero price elasticities of substitution) provide the best fit for the US data. In his calibrations based on 45 economies, Tomasz Święcki (2017) uses very low elasticities of substitution for manufacturing (–0.09 for the substitutability of manufacturing with services and –0.06 with agriculture).

Price and income elasticities tend to be higher in final demand specifications. Studies of structural change in the composition of final demand also find a greater role for income effects.

Timo Boppart (2014) uses a US sample. Although final demand price and income elasticities change in his model, they are generally close to 0.5. Diego Comin, Danial Lashkari, and Martí Mestieri (2021) use an international data sample. They find that final demand substitution elasticities are about 0.7 for all three sectors the parameter used in the model here. They also find that income demand elasticity is about 0.8 percentage point higher in manufacturing than in agriculture and 0.32 percentage point higher in services than in manufacturing. These results are consistent with the model's assumptions about the relative magnitudes of income elasticities.

There is considerable debate in the literature over whether income or relative price effects are more important in explaining structural change. Using final expenditure data, Comin, Lashkari, and Mestieri (2021) find

---

14. See Bureau of Economic Analysis, "Interactive Data Application," https://www.bea.gov/itable/.

that 80 percent of the change in final expenditures globally is from income effects. Also using final expenditure data, Boppart (2014) finds an equal role for price and income effects in US structural change.

Herrendorf, Rogerson, and Valentinyi (2013) argue that the results are sensitive to whether the change in final expenditures or industry value added is the dependent variable. Low price elasticities imply that changes in (nominal) value added shares attributable to productivity growth will be driven mainly by changes in relative prices rather than quantities. They find that price effects are generally more important for structural change in value added and income effects more important for structural change in final expenditures.

Święcki (2017) compares four sources of structural change: income effects, substitution effects, trade, and differences in sector markups. He finds that sector-biased technological change is the most important mechanism behind structural change, explaining 43 percent of the labor relocation for the median economy. He also finds differences in the roles played by income and productivity at different stages of development: "While income effects have on average less power to account for broad shifts in sectoral employment, they remain an important force. Nonhomotheticity of preferences, i.e., differences in sector income elasticities, play a key role in generating the transition of labor out of agriculture and are thus very relevant for economies at earlier stages of economic development" (p. 93). The relative importance of the two channels depends on how far along an economy is in the process of structural change, but, Święcki argues, both mechanisms are necessary to provide a fully satisfactory account of a complete transition from an agriculture-based to a service-based economy.

Postwar data provide mixed support for the assumed sector rankings in productivity growth assumed in the closed economy model used in this chapter. Margarida Duarte and Diego Restuccia (2010) report that between 1956 and 2004, US labor productivity growth was 3.8 percent in agriculture, 2.4 percent in industry, and 1.3 percent in services.[15] This ranking holds in 23 of the 29 economies in their sample; only in Venezuela do services not show the slowest productivity growth.

Using data for about 50 economies for 1967–92, Will Martin and Devashish Mitra (2001) find that at all levels of development, technological progress appears to have been faster in agriculture than in manufacturing, with both sectors enjoying faster productivity growth than services. In contrast, in the World Input-Output Database (http://www.wiod.org/

---

15. Duarte (2020) finds that the relative price of manufacturing tends to decline with income.

release16) used for empirical work later in this study, labor productivity growth rate in manufacturing is often higher than in agriculture, especially in Asia.[16]

Implications for Aggregate Growth Rates

Increases in output per worker result from a combination of structural change (the changing shares of sectors) and differences in productivity growth across sectors. During the early stages of development, agriculture has the lowest level of output per worker but the fastest labor productivity growth. Agricultural productivity growth can thus be an important source of rapid aggregate growth, both because its productivity growth rate is the highest and because average productivity increases when labor moves from agriculture, where output per worker is low, to manufacturing and services, where output per worker is higher. In the early stages of development, when the agricultural sector is large, these effects can be very strong. Changes in sector output shares can therefore be a powerful source of economic growth in the early stages of development, as they were in Japan between 1950 and 1974 and China between 1980 and 2010. Growth is likely to slow once the potential for moving people with low productivity off the farms is exhausted; once this happens, the share of agriculture in overall productivity growth declines.

Kiminori Matsuyama (1992) challenges the conventional view of the growth benefits from technological progress in agriculture. He argues that in an open economy, rapid agricultural productivity growth could create a comparative advantage that attracts resources into rather than releases them from the sector, possibly resulting in a smaller manufacturing sector. As his model includes learning by doing in manufacturing, long-run growth is slower, as the losses in the potential productivity-enhancing experience that would be gained from manufacturing more than offset the static gains from trade. A similar mechanism occurs if an abundance of natural resources attracts resources to the agricultural (or primary commodity) sector and away from manufacturing, a phenomenon known as the Dutch disease, after the effect the Netherlands' discovery of gas in the North Sea had on its economy (Corden 1984).

---

16. Once account is taken of trade, faster productivity growth in agriculture than manufacturing is no longer necessary to generate the hump-shaped MES as countries develop, as shown in the next chapter. The database was developed by Timmer, de Vries, and de Vries (2015).

Conclusion

This chapter documents the pervasiveness of the hump-shaped profile of the MES as countries develop. It shows how a parsimonious three-sector model can generate this profile as it simulates economic growth. This model makes three assumptions:

- Manufacturing productivity growth is lower than productivity growth in agriculture but higher than in services.
- The income elasticity of demand in manufacturing is higher than in agriculture but lower than in services.
- Demand is price inelastic in all three sectors.

There is considerable support in the literature for the second and third set of assumptions; productivity growth in agriculture is not always faster than in manufacturing, however. Chapter 2 shows that once trade is introduced, this condition is no longer necessary for the humped MES curve to emerge. The model here also helps explain why growth can be rapid during the transition from agriculture and why once this growth occurs countries are likely to grow more slowly.

2

The Curve in the Open Economy

In the special case in which the income demand elasticities of all sectors are unity (so that income has no impact on spending shares), differences in sector productivity growth are the key driver of structural change. As shown in the last chapter, in the closed economy, the falling share of agriculture, the rising share of services, and the hump-shaped profile for manufacturing all emerge naturally when productivity growth in manufacturing lies between that of agriculture and services. If productivity increases more rapidly in manufacturing than in agriculture and services, in a closed economy with unitary income elasticities, however, the manufacturing employment share (MES) *declines* continuously, because the prices of manufactured goods fall more rapidly than the prices of both services and agricultural products. In this case, explaining the structural evolution of the economy requires introducing another source of change that could offset this tendency, the most natural of which is international trade.

This chapter examines the effect of trade and capital flows on the MES. It is organized as follows. Given the conventional wisdom that running a trade surplus in manufacturing can prevent the inverted *U*-shaped profile of the MES by allowing the MES to continuously rise if countries are sufficiently competitive internationally, it first provides some surprising evidence that suggests the hump-shaped profile exists even when economies run large trade surpluses in manufactured goods. Equally surprising, it shows the hump is also present when countries run large trade deficits. It then turns to theory, which confirms that although introducing trade can change the location of the inverted curve, it does not change its shape over the long run. The chapter then uses regression analysis to show empirically how taking manufactured trade into account affects the position of the estimated manufacturing employment path but does not change the inverted U-shaped path.

In an open economy, both the price of manufactured goods relative to the prices of services and agricultural products at home and the costs of domestic manufactured goods relative to foreign substitutes matter. Including foreign demand has implications for sectoral employment, because, in addition to the negative impact on domestic spending on manufactured goods when domestic demand is inelastic, productivity growth in manufacturing can affect an economy's comparative advantage. Especially if exports are small relative to the global market and goods are homogeneous, the demand for manufactures could be infinitely elastic (economies could be pure price takers). In this case, higher productivity in manufacturing could increase the MES. An economy with a growing comparative advantage in manufacturing could therefore move along a higher rising MES path as it grows, reaching a higher manufacturing employment peak than without trade.

Although the trade effect on manufacturing employment may be positive initially, as an economy develops and its economy and trade become larger, the employment response to additional increases in productivity could dissipate, for two reasons. First, the country may no longer be a price taker in the world market, especially if products are differentiated, and the marginal foreign response to improvements in domestic manufacturing productivity and the lower relative prices of its manufacturing goods exports could decline. Second, if its output price falls, and domestic spending rises, the negative impact of productivity growth on its own manufacturing spending could be larger than the positive trade effects. Once trade is considered, therefore, the hump can emerge even when economies have a comparative advantage in manufacturing and productivity growth in manufacturing is faster than in agriculture.[1] This can occur even if all income elasticities are unity (Uy, Yi, and Zhang 2013).

---

1. Sposi (2018) develops an alternative explanation of the hump in an open economy, arguing that the share of manufacturing value added reflects patterns of changing comparative advantage that vary systemically with levels of economic development.

Evidence of the Hump in Deficit and Surplus Countries

Figure 2.1 shows the MES curves of economies with the largest average manufacturing trade deficits for the countries available in the Groningen Growth and Development Centre (GGDC) database between 1960 and 2010. Some low-income countries (Bolivia, Kenya, Malawi, and Tanzania) that ran large manufacturing trade deficits relative to their GDPs nonetheless still moved along the upward slope of the hump, presumably because of positive domestic demand spillovers that outweighed the negative impact of their negative manufacturing trade balances. Other countries (Egypt, Ghana, Mauritius, and Singapore) had already progressed farther along typical hump-shaped paths and were on the downward-sloping part of the curve. Hong Kong for example experienced a major decline in its MES curve, from above forty percent to a share in single digits as its manufacturing jobs relocated to China.

Figure 2.2 shows the MES of the 10 economies with the *largest* average manufacturing trade surpluses relative to GDP among the economies for which data were available in the GGDC database. Despite their trade surpluses, the MES of the most developed economies (France, Germany, Sweden, and the United Kingdom) peaked in the 1960s and declined thereafter. In contrast, Italy, Japan, South Korea, Taiwan, and Zambia experienced hump-shaped curves, but the employment share eventually fell in Italy, Japan, and South Korea.

Until 2013, China was on the upward-sloping part of the hump. At its peak, in 2013, the manufacturing sector accounted for 19.3 percent of employment). By 2017, that share had declined to 17.9 percent (figure 2.3). It fell further to 17.6 percent in 2018, and between 2013 and 2018 Chinese manufacturing employment fell by 10.4 percent from 148.485 million to 133.082 million.[2]

As in other economies, the MES in China displays a hump, even though China had the largest share of manufacturing in value added in GDP among the 60 economies in the OECD Trade in Value Added (TiVA) database. The challenge is explaining why the hump is evident in both deficit and surplus economies.

---

2. For total employment in 2018, see Statista, https://www.statista.com/statistics/251380/number-of-employed-persons-in-china/. For Chinese manufacturing employment, see The Conference Board, https://www.conference-board.org/ilcprogram.

Figure 2.1

Share of manufacturing employment in economies with largest average manufacturing trade deficits relative to GDP, 1960–2010 (earliest available data)

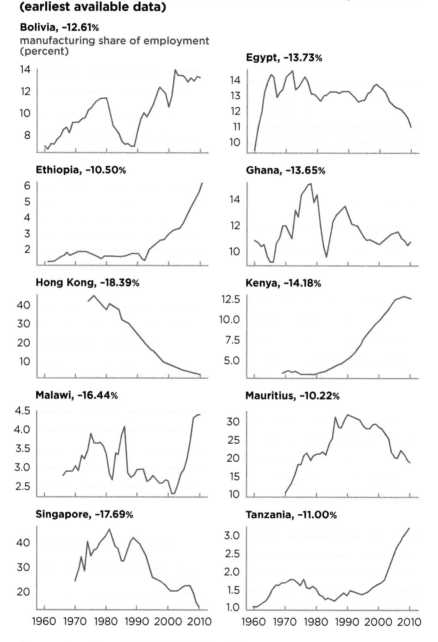

Bolivia, –12.61%
manufacturing share of employment (percent)

Egypt, –13.73%

Ethiopia, –10.50%

Ghana, –13.65%

Hong Kong, –18.39%

Kenya, –14.18%

Malawi, –16.44%

Mauritius, –10.22%

Singapore, –17.69%

Tanzania, –11.00%

Sources: Data from COMTRADE, the World Bank, and the Groningen Growth and Development Centre.

Figure 2.2

Share of manufacturing employment in economies with largest average manufacturing trade surpluses relative to GDP, 1960–2010 (earliest available data)

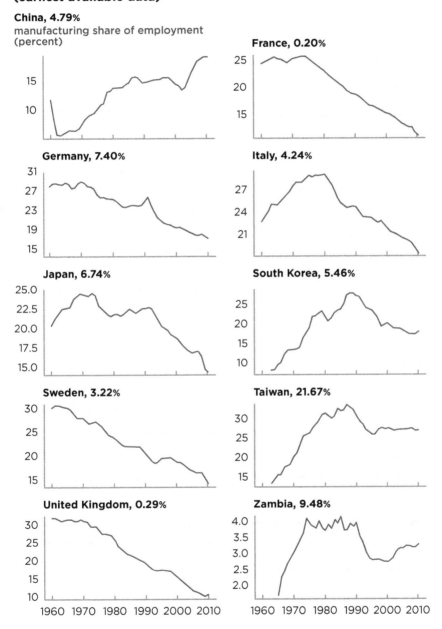

Sources: Data from COMTRADE, the World Bank, and the Groningen Growth and Development Centre (GGDC). Data for Germany come from a previous version of the GGDC database.

Figure 2.3

Share of manufacturing employment in China, 1999–2017

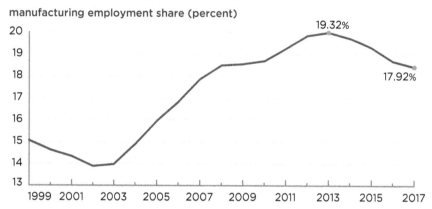

manufacturing employment share (percent)

Source: The Conference Board Total Economy Database.

How Trade Impacts the Manufacturing Employment Share

Opening the economy to trade and net capital flows breaks the identity between domestic production and domestic expenditure. In an open economy, domestic production will be equal to domestic expenditure $(C + I + G)$ (where C is consumption, I investment, and G government spending) plus net exports $(X - M)$ (where X is exports and M imports).

The determinants of net exports have the potential to alter the predictions about structural change that are derived in a closed economy framework. They can affect relationships at the level of a sector and the economy as a whole. This section considers the impact on manufacturing employment in an economy with balanced overall trade (although it allows for deficits and surpluses in manufacturing). The following section analyzes the effects of aggregate trade deficits and surpluses, under the assumption that all trade is in manufactured goods.

The MES is a function of the manufacturing labor embodied in the home economy's manufacturing expenditure share plus the labor embodied in the manufacturing net export ratio. Growth of domestic productivity in manufacturing will generally operate through its effects on sectoral net exports (by changing comparative advantage) and domestic spending (through the impact of trade on income and the relative prices of traded and nontraded goods and services).

In Ricardo's model, comparative advantage is determined by labor productivity differentials across products and economies. The Ricardian model is a natural complement to a closed economy model, such as the model of Rachel Ngai and Christopher Pissarides (2007), in which structural change reflects differences in labor productivity growth rates across sectors.[3] Several papers use versions of the Ricardian model to introduce trade into explanations of structural change (e.g., Matsuyama 2009; Yi and Zhang 2010; Uy, Yi, and Zhang 2013; Święcki 2017).

Matsuyama (2009) has been vocal about the dangers of concluding that productivity growth in manufacturing will have a negative impact on manufacturing employment when economies are treated in isolation and assumed not to engage in trade. He uses Ricardian theory to show that in a two-economy model the relationship between manufacturing productivity growth and employment could be positive. An increase in manufacturing productivity growth that increases the home economy's comparative advantage in manufacturing could boost its net manufacturing exports and thus more than offset the reduction in employment caused by the response of its domestic expenditure to productivity growth in the face of inelastic demand. However, this employment expansion at home comes at the expense of manufacturing jobs abroad. In the foreign economy, the share of manufacturing employment can fall for two reasons. Foreign manufacturing producers will experience an employment decline because of their own higher productivity in manufacturing. If, however, their comparative disadvantage in manufacturing increases, they will also lose market share to imports. In the early stages of development, the MES curve will thus be higher in the home country than in a closed economy and lower in the foreign country. Depending on patterns of comparative advantage, "globalization" could thus either increase or decrease the MES across economies.

Countries with a growing comparative advantage in manufacturing will not always experience an increase in manufacturing employment growth, because faster manufacturing productivity affects manufacturing employment in two ways. On the one hand, higher productivity increases the demand for exports by affecting relative prices (the comparative advantage productivity effect). On the other hand, the amount of labor required to produce a given quantity of output will decline (the absolute productivity effect). If the demand elasticity for exports is high, the comparative advantage productivity effect will dominate, and the employment impact will be positive. If the demand response to a comparative advantage productivity increase is relatively low, it could be offset by the negative absolute

---

3. The Ricardian framework with only one factor of production is used here because it is the simplest way to integrate structural change and trade. More realistic models of structural change and trade can be developed by assuming more factors of production and goods whose production differs in factor intensity. For a model in which land-scarce countries initiate manufacturing at a lower level of per capita income and specialize more intensively in manufactures, see Leamer (1987).

productivity effect. In this case, even in an open economy, the employment impact of faster productivity growth could be negative.

Kei-Mu Yi and Jing Zhang (2010) note that as economies capture a larger share of a foreign market in a particular product, the comparative advantage productivity effect is likely to diminish as export shares increase. Their point can be illustrated by thinking about two extreme cases:

- Case 1: The home economy is too small to affect the world price of its exports; it can sell as much as it can produce competitively without reducing prices (i.e., the demand elasticity it faces is infinite). If faster manufacturing productivity growth increases its comparative advantage in manufacturing and shifts its export supply curve outward, manufacturing employment will increase.
- Case 2: Economies are specialized, and home economy exports account for the entire foreign market for manufactured goods. In this case, as demand for manufactured goods abroad (and world demand) is inelastic, the employment response to faster manufacturing productivity that operates through the trade channel will be negative and complement the negative effect that operates through price-inelastic domestic spending in the home economy (though the two effects may differ in magnitude).

As economies increase their shares in foreign markets, they will be moving from the first case toward the second. As the elasticity of demand is likely to be inversely related to their foreign market share, the Matsuyama critique will eventually lose its relevance for large net-exporting economies. Together with the inelastic response that operates through domestic spending in the home economy, the increase in the MES associated with trade will eventually decline. Therefore, even in economies with manufacturing trade surpluses, the profile of manufacturing employment as income rises will be hump-shaped, as the negative impacts of more rapid manufacturing productivity growth on both domestic spending and net exports dominate the declining positive spillovers from agriculture.

Following in the tradition of Matsuyama, Timothy Uy, Kei-Mu Yi, and Jing Zhang (2013) explore structural change in an open economy using the sophisticated version of the Ricardian model developed by Jonathan Eaton and Samuel Kortum (2002). Their two-economy model has two traded goods (manufactures and agriculture) and a third sector (services) that is nontradable. They trace how productivity growth in manufacturing at home affects the MES through changes in the manufacturing employment content of domestic expenditure $(C + I + G)$ and the manufacturing content of net exports of manufactures $(X - M)$.

The simplest version of their model suppresses the employment effects that operate through domestic spending by assuming that income and price elasticities in both economies equal unity. Each economy spends fixed shares on the products of each sector, and productivity and price effects offset each other, keeping the share of labor demanded in each sector by domestic spending constant. If the economies were closed, without either income or productivity effects, there would be no structural change and no hump-shaped profile for the MES. With these assumptions, any shape that emerges in an open economy will be caused only by the effects of manufacturing productivity that operate through trade. Given unitary income and price elasticities, both economies will still have the same employment shares in nontraded services, even if they are allowed to trade. However, if an economy's manufacturing productivity increases by more than its agriculture productivity, it will export more manufactured goods and import more agricultural products—the classic Ricardian comparative advantage effect under balanced trade. Overall spending on agriculture will by assumption remain fixed, but more of these products will be imported. If overall trade is assumed to be balanced, employment in home manufacturing therefore initially rises, as the economy experiences a growing export surplus in manufactures. Labor moves from agriculture to manufactures. As a result, the MES rises and the employment share in agriculture declines. Because by assumption employment changes caused by domestic spending effects are suppressed, the domestic labor content of the net manufacturing surplus provides an exact measure of the impact of trade on manufacturing employment, and the growing surplus in manufacturing accounts for the upward slope of the hump.[4]

Initially, as the price of the home economy's manufactured goods declines and the home economy's share of the foreign market grows, an increasing share of its labor is involved in meeting foreign manufacturing demand. However, according to Uy, Yi, and Zhang (2013, 13):

> As time passes, the continuing increase in productivity growth implies that eventually the home economy will be fully supplying the demand for manufactures abroad. In this case, any further increase in productivity will lead to fewer manufacturing workers being needed to produce the net trade surplus in manufactures *since by assumption the value of foreign spending on manufactures (and thus on exports from the home economy) is fixed* [italics added].

---

4. The assumptions used in this model are sufficient to use the job content of the trade balance in manufacturing as an indicator of the net impact of trade on employment. In other words these assumptions suppress a role for changes in domestic spending *(C+I+G)* on employment, and only the net trade impact matters.

Over time, as its manufacturing sector becomes more productive, a smaller share of the home economy's labor is used to meet the foreign economy's manufacturing demand, and the manufacturing labor share in the home economy declines. The labor that is released from manufacturing employment moves into services. Thus, even if the home economy is a net exporter of manufactures and the MES producing for home demand remains constant, the MES will have a humped shape, because a declining share of employment will be required for trade.

The assumptions of unitary price and income elasticities at home and abroad can be relaxed to allow the expenditure channels to operate in both economies. Doing so strengthens the prediction of a hump-shaped manufacturing employment profile, because it brings into play the domestic sources of the hump that are captured in the closed economy model. When faster productivity growth in manufacturing at home reduces the domestic prices of manufactured goods, the MES falls, because of the inelastic response of domestic expenditures. Compared with the case of unitary price elasticity, the curve relating manufacturing employment to income growth will be lower. In addition, given the faster productivity growth in manufacturing, the relative wages—and thus the relative weight of the home economy, where labor is the only factor of production—will rise, increasing the importance of declining home expenditure relative to the trade effect. Initially, because its share of the foreign market is growing, the home economy's manufacturing employment still rises, through its net exports. As the home economy increases in size relative to the foreign economy, however, the (negative) impact of its domestic spending on manufacturing employment grows relative to the initially positive impact on manufacturing employment that operates through trade. Driven by faster manufacturing productivity growth, both trade and domestic demand eventually become sources of declining manufacturing labor demand. Over time, the MES in the home economy moves along the declining slope of the curve.

These models suggest that although a comparative advantage in trade could initially boost manufacturing employment, the effect will eventually peak and then reverse itself. As in a closed economy, the MES eventually declines. Allowing for trade introduces the possibility that in the early stages of development the MES could be either higher or lower than if the economy is in autarky. Once trade is taken into account, the hump-shaped profile can emerge even when the economy has a growing comparative advantage in manufacturing and productivity growth in manufacturing is more rapid than in agriculture. The prediction of a hump-shaped MES curve is thus more robust in an open economy than in a closed one.

Some caveats are in order. The models considered here assume that labor is the only factor of production; by definition, the factor intensity of manufacturing trade is thus unchanged. In reality, as economies develop and accumulate more physical and human capital, the composition of their exports is likely to become more intensive in both physical and human capital, potentially further reducing the employment impact of additional export growth. Conversely, as their comparative disadvantage in labor-intensive products increases, more jobs could be lost to imports. The model also assumes that services are not traded. An increase in comparative advantage in services could cause an economy's MES to fall for any given aggregate trade balance.

How International Capital Flows Impact the Manufacturing Employment Share

When manufactured products dominate trade, changes in international borrowing and lending can affect the MES. Appendix 2A illustrates this phenomenon formally in a two-economy model that builds on the model in appendix 1A but assumes that there are only manufactured goods and services.[5] It is based on the simplest version of the transfer problem, which assumes that the trade (current account) balance reflects exogenous changes in savings and investment decisions, with the decision to increase/decrease saving relative to investment leading to a trade surplus/deficit in manufacturing.[6] Each economy produces services that are nontraded and a unique tradable manufactured good. The model assumes that the marginal propensity to consume that good is the same at home and abroad (this assumption allows the terms of trade impact of the transfer to be ignored). The trade balance is defined in terms of the ratio of consumption to production of manufacturing output.

In this case, increased domestic spending relative to income associated with a deficit (associated here with international transfers) raises demand for both manufactured goods and services. As services are nontraded, the increased spending is met partly by increased production of and employment in services, reducing the MES. In addition, increased spending increases the demand for manufactured goods. The gap between increased demand for and reduced domestic production of manufactured goods is met through increased imports. The MES therefore declines in the deficit

---

5. Appendix 2A is available in the online data package for this book at https://www.piie.com/bookstore/behind-curve-can-manufacturing-still-provide-inclusive-growth.

6. By assumption, this version suppresses terms of trade effects by assuming a single good. For a more complete discussion, see Johnson (1976).

Figure 2.4

Manufacturing employment shares of net exporters, of net importers, and in a closed economy

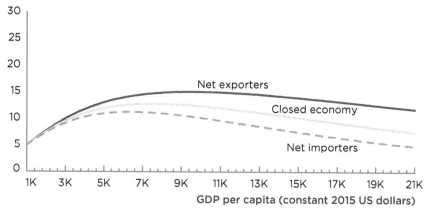

manufacturing employment share (percent)

Note: For parameters, see table 2A.1 in appendix 2A, available at https://www.piie.com/bookstore/behind-curve-can-manufacturing-still-provide-inclusive-growth.

economy. In the surplus economy, expenditure on and employment in services decline, and the MES increases to produce more exports. A net (manufacturing) exporter will thus have a larger share of manufacturing production and employment at every level of income and a smaller share of employment in services. Thus, the manufacturing employment–income curve will be lower and farther to the left in a deficit economy than in an economy with balanced trade and farther to the right in an economy with a surplus, as developed in appendix 2A[7] and illustrated in figure 2.4 for the case in which there is a deficit of 2 percent of output. As productivity in manufacturing grows, the manufacturing employment content of the trade deficits and surpluses declines, and the difference in the manufacturing employment–income curves between the closed and open economies narrows for both manufacturing surplus and deficit economies. The hump-shaped profile of MES is preserved.

---

7. Appendix 2A is available in the online data package for this book at https://www.piie.com/bookstore/behind-curve-can-manufacturing-still-provide-inclusive-growth.

Regression Analysis of the Effect of Trade on the Manufacturing Employment Share

The regressions reported in table 2.1 explore the impact of controlling for trade using the net manufacturing trade balance as a share of GDP. The data and variables are the same as in chapter 1.

A weakness of this approach is that the trade balance in manufacturing as a share of GDP is taken as exogenous and the regressions are estimated using ordinary least squares. Considerable effort was made to try to improve the identification of the net manufacturing trade balance impact using two-stage least squares.[8] They met with little success, both in combination and using the variables separately. Most of the variables failed the tests for relevance, exogeneity, or both, and several resulted in the coefficients on the trade variables having the wrong signs. It is possible that a better instrument might provide stronger results, but given the failure of these efforts, the regressions based on the ordinary least squares specification should be considered as statistical historical summaries of the association between the variables ex post rather than the results of a formal causal model.

At the global level, in the full sample, the coefficient on the trade balance (0.363) has the expected sign (positive) and is statistically significant. Similar estimates of the impact of trade are obtained when the sample includes only developed economies and Asian economies. The trade balance has weak explanatory power in the other regions and is not significant, possibly highlighting the endogeneity of the trade balance. If the trade balance is exogenous, its association with employment would be expected to be positive; if it is a response to domestic expenditure changes, the relationship could be negative. Taking trade into account still yields estimates of statistically significant hump-shaped MES curves in all groupings, although there are some differences in the coefficients on the GDP per capita variables compared with those in table 1.1. However, the implied per capita income at which the manufacturing share peaks is very similar for the samples with and without trade, except for Africa, for which the GDP coefficient is not statistically significant.[9]

---

8. The instrumental variables used a number of variables that are often used in trade equations, including a relative price competitiveness variable (the ratio of manufactured goods prices for each economy to a GDP-weighted average of manufactured goods prices of the other economies in the sample), the real exchange rate, commodity price indices (to capture Dutch disease effects), the ratio of national GDP to global GDP (to capture relative income effects), and product complexity (to capture nonprice effects).

9. Taking the derivative of the equation with respect to the log of per capita income and setting the result equal to zero to solve for the maximum income suggests that when trade is included, maximum incomes (in 2011 dollars) are $8,850 with trade and $9,090 without trade globally.

Table 2.1

Regression results on the manufacturing employment share in open economies, by region and level of development, 1960–2011

Variable	(1) Global	(2) Africa	(3) Asia	(4) Latin America	(5) Europe	(6) Developed economies	(7) Developing economies
Log GDP per capita	1.138*** (0.207)	0.403 (0.322)	1.598*** (0.243)	2.543*** (0.491)	2.888*** (0.309)	1.811*** (0.169)	0.897*** (0.246)
Log GDP per capita squared	-0.261*** (0.0347)	-0.159* (0.0842)	-0.314*** (0.0506)	-0.586*** (0.108)	-0.526*** (0.0600)	-0.362*** (0.0342)	-0.204*** (0.0656)
Log population	0.318* (0.160)	0.489 (0.609)	0.294 (0.413)	0.148 (0.194)	-0.959 (1.391)	-0.109 (0.836)	0.284 (0.176)
Log population squared	-0.0659* (0.0341)	-0.0473 (0.128)	-0.106** (0.0372)	-0.0632 (0.0385)	-0.0421 (0.133)	-0.0575 (0.0634)	-0.0518 (0.0386)
Ln share mfg trade balance	0.363*** (0.0423)	-0.152 (0.540)	0.364*** (0.0170)	-0.407 (0.270)	1.109 (1.006)	0.349*** (0.0416)	0.262 (0.361)

Constant	-3.153*** (0.356)	-3.769*** (0.774)	-2.562** (1.032)	-4.416*** (0.561)	-1.777 (2.945)	-2.502 (1.821)	-3.266*** (0.392)
Observations	1,876	533	474	448	372	627	1,249
R-squared	0.416	0.144	0.663	0.468	0.879	0.746	0.206
Number of economies	42	13	11	9	8	14	28

Note: Robust standard errors are in parentheses.

*** $p < 0.01$, ** $p < 0.05$, * $p < 0.1$.

Sources: Data from the Groningen Growth and Development Centre; the OECD; the World Bank; and the Maddison Project Database, version 2020.

These regressions suggest that although trade can affect sector employment shares in individual economies, its effects on the aggregate curves that capture common and shared features of structural change are diverse and often small. This finding should not be surprising, because in large samples with a diverse set of economies, economy-specific dummies are likely to be offset or captured by trade surpluses and deficits. This result is consistent with the findings of Święcki (2017), who constructs a more complex simulation model, calibrated using data from 45 economies. He finds that "ignoring trade would not lead to a systematic bias in predicting the changes in labor allocation across time" (p. 96).[10]

Conclusion

Rapid sectoral productivity may have different effects on employment in an open economy than in a closed one. Especially if the economy is small, the ability to export may make demand elastic. In this case, increased manufacturing employment could be associated with more rapid productivity growth in manufacturing. An economy with a growing comparative advantage in manufacturing could have a higher manufacturing employment curve and peak than under autarky. Conversely, if comparative disadvantage in manufactures increases, because of relatively rapid productivity growth in agriculture (or mining), economies with growing trade deficits in manufacturing trade could reach lower peaks of manufacturing employment.

The fact that a second humped path from trade arises in the face of more rapid increases in labor productivity in manufacturing strengthens the argument that the overall profile of manufacturing employment will be hump shaped. It means that the hump can emerge even when productivity growth is faster in manufacturing than in agriculture. Over time, the negative effects that operate through inelastic domestic demand in reducing the MES will be reinforced by those that operate through trade. Once past their peaks, therefore, more advanced economies will also experience declining MES despite trade surpluses in manufacturing.

---

10. Święcki (2017, 97) observes that "even in South Korea, sector-biased productivity growth and nonhomothetic preferences are quantitively more important than trade as drivers of structural change."

3

Larger Trade Balances and Declines in the Manufacturing Employment Share

It seems plausible that larger manufacturing trade surpluses would be associated with rising manufacturing employment shares (MES). Based on this assumption, many countries have adopted new industrial policies in the belief that better manufacturing technologies and higher manufacturing productivity will lead to higher manufacturing employment and allow more workers to obtain decent high-paying jobs (as described in part III).

This view is at odds with the theory developed in the previous chapter, which shows that the hump-shaped profile of the MES is typical for most economies. The theory indicates that once past their peak MES, countries will experience declining MES as they grow, whether they have trade deficits or surpluses.

The theory also highlights that increased productivity in manufacturing can be a double-edged sword. It can reduce the prices of manufactured goods at home and make manufactured exports more internationally competitive. But even if domestic production of manufactures expands, if the combination of domestic spending and international demand is insufficiently responsive to these lower prices, manufacturing employment can fall.

This chapter provides powerful empirical evidence that supports the theory. Using data from 60 economies, it examines the employment changes associated with levels and changes in the trade balance in manufacturing. It shows that between 1995 and 2011, economies with trade surpluses in manufacturing value added experienced average declines in the MES that were slightly larger than the declines in MES in economies with manufacturing trade deficits. It also shows that the declines in the MES were as large in economies in which the MVA trade balance increased as a share of GDP as in those economies where this share declined. These findings suggest that even if policies (or increased productivity in manufacturing) generate larger trade surpluses in manufacturing, they are unlikely to reverse declines in the MES that have persisted in many economies for several decades.

This chapter is organized as follows. The first section argues that rather than the more commonly used gross trade and final expenditure data, which include value-added outside of manufacturing, value-added data that isolate developments in the manufacturing industry are more appropriate for analyzing the determinants of the demand for manufacturing employment. The subsequent sections therefore use the manufacturing value added (MVA) data developed by the World Trade Organization (WTO) and the Organization for Economic Cooperation and Development (OECD) in their Trade in Value Added (TiVA) database to explore the association between levels and changes in net exports of MVA and manufacturing employment shares, drawing attention to the changes in the shares of MVA in national spending and production.

Using Value Added Rather than Gross Trade and Final Expenditure Data

Trade data are typically reported as the overall value of goods or services traded rather than the value of exports and imports that originate from particular industries. Expenditure data are similar, indicating the values of spending on goods and services sold as finished products rather than the value added in the industries in which they were produced. But the demand for workers in manufacturing reflects demand for value added in manufacturing alone. To measure this demand, it is necessary to subtract the nonmanufacturing inputs from the gross measures of manufactured goods output in both final expenditure and trade.

For example, the value of an automobile includes the value added not only of the automobile and other manufacturing industries but also of the industries that produce the raw materials (iron ore, glass sand, and rubber) and services (distribution, transportation, banking, advertising) used to produce the car, all of which are reflected in the final purchase price. Similarly, the value of final sales of services reflects the use of manufactured goods (computers and other equipment) to provide these services; the value of the sales of food (an agricultural product) also reflects the value of manufactured goods (tractors, trucks, irrigation pipes) used in agriculture. These MVA estimates can be derived from input-output tables that measure the industry sources of value added in trade and final spending on goods and services. When some MVA is imported as intermediate inputs from other economies, imported value added needs to be subtracted to determine the value-added measure that creates demand for domestic manufacturing labor.

Fortunately, the joint OECD/WTO project on TiVA links the input-output matrices of economies that account for over 90 percent of global manufacturing output. It provides data on the value added by each economy to both final demand and exports from 36 sectors. The TiVA analysis originally covered 61 economies, using data and classification methods for selected years between 1995 and 2011. A more recent version includes 64 economies.[1]

The data cover economies with per capita incomes that averaged $27,790 in 2022 (in 2021 purchasing power parity [PPP] dollars).[2] They range from $1,091 in the Democratic Republic of the Congo to $122,940 in Luxembourg. The sample is heavily weighted with upper-income economies, including 48 with per capita incomes above $30,000 and 63 above $20,000.

Most of these economies are likely to have passed their MES peak. This feature makes the sample particularly appropriate for analyzing the sources of changes in manufacturing labor demand in economies on the downward slope of the curve.

Relationships among Variables Linking the Trade Balance in Manufacturing Value Added to the Manufacturing Employment Share

This section explores the ex post relationships that determine the demand for manufacturing labor. These components of demand are not independent of their causes, but their association can provide some important

---

1. The TiVA data are available at https://www.oecd.org/sti/ind/measuring-trade-in-value-added.htm (accessed on June 21, 2016). A more recent version of the data (2005–15) is available for 64 countries, but the estimates differ, because of data revisions and different classification methods. As a result, the two versions give slightly different results even for the same years. In order to ensure consistency in comparisons over time, this analysis uses the 1995–2011 data. Conducting the analysis using the 2005–15 data yielded results that were qualitatively similar to those reported here. In particular, the declines in MES over this period were similar in trade-surplus and trade-deficit countries.

2. Data are from The Conference Board Total Economy Database, https://www.conference-board.org/data/economydatabase/total-economy-database-productivity (accessed in April 2022).

clues about the relevance of the theory developed in the previous chapter. It suggests that relatively rapid productivity growth in manufacturing could enhance a country's comparative advantage in manufacturing but that it could also reduce domestic spending on manufacturing. As the analysis indicates, this negative association between the trade balance in manufacturing and the share of domestic spending on manufacturing is not simply a theoretical possibility but a common feature of the data.

The definition of the components of value added in manufacturing follows from the definition of GDP. Just as GDP (Y) is defined as the sum of consumption (C), investment (I), and government spending (G) plus the trade balance ($X-M$), value added in manufacturing is defined as the sum of MVA in national consumption (C_m), investment (I_m), and government (G_m) spending and on exports (X_m) minus imports (M_m): $Y_m = C_m + I_m + G_m + (X_m - M_m)$. These variables can be used to explore three relationships: between trade balances in MVA and the MES, between (levels of) trade balances in MVA and changes in the MES, and between *changes* in trade balances in MVA and *changes* in the MES.

Table 3A.1 in appendix 3A uses TiVA data for 60 economies for 1995–2011 to calculate the averages of the components that define MVA production as a share of GDP.[3] These data include the MVA trade balance in goods and services ($X_m - M_m$), the MVA in domestic spending ($C_m + I_m + G_m$), and domestic production of MVA ($C_m + I_m + G_m + [X_m - M_m]$). Table 3A.1 also reports MVA in domestic investment (I_m) and domestic consumption (C_m), average per capita incomes (in 2017 PPP dollars), and the MES. The 60 economies are ranked by the ratio of their net exports of MVA to GDP (column 1). Table 3.1 shows the results for the averages of surplus economies and deficit economies as well as the averages of the top 10 and bottom 10 economies, as ranked by their average MVA trade balances.

The top 10 economies ranked by their net trade balances in MVA as a share of GDP are five in Asia (Singapore, South Korea, Taiwan, Malaysia, and Thailand) and five in Europe (Ireland, Finland, Germany, the Czech Republic, and Sweden). The important role of trade in the share of MVA production in GDP can be seen by the fact that 8 of these economies in table 3A.1 are also in the top 15 when ranked by share of MVA production in GDP.

---

3. Appendix 3A appears at the end of this chapter. Brunei Darussalam is in the TiVA data but is not included here because annual data on its MES are not readily available. Annual data for all countries in appendix 3A are not available for all years; reported averages for 1995–2011 therefore use data for only seven years: 1995, 2000, 2005, and 2008–11.

Figure 3.1 shows the close relationship between MVA trade balances and the share of MVA production in GDP. Fitting a linear trend line to capture the association between the production and net trade columns in table 3A.1 yields a coefficient that is very close to 1 and statistically significant (0.94). This result indicates that each 1 percent increase in the ratio of the MVA trade balance to GDP is associated with about a 1 percent increase in the share of MVA production in GDP.

The composition of national spending also helps explain the large share of manufacturing production in several economies. Final spending on investment (plant, equipment, and inventories) is far more intensive in MVA than final spending on consumption (Lawrence 2019) (see table 4.8).

An important source of the large MVA share in Asian economies' GDP is the level of investment spending. China—the economy with the largest share of manufacturing in GDP in the sample—is the leader in this respect, with 15.6 percent of its GDP spent on MVA in investment on average during the sample period, almost three times the average of the economies in the sample (box 3.1). Shares of MVA in GDP that stem from investment are also high in Vietnam (11.2 percent), Thailand (10.4 percent), South Korea (10.3 percent), Malaysia (10.0 percent), and Taiwan (7.8 percent), all of which are above the sample average of 6.3 percent. In contrast, the shares of spending on MVA in consumption in China (12.4 percent), Taiwan (11.8), and South Korea (11.4 percent) are very close to the 11.4 percent average of all the economies in the sample.

The large share of investment and hence manufacturing in these Asian economies is closely related to their rapid growth. If growth in these economies slows, investment and the share of MVA are likely to decline (Lawrence 2019). The relationships between the variables that connect the trade balance to manufacturing employment emerge clearly when economies are grouped into two categories. The key link is the level of manufacturing labor productivity, which as table 3.1 shows is substantially higher in manufacturing trade surplus countries.

Surplus versus Deficit Economies

In the full sample reported in table 3A.1, 26 economies had trade surpluses in MVA (averaging 3.4 percent of GDP) and 34 had deficits (averaging 3.2 percent of GDP). The average shares of MVA in overall spending $(C_m + I_m)$ were similar in both deficit and surplus countries, at about 18 percent of GDP. In contrast, the shares of GDP in manufacturing production were very different: On average, the surplus economies produced 21.9 percent of their GDP in manufacturing and the deficit economies just 15.2 percent. Although the average MES of 18.1 percent in

Table 3.1

Measures of manufacturing value added (MVA) as a share of GDP and associated variables, 1995–2011 average values

Grouping	Net trade in MVA as share of GDP	Production of MVA as share of GDP	Spending on MVA as share of GDP	Consumption of MVA as share of GDP
Average of 60 economies	-0.003	0.181	0.184	0.114
Surplus economy average	0.034	0.219	0.185	0.109
Deficit economy average	-0.032	0.152	0.183	0.119
Top 10 (largest surplus) economy average	0.059	0.245	0.186	0.104
Bottom 10 (largest deficit) economy average	-0.059	0.135	0.195	0.120

Grouping	Investment in MVA as share of GDP	Manufacturing employment share in total employment	Per capita income (2017 PPP US dollars)	Relative value added per worker in manufacturing[a]
Average of 60 economies	0.063	0.162	29,563	1.12
Surplus economy average	0.070	0.181	32,592	1.21
Deficit economy average	0.058	0.148	27,247	1.02
Top 10 (largest surplus) economy average	0.075	0.189	34,810	1.30
Bottom 10 (largest deficit) economy average	0.067	0.137	21,769	0.99

PPP = purchasing power parity

Definitions:

Net trade = $X_m - M_m$

Production = $C_m + I_m + G_m + (X_m - M_m)$

Spending = $C_m + I_m + G_m$

Consumption = C_m

Investment = I_m

a. Relative value added per worker in manufacturing calculated as MVA per worker in manufacturing divided by value added per worker in the whole economy = $(MVA/L_m)/(GDP/L)$.

Note: Countries ranked by average net trade in MVA as share of GDP.

Source: Table 3A.1 in appendix 3A.

Figure 3.1

Association between domestic production of manufacturing value added (MVA) and net exports of MVA as a share of GDP

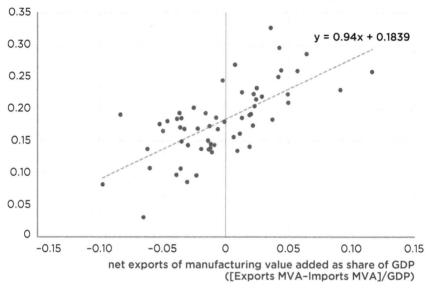

manufacturing value added production as share of GDP (MVA/GDP)

y = 0.94x + 0.1839

net exports of manufacturing value added as share of GDP
([Exports MVA–Imports MVA]/GDP)

Source: Data are averages for 1995–2011 from table 3A.1 in appendix 3A.

surplus economies was higher than the 14.8 percent in deficit economies, this 3.3 percentage point difference in employment was much smaller than the 6.7 percentage point difference in the shares of manufacturing production.[4] This suggests that aside from the MVA in their trade balances (which all else equal would have resulted in very large differences in MESs), differences in relative manufacturing labor productivity levels help explain the gap.

As shown in the far right-hand column of table 3.1, MVA per worker relative to GDP per worker was around 19 percent higher in economies with trade surpluses than in deficit economies, offsetting some of the employment impact of the higher manufacturing output shares in surplus

---

4. Data on the employment share in manufacturing are from The Conference Board's International Labor Comparisons program (July 2018), https://www.conference-board.org/topics/productivity-competitiveness/International-Productivity-Labor-Unit-Cost-Map (accessed on March 29, 2019), and the International Labor Organization Department of Statistics, https://www.ilo.org/ilostat/faces/oracle/webcenter/portalapp/pagehierarchy/Page3.jspx?locale = EN&MBI_ID = 538 (accessed on May 25, 2020).

Box 3.1

Sources of demand for manufacturing in the United States and China

The United States ran an average trade deficit in MVA equal to 1.2 percent of GDP between 1995 and 2011 (see table 3A.1 in appendix 3A to this chapter). This figure represents the difference between the 13.9 percent of GDP accounted for by manufacturing production and the 15.1 percent of GDP accounted for by MVA in US final expenditures. To a considerable extent, the relatively low spending share on MVA in the United States reflected its low investment share, which increased demand for MVA by just 3.7 percent of GDP (the sample average was 6.3 percent). US MVA consumption accounted for 11.3 percent of GDP, in line with the sample average of 11.4 percent.

Had the United States maintained its level of MVA spending at 15.1 percent of GDP over this period but produced all of the value added domestically, its production of MVA would have been 8.6 percent higher. In 2015, US MVA in domestic spending and the trade deficit were equal to 14.7 percent and 2.2 percent of GDP, respectively. Manufacturing production was thus 12.5 percent of GDP. The number of full-time equivalent manufacturing employees was 12.08 million (9.1 percent of total employment) in 2015. *With balanced trade in MVA and the same dollar level of spending on MVA, US manufacturing production would have been 17.6 percent higher*, employment in manufacturing would have been 2.12 million higher, and the MES would have been 10.7 percent rather than 9.1 percent. Of course, these data represent after-the-fact outcomes; the ultimate outcome would have been sensitive to how the trade deficit was eliminated. Thus the size of the US manufacturing sector would have been significantly larger but manufacturing's role in US employment would remain relatively small.

China's average trade surplus in MVA was 3.5 percent of GDP in 1995–2011 and the focus of considerable attention and controversy. But the primary source of China's very large share of manufacturing production, which averaged 32.6 percent of GDP, was its MVA of 29.1 percent of GDP, which resulted from its domestic spending. High domestic spending reflected the value added in the economy's extraordinarily large share of investment spending, which accounted for MVA of 15.6 percent of GDP. In contrast, Chinese consumption spending was typical of the economies in the sample, accounting for MVA equal to 12.4 percent of GDP—not much greater than the sample average of 11.4 percent.

By 2015, the share of GDP accounted for by production had declined to 30.7 percent in China, and its MVA trade surplus had grown to 4.0 percent of GDP. Had China been self-contained (or had balanced trade) but maintained its nominal level of domestic spending on MVA at 30.7 percent,

box continues

Box 3.1 continued
Sources of demand for manufacturing in the United States and China

its MVA and manufacturing employment would have been 11.5 percent smaller (30.7/34.7). According to The Conference Board, in 2015 the manufacturing employment share in China was 18.5 percent; without its trade surplus, it would have been 16.3 percent.

In sum, although much of the focus has been on trade balances, in both the United States and China by far the most important source of the demand for manufacturing output and employment has been domestic spending and the most important source of the difference in their domestic spending has been their different investment rates. Even with balanced trade in manufacturing, in both countries the employment shares in manufacturing would not be very different.

economies. Assuming international convergence of the prices of manufactured goods, the association between higher (labor) productivity in manufacturing (compared with labor productivity in the rest of the economy) and manufacturing trade surpluses is consistent with the basic Ricardian model of trade, which predicts comparative advantage based on the relative productivity of labor across products and that countries with such a comparative advantage will be net exporters of manufactured products.

Results for the Top 10 and Bottom 10 Economies

These conclusions are even stronger at the extremes. The 10 economies with the largest trade surpluses in MVA (relative to GDP) are richer than the 10 economies with the smallest surpluses (with per capita income in 2017 PPP of $34,810 and $21,769, respectively). On average, the top 10 had trade surpluses equal to 5.9 percent of GDP, and those in the bottom 10 had deficits of 5.9 percent of GDP. The two groups spent similar shares of their GDP on MVA, but the share of MVA production in GDP was 24.5 percent in the top 10 economies and just 13.5 percent in the bottom 10. But relative MVA per worker in the top 10 was around 31 percent higher than in the bottom 10. This finding explains why the differences in the MES (18.9 percent versus 13.7 percent) are much narrower than the differences in manufacturing production shares.

Regressions confirm both that larger trade balances in manufacturing are associated with larger shares of MVA in GDP and that higher MVA per worker in manufacturing is associated with large trade balances in MVA. Figure 3.2 shows the strong linear relationship between changes in the

Figure 3.2

Relationship between changes in the manufacturing value added (MVA) trade balance and changes in the ratio of MVA per worker to GDP per worker

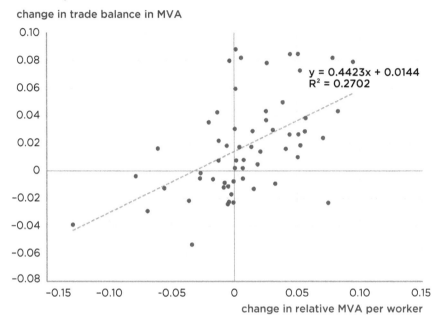

change in trade balance in MVA

$y = 0.4423x + 0.0144$
$R^2 = 0.2702$

change in relative MVA per worker

Source: Data are averages for 1995–2011 from table 3A.2 in appendix 3A.

trade balance in MVA and changes in relative MVA per worker (the ratio of MVA per worker to economywide value added).

On average, shares of spending on MVA are similar in deficit and surplus economies, but economies with larger trade surpluses have higher relative productivity in manufacturing (panel a of figure 3.3) and smaller shares of spending on MVA relative to GDP (panel b in figure 3.3).

Changes in the Manufacturing Employment Share: Does the Manufacturing Trade Balance Make a Difference?

Table 3A.2 in appendix 3A ranks economies by the size of their average net trade balance in manufacturing to GDP between 1995 and 2011 and shows the relationships between changes in the MES in total employment in percentage points and changes in the underlying determinants of the demand for manufacturing employment as a percent of GDP. These underlying variables are changes in net trade in MVA, changes in spending on MVA, and changes in MVA production, all expressed as shares of GDP.

Figure 3.3

Association between trade balance in manufacturing value added (MVA) and relative productivity in manufacturing and relative spending on MVA

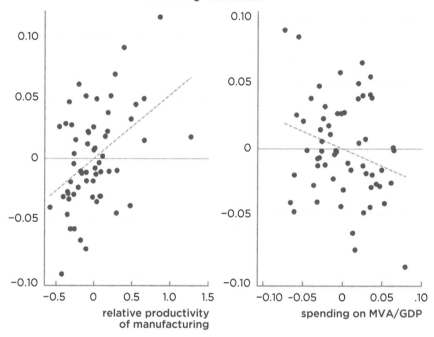

Relative manufacturing productivity
b = 0.0527 (robust) t = 3.09

Spending on manufacturing value added
b = -0.2641 (robust) t = -1.74

trade balance in manufacturing value added

relative productivity of manufacturing

spending on MVA/GDP

Note: b is the coefficient in regression Y = a + bx
Source: Data are from table 3A.1 in appendix 3A.

Changes in the MES are also reported in percentage points. The change in relative MVA per worker is obtained by subtracting changes in the MES from changes in the manufacturing output share.[5]

Over the full sample period, the 60 economies had divergent experiences in their trade balances as a share of GDP. Only three (Argentina, Cambodia, and Vietnam) did not experience a decline in MVA spending as

---

5. MVA per worker is given by $(MVA/L_m)/(GDP/L)$ or $(MVA/GDP)/(L_m/L)$. Expressed in logs, the log of the relative MVA per worker equals the log of manufacturing output share (MVA/GDP) minus the log of manufacturing employment share (L_m/L). Taking first differences yields an expression in terms of approximate percentage changes. Thus, the change in relative MVA per worker can be obtained by subtracting changes in the manufacturing employment share from changes in the manufacturing output share.

a share of GDP, however; on average the declines were 5 percent of GDP. The MES declined in 52 of the 60 economies, with an average decline of 4.0 percentage points (table 3.2).

Surplus and deficit economies increased their MVA net trade balances between 1995 and 2011 by 3 and 1 percent of GDP, respectively (second column in table 3.2), implying that economies in the rest of the world that are excluded from the sample saw declines in their net trade in MVA with the economies in the sample. Some of the differences in the changes in the net trade balances of surplus and deficit economies were offset by differences in the declines in spending on MVA, however. As a result, manufacturing production as a share of GDP fell by only 1.1 percentage points less in surplus than in deficit economies.

Despite the differences in the size of average manufacturing trade surpluses and in the changes in trade balances, *the declines in the MES were very similar*. Indeed, because of the larger increases in relative MVA per worker, the decline in the MES in the surplus economies was actually 0.6 percentage point greater than in the deficit economies (4.4 percentage points and 3.8 percentage points, respectively). *Clearly, large trade balances in manufacturing trade do not necessarily imply smaller declines in manufacturing employment.*

A similar and even starker picture emerges when economies at the extremes are considered in greater detail. The 10 economies with the largest MVA trade surpluses experienced average increases in their MVA net trade equal to 4.6 percent of their GDP. In the bottom 10 trade deficit economies, the figure increased by an average of 2.1 percentage points. However, the declines in spending on MVA were larger in the top surplus economies: 5.7 percent of GDP compared with 3.5 percent of GDP for the 10 economies with the largest deficits. As a result, the decline in MVA production of around 1 percent of GDP was almost identical in both groups. However, because MVA per worker in manufacturing relative to overall output per worker grew more rapidly in the trade surplus economies, their shares of manufacturing employment declined by 0.5 percentage point more than it did in economies with large deficits. Of the 10 economies, only 2 (Taiwan and Thailand) did not experience declines in their MES (table 3A.2).

These numbers highlight the two sources of convergence in the changes in the MES in trade surplus and deficit economies. Trade surplus economies tended to experience larger declines in domestic spending on MVA but they had larger increases in relative MVA per worker. Thus their faster manufacturing productivity growth resulted in greater declines in their spending on MVA and thus they had large declines in MES.

Table 3.2

Average net trade in manufacturing value added (MVA) and changes in the determinants of the manufacturing employment share, 1995–2011

Grouping	Average net trade in MVA as share of GDP	Change in net trade in MVA as share of GDP	Change in spending on MVA as share of GDP	Change in production of MVA as share of GDP
Average of 60 economies	-0.003	0.019	-0.050	-0.031
Surplus economy average	0.034	0.030	-0.055	-0.025
Deficit economy average	-0.032	0.010	-0.046	-0.036
Average of 10 largest surplus economies	0.059	0.046	-0.057	-0.011
Average of 10 largest deficit economies	-0.059	0.021	-0.035	-0.014

Grouping	Change in relative value added per worker in manufacturing	Change in manufacturing employment share in total employment	Per capita income (2017 PPP US dollars)
Average of 60 economies	0.009	-0.040	29,563
Surplus economy average	0.019	-0.044	32,592
Deficit economy average	0.002	-0.038	27,247
Average of 10 largest surplus economies	0.027	-0.038	34,810
Average of 10 largest deficit economies	0.019	-0.033	21,769

PPP = purchasing power parity

Note: See definitions below table 3.1. Countries ranked by average net trade in MVA as share of GDP.

Source: See table 3.A2 in appendix 3A.

What is striking are the pervasive declines in the domestic shares of MVA spending in these 10 economies: Half of them experienced declines in the share of nominal manufacturing production in GDP. The spending declines on MVA as a share of GDP were especially large in Singapore (11.4 percentage points), Malaysia (9.1 percentage points), the Czech Republic (8.9 percentage points), and Ireland (7.3 percentage points). Singapore and South Korea stand out for the very rapid relative productivity growth in manufacturing; despite their large trade surpluses, they experienced large declines in their MESs.

Germany's trade surplus in MVA as a share of GDP increased by 3.8 percentage points, but it was almost fully offset by the decline in its domestic spending on MVA. Because of its rapid relative growth in MVA per worker, Germany's MES fell by 4.9 percentage points.

All of these data reinforce the conclusion that economies that had larger trade surpluses saw larger declines in their domestic spending and larger increases in their relative MVA per worker that reduced the manufacturing employment effects of their surpluses.

Changes in the Trade Balance and the Manufacturing Employment Share

A third relationship that is revealing is between changes in the net export surplus in MVA and changes in the MES. For this analysis, economies are ranked according to changes in their net MVA exports between 1995 and 2011. Two-thirds of the sample (39 of the 60 economies) had positive changes, and a third experienced declines. For the sample as a whole, average net exports of manufacturing increased by 1.9 percent of GDP, allowing these economies to achieve nearly balanced MVA trade over the period.

Despite their balanced MVA trade, these economies' MES fell by 4.0 percentage points. The decline was driven mainly by decreases in the share of spending on manufacturing of 5 percent of GDP, decreases in in the MVA production share of 3.1 percent of GDP, and increases in relative MVA per worker of 0.9 percent. This example vividly illustrates how spending patterns and productivity rather than trade dominated the average MES experience over the period.

Table 3.3 reports averages for two groups of economies. The first compares economies with positive changes in net MVA exports with those with negative changes. On average the declines in MESs in both groups were virtually identical, at 4.0 percentage points, as the shaded column shows. Trade performance increased output in the economies with positive changes, but those economies had larger declines in domestic spending and much faster relative productivity growth in manufacturing. Moreover, in the economies with declining net MVA trade balances, relative output per worker in manufacturing grew more slowly than it did in other sectors.

The second group compares the top 10 and bottom 10 economies ranked by changes in their MVA trade balances as a share of GDP. The MES declined by 1.2 percentage points less in the economies with the largest trade balance increases than in those with the largest decreases (3.5 versus 4.7 percentage points), but this difference was far less than the 10.6 percentage point difference in their trade performance (7.9 versus −2.7 percentage points). Part of the explanation for the difference is the larger declines in spending shares in the economies with positive net export changes (7.9 versus 4.0 percentage points) and the larger increases in manufacturing output per worker (3.5 versus −1.9 percentage points).

Table 3A.3 describes the economies with the largest increases in net trade balances in manufacturing between 1995 and 2011. With the exception of Cambodia (by far the poorest economy in the sample), all of the top 10 economies experienced declines in domestic spending on MVA that on average were as large as the increases in their trade balances. Theory suggests that small economies will be price takers in world markets; with a comparative advantage in manufacturing, they could experience a rising MES. This is precisely what happened in Cambodia (Matsuyama 2009). In all other economies, both spending and manufacturing employment declined, with most experiencing relatively rapid productivity growth in MVA per worker.

Manufacturing trade balances are not determined in a vacuum. This analysis points to a major role for levels and changes in MVA per worker in manufacturing compared with developments in value added per worker in other sectors. When increases in the relative value added per worker in manufacturing are large, economies are likely to have a growing comparative advantage in manufacturing and thus run larger net trade balances (or smaller deficits) in manufacturing, as figure 3.2 shows. With higher value added per worker, the job content of any given trade balance is likely to be lower. This finding helps explain why despite their relatively larger shares of manufacturing output, employment shares in economies with manufacturing trade surpluses may be relatively close to those of economies with trade deficits. Similarly, rapid growth in relative manufacturing productivity is likely to lead to lower prices for domestic goods. Although the decline could mean more net exports, it could also lead to larger reductions in nominal domestic spending on MVA and the employment associated with it.

Table 3.3

Average changes in net exports in manufacturing value added (MVA) and changes in determinants of the manufacturing employment share, 1995–2011

Grouping	Average net exports in MVA as share of GDP	Change in net exports in MVA as share of GDP	Change in spending on MVA as share of GDP	Change in production of MVA as share of GDP
Average changes in net exports in 60 economies	-0.003	0.019	-0.050	-0.031
Economies with positive changes in net exports	0.002	0.037	-0.054	-0.017
Economies with negative changes in net exports	-0.012	-0.017	-0.042	-0.058
Top 10 (largest surplus) country average	0.020	0.079	-0.079	0.000
Bottom 10 (largest deficit) country average	-0.010	-0.027	-0.040	-0.066

Grouping	Change in relative value added per worker in manufacturing	Change in manufacturing employment share in total employment	Per capita income (2017 PPP US dollars)
Average changes in net exports in 60 economies	0.009	-0.040	29,563
Economies with positive changes in net exports	0.024	-0.041	28,337
Economies with negative changes in net exports	-0.018	-0.040	31,841
Top 10 (largest surplus) country average	0.035	-0.035	22,398
Bottom 10 (largest deficit) country average	-0.019	-0.047	40,370

Note: See definitions below table 3.1. Countries ranked by changes in net exports in MVA as share of GDP.

Sources: See table 3A.3 in appendix 3A.

Conclusion

Many economies have implemented industrial policies in the hope of enhancing national technological capabilities and thus increasing productivity and employment in manufacturing. The experience of the economies analyzed in this chapter raises serious questions about the efficacy of such policies. The data provide overwhelming evidence of the impact of being on the downward slope of the hump. The key finding is that neither the level of the net trade balance as a share of GDP nor changes in the net trade balance was an important contributor to the decline in the MES. Underlying this outcome is the finding that countries with larger MVA trade balances have higher levels and rates of change in relative labor productivity in manufacturing. As a result the positive impacts of the value of their trade balances on employment are generally offset by the lower manufacturing labor content of their trade balances and their domestic spending.

APPENDIX 3A Country Data

Table 3A.1

Measures of manufacturing value added (MVA), 1995–2011 average values, full sample (unless indicated otherwise all variables expressed as share of GDP)

Countries ranked by average net trade in MVA as share of GDP (column 1). Shading indicates top and bottom 10 economies.

	Country	Net trade in MVA	Production of MVA	Spending on MVA	Consumption of MVA	Investment in MVA	Manufacturing employment share in total employment	Per capita income (2017 PPP US dollars)
1	IRL: Ireland	0.116	0.258	0.142	0.090	0.047	0.139	44,738
2	SGP: Singapore	0.091	0.229	0.138	0.053	0.074	0.167	61,365
3	KOR: Korea	0.064	0.286	0.222	0.114	0.103	0.181	26,005
4	TWN: Taiwan	0.057	0.259	0.202	0.118	0.078	0.253	33,687
5	FIN: Finland	0.050	0.210	0.160	0.102	0.054	0.163	39,542
6	DEU: Germany	0.049	0.223	0.174	0.111	0.058	0.221	41,835
7	MYS: Malaysia	0.044	0.260	0.216	0.106	0.100	0.198	19,947
8	THA: Thailand	0.042	0.295	0.253	0.137	0.104	0.142	12,189
9	CZE: Czech Republic	0.042	0.250	0.208	0.121	0.083	0.272	26,274
10	SWE: Sweden	0.037	0.183	0.146	0.091	0.051	0.153	42,514

table continues

71

Table 3A.1 continued

Measures of manufacturing value added (MVA), 1995–2011 average values, full sample (unless indicated otherwise all variables expressed as share of GDP)

Countries ranked by average net trade in MVA as share of GDP (column 1). Shading indicates top and bottom 10 economies.

	Country	Net trade in MVA	Production of MVA	Spending on MVA	Consumption of MVA	Investment in MVA	Manufacturing employment share in total employment	Per capita income (2017 PPP US dollars)
11	CHN: China	0.035	0.326	0.291	0.124	0.156	0.154	6,550
12	CHL: Chile	0.029	0.219	0.191	0.117	0.068	0.131	17,575
13	SVK: Slovak Republic	0.024	0.232	0.208	0.125	0.076	0.267	21,048
14	HUN: Hungary	0.024	0.215	0.191	0.116	0.067	0.243	22,058
15	JPN: Japan	0.023	0.204	0.181	0.110	0.071	0.180	38,023
16	SVN: Slovenia	0.022	0.223	0.201	0.122	0.072	0.292	27,483
17	RUS: Russia	0.021	0.174	0.153	0.106	0.039	0.182	19,284
18	CHE: Switzerland	0.020	0.192	0.172	0.094	0.073	0.149	54,126
19	NLD: Netherlands	0.019	0.141	0.122	0.084	0.034	0.132	47,018
20	AUT: Austria	0.019	0.190	0.172	0.099	0.065	0.184	43,719
21	ITA: Italy	0.013	0.186	0.173	0.111	0.059	0.214	39,404

22	PHL: Philippines	0.013	0.226	0.213	0.143	0.065	0.089	4,911
23	BEL: Belgium	0.011	0.161	0.150	0.091	0.052	0.172	41,501
24	DNK: Denmark	0.009	0.135	0.125	0.078	0.043	0.143	45,492
25	IDN: Indonesia	0.007	0.269	0.262	0.166	0.089	0.127	41,325
26	ISR: Israel	0.006	0.156	0.150	0.097	0.047	0.153	29,789
27	ARG: Argentina	-0.001	0.180	0.181	0.119	0.056	0.143	17,251
28	ROU: Romania	-0.003	0.244	0.247	0.170	0.074	0.215	13,895
29	BRA: Brazil	-0.006	0.168	0.175	0.133	0.039	0.142	13,430
30	POL: Poland	-0.008	0.186	0.194	0.127	0.060	0.201	17,845
31	CAN: Canada	-0.009	0.144	0.153	0.096	0.052	0.137	41,685
32	FRA: France	-0.011	0.132	0.143	0.100	0.040	0.161	38,451
33	NZL: New Zealand	-0.012	0.145	0.157	0.100	0.051	0.116	32,504
34	USA: United States	-0.012	0.139	0.151	0.113	0.037	0.124	51,005
35	IND: India	-0.013	0.173	0.186	0.088	0.087	0.118	3,408
36	ISL: Iceland	-0.014	0.137	0.150	0.106	0.034	0.130	44,738
37	ESP: Spain	-0.014	0.151	0.165	0.107	0.056	0.164	33,771

table continues

Table 3A.1 continued

Measures of manufacturing value added (MVA), 1995–2011 average values, full sample (unless indicated otherwise all variables expressed as share of GDP)

Countries ranked by average net trade in MVA as share of GDP (column 1). Shading indicates top and bottom 10 economies.

	Country	Net trade in MVA	Production of MVA	Spending on MVA	Consumption of MVA	Investment in MVA	Manufacturing employment share in total employment	Per capita income (2017 PPP US dollars)
38	MEX: Mexico	-0.016	0.193	0.209	0.141	0.048	0.168	17,482
39	GBR: United Kingdom	-0.020	0.137	0.157	0.116	0.036	0.132	38,205
40	ZAF: South Africa	-0.022	0.169	0.191	0.129	0.059	0.156	11,610
41	NOR: Norway	-0.023	0.096	0.119	0.070	0.040	0.138	66,226
42	TUR: Turkey	-0.025	0.202	0.227	0.149	0.075	0.199	15,371
43	PRT: Portugal	-0.030	0.143	0.173	0.115	0.055	0.188	28,321
44	LUX: Luxembourg	-0.030	0.086	0.116	0.062	0.048	0.087	91,204
45	MLT: Malta	-0.033	0.169	0.201	0.137	0.059	0.192	28,226
46	COL: Colombia	-0.035	0.149	0.184	0.126	0.054	0.131	10,595
47	LTU: Lithuania	-0.035	0.186	0.221	0.161	0.055	0.180	17,714
48	AUS: Australia	-0.036	0.107	0.142	0.085	0.055	0.104	42,645

#	Country							
49	EST: Estonia	-0.036	0.171	0.207	0.120	0.079	0.204	21,082
50	CRI: Costa Rica	-0.037	0.193	0.230	0.173	0.052	0.137	12,044
51	TUN: Tunisia	-0.039	0.184	0.223	0.131	0.088	0.190	9,329
52	SAU: Saudi Arabia	-0.039	0.097	0.136	0.063	0.066	0.067	49,327
53	BGR: Bulgaria	-0.046	0.181	0.227	0.139	0.077	0.245	13,886
54	KHM: Cambodia	-0.050	0.165	0.215	0.154	0.055	0.105	1,926
55	HRV: Croatia	-0.052	0.176	0.229	0.149	0.072	0.181	19,372
56	GRC: Greece	-0.060	0.108	0.168	0.114	0.051	0.128	30,680
57	LVA: Latvia	-0.062	0.137	0.199	0.129	0.063	0.152	16,359
58	HKG: Hong Kong	-0.065	0.031	0.096	0.042	0.039	0.048	43,177
59	VNM: Vietnam	-0.083	0.191	0.274	0.154	0.112	0.137	3,440
60	CYP: Cyprus	-0.098	0.082	0.180	0.125	0.046	0.115	30,197
	Average	**-0.003**	**0.181**	**0.184**	**0.114**	**0.063**	**0.162**	**29,563**

Definitions:

Net trade = $X_m - M_m$

Production = $C_m + I_m + G_m + (X_m - M_m)$

Spending = $C_m + I_m + G_m$

Consumption = C_m

Investment = I_m

Sources: Author's calculations based on Trade in Value Added (TiVA) database.

Table 3A.2

Changes in determinants of manufacturing employment shares in 1995–2011 (unless indicated otherwise all variables expressed as share of GDP)

Countries ranked by average net trade in MVA as share of GDP (column 1). Shading indicates top and bottom 10 economies.

	Country	Average net trade in MVA	Change in net trade in MVA	Change in spending on MVA	Change in production of MVA	Change in relative value added per worker in manufacturing	Change in manufacturing employment share in total employment	Per capita income (2017 PPP US dollars)
1	IRL: Ireland	0.116	0.050	-0.073	-0.023	0.039	-0.062	44,738
2	SGP: Singapore	0.091	0.073	-0.114	-0.041	0.053	-0.094	61,365
3	KOR: Korea	0.064	0.079	-0.038	0.041	0.095	-0.054	26,005
4	TWN: Taiwan	0.057	0.043	-0.043	-0.000	-0.014	0.013	33,687
5	FIN: Finland	0.050	-0.053	-0.018	-0.071	-0.034	-0.037	39,542
6	DEU: Germany	0.049	0.038	-0.031	0.008	0.057	-0.049	41,835
7	MYS: Malaysia	0.044	0.085	-0.091	-0.006	0.045	-0.051	19,947
8	THA: Thailand	0.042	0.078	-0.047	0.031	0.026	0.005	12,189
9	CZE: Czech Republic	0.042	0.088	-0.089	-0.000	0.001	-0.002	26,274
10	SWE: Sweden	0.037	-0.023	-0.028	-0.051	-0.001	-0.051	42,514

11	CHN: China	0.035	0.016	-0.044	-0.027	-0.061	0.034	6,550
12	CHL: Chile	0.029	0.030	-0.064	-0.035	0.031	-0.065	17,575
13	SVK: Slovak Republic	0.024	0.014	-0.064	-0.050	0.021	-0.071	21,048
14	HUN: Hungary	0.024	0.082	-0.077	0.005	0.078	-0.074	22,058
15	JPN: Japan	0.023	0.005	-0.043	-0.039	0.019	-0.057	38,023
16	SVN: Slovenia	0.022	0.019	-0.075	-0.056	0.053	-0.109	27,483
17	RUS: Russia	0.021	-0.007	-0.036	-0.044	-0.001	-0.043	19,284
18	CHE: Switzerland	0.020	0.027	-0.033	-0.007	0.051	-0.058	54,126
19	NLD: Netherlands	0.019	0.017	-0.053	-0.035	0.004	-0.039	47,018
20	AUT: Austria	0.019	0.037	-0.038	-0.001	0.025	-0.027	43,719
21	ITA: Italy	0.013	-0.012	-0.040	-0.052	-0.009	-0.043	39,404
22	PHL: Philippines	0.013	0.060	-0.079	-0.019	0.001	-0.020	4,911
23	BEL: Belgium	0.011	-0.017	-0.043	-0.059	-0.002	-0.057	41,501
24	DNK: Denmark	0.009	0.002	-0.057	-0.055	0.007	-0.062	45,492
25	IDN: Indonesia	0.007	0.008	-0.030	-0.022	-0.013	-0.010	41,325
26	ISR: Israel	0.006	0.043	-0.077	-0.033	0.025	-0.059	29,789

table continues

Table 3A.2 continued

Changes in determinants of manufacturing employment shares in 1995–2011 (unless indicated otherwise all variables expressed as share of GDP)

Countries ranked by average net trade in MVA as share of GDP (column 1). Shading indicates top and bottom 10 economies.

	Country	Average net trade in MVA	Change in net trade in MVA	Change in spending on MVA	Change in production of MVA	Change in relative value added per worker in manufacturing	Change in manufacturing employment share in total employment	Per capita income (2017 PPP US dollars)
27	ARG: Argentina	-0.001	0.010	0.012	0.022	0.051	-0.029	17,251
28	ROU: Romania	-0.003	0.024	-0.037	-0.013	0.071	-0.083	13,895
29	BRA: Brazil	-0.006	-0.006	-0.035	-0.041	-0.017	-0.024	13,430
30	POL: Poland	-0.008	-0.009	-0.024	-0.032	-0.008	-0.025	17,845
31	CAN: Canada	-0.009	-0.029	-0.039	-0.068	-0.069	0.001	41,685
32	FRA: France	-0.011	-0.024	-0.035	-0.059	-0.005	-0.054	38,451
33	NZL: New Zealand	-0.012	-0.002	-0.069	-0.070	-0.027	-0.043	32,504
34	USA: United States	-0.012	-0.006	-0.039	-0.045	0.007	-0.051	51,005
35	IND: India	-0.013	-0.004	-0.039	-0.043	-0.079	0.036	3,408
36	ISL: Iceland	-0.014	0.029	-0.052	-0.023	0.015	-0.038	44,738
37	ESP: Spain	-0.014	0.002	-0.055	-0.053	0.000	-0.053	33,771

38	MEX: Mexico	-0.016	-0.005	-0.029	-0.035	-0.028	-0.007	17,482
39	GBR: United Kingdom	-0.020	-0.022	-0.074	-0.096	-0.036	-0.060	38,205
40	ZAF: South Africa	-0.022	-0.012	-0.059	-0.071	-0.056	-0.016	11,610
41	NOR: Norway	-0.023	0.018	-0.060	-0.042	-0.006	-0.036	66,226
42	TUR: Turkey	-0.025	-0.039	-0.056	-0.095	-0.129	0.034	15,371
43	PRT: Portugal	-0.030	0.016	-0.059	-0.043	0.041	-0.084	28,321
44	LUX: Luxembourg	-0.030	-0.022	-0.044	-0.066	-0.004	-0.062	91,204
45	MLT: Malta	-0.033	0.080	-0.159	-0.079	-0.004	-0.075	28,226
46	COL: Colombia	-0.035	0.018	-0.022	-0.005	0.014	-0.018	10,595
47	LTU: Lithuania	-0.035	0.043	-0.034	0.009	0.083	-0.074	17,714
48	AUS: Australia	-0.036	-0.011	-0.043	-0.054	-0.005	-0.049	42,645
49	EST: Estonia	-0.036	0.085	-0.115	-0.030	0.051	-0.081	21,082
50	CRI: Costa Rica	-0.037	-0.013	-0.034	-0.047	0.015	-0.062	12,044
51	TUN: Tunisia	-0.039	0.022	-0.071	-0.049	-0.012	-0.037	9,329
52	SAU: Saudi Arabia	-0.039	0.008	-0.007	0.001	0.007	-0.006	49,327
53	BGR: Bulgaria	-0.046	0.029	-0.023	0.006	0.056	-0.051	13,886

table continues

Table 3A.2 continued

Changes in determinants of manufacturing employment shares in 1995–2011 (unless indicated otherwise all variables expressed as share of GDP)

Countries ranked by average net trade in MVA as share of GDP (column 1). Shading indicates top and bottom 10 economies.

Country	Average net trade in MVA	Change in net trade in MVA	Change in spending on MVA	Change in production of MVA	Change in relative value added per worker in manufacturing	Change in manufacturing employment share in total employment	Per capita income (2017 PPP US dollars)
54 KHM: Cambodia	-0.050	0.082	0.018	0.100	0.005	0.095	1,926
55 HRV: Croatia	-0.052	0.035	-0.088	-0.052	-0.020	-0.032	19,372
56 GRC: Greece	-0.060	0.031	-0.046	-0.016	0.000	-0.016	30,680
57 LVA: Latvia	-0.062	-0.009	-0.061	-0.070	0.033	-0.103	16,359
58 HKG: Hong Kong	-0.065	-0.023	-0.028	-0.051	0.075	-0.126	43,177
59 VNM: Vietnam	-0.083	0.027	0.018	0.044	0.044	0.000	3,440
60 CYP: Cyprus	-0.098	0.008	-0.063	-0.056	0.002	-0.057	30,197
Average	**-0.003**	**0.019**	**-0.050**	**-0.031**	**0.009**	**-0.040**	**29,563**

MVA = manufacturing value added

a. Relative value added per worker in manufacturing calculated as MVA per worker in manufacturing divided by value-added per worker in the whole economy = $(MVA/L_m)/(GDP/L)$.

Note: See other definitions below table 3A.1.

Sources: Author's calculations based on Trade in Value Added (TiVA) database, International Labor Organization (ILO) Department of Statistics, and The Conference Board's International Labor Comparison Program.

Table 3A.3

Changes in determinants of manufacturing employment shares in 1995–2011 (unless indicated otherwise all variables expressed as share of GDP)

Countries ranked by changes in their net exports in MVA between 1995 and 2011 (column 2). Shading indicates top and bottom 10 economies.

	Country	Average net trade in MVA	Change in net trade in MVA	Change in spending on MVA	Change in production of MVA	Change in relative value added per worker in manufacturing	Change in manufacturing employment share in total employment	Per capita income (2017 PPP US dollars)
1	CZE: Czech Republic	0.042	0.088	-0.089	-0.000	0.001	-0.002	26,274
2	EST: Estonia	-0.036	0.085	-0.115	-0.030	0.051	-0.081	21,082
3	MYS: Malaysia	0.044	0.085	-0.091	-0.006	0.045	-0.051	19,947
4	KHM: Cambodia	-0.050	0.082	0.018	0.100	0.005	0.095	1,926
5	HUN: Hungary	0.024	0.082	-0.077	0.005	0.078	-0.074	22,058
6	MLT: Malta	-0.033	0.080	-0.159	-0.079	-0.004	-0.075	28,226
7	KOR: Korea	0.064	0.079	-0.038	0.041	0.095	-0.054	26,005
8	THA: Thailand	0.042	0.078	-0.047	0.031	0.026	0.005	12,189
9	SGP: Singapore	0.091	0.073	-0.114	-0.041	0.053	-0.094	61,365

table continues

81

Table 3A.3 continued

Changes in determinants of manufacturing employment shares in 1995–2011 (unless indicated otherwise all variables expressed as share of GDP)

Countries ranked by changes in their net exports in MVA between 1995 and 2011 (column 2). Shading indicates top and bottom 10 economies.

	Country	Average net trade in MVA	Change in net trade in MVA	Change in spending on MVA	Change in production of MVA	Change in relative value added per worker in manufacturing	Change in manufacturing employment share in total employment	Per capita income (2017 PPP US dollars)
10	PHL: Philippines	0.013	0.060	-0.079	-0.019	0.001	-0.020	4,911
11	IRL: Ireland	0.116	0.050	-0.073	-0.023	0.039	-0.062	44,738
12	ISR: Israel	0.006	0.043	-0.077	-0.033	0.025	-0.059	29,789
13	LTU: Lithuania	-0.035	0.043	-0.034	0.009	0.083	-0.074	17,714
14	TWN: Taiwan	0.057	0.043	-0.043	-0.000	-0.014	0.013	33,687
15	DEU: Germany	0.049	0.038	-0.031	0.008	0.057	-0.049	41,835
16	AUT: Austria	0.019	0.037	-0.038	-0.001	0.025	-0.027	43,719
17	HRV: Croatia	-0.052	0.035	-0.088	-0.052	-0.020	-0.032	19,372
18	GRC: Greece	-0.060	0.031	-0.046	-0.016	0.000	-0.016	30,680
19	CHL: Chile	0.029	0.030	-0.064	-0.035	0.031	-0.065	17,575

20	ISL: Iceland	-0.014	0.029	-0.052	-0.023	0.015	-0.038	44,738
21	BGR: Bulgaria	-0.046	0.029	-0.023	0.006	0.056	-0.051	13,886
22	CHE: Switzerland	0.020	0.027	-0.033	-0.007	0.051	-0.058	54,126
23	VNM: Viet Nam	-0.083	0.027	0.018	0.044	0.044	0.000	3,440
24	ROU: Romania	-0.003	0.024	-0.037	-0.013	0.071	-0.083	13,895
25	TUN: Tunisia	-0.039	0.022	-0.071	-0.049	-0.012	-0.037	9,329
26	SVN: Slovenia	0.022	0.019	-0.075	-0.056	0.053	-0.109	27,483
27	NOR: Norway	-0.023	0.018	-0.060	-0.042	-0.006	-0.036	66,226
28	COL: Colombia	-0.035	0.018	-0.022	-0.005	0.014	-0.018	10,595
29	NLD: Netherlands	0.019	0.017	-0.053	-0.035	0.004	-0.039	47,018
30	CHN: China	0.035	0.016	-0.044	-0.027	-0.061	0.034	6,550
31	PRT: Portugal	-0.030	0.016	-0.059	-0.043	0.041	-0.084	28,321
32	SVK: Slovak Republic	0.024	0.014	-0.064	-0.050	0.021	-0.071	21,048
33	ARG: Argentina	-0.001	0.010	0.012	0.022	0.051	-0.029	17,251
34	SAU: Saudi Arabia	-0.039	0.008	-0.007	0.001	0.007	-0.006	49,327
35	CYP: Cyprus	-0.098	0.008	-0.063	-0.056	0.002	-0.057	30,197

table continues

Table 3A.3 continued

Changes in determinants of manufacturing employment shares in 1995–2011 (unless indicated otherwise all variables expressed as share of GDP)

Countries ranked by changes in their net exports in MVA between 1995 and 2011 (column 2). Shading indicates top and bottom 10 economies.

Country	Average net trade in MVA	Change in net trade in MVA	Change in spending on MVA	Change in production of MVA	Change in relative value added per worker in manufacturing	Change in manufacturing employment share in total employment	Per capita income (2017 PPP US dollars)
36 IDN: Indonesia	0.007	0.008	-0.030	-0.022	-0.013	-0.010	41,325
37 JPN: Japan	0.023	0.005	-0.043	-0.039	0.019	-0.057	38,023
38 ESP: Spain	-0.014	0.002	-0.055	-0.053	0.000	-0.053	33,771
39 DNK: Denmark	0.009	0.002	-0.057	-0.055	0.007	-0.062	45,492
40 NZL: New Zealand	-0.012	-0.002	-0.069	-0.070	-0.027	-0.043	32,504
41 IND: India	-0.013	-0.004	-0.039	-0.043	-0.079	0.036	3,408
42 MEX: Mexico	-0.016	-0.005	-0.029	-0.035	-0.028	-0.007	17,482
43 USA: United States	-0.012	-0.006	-0.039	-0.045	0.007	-0.051	51,005
44 BRA: Brazil	-0.006	-0.006	-0.035	-0.041	-0.017	-0.024	13,430
45 RUS: Russia	0.021	-0.007	-0.036	-0.044	-0.001	-0.043	19,284
46 POL: Poland	-0.008	-0.009	-0.024	-0.032	-0.008	-0.025	17,845

								MVA
47	LVA: Latvia	-0.062	-0.009	-0.061	-0.070	0.033	-0.103	16,359
48	AUS: Australia	-0.036	-0.011	-0.043	-0.054	-0.005	-0.049	42,645
49	ITA: Italy	0.013	-0.012	-0.040	-0.052	-0.009	-0.043	39,404
50	ZAF: South Africa	-0.022	-0.012	-0.059	-0.071	-0.056	-0.016	11,610
51	CRI: Costa Rica	-0.037	-0.013	-0.034	-0.047	0.015	-0.062	12,044
52	BEL: Belgium	0.011	-0.017	-0.043	-0.059	-0.002	-0.057	41,501
53	GBR: United Kingdom	-0.020	-0.022	-0.074	-0.096	-0.036	-0.060	38,205
54	LUX: Luxembourg	-0.030	-0.022	-0.044	-0.066	-0.004	-0.062	91,204
55	SWE: Sweden	0.037	-0.023	-0.028	-0.051	-0.001	-0.051	42,514
56	HKG: Hong Kong	-0.065	-0.023	-0.028	-0.051	0.075	-0.126	43,177
57	FRA: France	-0.011	-0.024	-0.035	-0.059	-0.005	-0.054	38,451
58	CAN: Canada	-0.009	-0.029	-0.039	-0.068	-0.069	0.001	41,685
59	TUR: Turkey	-0.025	-0.039	-0.056	-0.095	-0.129	0.034	15,371
60	FIN: Finland	0.050	-0.053	-0.018	-0.071	-0.034	-0.037	39,542
	Average	**-0.003**	**0.019**	**-0.050**	**-0.031**	**0.009**	**-0.040**	**29,563**

MVA = manufacturing value added

Note: See definitions below tables 3A.1 and 3A.2.

Sources: Author's calculations based on Trade in Value Added (TiVA) database, International Labor Organization (ILO) Department of Statistics, and The Conference Board's International Labor Comparison Program.

4

Why Did the Manufacturing Employment Share Curve Shift over Time?

Developing economies seeking to achieve export-driven economic growth, higher living standards, and healthy manufacturing sectors often rely on what they view as time-tested models offered by richer economies over the last few centuries. But compared with the manufacturing employment shares (MES) attained by today's developed economies, even the most rapidly growing developing economies that only recently began exporting manufactured goods have lower MES at every level of real per capita GDP, with their peak MES occurring at lower levels of real per capita GDP, a phenomenon dubbed *premature deindustrialization* (Dasgupta and Singh 2006, Rodrik 2016).

After describing the implications of this development, reviewing the state of the literature, and providing visual evidence of its persistence and prevalence globally, this chapter shows how in theory large trade deficits in manufacturing, relatively faster productivity growth in manufacturing compared with other sectors, and changes in the composition of spending, operating either separately or together, can result in premature deindustrialization. It then explores how each of these potential explanatory variables has behaved over time and assesses the power of each to explain the downward shifts in the curves that have occurred over five decades.

Why Does Premature Deindustrialization Matter?

Premature deindustrialization poses serious problems for developing economies seeking to raise their living standards. Traditionally, moving workers out of agriculture, where labor productivity levels are typically low, into manufacturing, where labor productivity is substantially higher, has been an important source of economic growth in the early stages of economic development (Lewis 1954; Diao, McMillan, and Rodrik 2017). Premature deindustrialization implies that a larger share of workers will either remain working in low-productivity agriculture or have to earn a living working in urban services, often in the informal sector. This path could lead to slower aggregate growth and fewer opportunities for less educated workers to obtain jobs in manufacturing industries that often pay premium wages.

If the share of real output in manufacturing declines along with the share of employment, the implications for growth could be even worse (Matsuyama 1992). Smaller manufacturing industries could lose potential economies of scale, the classic justification for infant industry protection. There could also be fewer dynamic benefits from "learning by doing" (Arrow 1962), and a smaller share of manufacturing output could generate less output in other sectors through forward and backward linkages (Hirschman 1958).

Policymakers in developing economies often view developed economies as role models and benchmark their goals based on the historical achievements of developed economies, which have included a peak MES of at least 18 percent in all of today's rich nonoil economies (Felipe, Mehta, and Rhee 2019). Given the changes that have occurred over five decades, however, emerging-market economies are not likely to reproduce the manufacturing employment experience of today's industrial economies; by comparing themselves to those that have industrialized earlier, their expectations and manufacturing employment targets may be unrealistically high. As awareness of premature deindustrialization has grown, it has sparked a debate over whether services can take over some of the historic role played by manufacturing in generating development or whether the future of economic development has become bleaker (Ghani and O'Connell 2014, Amirapu and Subramanian 2015, Dadush 2015, Rodrik 2018, Baldwin 2019, Stiglitz and Rodrik 2024).[1]

The downward shift in the MES path has not been confined to developing economies. If anything, it has been stronger in developed economies.

---

1. Some economists have questioned whether manufacturing has become a less important source of economic development. Haraguchi, Cheng, and Smeets (2017) do not dispute that manufacturing's value added and employment have declined but argue that there has been a shift in manufacturing activities toward a small number of populous countries. When countries are considered in the aggregate, "the sector's contribution to world GDP and employment has not diminished" (p. 293). This conclusion rests heavily on China's heavy weight in aggregate data. Around 2013, China passed its employment peak at a considerably lower per capita GDP and a smaller MES than many of today's developed economies (Lawrence 2019).

In these economies, even when manufacturing output has maintained or even increased its share in GDP, over time manufacturing has provided a smaller share of employment at every level of per capita income. As is explored in more detail in Part II of this book, in the United States, this development has had detrimental effects on opportunities for less educated workers, sometimes with devastating effects on the communities in which they live (Charles, Hurst, and Schwartz 2019; Autor, Dorn, and Hanson 2013).

Literature Review

In the literature, explanations for these shifts in the curve almost exclusively highlight two major causes: labor-saving technological change and trade. Few take account of the role of changes in the level and composition of demand. Dani Rodrik (2016), for example, discusses this possibility theoretically, but his empirical work concentrates on the roles of technological change and trade. He finds that the relative importance of technological change and trade has been different in different parts of the world. In developed economies, he argues, technological change has played the dominant role in the downward shifts; in developing economies—mostly in Africa and Latin America—trade has been more important. Rodrik also ascribes the ability of Asian economies to avoid premature deindustrialization to their trade performance.

Rodrik infers the relative importance of these causes in different regions mainly by their effects. He emphasizes that although more rapid technological change and trade could both reduce the MES, the implications for manufacturing output differ. If productivity growth is faster in manufacturing than in the rest of the economy, the MES will decline but the share of real manufacturing output in real GDP should remain constant or increase. In contrast, if trade causes deindustrialization, the shares of both employment and real output will decline.

Once controls such as GDP per capita and population and unique economy characteristics are used, Rodrik finds no decline in the real manufacturing output share over time in developed economies. He does find a downward shift in manufacturing employment, however, and concludes that relatively rapid labor productivity growth in manufacturing is the main cause of the downward shift in the MES curve in these economies.

Using similar controls, he finds that the shares of both manufacturing employment and manufacturing output declined in Latin America and Africa. He therefore concludes that trade was the source of premature deindustrialization in these regions. He attributes this combination of deindustrialization in employment and output to changes in these regions' trade policy reorientation from import substitution in the 1960s and 1970s to trade liberalization thereafter. By reducing their import barriers, he argues, these economies exposed their manufacturing firms to more international competition from developed economies and countries such as China, which resulted in both lower manufacturing output and smaller employment shares. He does not find statistically significant evidence of downward shifts in Asia.

Other studies reach different conclusions. Several claim a greater role for trade in employment deindustrialization in developed economies (Felipe, Mehta, and Rhee 2019; Coricelli and Ravasan 2017; and Spence and Hlatshwayo 2011). These studies argue that that the internationalization of supply chains and convergence toward leading economy productivity by some developing economies has made it more difficult for developed economies to sustain their MES. Several other studies argue that manufacturing output growth (and thus labor productivity growth) has been much weaker than indicated by the official output data because of measurement issues involving computers, especially in the United States (Baily and Bosworth 2014, Houseman 2018), suggesting a greater role for trade.

Some important issues have not been fully explored in the literature. First, several studies (especially Felipe, Mehta, and Rhee 2019) show empirically that the MES curve has shifted both downward and inward, globally and in many economies. But the theories explaining this combination of inward and downward shifts have not always been spelled out.

Second, researchers such as Coricelli and Ravasan (2017) and Felipe, Mehta, and Rhee (2019) draw their conclusions about the relative importance of trade and technological change in the shifts in the MES curve over time primarily from the association between employment and output outcomes rather than by using explicit measures of trade and productivity as independent variables and exploring empirically the association between these variables and the outcomes.[2]

---

2. Rodrik is an exception. He splits his sample into manufacturing exporters and nonmanufacturing exporters. He finds that manufacturing exporters experienced more robust output growth and smaller employment declines than nonexporters—this result, he argues, strengthens the case that trade has played an important role. However, although he finds that exporters have had more robust output growth than nonexporters, he still finds that over five decades, declines in the MES curve in manufacturing exporters were larger than the difference between the MES declines of exporters and nonexporters (i.e., differences attributable to trade). This result suggests that even among manufacturing exporters, factors other than their exports (presumably rapid relative productivity growth and demand changes) have played a larger role in their MES deindustrialization than their trade performance.

Third, changes in the behavior of domestic demand for manufactured workers as a result of changes in the level and composition of investment have generally not been taken into account. Final spending on investment is much more intensive in manufacturing value added than final spending on consumption—a difference not captured by the per capita income measures used in the regressions of manufacturing employment and output shares found in the literature. In addition, the nature of investment has changed because of the growing role of software, databases, and other forms of intellectual property in the fixed assets of manufacturing. Declines in both the share of GDP devoted to investment and the manufacturing-labor intensity of investment because of intangibles could shift the MES and manufacturing output curves.

This chapter attempts to fill some of these gaps. It shows that in the global sample and almost all groupings of economies by level of development and region, the inclusion of trade variables often increases rather decreases the downward shifts that need to be explained. In contrast, a measure of the ratio of labor productivity in manufacturing relative to labor productivity in services is generally associated with a substantial share of the decline in the MES curve over time, especially in developed economies. In Europe and Latin America, investment levels and trends also have a very strong association with the declines in the curve. In sum, this study finds an association between curve shifts and demand that is ignored by the literature and results in the literature placing a greater weight on trade.

The rest of this chapter is organized as follows. Section 3 presents graphical and regression evidence of the pervasive downward and inward shifts of the MES curves in all regions. It considers how the three potential explanations for the shifting MES curve might operate in theory. Section 4 examines the independent variables that represent each of the three causes of the shifts in the MES curves. It considers whether, after controlling for GDP per capita and economy effects, both globally and regionally, the productivity of manufacturing has been rising relative to productivity in services. It then explores the behavior of the trade balance in manufacturing, especially in Africa and Latin America, where it has been argued that trade has been a key factor in premature deindustrialization. Controlling for GDP per capita incomes, it explores trends in the share and composition of gross investment in GDP. Section 5 then considers the impact of adding measures of each of these variables to regressions that estimate the downward shifts in the MES curve over time and explores how they change the dummy variables that capture downward shifts in the manufacturing employment and output curves. Section 6 summarizes the major results and presents questions that deserve further research.

Evidence of Shifts in the Manufacturing Employment Share Curve

Figure 4.1 illustrates the downward shifts in MES curves between the 1960s and 2000s for the full sample and for various groupings, based on the regressions in table 4.1. The regressions fitted on data from 1962 to 2011 include dummy variables for each decade (to allow for shifts in the curves) and economy dummy variables (to allow for unique features of each economy). Implicit in this formulation is the assumption that real purchasing power parity GDP per capita is sufficient to capture the demand and productivity effects that are associated with given levels of per capita income in all economies in all periods and that it is not necessary to distinguish between income and productivity effects.

The regressions in table 4.1 in all groupings capture inverted U-shaped relationships between the MES and GDP per capita. They have the expected positive and statistically significant coefficients on GDP per capita and negative and coefficients on GDP per capita squared, indicating that as GDP per capita increases, the curve turns negative. In all samples except Africa, the coefficients are statistically significant. The impact of population is significant in the global, Africa, Latin America, and developing economy samples; the coefficients on the squared population variables are mostly negative but not statistically different from zero. Over successive decades, all the samples indicate downward shifts in the curve, with the smallest shifts from the 1960s to the 2000s indicated by the coefficient for the dummy in Asia (–22.9 log points) and the largest for the developed economy group (–54.7 log points), although not all coefficients are highly statistically significant.

Figure 4.1 does not capture the second feature of premature deindustrialization—the leftward shift in the curve. It fails to do because the specification estimates only a single coefficient on the per capita income variables, which prevents detection of inward shifts in the GDP per capita associated with the peak.

Following Felipe, Mehta, and Rhee (2019), changes in the peak MES and the income level at which it occurs can be captured with a specification that uses a time variable that isolates the pure downward (or upward) shifts in the curve. A term that interacts the time variable with GDP per capita can potentially capture additional downward and inward shifts of the income level at which the peak occurs. The basic regression in this case is:

$$MES_t = \alpha_t + \beta_1 \times T + \beta_2 \times Y_t + \beta_3 \times Y_t^2 + \beta_4 \times T \times Y_t + \beta_5 \times P_t + \beta_6 \times P_t^2, \qquad (4.1)$$

Figure 4.1
Manufacturing employment share curves of selected groupings of economies, 1960s–2000s

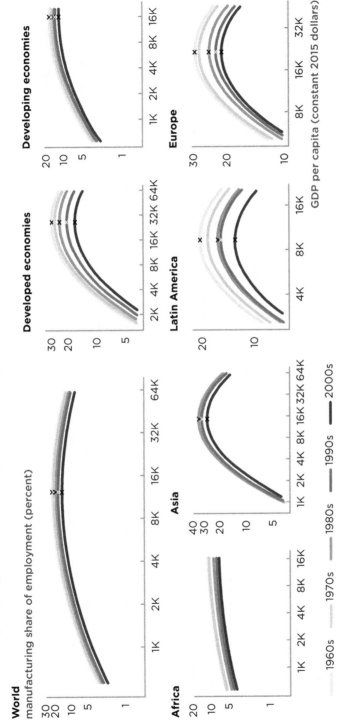

Note: Developed economies include European countries, the United States, Japan, Hong Kong, South Korea, Singapore, and Taiwan. Developing economies include economies in the Middle East and North Africa; sub-Saharan Africa; and nondeveloped Asia and Latin America. The Asia, Latin America, Africa, and Europe panels each include their respective regional economies in the sample.
Source: See table 4.1.

Table 4.1

Estimations of downward shifts in the manufacturing employment share curve between 1962 and 2011

Variable	(1) Global	(2) Africa	(3) Asia	(4) Latin America	(5) Europe	(6) Developed economies	(7) Developing economies
Log GDP per capita	1.025*** (0.163)	0.310* (0.164)	1.702*** (0.356)	2.311*** (0.573)	3.033*** (0.464)	1.674*** (0.226)	0.808*** (0.158)
Log GDP per capita squared	-0.205*** (0.0370)	-0.0492 (0.0574)	-0.317*** (0.0676)	-0.517*** (0.137)	-0.498*** (0.0796)	-0.255*** (0.0250)	-0.145*** (0.0492)
Log population	0.586*** (0.161)	1.265*** (0.344)	0.464 (0.561)	0.456** (0.162)	-0.157 (1.862)	-0.738 (1.235)	0.629** (0.236)
Log population squared	-0.0463* (0.0267)	-0.116* (0.0575)	-0.100 (0.0628)	-0.0459 (0.0282)	-0.191 (0.216)	0.00154 (0.0974)	-0.0534* (0.0293)
Dummy 1970s	-0.0535 (0.0443)	-0.0333 (0.0907)	0.0307 (0.0947)	-0.0901 (0.0582)	-0.0486 (0.0412)	-0.0669** (0.0273)	-0.0699 (0.0763)
Dummy 1980s	-0.151* (0.0817)	-0.214 (0.155)	-0.0130 (0.158)	-0.214* (0.108)	-0.166** (0.0652)	-0.180*** (0.0520)	-0.173 (0.144)
Dummy 1990s	-0.221** (0.0988)	-0.306* (0.165)	-0.0891 (0.259)	-0.243 (0.155)	-0.239** (0.0864)	-0.349*** (0.0770)	-0.208 (0.179)
Dummy 2000s	-0.383*** (0.116)	-0.360* (0.173)	-0.229 (0.368)	-0.428** (0.183)	-0.286** (0.111)	-0.547*** (0.122)	-0.346 (0.209)

Constant	-4.230*** (0.448)	-5.139*** (0.571)	-3.542** (1.271)	-5.120*** (0.764)	-3.229 (3.959)	-1.535 (2.513)	-4.301*** (0.702)
Observations	1,986	614	495	448	380	656	1,330
R-squared	0.446	0.425	0.553	0.532	0.891	0.686	0.374
Number of countries	42	13	11	9	8	14	28

Note: Robust standard errors are in parentheses.

*** $p < 0.01$, ** $p < 0.05$, * $p < 0.1$.

Sources: Groningen Growth and Development Centre (GGDC) database, https://www.rug.nl/ggdc/structuralchange/previous-sector-database/10-sector-2014?lang = en; and the Maddison Project Database, version 2020, https://www.rug.nl/ggdc/historicaldevelopment/maddison/releases/maddison-project-database-2020.

Figure 4.2

Global manufacturing employment share curves estimated to capture both downward and inward shifts of the curve

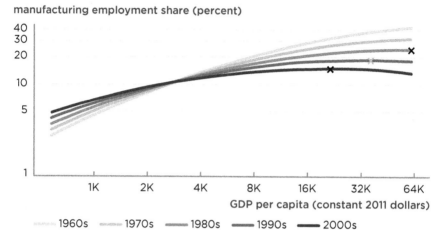

manufacturing employment share (percent)

GDP per capita (constant 2011 dollars)

.... 1960s   -------- 1970s   ——— 1980s   ——— 1990s   ——— 2000s

Note: Peaks available are marked by black or gray crosses in decades.
Source: See table 4.2.

where all variables except time are in logarithms, Y_t is per capita GDP measured in 2011 PPP dollars, P_t is population measured in millions, and T is the number of years since 1962.

Figure 4.2 illustrates the curve fitted for the global sample derived using the regressions reported in table 4.2, based on the specification in equation 4.1. In the early years, too few economies have passed their peaks; as a result, the downward slope in the curve cannot be estimated. After 1980, as more countries pass their peaks, the leftward and the downward shifts in the peaks are evident.

Table 4.2 provides estimations of the downward shifts of the MES curves for the other groups. These equations generate negative coefficients on the interaction term of GDP per capita and years since 1962. The coefficients on the interactive term are also statistically significant in the global sample and Latin America at a 1 percent confidence level and in the developed and developing countries. The downward and inward shifts for the global samples are clearly evident in figure 4.2.

Taking the derivative of the regressions in tables 4.1 and 4.2 with respect to GDP and setting it equal to zero yields an expression that can be used to solve for the GDP per capita associated with the peak manufacturing share in each year. This value can be substituted in the full specification to predict the peak MES associated with that GDP. The Asia regression, although not

Table 4.2

Estimations of changes in the levels and slopes of manufacturing employment share curves, 1962–2010

Variable	(1) Global	(2) Africa	(3) Asia	(4) Latin America	(5) Europe	(6) Developed economies	(7) Developing economies
Log GDP per capita	0.933*** (0.137)	0.364** (0.166)	1.514*** (0.306)	0.656 (0.743)	1.780* (0.787)	1.114*** (0.223)	0.677*** (0.131)
Log GDP per capita squared	-0.0866** (0.0429)	0.0654 (0.142)	-0.185 (0.109)	-0.0465 (0.179)	-0.186 (0.154)	-0.0741 (0.0631)	0.0253 (0.0666)
Log population	0.328 (0.253)	1.179 (0.743)	0.276 (0.700)	1.157*** (0.181)	-0.293 (1.652)	-1.083 (1.206)	0.643 (0.387)
Log population squared	-0.0545** (0.0264)	-0.0929 (0.0650)	-0.0886 (0.0948)	-0.0103 (0.0232)	-0.116 (0.186)	0.0582 (0.0999)	-0.0528 (0.0326)
Years since 1962	0.00964 (0.00992)	-0.00875 (0.0240)	0.0104 (0.0297)	-0.00813 (0.00575)	-0.0164 (0.0111)	0.0101 (0.0130)	0.000543 (0.0140)
LnGDP per capita * years since 1962	-0.00914*** (0.00289)	-0.00597 (0.00886)	-0.00991 (0.00835)	-0.0101*** (0.00137)	-0.00228 (0.00400)	-0.0102** (0.00458)	-0.00870** (0.00349)
Constant	-3.622*** (0.701)	-5.143*** (1.383)	-3.030 (2.497)	-5.739*** (0.551)	-2.399 (3.468)	-0.787 (2.456)	-4.473*** (1.194)

table continues

Table 4.2 continued

Estimations of changes in the levels and slopes of manufacturing employment share curves, 1962–2010

Variable	(1) Global	(2) Africa	(3) Asia	(4) Latin America	(5) Europe	(6) Developed economies	(7) Developing economies
Observations	1,986	614	495	448	380	656	1,330
R-squared	0.522	0.435	0.575	0.652	0.921	0.714	0.462
Number of economies	42	13	11	9	8	14	28

Note: Robust standard errors are in parentheses.

*** $p < 0.01$, ** $p < 0.05$, * $p < 0.1$.

Sources: Data from the Groningen Growth and Development Centre (GGDC) database, https://www.rug.nl/ggdc/structuralchange/previous-sector-database/10-sector-2014?lang = en; and the Maddison Project Database, version 2020, https://www.rug.nl/ggdc/historicaldevelopment/maddison/releases/maddison-project-database-2020.

significant, indicates a decline in both the peak employment share and the associated incomes between the 1970s and the 2000s. The peak MES fell from 50.5 percent in the 1970s to 25.8 percent in the 2000s, and the peak GDP per capita fell from around $48,000 in the 1960s to around $22,000 in the 2000s.[3] These results suggest that there may have been premature deindustrialization in Asia that was not apparent when analyzing the data using only the downward decade-dummy specification reported in table 4.1. The lack of statistical significance, however, suggests that the evidence is not very strong.

Variables That May Explain Structural Shifts

The models developed in chapters 1 and 2 emphasize the role played by technological change, trade, and changes in demand and investment. Changes in these forces could explain why the MES curve has shifted downward and leftward over time. This section concludes with a regression analysis and interpretation of equations based on these considerations and variables.

Technological Change

If economies that develop later have higher productivity levels at every level of income in manufacturing than in services, their MES curves would shift downward and to the left compared with those of economies that developed earlier. The downward shifts would reflect a pure productivity effect (the ability to produce the goods associated with any given level of per capita income with fewer manufacturing workers). However, as there is an inverse relationship between productivity and prices, if manufacturing productivity is higher in the economies that develop later, the relative price of manufactured goods will be lower and the relative prices of services higher. If domestic demand for manufactures is inelastic, the increased output demanded at every level of per capita income will be less than proportional to the productivity growth; these late developers will therefore devote smaller shares of domestic spending and employment to manufacturing output at every level of income and more to services. The inverted U-shaped path of the MES curve of late developers will therefore lie closer to the origin. The manufacturing employment shares previously

---

3. The values of the other variables were substituted by their respective average regional values for the whole period. For example, for Asia, the average population value substituted in the regression to predict peak MES was the average population of all Asian countries in the dataset for all years between 1962 and 2011. For Asia, GDP per capita = $\exp([1.514 - 0.00991 * (\text{years since 1962})]/(2 * 0.185))$. For 1970 ($t = 8$) this indicates a peak share of 48.31. For 2000 ($t = 38$) it indicates a peak share of 21.63 percent.

associated with particular per capita income levels are now associated with higher per capita incomes, because at each level of income the employment share of services is now higher.

Faster manufacturing productivity growth and higher productivity levels in manufacturing at given per capita income levels are likely in late developers. It is easier to copy than to innovate, as economic historian Alexander Gerschenkron (1951) noted when he famously spoke of "the advantages of relative backwardness." Developing economies can enjoy rapid productivity growth by adopting technologies that have been developed by and are already used by more advanced economies. This advantage appears to be stronger in manufacturing than in services, as confirmed by evidence showing that productivity catch-up in poor economies has been more rapid in manufacturing than in other sectors.

Duarte and Restuccia (2010) report that differences in labor productivity levels between rich and poor economies are larger in agriculture and services than in manufacturing. They find that productivity gaps narrowed much less in services than in agriculture and manufacturing. Rodrik (2013) finds that manufacturing is an unusual sector because labor productivity in lagging economies converges toward labor productivity in leading economies (the global technological frontier) regardless of other factors, such as human capital, institutions, geography, and the quality of policies. He characterizes this behavior as "unconditional convergence," because it is not associated with particular institutions and policies but rather with the quantity of manufacturing output.

Unconditional convergence suggests that productivity growth in manufacturing in lagging economies is related to productivity in the leading economy. This convergence could occur through a number of channels. Some economies could simply copy technologies that have been developed elsewhere; others could pay to use these better technologies through licensing, gain access to new technologies by attracting foreign investment from multinational corporations that transfer them, or simply import equipment and other capital goods that embody newer technologies. The key in all these cases is that the later domestic adoption of technologies can lead to higher manufacturing productivity, thereby affecting manufacturing employment shares at every level of income.

Unconditional convergence can therefore help explain premature deindustrialization in developing economies. Convergence implies that economies that are far behind the technological frontier experience faster productivity growth than economies that are closer to the frontier. If the frontier is continuously moving outward, new starters will have farther to catch up in manufacturing and experience more rapid manufacturing productivity growth at every level of per capita income.

The increased relative productivity of manufacturing is not confined to developing economies. National technological capabilities are likely to differ; as communications and integration among economies improve, leading technologies could also be diffused more rapidly among economies at advanced levels of development. Indeed, to the degree that new technologies require advanced skills for their adoption, the diffusion could be more rapid in economies with larger shares of educated workers. Thus, even advanced economies with similar per capita incomes could over time experience higher productivity changes in manufacturing than in other sectors. This is likely to have happened, as economies have become more integrated, because of improvements in communications technology, increased multinational investment, and the integration of global supply chains. In addition, at least until the financial crisis in 2008, labor productivity growth in manufacturing appeared to have accelerated in leading economies because of the digital revolution (Jorgenson 2001).

Simulation of the effect of technological change

Table 4.3 uses the model laid out in appendix 1A to chapter 1[4] to simulate the impact of faster manufacturing productivity growth on the MES as per capita GDP grows. The simulation changes reported annual productivity growth rates in manufacturing upward or downward by 50 percent.

The results of the simulation, shown in figure 4.3, show that productivity growth rates in manufacturing that are higher or lower than a baseline lead to an MES curve that is lower and to the left of the curve generated by the baseline and that slower productivity growth in manufacturing leads the curve to shift upward and to the right. If manufacturing productivity is higher at every income level, the path followed by the MES in latecomers will be lower and to the left of those that industrialize earlier.

Figure 4.4 uses the same simulation to show that when the manufacturing employment curve shifts downward and to the left because of faster productivity growth, there is a simultaneous upward shift in the light gray curve that tracks the share of employment in services. In other words, with faster productivity growth in manufacturing, the share of services is larger and the share of manufacturing smaller at every level of income. (To keep things simple, the model assumes that the agricultural income and substitution elasticities are identical, so there is no impact on the share of employment in agriculture.) Higher productivity in manufacturing relative to services at a given level of GDP per capita will shift the MES curve

---

4. Appendix 1A is available in the online data package for this book at https://www.piie.com/bookstore/behind-curve-can-manufacturing-still-provide-inclusive-growth.

Table 4.3
Parameters used in figures 4.3 and 4.4

Parameter	Value
Manufacturing productivity (percent)	
Faster	3
Slower	1
Income elasticity	
Agriculture (ε_A)	0.7
Manufacturing (ε_M)	1.4
Services (ε_S)	1.5
Initial employment share (percent)	
Agriculture (L_{A0})	80
Manufacturing (L_{M0})	5
Services (L_{S0})	15
Baseline productivity growth rate (percent)	
Agriculture (τ_A)	8
Manufacturing (τ_M)	2
Services (τ_S)	0
Other	
Elasticity of substitution (σ)	0.7
Initial GDP per capita (Y_0) (2015 dollars)	1,000

downward and toward the origin and shift the services employment share outward and upward, indicating one possible explanation for premature deindustrialization.

Evidence on the effect of technological change

The Groningen Growth and Development Centre (GGDC) database used in the regressions in tables 4.1 and 4.2 was used to explore what happened to the relative productivity of manufacturing between 1960 and 2011

Figure 4.3

Impact of positive and negative productivity shocks on the manufacturing employment share at various levels of GDP per capita

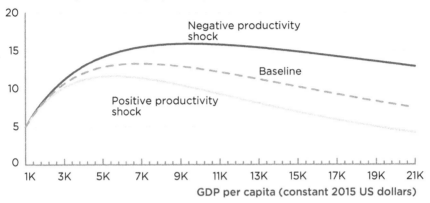

manufacturing share of employment (percent)

Negative productivity shock

Baseline

Positive productivity shock

GDP per capita (constant 2015 US dollars)

Source: Author's simulations.

using the log of per capita income and economy fixed effects as controls (table 4.4). Over these five decades, the labor productivity of manufacturing relative to the labor productivity of services increased steadily in the global sample. In the developed economies sample (column 6), the dummy variable for the 2000s is 73.5 log points higher than for the 1960s (an average annual increase of about 1.5 percent) and close to the pace assumed in the simulations. These large changes would be expected to lead to lower (nominal) manufacturing employment and expenditure shares at every level of per capita GDP. In developing economies (column 7), the trend increases are smaller but are still 31.3 log points higher for the 2000s than the 1960s. The increases are large in Latin America (69.4 log points) and highly significant and positive, and smaller (but not statistically significant) in Asia. In Africa through the 1990s there is a small increase, but it disappears in the 2000s.

These results confirm a potential role for rising labor productivity in manufacturing relative to services in explaining shifts in the MES curve over time in both developed and developing economies, but Africa seems an exception.

Trade Performance

A second mechanism that could be associated with premature deindustrialization is trade performance. If an economy enjoys faster technological progress in manufacturing than its trading partners (or other factors

Figure 4.4

Impact of a positive productivity shock in manufacturing on employment shares in services and manufacturing

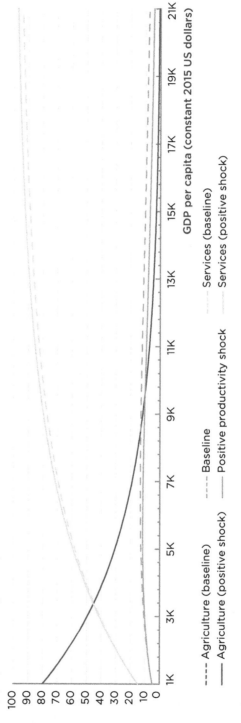

employment share (percent)

GDP per capita (constant 2015 US dollars)

- - - - Agriculture (baseline)
——— Agriculture (positive shock)
- - - - Baseline
——— Positive productivity shock
Services (baseline)
Services (positive shock)

Note: Parameters for agriculture are chosen to keep its share constant.
Source: Author's simulations.

Table 4.4

Regression results on the ratio of labor productivity in manufacturing to services over time, by region (log specification)

Variable	(1) Global	(2) Africa	(3) Asia	(4) Latin America	(5) Europe	(6) Developed economies	(7) Developing economies
Log GDP per capita	0.280** (0.129)	0.157 (0.148)	0.416 (0.252)	-0.0232 (0.109)	0.569** (0.168)	0.230 (0.292)	0.187 (0.125)
Dummy 1970s	0.185** (0.0699)	0.243 (0.182)	0.0667 (0.112)	0.184** (0.0572)	0.118 (0.0772)	0.220* (0.108)	0.194** (0.0875)
Dummy 1980s	0.292*** (0.105)	0.341 (0.272)	0.0712 (0.166)	0.334*** (0.0467)	0.226* (0.116)	0.358* (0.168)	0.304** (0.132)
Dummy 1990s	0.339*** (0.112)	0.269 (0.228)	0.118 (0.252)	0.435*** (0.0819)	0.319* (0.150)	0.536** (0.239)	0.313** (0.125)
Dummy 2000s	0.373** (0.142)	0.0935 (0.239)	0.174 (0.299)	0.694*** (0.0822)	0.442* (0.216)	0.735** (0.282)	0.313* (0.155)
Constant	-0.798*** (0.186)	-0.325 (0.188)	-0.939** (0.343)	-0.144 (0.192)	-2.166*** (0.430)	-1.307* (0.729)	-0.399*** (0.128)

table continues

Table 4.4 continued

Regression results on the ratio of labor productivity in manufacturing to services over time, by region (log specification)

Variable	(1) Global	(2) Africa	(3) Asia	(4) Latin America	(5) Europe	(6) Developed economies	(7) Developing economies
Observations	2,028	627	502	466	382	662	1,366
R-squared	0.398	0.111	0.609	0.760	0.866	0.739	0.237
Number of economies	42	13	11	9	8	14	28

Note: Robust standard errors are in parentheses.

*** $p < 0.01$, ** $p < 0.05$, * $p < 0.1$.

Sources: Data from the Groningen Growth and Development Centre (GGDC) database, https://www.rug.nl/ggdc/structuralchange/previous-sector-database/10-sector-2014?lang = en; and the Maddison Project Database, version 2020, https://www.rug.nl/ggdc/historicaldevelopment/maddison/releases/maddison-project-database-2020.

that increase its comparative advantage in manufacturing), it could create a growing trade surplus in manufacturing that could increase manufacturing employment at home while reducing it abroad. If, over time, the manufacturing trade surpluses of just a few large economies absorb a larger share of overall global manufacturing demand, the remaining economies could find that both their manufacturing employment and output shares decline. In the surplus economies, manufacturing employment would then move along a higher curve; in the deficit economies, manufacturing employment and output would be lower at every level of income. In addition, if demand is inelastic, with cheaper manufactured imports, employment in manufacturing would be lower and employment in services higher. If the deficit economies experience deindustrialization as a result of the loss of competitiveness in labor-intensive products, the shift to the left and downward could be even more pronounced, because the loss of manufacturing jobs would be proportionately larger.

At the global level, of course, trade must be balanced. Thus, although trade performance over time might offer an explanation of employment deindustrialization for some economies, it is unlikely to provide a complete explanation for a phenomenon that is globally pervasive. Indeed, at the global level, if manufacturing production shifts toward more labor-abundant economies that use more labor-intensive production methods, manufacturing employment globally could remain stable or even increase (Felipe and Mehta 2016).

Simulation of trade performance

This mechanism can be illustrated in a simulation using the model of the trade balance introduced in appendix 2A to chapter 2.[5] Figure 4.5 simulates the paths followed by economies with manufacturing trade deficits and trade surpluses of similar magnitudes, where the change in log share of manufacturing output of net importers or net exporters is equal to 0.2 percent of manufacturing output. Table 4.5 shows the parameters used in the simulation.

As shown in figure 4.5, which repeats figure 2.4 for convenience, moving from balanced trade to a deficit shifts the MES curve downward and inward and moving to a surplus shifts the curve upward and outward. As shown in figure 4.6 the services employment path of net importers is higher in an open economy than in a closed economy (or one with balanced trade). As a result, the MES curve shifts inward as well as downward in deficit econo-

---

5. Appendix 2A is available in the online data package for this book at https://www.piie.com/bookstore/behind-curve-can-manufacturing-still-provide-inclusive-growth.

Figure 4.5
Impact of trade balances on manufacturing employment shares

manufacturing employment share (percent)

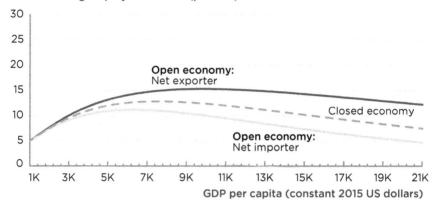

Source: Author's simulations.

mies. Thus larger deficits over time could explain premature deindustrialization.

Evidence on the effect of trade performance

Rodrik (2016, 4) attributes the premature deindustrialization in developing economies in Africa and Latin America to the shift in their policies from import substitution in the 1960s and 1970s to freer trade with less tariff protection after 1980:

> As developing economies opened up to trade, their manufacturing sectors were hit by a double shock. Those without a strong comparative advantage in manufacturing became net importers of manufacturing, reversing a long process of import-substitution. In addition, developing economies "imported" deindustrialization from the advanced economies, because they became exposed to the relative price trends originating from advanced economies. The decline in the relative price of manufacturing in the advanced economies put a squeeze on manufacturing everywhere, including the economies that may not have experienced much technological progress.

To explore changes in trade balances in manufacturing over time, the analysis that follows weights manufacturing trade balances as a share of GDP by economy GDP and derives a regional average. On average economies typically ran *smaller* trade deficits in manufacturing relative to GDP in the 1980s, 1990s, and 2000s than they did in the 1960s and 1970s, as evident in both Africa and Latin America. There were small declines in the manufacturing trade balances of Europe and larger declines in the United

Table 4.5

Parameters used to simulate trade

Parameter	Value
Elasticity of substitution (σ)	0.7
Income elasticity	
For agricultural goods (ε_A)	0.8
For manufactured goods (ε_M)	1.4
For services (ε_S)	1.5
Initial employment share (percent)	
In agriculture (L_{A0})	80
In manufacturing (L_{M0})	5
In services (L_{S0})	15
Initial GDP per capita (Y_0) (2015 dollars)	1,000
Productivity growth rate (percent)	
In agriculture (τ_A)	8
In manufacturing (τ_M)	2
In services (τ_S)	0
Change in log share of manufacturing output demanded domestically (λ) (percent)	
If importer	0.2
If exporter	−0.2

States; Asia experienced a substantial increase in its manufacturing trade surplus. Regional effects thus appear mainly between developed economies with declining trade balances and the Asian and (surprisingly) African economies in which manufacturing net trade increased (i.e., became less negative). Thus these are outcomes at odds with Rodrik's explanation.

Table 4.6 reports the trade balance and incomes measured in nominal terms. A more relevant measure might be the impact of these trade balances on the demand for labor (table 4.7). Accordingly, measures of value added per worker in manufacturing relative to overall value added per worker in

Figure 4.6

Sectoral employment shares in a closed economy and for net importers in an open economy

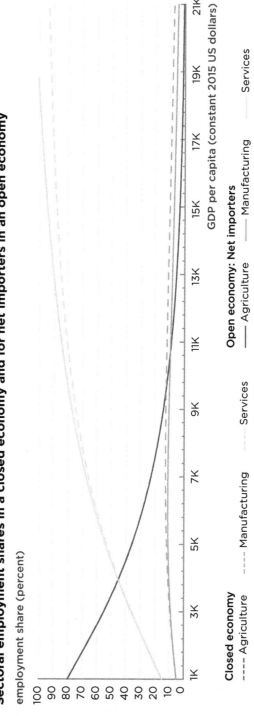

employment share (percent)

Closed economy
- - - - Agriculture   - - - - Manufacturing   .... Services

Open economy: Net importers
——— Agriculture   ——— Manufacturing   ——— Services

GDP per capita (constant 2015 US dollars)

Source: Author's simulations.

Table 4.6

Manufacturing trade balance as percent of GDP, by decade and region

Decade	Africa	Asia	Europe	Latin America	United States
1960s	-9.07	1.27	1.83	-4.43	0.79
1970s	-11.48	3.74	3.79	-4.72	0.39
1980s	-7.85	5.36	2.89	-1.91	-1.50
1990s	-7.61	4.61	1.30	-2.43	-1.50
2000s	-6.32	8.66	0.96	-2.07	-3.27
Net change	2.76	7.39	-0.87	2.36	-4.06

Note: Figures are weighted by the GDP of the economies included in each region. Africa includes economies in the Middle East, North Africa, and sub-Saharan Africa.
Sources: Data from COMTRADE, World Bank, and IMF.

Table 4.7

Domestic labor equivalence of the manufacturing trade balance as a share of total employment, by region and decade, 1960–2000 (percent)

Decade	Africa	Asia	Europe	Latin America	United States
1960s	-2.19	0.78	2.27	-1.69	0.39
1970s	-2.95	1.62	0.77	-2.16	0.20
1980s	-2.01	2.30	0.30	-1.62	-0.73
1990s	-2.24	1.38	0.06	-1.04	-0.68
2000s	-2.99	1.91	-0.55	-0.87	-1.38
Net change	-0.80	1.13	-2.82	0.82	-1.76

Note: Labor equivalence is calculated by using the nominal production per worker in manufacturing to convert manufacturing trade balance in dollars. Figures are weighted by the GDP of the economies included in each region. Africa includes economies in the Middle East, North Africa, and sub-Saharan Africa.
Sources: Data from COMTRADE, IMF International Financial Statistics, and the Groningen Growth and Development Centre database.

GDP are used to estimate the share of total domestic employment represented in the manufacturing trade balance.[6]

In the 1960s, for example, Africa's nominal output per worker was much higher in manufacturing than it was in the economy as whole. As a result, the manufacturing trade deficit of 9.1 percent of GDP translated into a deficit equal to just 2.2 percent of employment in terms of estimated labor content. Over time, however, the growth in African manufacturing output per worker in manufacturing lagged that in the rest of the economy, so that in the 2000s, the smaller nominal deficit of 6.3 percent of GDP translated into a labor content deficit of 3.0 percent. In Latin America, the manufacturing trade balance fell from 4.4 percent of GDP in the 1960s to 2.1 percent in the 2000s. What stands out is the decline in the labor share of manufacturing in both regions between the 1970s and the 1980s, despite the policy switch from import substitution to trade liberalization. The more sizable changes in nominal balances in Asia and North America were offset to a considerable degree by the more rapid increases in relative manufacturing value added per worker.

There is, of course, a danger in using ex post data, because the trade balance is an endogenous variable, and although under some assumptions it may be an indicator of the impact of manufacturing trade on employment, under others it may not. If, for example, manufacturing demand is particularly sensitive to economic growth, slower growth could lead to slower import growth at the same time as it reduces manufacturing employment. In this case, if Africa and Latin America experienced slower domestic growth after they liberalized in the 1980s and 1990s, *they might have experienced smaller deficits as a result of slower growth rather than liberalization*. Nonetheless, if the direction of causation is from domestic growth to the trade balance, trade may have operated as a stabilizer of manufacturing employment rather than a source of deindustrialization, suggesting that it may be a less important factor than often assumed.

Changes in Demand: Role of Investment

The empirical evidence on the role of demand in the papers on premature deindustrialization is conspicuous by its absence. This could lead to serious attribution errors if ex post outcomes are used to infer causation. For example, the impact of a declining share of capital spending at every level of GDP could reduce the shares of both output and employment in manufacturing. Finding a positive relationship between output and employment

---

6. To account for the fact that manufacturing trade balances are gross measures that include value added from other sectors, only half the value added in the gross manufacturing trade balance is attributed to the manufacturing sector.

Table 4.8
Ratio of share of manufacturing value added (MVA) in global gross fixed capital formation to share of MVA in global consumption, 1995–2010

Ratio	1995	2000	2005	2010
a. Manufacturing value added/gross fixed capital formation	0.31	0.30	0.28	0.29
b. Manufacturing value added/global consumption	0.17	0.16	0.15	0.14
a/b	1.83	1.88	1.93	2.10

Source: Trade in Value Added (TiVA) database.

changes could thus indicate the effects of demand rather than the impact of trade, as assumed in the literature.

In the formulation used in most of the MES regressions in the literature, the use of per capita GDP as an independent variable is implicitly intended to capture both demand and productivity at given levels of economic development. However, changes in the composition of demand between consumption and investment could materially affect the shares of manufacturing production and employment at given levels of GDP per capita. Indeed, as shown in table 4.8, Trade in Value Added (TiVA) data indicate that, globally, spending on gross fixed capital formation (plant, structures, and equipment) is generally about twice as intensive in manufacturing value added (MVA) as spending on consumption. In addition, changes in the labor intensity of manufacturing used in investment could have an important impact on the MES curve—for example, if investment becomes less manufacturing intensive because of an increased role of intangible fixed assets, such as software, databases, design, branding, and research and development, the effects on manufacturing labor demand could be smaller.

Simulation of the effect of changes in investment

One way to simulate the effect of a declining investment share in spending is to reduce the income elasticity of demand for manufactures. Figure 4.7 shows the results of making this change in a simulation of the sector shares of employment using the model from chapter 1. The income elasticity for manufacturing is simulated for income demand elasticities between 1.5 and 1.1, as indicated in table 4.9. With the highest elasticity (1.5, simulation 1), the MES curve lies above and peaks to the right of the other curves.

Figure 4.7

Effect of declining income elasticity of manufacturing on employment shares

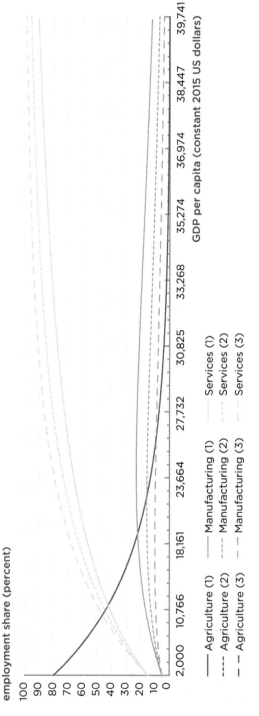

(1) income elasticity of manufacturing = 1.5; (2) income elasticity of manufacturing = 1.3; and (3) income elasticity of manufacturing = 1.1 (see table 4.9).
Note: Agricultural share is unchanged because of assumed equality of income and substitution elasticities.
Source: Author's simulations.

Table 4.9
Parameters used in figure 4.7 simulation

Parameter	Value
Curve for income elasticity of manufactured goods	
ε_{M1}	1.5
ε_{M2}	1.3
ε_{M3}	1.1
Elasticity of substitution (σ)	0.7
Income elasticity	
Agricultural goods (ε_A)	0.7
Services (ε_S)	1.3
Initial employment share (percent)	
Agriculture (L_{A0})	80
Manufacturing (L_{M0})	5
Services (L_{S0})	15
Initial GDP per capita (Y_0) (2015 dollars)	2,000
Productivity growth rate (percent)	
Agriculture (τ_A)	10
Manufacturing (τ_M)	2.5
Services (τ_S)	0

In simulation 2, with an elasticity of 1.3, the manufacturing curve is lower, and its peak lies to the left of simulation 1. In simulation 3, with an elasticity of 1.1, it lies even farther below and peaks to the left of simulation 2. These results imply that a reduction in the share of investment in GDP is likely to shift the curve downward and to the left, reducing the MES at every level of per capita GDP. It will also increase the share of employment in services at every level of GDP per capita (the light gray lines). (As earlier, the parameters were chosen to keep the employment share in agriculture constant, in order to simplify the discussion.)

Evidence of changes in investment

Table 4.10 displays the results of regressions that track the share of capital formation, i.e., investment in GDP, over time for the 42 economies and regional groupings in the GGDC sample. In most groupings, there is a statistically significant decline in the share of GDP devoted to spending on capital formation.

Consider the global regression reported in table 4.10. Controlling for GDP per capita, the full global sample shows a decline from 17.3 log points in the 1970s to –11.1 log points in the 2000s (i.e., by 28.7 log points since the 1970s). Between the 1960s and 2000s, the declines were 28.9 log points in Europe (minus Germany), 50.6 log points in Latin America, and 36.3 log points in developed economies. These figures suggest that weaker investment shares, perhaps due to slower European growth rates after the mid-1970s and steady declines in Latin America over time, may have played a role in these regions' premature deindustrialization. A similar development could also be responsible for some of the decline in manufacturing employment in the United States since the capital-formation-to-GDP dummy declines by 31.7 log points over the five decades. [7]

A second consideration could be the fact that intangible capital has become an increasingly important source of capital formation (Haskel and Westlake 2017). Since 2008, when the national income accounts were revised, intellectual property products such as software have been classified as part of gross fixed capital formation in most economies. The share of gross fixed capital formation contributed by intellectual property grew very rapidly (figure 4.8). In 1985, it accounted for 16.3 percent of gross fixed capital in France, 10.9 percent in Germany, and 17.2 percent in the United States. By 2015, these shares had almost doubled, reaching 24.0 percent in France, 17.7 percent in Germany, and 25.6 percent in the United States.[8] This increased share of intellectual property could further bias demand toward more skilled labor implying lower manufacturing value added and employment for any given investment share (Haskel and Westlake 2017).

---

7. The share of manufacturing value added in GDP from gross fixed investment in the United States averaged just 3.7 percent between 1995 and 2011. This share was greater than that of just three other countries (Iceland, the United Kingdom, and the Netherlands) in the 60-country TiVA sample and just 58 percent of the average country in the sample.

8. Ireland stands out for its very large share of intellectual property assets—this could be evidence of the effect of the incentives given to multinationals to transfer intellectual property to their Irish subsidiaries at low prices in order to take advantage of Ireland's low tax regime.

Table 4.10
Regression results on share of gross fixed capital formation to GDP (in logs), by region, 1960–2011

	(1)	(2)	(3)	(4)	(5)	(6)	(7)	(8)
Variable	Global	Africa	Asia	Latin America	Europe	Developed economies	Developing economies	United States
Log GDP per capita	0.279*** (0.0794)	0.120 (0.227)	0.203* (0.0971)	0.687*** (0.135)	0.190 (0.148)	0.304*** (0.0603)	0.378*** (0.124)	0.271*** (0.0855)
Dummy 1970s	0.173*** (0.0613)	0.332** (0.130)	0.289** (0.111)	-0.119 (0.0985)	0.0335 (0.0425)	0.0877 (0.0883)	0.140* (0.0710)	-0.0905*** (0.0268)
Dummy 1980s	0.0965 (0.0797)	0.361* (0.183)	0.282 (0.169)	-0.234** (0.0725)	-0.145* (0.0725)	-0.0781 (0.0955)	0.101 (0.0953)	-0.116*** (0.0410)
Dummy 1990s	0.0229 (0.0969)	0.281 (0.182)	0.277 (0.199)	-0.326*** (0.0769)	-0.242** (0.0959)	-0.211** (0.0908)	0.0388 (0.117)	-0.255*** (0.0576)
Dummy 2000s	-0.111 (0.113)	0.217 (0.224)	0.0492 (0.240)	-0.506*** (0.0981)	-0.289** (0.111)	-0.363*** (0.0832)	-0.119 (0.142)	-0.317*** (0.0792)
Constant	2.529*** (0.121)	2.683*** (0.190)	2.710*** (0.104)	1.834*** (0.263)	2.673*** (0.414)	2.394*** (0.155)	2.495*** (0.139)	2.321*** (0.258)
Observations	1,826	451	510	458	355	605	1,221	52
R-squared	0.192	0.147	0.417	0.311	0.447	0.388	0.207	0.383
Number of countries	41	13	10	9	8	13	28	1

Note: Robust standard errors are in parentheses.

*** $p < 0.01$, ** $p < 0.05$, * $p < 0.1$.

Sources: Data from the IMF *World Economic Outlook*, the World Bank, and the Penn World Tables.

Figure 4.8
Share of intellectual property in gross fixed capital formation, by economy, 1975–2020

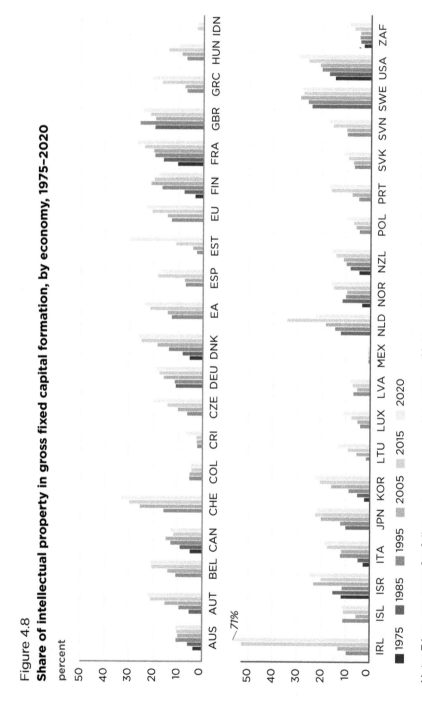

Note: EA = euro area; for full country names, see list at https://wits.worldbank.org/wits/wits/witshelp/content/codes/country_codes.htm.

Source: OECD, https://data.oecd.org/gdp/investment-by-asset.htm.

Regression Analysis of Premature Deindustrialization

The standard specification used in the literature to track premature deindustrialization, such as Rodrik (2016), inserts decade dummies into the regression that explains the MES for per capita incomes, population, and country. These dummies capture how the employment curve shifts downward vertically, but as noted above the specification constrains the curves to reach their peaks at the same income level throughout the sample period. It therefore does not allow for changes in the income associated with the peak. To facilitate interpretation, however, the following analysis will focus on the downward shifts.

The decade dummies do allow the shifts to differ in each decade and easy measurement of the downward shifts in the dummies controlling for the other variables in the specification.[9] In the analysis that follows, five specifications explaining the MES curve are estimated for seven groupings using the countries in the GGDC data. The first regressions for each of the groupings reported in table 4A.1 are called the standard specification.[10] As explanatory variables, they use GDP per capita, population, and their squares, all expressed in logs, in addition to unique economy characteristics captured by economy dummy variables. In addition, dummy variables are inserted to capture vertical shifts of the curve over time. Each of the potential explanatory variables is then added to the standard specification separately, with trade variables used in regression 2, the ratio of labor productivity in manufacturing to labor productivity in services in regression 3, and the share of investment and a time dummy in regression 4; regression 5 includes all three variables.[11]

---

9. The term *association* is used here to emphasize that the results are ex post historical summaries of the relationship between the variable rather than the outcome of a full-fledged estimation of a model capturing causation.

10. Table 4A.1 is in appendix 4A in the online data package for this book at https://www. piie.com/bookstore/behind-curve-can-manufacturing-still-provide-inclusive-growth.

11. In regression 2, the independent variables are the variables in the standard regression plus two trade variables: the log of the share of manufacturing exports and the log of the share of manufacturing imports. In regression 3, the independent variables are the variables in regression 1 plus the log of the relative labor productivity of manufacturing and services. In regression 4, the independent variables are the variables in regression 1 plus the log of the share of capital formation in GDP and a variable that captures the interaction between the investment share and time. Regression 5 (the full specification) includes all three potential explanatory effects. A set of tables for each of the groups explores the association between these variables and the share of manufacturing output in GDP, both measured in 2011 dollars. These tables are available in appendix 4A, which is in the online data package for this book at https://www.piie.com/bookstore/behind-curve-can-manufacturing-still-provide-inclusive-growth.

The variables introduced into the regressions, especially the trade variables, are not strictly exogenous. Numerous efforts to use instrumental variables to control for endogeneity were unsuccessful. The reported regressions, which are all ordinary least squares, should therefore be thought of as statistical descriptions of ex post associations rather than the outcome of a rigorous econometric analysis that identifies causation.

Interpreting the Equations

As the dummy variable for the 1960s is omitted in all specifications, its impact is included in the constant term; the dummy variable for the 2000s therefore provides estimates of the cumulative shifts of the curve over the five decades that are unexplained by the independent variables. The methodology used by Rodrik (2016) and others for determining causation based on outcomes involves comparing the dummies in the regressions that explain the MES with those in a similar regression that explains the manufacturing output share (MOS) of real GDP. If the dummy variable in the MES equation becomes more negative over time but the dummy variable in the MOS becomes more positive, the result is interpreted as confirmation of relative productivity, because higher relative manufacturing productivity will reduce relative manufacturing prices and thus be associated with lower employment but higher output. If the coefficient on the dummy variables for both the employment and output shares become more negative over time, trade seems the more likely explanation, because trade affects employment and output in the same direction.

The addition of the demand variable makes the interpretation more complicated, because similar directional changes in output and employment are consistent with both demand and trade. It is also possible that a combination of variables is responsible. Thus, a combination of productivity and trade or demand as the explanation could lead to a larger decline in the MES dummy than in the MOS dummy.

Interpreting the Regression Results after Adding Variables

The dummy variable for the 2000s is of particular interest, because it captures the full shift over the five decades. If it becomes less negative (or more positive) over time, it implies that the added variable is reducing the unexplained decline in the curve and thus helping explain the downward shift in dummy variables over the decades. If instead the dummy becomes more negative or less positive when the additional variable is inserted, the variable reduces the ability of the regression to track downward shifts of the curve.

Table 4.11 reports the dummy coefficients for the 2000s obtained from regressions explaining the log of the MES curves and the (log) of the MOS in the seven groupings that are reported in appendix 4A.[12]

Standard specification

The first column of table 4.11 reports the dummies for the 2000s. They measure the cumulative downward shifts between the 1960s and 2000s without controlling for any of the explanatory variables. If either trade or investment were the only reason for the downward shifts of the dummies, the coefficients of negative dummies in MES and MOS regressions in table 4.11 might be expected to be similar.[13]

In fact, as shown in the first column in the groupings with negative declines in the coefficients on *both* employment and output, the declines in output are generally much smaller than those for employment, suggesting a role for increases in the relative productivity in manufacturing even where investment or trade move the employment curves downward. The estimated declines in the manufacturing employment shares are –38.3, –54.7, –34.6, and –28.6 log points in the global, developed, developing, and European samples, respectively; the declines in the manufacturing output shares in these groupings are all very small and insignificantly different from zero. These estimates hint at much larger effects for productivity as an explanation than for trade or investment.

The African sample, though less significant statistically, is qualitatively similar: –36 log points in the dummy for the MES regression and –7.62 for the MOS regression. Neither of the Asian coefficients is significant. The Latin American coefficients are both negative and large, at –42.8 log points for employment and –46.3 for output.

Thus, using the standard specifications, with the exceptions of Asia and Latin America, the downward shifts appear to be explained by higher productivity in manufacturing relative to services over time with neither trade nor demand an important factor. In contrast, in Latin America, the large negative coefficients on the MES and MOS dummies point to possible roles for trade and/or investment.[14]

---

12. Appendix 4A is available in the online data package for this book at https://www.piie.com/bookstore/behind-curve-can-manufacturing-still-provide-inclusive-growth.

13. If net trade in manufacturing is more labor intensive than output in general, shortfalls in output could lead to greater declines in employment shares.

14. With the exception of the Africa results and the omission of demand as a possible explanatory variable, these results are all consistent with the findings of Rodrik (2016).

Table 4.11

Dummies for the 2000s explaining manufacturing employment and real output shares in regressions in appendix 4A[a]

Country grouping/variable	(1) Standard	(2) Plus trade	(3) Plus productivity	(4) Plus investment	(5) All three
Global					
Employment	-0.383*** (0.116)	-0.326** (0.157)	-0.145 (0.124)	-0.0804 (0.0739)	-0.0885 (0.0762)
Output	-0.0395 (0.134)	-0.197 (0.119)	-0.251** (0.116)	-0.00478 (0.0733)	-0.0640 (0.0633)
Developed economies[a]					
Employment	-0.547*** (0.122)	-0.246* (0.136)	-0.256** (0.114)	-0.0961 (0.0782)	-0.0445 (0.136)
Output	-0.0325 (0.206)	-0.114 (0.142)	-0.224** (0.0928)	-0.0461 (0.0952)	0.0155 (0.127)
Developing economies					
Employment	-0.346 (0.209)	-0.379 (0.230)	-0.124 (0.163)	-0.143 (0.107)	-0.129 (0.109)
Output	0.0191 (0.193)	-0.223 (0.158)	-0.202 (0.148)	-0.0328 (0.0991)	-0.127 (0.0873)

Latin America

Employment	−0.428**	−0.380*	−0.244*	−0.142	−0.0813
	(0.183)	(0.190)	(0.130)	(0.0875)	(0.0659)
Output	−0.463***	−0.415***	−0.502***	−0.213***	−0.206***
	(0.107)	(0.141)	(0.110)	(0.0633)	(0.0587)

Asia

Employment	−0.229	−0.0822	0.0154	−0.0856	0.189
	(0.368)	(0.222)	(0.250)	(0.262)	(0.105)
Output	−0.142	−0.186	−0.178	0.141	0.167
	(0.279)	(0.183)	(0.213)	(0.171)	(0.130)

Africa

Employment	−0.360*	−0.401*	−0.189	−0.246	−0.313*
	(0.173)	(0.214)	(0.185)	(0.149)	(0.167)
Output	0.0762	−0.157	−0.121	−0.122	−0.146
	(0.280)	(0.196)	(0.158)	(0.113)	(0.112)

Europe

Employment	−0.286**	−0.322***	−0.285**	−0.0802	−0.137*
	(0.111)	(0.0660)	(0.116)	(0.0654)	(0.0717)
Output	−0.0380	−0.204**	−0.262**	−0.0339	−0.0779
	(0.160)	(0.0812)	(0.0817)	(0.108)	(0.0495)

a. Appendix 4A is available in the online data package for this book at https://www.piie.com/bookstore/behind-curve-can-manufacturing-still-provide-inclusive-growth.

Sources: Data from the Groningen Growth and Development Centre (GGDC) database, https://www.rug.nl/ggdc/structuralchange/previous-sector-database/10-sector-2014?lang = en; and the Maddison Project Database, version 2020, https://www.rug.nl/ggdc/historicaldevelopment/maddison/releases/maddison-project-database-2020.

Trade

Table 4.11 provides estimates of the effects of adding measures of the three explanatory variables to the standard regression. Trade is measured as the shares of manufactured exports and imports in GDP. The impact of adding these trade variables to the employment specification is mixed, as can be seen by comparing regressions 1 and 2. In the global sample, adding trade does not have much of an impact on the employment regression dummy, which increases from –38.3 to –32.6 log points, but the MOS regression dummy falls from –3.95 log points to –19.7 log points, which although not statistically significant suggests that trade effects *increased* manufacturing output (requiring a more negative dummy) and that trade did not play a role in the declining MOS curve.

In the developed country sample, adding trade causes the dummy on manufacturing employment to rise from –54.7 to –24.6 log points, suggesting a potential role for trade since it means that it has a negative impact so that a smaller negative dummy (in absolute terms) is required to track the downward movement. In the output equation, however the dummy falls from –3.25 to –11.4 log points, indicating trade has a positive impact on the dummy, which casts doubts about trade as the explanation. In the developing country sample, the employment dummy decreases slightly but none of the variables are significant in any of the specifications. All told, in these three aggregate measures, the support for trade as an explanation for the negative dummies is weak.

In the Asian MES regression, adding trade raises the dummy from –22.9. to –8.2 log points, which would be consistent with trade playing a role but it is not statistically significant; the output dummy falls from –14.2 to –18.6 log points, which is inconsistent with trade as the explanation. The result is thus mixed.

In the Latin American sample, the coefficients on both employment and output dummies changed by a few points, casting doubt on trade as the explanation and suggesting that investment could be playing a role in the large negative coefficients obtained for both the MES and MOS dummies.

In Africa and Europe, the changes in the dummies in the employment regressions become more negative, allowing rejection of trade as a cause because taking account of the impact of trade requires a bigger (in absolute terms) negative dummy, which means that the impact of trade is positive and thus cannot help explain a downward shift. Overall, therefore, with the exception of the Asian sample, where the coefficients are not statistically significant and the MES and MOS yield different interpretations, these results do not suggest a role for trade.

Relative manufacturing productivity

Adding the ratio of output per worker in manufacturing to output per worker in services (relative productivity) generally has powerful effects on the negative MES dummy variable, reducing its absolute size (column 3 of table 4.11). This change in the dummies that become smaller points to productivity as an important part of the explanation for the initially large negative dummies in the employment regressions. Although some of the variables are not significant, with the exception of Europe, all suggest that taking account of productivity has a substantial impact on reducing the employment dummy. The employment share dummy rises from –38.3 to –14.5 log points in the global sample , from –54.7 to –25.6 log points in the developed economy sample, from –34.6 to –12.4 log points in the developing economy sample, and from –42.8 to –24.4 log points in the Latin American sample. The Asian dummy rises from –22.9 log points to effectively zero, although neither the MES or MOS dummies are statistically significant. In Africa, the coefficient on employment rises from –36.0 to –18.9 log points. In Europe, the coefficient barely changes.[15] Thus, with the exception of Europe, the changes in the employment dummy when productivity is introduced indicate an important role for relative productivity in all groupings.

Once productivity is controlled for, the output variables still remain significant and large (absolutely) in the global sample (–25.1 log points), in developed economies (–22.4 log points), in developing economies (–20.2 log points), and in Latin America (–50.2 log points). These results (with the European exception) are consistent with the notion that relatively rapid productivity growth in manufacturing has an important impact on employment but a smaller impact on output. They suggest that although productivity has played a role, demand may also have had an impact.

Investment (demand)

Adding the investment variables to the standard regression reduces the employment dummies (see column 4 of table 4.11), in most cases by more than the reductions from the productivity equations. For employment, the dummies fall from 38.3 to –8.0 log points in the global sample, from 54.7 to 9.6 log points in the developed economy sample, and from 28.6 to –8.0 in the Europe equation, and none is statistically significant. These results suggest that investment is also an important contributor to the downward

---

15. In the Europe MOS regression, the coefficient on the relative productivity is unusually large and close to unity, implying that demand is sufficiently responsive (elastic) that relative productivity increases leave manufacturing employment unchanged.

shifts in the curve in developed economies. In developing economies, the reduction from –34.6 percent to –14.3 percent also suggests that much of the declining dummy in the standard equation stems from investment. The dummy coefficient falls from –42.8 to –14.2 log points in Latin America, from –22.9 to –8.5 log points in Asia, and from 36.0 to 24.6 log points in Africa.

In the MOS regressions, none of the MOS dummies remains significant except in Latin America, and even there the dummy falls from –46.3 to –21.3 log points. With the exception of Africa, where the results are not significant, these results strongly suggest that investment shifts have been very important in both developed and developing economies, especially in Latin America.

All three variables

Adding all three sets of explanatory variables goes a long way in reducing the dummy found in the standard equations, eliminating its statistical significance in the global, developed country, and Latin American samples The reductions in the dummy variables are large in all groups other than Africa, falling from –38.3 to –8.9 log points for the global sample, from –54.7 to –4.5 log points in developed economies, and from –36.6 to –12.9 log points in developing economies.

The employment equation results, especially on the MOS dummies, do not point to a major role for trade. In contrast, the relative productivity and investment variables both appear to play important roles in explaining the downward shifts of the MES curves.

Conclusion

The evidence in tables 4.1 and 4.2 for premature deindustrialization in developing economies is overwhelming (and disconcerting): Poor and middle-income economies that develop later have smaller MES than economies that attain similar levels of development earlier. The later these economies develop, they more limitations they face. Premature deindustrialization is also occurring in developed economies, which achieve lower peak manufacturing shares at lower per capita incomes. This behavior is evident in global samples of economies and in samples that group economies by region.

The explanations for premature deindustrialization in the literature focus on the relative roles of trade and technological change in shifting the MES curve. This chapter considers investment as an additional potential cause. The models of structural change in chapters 1 and 2 show how each of these causes could shift the MES curve downward and inward toward the origin: Faster relative productivity in manufacturing relative to services allows countries to meet the demand for manufactured goods with fewer workers, shifting the curve down; when manufactured goods are cheaper, people reduce the share of their spending on manufactures and increase it on services, shifting the MES curve inward. Similarly, less responsive demand for investment as income grows reduces spending on manufacturing, lowering the MES, and increases in spending on services shift the MES curve inward. Larger trade deficits in manufactures can reduce output and employment in manufacturing and increase spending on domestic services.

After controlling for GDP per capita and individual economy characteristics, two of these explanations appear to be relevant in most cases. First, given GDP per capita, the productivity of manufacturing relative to services increased strongly almost everywhere. Second, the share of gross fixed capital formation in GDP declined pervasively, and the intellectual property intensity of manufacturing investment increased. Both forces reduce the responsiveness of manufacturing employment to income growth. Trade (or globalization) is often said to be the most important reasons for the downward shift in the employment curve. But its explanatory power is weak. Although it is sometimes associated with these shifts, its impact in explaining the shifts is much weaker than the other two variables and often moves the dummy in the wrong direction. Both trade and investment shocks have negative effects on output and employment, but investment has been the much more powerful source of deindustrialization, especially in Latin America.

The findings in this chapter validate Rodrik's conclusions that trade has not been a very important source of the long-run declines in the MES in developed economies. The evidence presented also suggests that declining investment is a major factor in explaining its decline in these countries. Unlike Rodrik's conclusions, however, the research presented here suggests that Asia has experienced downward shifts of the MES curve that are consistent with a role for relatively rapid productivity growth in manufacturing, although the effects are generally not statistically significant. Rodrik attributes much of explanation in Latin America to trade; the results here find its role much less important than the effects of investment.

Some questions need to be explored. Although the theory indicates that each of these variables could account for both downward and inward shifts of the MES curve, the regressions track only downward shifts. Research on both the downward and inward shifts is warranted. The results here are also relatively low in statistical significance with respect to Africa and Asia. Additional research on these regions is also warranted.

This chapter used ordinary least squares regressions in which the explanatory variables were assumed to be independent variables, because it was not possible to find robust instruments to control for their endogeneity. Although the results show an association between the three explanations for premature deindustrialization and the dependent variables, they do not establish causation. It is possible that better identification methods could yield a deeper understanding of causal linkages and identify a larger role for trade in some economies and regions.

Appendix 4A

The regression tables for all samples are available in the online data package for this book at https://www.piie.com/bookstore/behind-curve-can-manufacturing-still-provide-inclusive-growth.

II

THE EXPERIENCE OF THE UNITED STATES

Part II considers the role of manufacturing employment in generating inclusive growth in the United States. A brief survey of the literature suggests that the term *inclusive growth* means different things to different people and thus clarity about what is meant here is required.

Some writers use the term to denote growth that is concentrated among people at the lowest end of the income scale (i.e., growth that is pro-poor).[1] This concept can be misleading, because growth that raises the incomes of the poor can be accompanied by growth that raises the incomes of higher-income groups by even more, thereby exacerbating inequality (Ravallion and Chen 2003; Anand, Mishra, and Peiris 2013).

A second definition of the term refers to growth that raises the incomes of the poor by a larger percentage than the rest of the population (i.e., reduces income inequality) (Dollar and Kraay 2002). The term can also be expanded to take account of inclusive opportunities that allow for income growth at the bottom over time. The Organization for Economic Cooperation and Development (OECD) defines inclusive growth as "economic growth that is distributed fairly across society (equity) and creates opportunities for all."[2]

---

1. See Anand, Mishra, and Peiris (2013) for an analysis of pro-poor growth that synthesizes measures of increases in absolute incomes of the poor with those of relative incomes.

2. See OECD, "Inclusive Growth," https://www.oecd.org/inclusive-growth/.

The World Bank Commission on Growth and Development (2008) references policies that help people who may be hurt by economic growth or who need assistance to take advantage of the opportunities growth offers. In this expansive definition, "inclusive development" (or growth) encompasses equity, equality of opportunity, and protection in market and employment transitions.

Another possibility—relevant for the US experience—is to define inclusive growth as growth that does not exclude a significant group (such as lower-middle-class men) from the benefits of growth, which distinguishes the concept from income inequality.

These different definitions suggest that inclusive growth may not be synonymous with growth that leads to a more equal income distribution. Growth might provide opportunities for people at the bottom to become richer while at the same time making the income distribution less equal. If some previously poor people receive an education, for example, this could increase income inequality but making education open to all could increase inclusion.

No single notion of inclusive growth applies under all circumstances. Rather than searching for a perfect way to incorporate these dimensions of inclusion, it seems more fruitful to specify the criteria by which inclusion will be judged in this study. This part of the book therefore examines three narrower questions (in the case of the United States):

- Is growth shared with people without college education, even if they are not poor?
- Does growth increase income inequality, either by increasing wage inequality among workers with different levels of education or by increasing class inequality by reducing the share of labor relative to capital?
- Is growth associated with the convergence of incomes across regions within economies?

5

Rise and Fall of Inclusive Growth in the United States

Before the 1970s, growth in the United States was inclusive by most definitions. Since the early 1970s, income growth has been much slower and less inclusive judged by the three criteria mentioned above.

If real incomes grow at 2 percent a year, they will double every 35 years, enabling successive generations to live twice as well as their parents did. Between 1947 and 1973, real per capita GDP in the United States achieved an average growth rate of 2.5 percent, allowing millions of Americans to achieve the American dream (figure 5.1). Income growth was both rapid and widely shared across households (although not always by women and people of color). The real earnings of households in the bottom four quintiles increased slightly more rapidly than those in the top quintile, and earnings growth of the top 5 percent was (marginally) lower than earnings growth of the rest of the distribution.

Labor compensation data tell a similar story. Between 1947 and 1970, average real compensation for production and nonsupervisory workers—a category that accounts for more than two-thirds of US employment and 80 percent of private employment—increased at an annual rate of 2.6 percent, about the same as the 2.7 percent annual growth rate in the compensation of all workers (Lawrence 2016). Labor's share in income increased slightly between 1947 and the late 1960s, contributing to the robust growth of labor income.

Between 1973 and 2005, the lower a household ranked on the income distribution, the slower its income growth was (see figure 5.1), and even households in the top quintile failed to see their incomes grow at 2 percent

Figure 5.1

Annual growth in real household income in the United States, by income quintile, 1947–73 and 1973–2005

annual growth in real household income (percent)

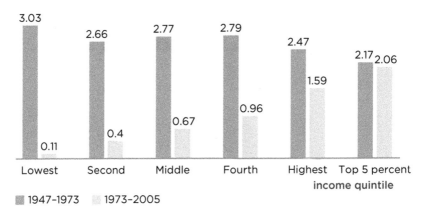

■ 1947–1973 ▨ 1973–2005

Source: US Census Bureau, Table F3, updated September 15, 2006.

pace that would double their income every 35 years. Only people in the top 5 percent enjoyed growth above that threshold.

The individual wage data shown in figure 5.2 reveal a similar story. Between 1970 and 2011, estimated real wage growth of production and nonsupervisory workers increased by just 0.48 percent a year,[1] and the real wages of workers in the bottom 90 percent of the wage distribution grew by just 0.68 percent a year.[2] In contrast, real wages of workers in the 90th–99th percentile increased at an annual pace of 1.37 percent. Thus, even workers with earnings rankings just below the 99th percentile saw their wages grow at a rate that was slower than required to achieve the American dream.

---

1. Nominal wages for production and nonsupervisory workers are from Federal Reserve Bank of St. Louis, Federal Reserve Economic Data, "Average Hourly Earnings of Production and Nonsupervisory Employees, Total Private," https://fred.stlouisfed.org/series/AHETPI. It was adjusted using the Personal Consumption Expenditures price index from the US Bureau of Economic Analysis, https://apps.bea.gov/iTable/iTable.cfm?reqid = 19&step = 3&isuri = 1&1921 = survey&1903 = 84.

2. Saez and Piketty (2003) provide time series data for the shares of wage earnings at different levels of the wage distribution. They use these data to allocate annual aggregate nominal wage measures in the national accounts. They calculate real wages using the Personal Consumption Expenditures (PCE) deflator. Data on personal income and its disposition are available at https://apps.bea.gov/iTable/index_nipa.cfm for workers at different points on the wage distribution. National income accounts data on full-time equivalent employment are available at https://apps.bea.gov/iTable/?reqid = 19&step = 2&isuri = 1&1921 = survey.

Figure 5.2

Real wages of US workers in selected income percentiles, 1970–2011

index (1970 = 100)

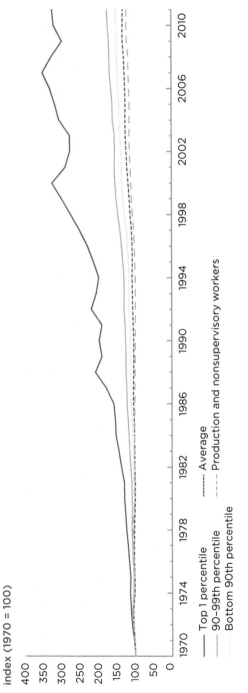

Sources: Piketty and Saez (2003) and national income accounts of the US Bureau of Economic Analysis.

Remarkably, even the growth in the annual real wages of the top 1 percent (2.9 percent a year) was not much faster than the 2.7 percent growth in average compensation of *all* workers between 1947 and 1970. Had the pace of real wage growth between 1947 and 1973 been maintained and shared proportionately, the earnings of *all* US workers would have risen almost at the pace of those in the top 1 percent after 1973.[3]

The 0.48 percent a year increase in annual wages of US production workers amounted to just 21.6 percent over the 41 years from 1970 and 2011. Had all workers enjoyed the same 2.7 annual rise in real compensation they did in 1947–70, the real compensation of production workers would have more than doubled. Increased inequality contributed significantly to workers' weak real earnings growth.

Education and Gender

Differentiating workers by education and gender yields further insight into these wage growth divergences. The Current Population Survey provides data on the earnings of full-year, full-time workers.[4] Median annual earnings of men without a college degree rose 6.3 percent between 2015 and 2019 (figure 5.3).[5] Despite this rise, in 2019, deflated by the consumer price index, median earnings of $39,000 were 15.3 percent *lower* than in 1970—an annual average decrease of 0.34 percent between 1970 and 2019. In contrast, the $76,000 earned in 2019 by the median man with a college degree was 5.0 percent higher than it was in 1970. As a result, the college earnings premium (defined as the median college wage divided by the median noncollege wage) for men increased by 37.7 percent.

In contrast, the gap in wages of women with and without college degrees narrowed over this period. In 2019, the median salary of a woman with a college degree was $52,000, 25.8 percent more than in 1970 ($41,329), and the median salary for a woman without a college degree was $26,000 in 2019, 27.5 percent more than in 1970 ($20,395).

---

3. In addition, labor compensation failed to keep up with income growth.

4. See Current Population Survey Data for Social, Economic and Health Research, https://cps.ipums.org/cps/.

5. These earnings data were converted into 2019 dollars using the Urban Consumer Price Index of the US Bureau of Labor Statistics. Deflating the real wage growth of non-college-educated men between 1970 and 2019 by the personal consumption expenditures (PCE) deflator rather than the CPI would indicate a minimal increase of 6.5 percent over the 39 years rather than a decline of 15.3 percent.

Figure 5.3

Real annual median earnings of men and women in the United States with and without college degrees, 1970-2019

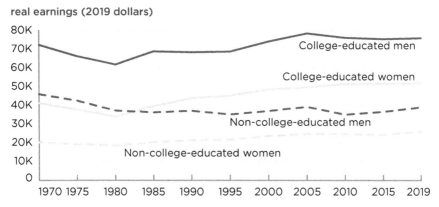

real earnings (2019 dollars)

Source: Ruggles et al. (2022).

Although women still earned less than men with similar educational levels, the gender gap narrowed between 1970 and 2019 (figure 5.4).[6] In 1970, non-college-educated men earned 126 percent more than non-college-educated women. In 2019, they earned 50 percent more. Although factors such as experience, race, and region explain some of the remaining gap, a marked difference in gender earnings that cannot be explained by the normal determinants of wages, such as age, qualifications, and experience remained.

In 2015, the median man without a college degree earned substantially less in real terms than his similarly educated father earned 45 years earlier. As these data are based only on men who were employed full time, they overstate the earnings growth of such men, because a growing share of these men dropped out of the labor force. In 1970, for example, 95.8 percent of men between the ages of 25 and 54 that did not have a college degree participated in the labor force. By 2015, that share had fallen by almost 10 percentage points to 86.5 percent. Over the same period, the participation rate for prime-age men with college degrees fell by just over 2 percentage points, from 97.1 percent to 94.7 percent (Ruggles et al. 2022).

---

6. Blau and Kahn (2017) report that the gender gap fell from 0.477 log points in 1980 to 0.230 log points in 2010. This gap—the difference in earnings that cannot be explained by (nongender) variables such as education, experience, race, region, unionization, industry, and occupation—fell from 0.230 log points to 0.088 log points over this period.

Figure 5.4

Growth in median real wages of men and women in the United States with and without college degrees between 1970 and 2019

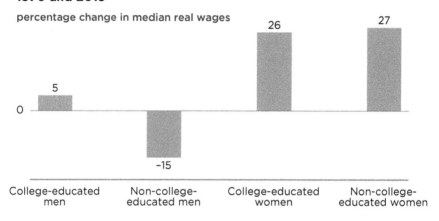

percentage change in median real wages

College-educated men / Non-college-educated men / College-educated women / Non-college-educated women

Source: Ruggles et al. (2022).

Fatih Guvenen et al. (2017) provide additional evidence of stagnation in the earnings of the median incomes of men. They use longitudinal Social Security data to estimate real earnings over 31 working years (from age 25 to 55). They find that even when compensation and benefits are included there was little to no rise in the lifetime income of men in the bottom three-quarters of the income distribution who started working between 1967 and 1983. After adjusting for inflation, the median US male worker born in 1958 who started working in 1983 earned just 1 percent more during his career than the median male born in 1932 who started working in 1957. "The stagnation of median income is closely related to declining median income of young workers, which is not compensated for by faster average income growth later in the career," Guvenen et al. write (p. 4). The median income at age 25 declined steadily from the 1967 cohort to the 1983 cohort. In contrast, over the 27 cohorts they examine, men in the 90th percentile of the earnings distribution saw their real career wages climb 35 percent. Successive cohorts of prime-age women in all percentiles of income distribution also enjoyed significant gains in career earnings.

Polarization of Wages

The distribution of men's earnings has also become increasingly polarized, with the share of men earning close to the median wage declining markedly. In 2015, a larger share of men earned below the median economywide wage, and a larger share earned more than twice the median than in 1970

Figure 5.5
Distribution of men's earnings in the United States, 1970–2015

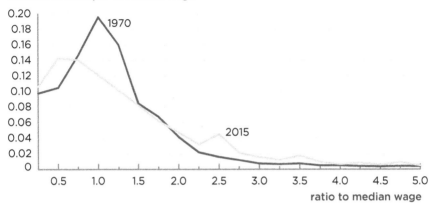

fraction or multiple of median wage

Source: Ruggles et al. (2022).

(figure 5.5). As a result, the mode, which had been close to the median, shifted to the left. David Autor and David Dorn (2013) find much slower growth in the share of jobs and the wages of occupations in the middle of the skills distribution.

Labor Compensation versus Capital Income

Figure 5.6 provides a long view of what happened to the share of labor compensation in gross domestic income over nine decades. It shows that between just after World War II and around 1970, declining income inequality was associated with a rising share of labor compensation in national income. Profits were more volatile than wages, and the shares fluctuated cyclically. But it is plausible to argue that the labor share remained fairly constant, at around 55–57 percent of domestic income, between 1970 and 2000 and perhaps even through 2008.[7] Rising income inequality since 1973 has primarily reflected rising income inequality of labor earnings rather than differences between the earnings of labor and capital, contrary to what Thomas Piketty (2014) and others claim.[8] After the Great Recession,

---

7. According to Dew-Becker and Gordon (2005, 71), "Labor's share was about the same in 2005 as eight years earlier. Over a longer period going back to 1954, labor's income share has been virtually constant." Lawrence (2008) argues that the profit share was basically constant between 1993 and 2007.

8. For an analysis of the profit share and a critique of Piketty, see Rognlie (2015).

Figure 5.6

Share of labor compensation in domestic income in the United States, 1929–2019

labor compensation as percent of domestic income

Source: US Bureau of Economic Analysis via Federal Reserve Bank of St. Louis, Federal Reserve Economic Data, https://fred.stlouisfed.org/.

the labor share of income declined through 2016, but it increased between 2016 and 2019 and rose sharply in 2020, during the unusual circumstances of the COVID pandemic.

Regional Convergence and Divergence

The first four decades of the postwar period were marked by income equalization not only across households but also across regions of the United States. Katheryn Russ and Jay Shambaugh (2019) report that that the poorest counties in the 1960s grew the most rapidly between 1960 and 1980. Robert Barro and Xavier Sala-i-Martin (1991) estimate that between 1963 and 1986, gross state product per capita and productivity gaps between the richest and poorest US states narrowed at an annual rate of about 2 percent a year.

Migration to more prosperous locations was the glue that enhanced income convergence when communities were dislocated by regional shocks. Olivier Blanchard and Lawrence Katz (1992) find that adverse demand shocks led to higher unemployment and lower wages in the short run but that over the longer run (periods of up to a decade), migration played the most important role in restoring unemployment rates and relative income levels, allowing unemployment and wage rates to revert to their previous levels. The long-run legacy of a negative shock was a smaller population and labor force; there was no permanently negative impact on local wages and per capita incomes.[9]

Starting around 1980, countervailing forces fundamentally changed the basis of economic growth and the patterns of regional location associated with it. These forces were primarily reflections of technological change, but they also reflected increased globalization. New digital technologies based on computers and semiconductors became increasingly important, as ever cheaper semiconductors were used to make smarter machines and many of the tasks performed using mainframe computers were taken over by desktop computers and other devices that used microprocessors. Although their impact on productivity was not initially evident, the effects of these technologies on patterns of employment, wages, and the location of production were profound.[10] These technological forces were reinforced by the emergence of increased international competition in industries such as clothing, electronics, automobiles, and steel.

The impact of these forces resulted in a "new geography of jobs" (Moretti 2013). Following the computer revolution, the creation of new jobs shifted toward cities with workers with analytical skills. The divergence in the subsequent growth of US cities can in no small part be explained by the complementarities between new technologies and their skill endowments. After 1975, the share of adults with college degrees increased more in cities with higher initial schooling levels (Berry and Glaeser 2005). Despite this increase in their supply, the wage premiums for college-educated workers in cities with already large shares of skilled workers rose especially rapidly. As a result, superstar cities—Seattle, San Jose, San Francisco, Raleigh-Durham, Austin, Dallas, Boston, New York, and Washington—which could attract more high-skilled workers and capital prospered by offering a growing number of high-paid jobs to college graduates in knowledge-intensive industries (Gyourko, Mayer, and Sinai 2013).

The responses of migration to these technology and trade shocks—the key adjustment mechanism demonstrated by Blanchard and Katz (1992)—slowed. Since the 1990s, shocks to local communities have become more persistent (Russ and Shambaugh 2019), but US workers, particularly those without a college degree, were much less willing to move.

---

9. Bound and Holzer (2000) find that positive (negative) labor demand shocks are followed by labor in-migration (out-migration).

10. Robert Solow famously said, "You can see the computer age everywhere but in the productivity statistics." See "We'd Better Watch Out," *New York Times Book Review*, July 12, 1987, http://www.standupeconomist.com/pdf/misc/solow-computer-productivity.pdf.

Conclusion

US growth was less inclusive after 1973 than it was between 1947 and 1973. Incomes increased much more slowly after 1973, and growth was more uneven than it had been. Incomes at the top rose far more rapidly than incomes in the middle or at the bottom. The earnings of men without college degrees declined after the 1970s and even those at the median did not share in what growth there was. After 2000, the share of income going to labor further declined.

Between 1940 and 1980, incomes converged regionally across US states. After the 1980s income convergence across states slowed markedly and by some measures diverged. Conditions of high and low unemployment in particular locations became far more persistent as migration between poor and rich locations slowed.

6

Why Did the Share of Manufacturing Employment Decline in the United States?

The manufacturing employment share (MES) in the United States has fallen steadily for many decades. The decline was especially severe between 2000 and 2010, when almost 6 million manufacturing jobs were lost.[1] Some economists argue that this absolute decline in manufacturing jobs after 2000 resulted from rapid labor productivity gains (Hicks and Devaraj 2017).[2] They point out that productivity growth in this period was substantially faster in computers and electronics (North American Industry Classification System [NAICS] 334) than in the rest of the manufacturing sector, suggesting that the experience reflected a more severe version of the long-run declining MES trend driven by relative rapid manufacturing productivity growth.

If, however, the inclusion of computers and electronics in output and productivity statistics distorted figures for the manufacturing sector, trade may have played a more important role in depressing employment than proponents of the rapid productivity growth explanation suggest, as Susan Houseman (2018) and Martin Baily and Barry Bosworth (2014) note. Thus other economists attribute the severe employment falloff to large manu-

---

1. Federal Reserve Bank of St. Louis, Federal Reserve Economic Data, "All Employees, Manufacturing," https://fred.stlouisfed.org/series/MANEMP.

2. Nager (2017) rejects relative productivity as the major factor in the decline, pointing out that growth in labor productivity in manufacturing relative to growth in the rest of the economy was similar in the 1990s and 2000s. He neglects the roles of slower output growth in both GDP and manufacturing output (see figure 6.3) in the later period, which resulted in no growth in aggregate employment and falling manufacturing employment.

facturing trade deficits, especially with China (Nager 2017). Studies of the "China shock" support the view that China played an important role in the large decline in US manufacturing employment after 2000 (Autor, Dorn, and Hanson 2013; Acemoglu et al. 2016; and Pierce and Schott 2016).

Trade and technology are not the only potential reasons for the absolute decline in manufacturing employment in the decade after 2000, however. The demand for manufactured goods is cyclically sensitive and responds disproportionately to changes in income in the short run. Slow GDP growth over the decade as shown in figure 6.1 should thus be expected to be associated with even slower manufacturing demand. The United States had two recessions between 2000 and 2010, which corresponded closely to the two periods of major losses in manufacturing employment. Over the decade, GDP grew at barely half the annual rate of any previous postwar decade. Regardless of the effects of productivity and trade, manufacturing employment growth should thus have been expected to be unusually slow.[3]

Figure 6.2 illustrates these developments. It shows (right axis) that manufacturing employment rose fairly steadily until 1979, declined in the recession of the early 1980s, and then fluctuated around 17.5 million for the next two decades (US Bureau of Labor Statistics, Current Employment Statistics).[4] US manufacturing employment then plummeted, falling from 17.3 million in 2000 to 11.5 million in 2010.[5] The trend decline in the MES was more steady (left axis). Between 1953 and 2000, total US nonfarm employment grew at an average annual rate of 2.1 percent, increasing from 50.3 million to 132.0 million. As a result, the share of manufacturing in nonfarm employment declined steadily, from 32.1 percent in 1953 to 13.1 percent in 2000 and then to 8.8 percent in 2010, after which the pace of the decline in the MES slowed.

The decline in manufacturing employment, which averaged 4 percent a year over the decade, came in three phases. Between 2000 and 2003, 2.76 million manufacturing job losses were associated with the recession that followed the bursting of the dot.com bubble. Between 2003 and 2007, although aggregate employment recovered, manufacturing's recovery was

---

3. Edwards and Lawrence (2013) show that a regression explaining manufacturing employment growth by aggregate employment growth fitted on data before 2000 predicts that flat employment growth over the decade would have been expected to lead almost precisely to an annual decline in manufacturing employment of about 4 percent, as actually happened.

4. Manufacturing employment fell by 1.37 million jobs between 1980 and 1982, as figure 6.2 shows. Lawrence (1983) finds that falling exports caused by a strengthening of the dollar accounted for about 34 percent of the decline.

5. The full-time equivalent employment series comes from national income accounts. It is available using the NAICS only after 1997.

Figure 6.1

Average growth in real GDP in the United States, by decade, 1950s–2010s (percent)

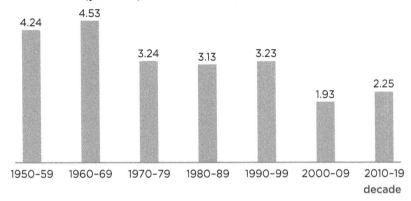

Source: US Bureau of Economic Analysis, National Income Accounts.

Figure 6.2

Total manufacturing employment and share of nonfarm employment in the United States, 1950–2018

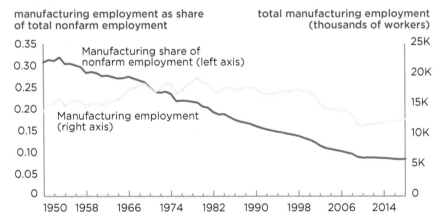

Source: Federal Reserve Bank of Saint Louis, Federal Reserve Economic Data, https://fred.stlouisfed.org/.

jobless, and an additional 631,000 manufacturing jobs were lost. Between 2007 and 2010, 2.3 million manufacturing jobs were lost in the Great Recession associated with the financial crisis. After 2010, the economy recovered steadily but slowly, and manufacturing employment rose, reaching a peak of 12.8 million in 2019 a few months before the COVID crisis. Despite this rise, in 2019 manufacturing employment was still 4.4 million jobs below its 2000 level, and the manufacturing share of employment declined between 2010 and 2019, albeit far more slowly than previously.

This chapter explains these developments in manufacturing employment. It is organized as follows. Section 1 focuses on the decade of the 2000s, when manufacturing employment declined absolutely. It shows that labor productivity growth in manufacturing was very rapid and that even in noncomputer manufacturing it was substantially faster than labor productivity in the rest of the economy. Relatively rapid productivity growth in manufacturing alone accounts for just over half the decline in noncomputer manufacturing employment. The impact of slow GDP growth accounts for much the rest. A reasonable estimate of the residual decline in employment remaining to be potentially explained by trade is around 11 percent of the decline.

Section 2 turns to the long-run trends in the MES. It shows that differences in the ways in which manufacturing output and productivity are measured are important in explaining declines in manufacturing's share over the long run. When NAICS 334 is included, manufacturing output grows as rapidly as GDP between 1948 and 2018; declining relative prices that match rapid productivity growth account fully for manufacturing's declining share in nominal output, and the real output share remains constant. This finding suggests, as the literature in chapter 1 indicated, that demand is very inelastic and points to a dominant role for relatively rapid productivity growth in the decline in the MES. However, when the computer and electronics industry is excluded the dominant source of the declining nominal share is real noncomputer manufacturing output, which is growing more slowly than real GDP. In other words, inelastic income demand is also an important reason for the declining employment trend in manufacturing industries.

Section 3 reviews the literature investigating the contributions of trade to the loss of manufacturing jobs, particularly in the decade of the 2000s. Using a variety of methodologies, studies show that although at the regional level in the United States the impact of trade and offshoring were significant, even between 2000 and 2010 much of the job loss from imports was offset by the gains from exports. Thus this literature confirms the finding that the contribution of aggregate trade flows to the overall decline in manufacturing employment was a relatively small share of loss.

Declining Share of Manufacturing Employment between 1987 and 2019: What Role for Trade?

Technology shocks can be distinguished from trade and demand shocks by examining the behavior of real manufacturing output and relative productivity growth. Houseman (2018) notes that one way to explore this relationship is to decompose the expression for the change in the log of the share of manufacturing in employment into changes due to the differences in output growth between manufacturing and GDP and changes due to differences in labor productivity growth between manufacturing and GDP. This decomposition can be achieved by using the formula for the log of output per worker and subtracting the log of the difference in the change in log of labor productivity in manufacturing from the change in the log of labor productivity in the economy. The change in the MES is thus equal to the difference between manufacturing and GDP output growth minus the difference between manufacturing and total labor productivity:

$$\Delta ln(L_m) - \Delta ln(L_t) = (\Delta ln(GDP_m) - \Delta ln(GDP_t)) - (\Delta ln(Prd_m) - \Delta ln(Prd_t)),^6 \quad (6.1)$$

where L stands for employment; GDP for output; Prd for output per worker; and the subscripts m and t for the manufacturing and total economy variables, respectively.

If the real output growth rate in the manufacturing sector is the same as in the rest of the economy then the full change in the MES reflects differences in labor productivity growth. If manufacturing productivity is the same as in the rest of the economy, the share changes will reflect differences in output growth. If trade is the dominant cause of the declining MES, it would depress manufacturing output, and a negative output difference would dominate the outcome. As discussed in chapter 4, as well as trade, declining manufacturing output relative to GDP could also indicate especially weak demand for manufacturing.[7]

This approach rests heavily on the assumption that manufacturing output is measured correctly. Houseman (2018) and Baily and Bosworth (2014) challenge that assumption. Houseman notes that in the official data,

---

6. Define total labor productivity (Prd_t) as GDP_t/L_t, where t refers to the total economy: $L_t = GDP_t/Prd_t$. Taking the natural log of each side, $ln(L_t) = ln(GDP_t/Prd_t)$. This equality can also be expressed as $ln(L_t) = ln(GDP_t) - ln(Prd_t)$. Expressing as changes implies $\Delta ln(L_t) = \Delta ln(GDP_t) - \Delta ln(Prd_t)$. Applying this expression to manufacturing yields $\Delta ln(L_m) = \Delta ln(GDP_m) - \Delta ln(Prd_m)$. Subtracting the first expression from the second one yields the expression used in the text for the change in the share of manufacturing employment in terms of the difference between output growth rates and productivity growth rates: $\Delta ln(L_m) - \Delta ln(L_t) = (\Delta ln(GDP_m) - \Delta ln(GDP_t)) - (\Delta ln(Prd_m) - \Delta ln(Prd_t))$, where $\Delta ln(L_m) - \Delta ln(L_t)$ is equal to the $\Delta(L_m/L_t)$ (the change in the MES in total employment).

7. Care needs to be taken in interpreting these measures, because the variables may not be independent. International competition could induce the substitution of capital for labor and thus affect labor productivity growth, for example, as Fort, Pierce, and Schott (2018) and Bloom, Draca, and Van Reenen (2016) note. Relatively rapid productivity growth in manufacturing could lead to lower prices for manufactured goods; by stimulating demand, it could increase manufacturing output.

the relatively stable growth in manufacturing output relative to GDP that is evident in both the long-run data and the data for 2000–10 are almost entirely related to measured output growth in just one industry—NAICS 334, which includes both computers and semiconductors.[8] The measurement of output in this sector rests heavily on adjustments that have been made to take account of quality improvements in semiconductors and computers that count as increased real output. These adjustments are extraordinarily large and sensitive to the methods used to estimate them.[9] If manufacturing output growth has been overstated, so, too, has labor productivity growth in manufacturing. If productivity growth in manufacturing was slower than measured, more of the explanation for the declining MES must reflect slower output growth in manufacturing than in the rest of the economy as equation (6.1) implies.[10] Such a finding could imply that trade has played a larger role in the declining MES than the official data suggest. It could also imply that weak demand for manufacturing output may have been important.[11]

Estimates of real output and labor productivity in noncomputer manufacturing (manufacturing excluding NAICS 334) are not readily available. The national income accounts report industry output measures in chained 2012 dollars for the 19 three-digit NAICS industries that include the manufacturing sector separately and provide estimates in chained 2012 dollars for aggregate manufacturing. However, because of weighting

---

8. For a description of the central role of information technology, especially semiconductors, in strong US productivity growth after 1995, see Jorgenson (2001).

9. For a review of this debate, see Byrne, Oliner, and Sichel (2017).

10. A concern that could also lead to overstatement of labor productivity growth in manufacturing and understatement of employment relates to the increased outsourcing of services by manufacturing firms to firms specialized in staffing services. Dey, Houseman, and Polivka (2012) estimate that this practice may have led to an overstatement of labor productivity by 0.5 percent a year between 1989 and 2000 and 0.2 percent a year between 2000 and 2012. However, these estimates imply that particularly for the decade of the 2000s, taking account of international outsourcing in the United States would not change the qualitative conclusions in this analysis.

11. Another concern, raised by Houseman et al. (2011), relates to the problem of deflating nominal output when account is not adequately taken of cheaper imported inputs when real output is obtained by deflating gross output and inputs. This problem leads to overstating input prices and thus understating changes in the quantity of imported inputs. The result would be an overstatement of growth in manufacturing value added. Houseman et al. claim that this faulty adjustment has overstated the growth in manufacturing value added by about 0.2 percent a year. Baily and Bosworth (2014) consider both bias from the treatment of offshored inputs and other possible measurement errors. They argue that although these errors may lead to an overstatement of output growth, especially in computers, they do not change "the basic story of the evolution of value added for the computer and electronics industry or for the rest of the manufacturing sector" (p. 9).

issues, output reported for individual industries cannot simply be aggregated to obtain the total reported for manufacturing output in 2012 dollars, because the aggregate is derived by aggregating the annual changes in the three-digit industry volumes with weights that change annually.[12] An output measure for noncomputer manufacturing cannot be obtained by simply subtracting the 2012 chained dollar series for the computer and electronics industry from the 2012 chained dollar measure of manufacturing aggregate output, because the weight assigned to the electronics industry in the aggregate is continuously changing. Instead, it is necessary to build up a separate estimate of noncomputer manufacturing output by aggregating the quantity indices of the individual nonelectronic industries using the Tornquist weighting method.[13]

Data for Noncomputer Manufacturing

For this analysis, the quantity indices provided by the Bureau of Economic Analysis for individual manufacturing industries other than computers and electronics (NAICS 334) have been summed using a Tornquist weighting procedure. Annual changes in real output (in logs) of the individual noncomputer industries in manufacturing are aggregated, with each annual change weighted by the share of each industry in the aggregate nominal value added for all the noncomputer industries for the years of the change. The exponents of these changes are then aggregated and converted into an index of noncomputer manufacturing output. Nominal output for noncomputer manufacturing is simply the total dollar value added for every industry other than NAICS 334. An implicit price index is obtained using the nominal and real output measures. Employment, measured on a full-time equivalent (FTE) basis, is taken from national income accounts. NAICS data on employment for the computer industry from the Current Employment Survey are available starting in 1987; they are available on an FTE basis only after 1998. Accordingly, to obtain a single FTE series, the Current Employment Survey employment series between 1987 and 1998 was converted into its FTE equivalence based on the assumption that changes in FTE employment are proportional to changes in the employment series. This assumption allows for an estimate of noncomputer manu-

---

12. As the Bureau of Economic Analysis notes, "Because the formula for the chain-type quantity indices uses weights of more than one period, the corresponding chained-dollar estimates are usually not additive" (see https://apps.bea.gov/iTable/iTable.cfm?reqid = 150&step = 2&isuri = 1&categories = gdpxind).

13. For a description and the formula of the methodology, see Houseman, Bartik, and Sturgeon (2015).

facturing per FTE worker from 1987 to 2019. A similar procedure was used to obtain an NAICS measure of total manufacturing employment on an FTE basis.

Decomposing Changes in the Manufacturing Employment Share into Relative Manufacturing Growth and Relative Productivity Growth

Table 6.1 reports the results of the decompositions of changes in employment shares for both manufacturing and noncomputer manufacturing. The first four columns use the annual data on changes in output and labor productivity that are required to track the change in the employment share in the last column, which is derived from their differences.

Results for Total Manufacturing

Between 1987 and 2000, manufacturing output and GDP increased at annual rates of 3.84 and 3.39 percent, respectively; annual growth rates in labor productivity in manufacturing and the total economy were 4.04 and 1.54 percent, respectively. Ex post, productivity differences thus played the main role in the annual decline in the manufacturing share of employment of –2.05 percent, which resulted in the share of FTE manufacturing employment falling from 17.9 percent in 1987 to 13.8 percent in 2000. Despite growing manufacturing trade deficits (which increased from 0.7 percent of GDP in 1991 to 2.7 percent of GDP in 2000 according to data from comtrade.un.org) the share of manufacturing output in real GDP rose for much of the period. The evidence thus does not support either a trade or demand explanation for the decline in MES over this period but indicates that relative productivity growth suffices to explain the declining MES before 2000.

Between 2000 and 2010, annual manufacturing output grew by only 0.30 percentage point less than GDP. In contrast, annual labor productivity growth in manufacturing was 3.69 percent faster than labor productivity growth for the economy as a whole. As in the earlier period, the dominant source of the decline in the MES was relative productivity growth.

Between 2000 and 2007, manufacturing output growth was 0.54 percent faster than GDP growth, and the productivity growth differential between manufacturing and GDP was 4.44 percent a year. For this period—the focus of studies of the China shock—relatively rapid productivity growth in manufacturing dominated differences in output growth and more than fully accounted for the annual 3.90 percent decline in the MES and 3.15 percent a year absolute declines in manufacturing employment.

Between 2007 and 2010, the –2.19 percent annual growth differential between manufacturing and GDP output was larger than the 1.96 percent

Table 6.1

Decomposition of annual changes in manufacturing and noncomputer manufacturing employment shares into growth and productivity differentials, 1987–2018 (percent)

Sector/period	Output		Labor productivity		Differences		Change in manufacturing share
	Sector (1)	GDP (2)	Sector (3)	GDP (4)	(1)–(2) (5)	(3)–(4) (6)	(5)–(6)
Total manufacturing							
1987–2000	3.84	3.39	4.04	1.54	0.45	2.50	–2.05
2000–10	1.46	1.76	5.73	2.04	–0.30	3.69	–3.99
2010–18	1.57	2.19	0.32	0.42	–0.62	–0.10	–0.52
2000–07	3.05	2.51	6.34	1.90	0.54	4.44	–3.90
2007–10	–2.13	0.05	4.33	2.37	–2.19	1.96	–4.15
Noncomputer manufacturing							
1987–2000	1.55	3.39	1.75	1.54	–1.84	0.20	–2.04
2000–10	–0.08	1.76	4.03	2.04	–1.84	1.99	–3.83
2010–18	1.08	2.19	–0.33	0.42	–1.11	–0.75	–0.36
2000–07	1.60	2.51	4.64	1.90	–0.91	2.74	–3.64
2007–10	–3.88	0.05	2.62	2.37	–3.93	0.25	–4.18

Sources: US Bureau of Economic Analysis and Federal Reserve Bank of St. Louis, Federal Reserve Economic Data, https://fred.stlouisfed.org/.

productivity differential. In this period, slow manufacturing output growth played a similar role to rapid productivity. However, as noted below, trade studies point to smaller impacts from the China shock in this period, and as these were the years of the Great Recession, it is more plausible that slow growth accounted for the part of the MES decline not caused by productivity.

For the decade, and especially during 2000–07, the main source of the large declines in MES was rapid manufacturing productivity growth in the context of slow overall economic growth. Over the decade, FTE employment in US manufacturing fell by 5.73 million. Had manufacturing output grown at the same rate as GDP (1.76 percent a year), the change in the MES would have been –3.51 percent rather than –3.99 percent. This change would have resulted in 689,000 more FTE workers in manufacturing. Slower output growth in manufacturing than in the economy as a whole, as a result of trade or other factors, thus could represent just 11.8 percent of the MES decline over the decade.

Between 2010 and 2018, productivity growth in both manufacturing and the economy as a whole was very slow (Lawrence 2017). Average annual manufacturing output growth of 1.57 percent lagged 0.62 percentage point behind the 2.19 percent growth rate of GDP. Given the very slow annual growth in manufacturing (0.32 percent) and total labor productivity (0.42 percent), the MES declined much less than earlier, and productivity growth in manufacturing played no role in the 0.52 percent a year decline.

Results for the Manufacturing Sector Excluding the Computer and Electronics Industry

Noncomputer manufacturing output grew at an annual rate of just 1.55 percent between 1987 and 2000, well below the 3.84 percent for manufacturing and 3.39 percent for GDP. As with aggregate manufacturing, the absolute level of employment in the noncomputer manufacturing sector remained fairly constant over the 13-year period. The sector's annual growth in output per worker (1.75 percent) was close to the rate for the economy as a whole (1.54 percent). The decline in the sector's share of noncomputer manufacturing employment (2.04 percent) was almost identical to the figure for manufacturing as a whole (2.05 percent). The main source of the declining noncomputer MES therefore was slower output growth rather than faster productivity growth. This outcome is compatible with a large role for trade or demand in the declining MES.

Between 2000 and 2010, noncomputer manufacturing output stagnated while GDP grew at 1.76 percent a year. Labor productivity growth in noncomputer manufacturing computed as changes in the log of ratio of noncomputer manufacturing output to FTE employment in noncomputer manufacturing increased at an annual rate of 4.03 percent, almost twice the rate for the economy as a whole (2.04 percent). For the decade, the average annual difference between the rate of noncomputer output growth and the rate of GDP growth was –1.84 percent, and the difference between labor productivity in noncomputer manufacturing and GDP was 1.99 percent. The contributions of productivity and output differentials to the annual 3.83 percent decline of in the employment share of noncomputer manufacturing were similar, with each accounting for about half the decline in the noncomputer manufacturing labor share.

In the two subperiods in the decade, the roles of productivity and output differentials were different. In 2000–07—the focus of the China shock—three-quarters of the declining noncomputer manufacturing employment share reflected faster annual productivity growth in noncomputer manufacturing (4.64 percent) than in the economy as a whole (1.90 percent), and about a quarter (0.91 percentage points of the 3.64 percent annual MES decline) reflected relatively slower output growth in noncomputer manufacturing.[14] Between 2007 and 2010, the 3.88 percent annual decline in noncomputer manufacturing output accounted for almost all of the decline in noncomputer manufacturing employment share of 4.18 percent. Thus, in the first seven years of the decade relative productivity growth was dominant, while in the final three years relative output was.

Between 2010 and 2018, output per worker declined by 0.33 percent a year in noncomputer manufacturing and increased by 0.42 for the economy as a whole. Total GDP increased by 2.19 percent, and noncomputer manufacturing output rose by 1.08 percent. Slower and negative productivity in noncomputer manufacturing increased employment 0.75 percent, but the slower noncomputer manufacturing output growth of 1.11 percent resulted in the noncomputer manufacturing employment share declining by 0.36 percent a year.

Differences in the Decomposition for Aggregate Manufacturing and Noncomputer Manufacturing

Differences in the decomposition results for aggregate manufacturing and noncomputer manufacturing reflect the slower labor productivity and output growth in noncomputer manufacturing. Between 1987 and 2000,

---

14. Houseman (2018) obtains similar results. She finds that differences in output growth account for 81.5 percent of the decline in the noncomputer manufacturing employment share between 1989 and 2000 and differences in labor productivity account for 74.5 percent of the declining noncomputer manufacturing employment share between 2000 and 2007.

Figure 6.3

Ratio of labor productivity in manufacturing and noncomputer manufacturing to GDP labor productivity in the United States, 1987–2018

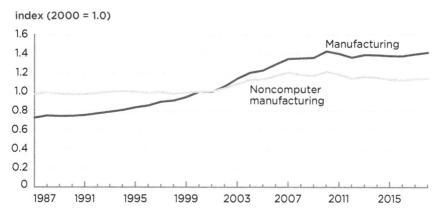

index (2000 = 1.0)

Source: US Bureau of Economic Analysis, Interactive Data, "Chain-Type Quantity Indexes for Gross Output by Industry," Interactive Access to Industry Economic Accounts Data (accessed on August 1, 2023).

aggregate manufacturing experienced rapid relative productivity growth, while labor productivity in noncomputer manufacturing grew at the same rate as labor productivity in the economy (figure 6.3).[15] Between 2000 and 2010, however, noncomputer manufacturing experienced relatively rapid productivity growth, albeit not as rapid as in manufacturing as a whole. Over this decade, the ratio of productivity in noncomputer manufacturing to productivity in GDP increased by 21 percent—about half the 43 percent relative productivity increase for the manufacturing aggregate. The difference suggests that even without the computer industry, relatively rapid productivity growth was a significant source of declining manufacturing employment over the decade. What remains is to explain the behavior of noncomputer manufacturing output, which fell by –0.80 percent over the decade compared with GDP output.

15. Baily and Bosworth (2014) and Houseman (2018) conclude that over the long run, productivity growth in noncomputer manufacturing was no faster than in other private industries (according to Houseman 2018) or the business sector (Baily and Bosworth 2014).

Explaining Output Demand for Noncomputer Manufacturing

Output demand can be captured by an equation in which noncomputer manufacturing output is assumed to depend on GDP and the relative price of noncomputer manufacturing to GDP. The results of two sets of regressions using data for 1960–2000 are illuminating.[16]

As the decade after 2000 was characterized by two sharp recessions, it makes sense to explore the cyclical nature of the demand for noncomputer manufacturing output using a first-difference specification. Regression 6.1 does so by explaining the change in log of noncomputer manufacturing output (*FLQNCMAN*) by the change in the log of GDP (*FLGDP*) and the change in the ratio of relative price deflator of noncomputer manufacturing to the GDP price deflator (*FLRPNCMAN*).

Regression 6.1:
$$FLQNCMAN = -0.045 + 1.89 \, FLGDP - 0.74 \, FLRPNCMAN$$
$$(0.005) \quad (0.122) \qquad (0.101)$$
41 observations, *R*-squared = 0.911, root mean square error = 0.0146.

Regression 6.1 estimated over 1960–2000 captures the highly cyclical nature of the demand for noncomputer manufacturing output (figure 6.4). It explains changes in noncomputer manufacturing accurately, with a root mean square error of 1.46 percent and an *R*-squared of 0.911; all variables have the expected signs and are statistically significant. Given the constant term of –0.045, the coefficient of 1.89 on changes in GDP indicates that assuming no change in relative prices, for noncomputer manufacturing output to remain constant, GDP needs to grow 2.4 percent a year (4.5/1.89). If GDP growth is flat, noncomputer manufacturing declines by 4.5 percent. Had GDP increased at the 3.3 percent it averaged between 1987 and 2000, the income effect would have increased demand for noncomputer manufacturing by 1.74 percent a year—an implied income elasticity of about a half (1.74/3.3). As GDP grew at an annual average rate of just 1.76 percent between 2000 and 2010—less than required for positive noncomputer manufacturing growth—the equation predicts that with no change in relative prices, noncomputer manufacturing would decline by 1.17 percent a year, just over 1 percent a year more than the actual annual decline of 0.08 percent.

Cumulating the predictions of the equation using actual data for the independent variables over the decade suggests that noncomputer manufacturing output growth was higher than might have been expected

---

16. The source of the data is US Bureau of Economic Analysis, https://www.bea.gov/data/economic-accounts/industry.

Figure 6.4

Actual and predicted first differences in the log of the output of noncomputer manufacturing in the United States (regression 6.1 results), 2001–18

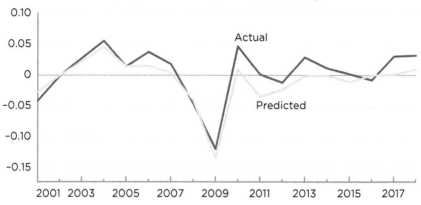

first difference of ln(output of noncomputer manufacturing)

Source: Author's calculations.

using the change regression. Between 2000 and 2010, GDP growth was 17.64 percent. Using the coefficient of 1.89 on *FLGDP* implies that GDP growth would raise noncomputer output by 1.89 * 17.64 (33.34 percent). Between 2000 and 2010, the price of noncomputer output declined relative to the GDP deflator by 3.81 percent. Given elasticity of –0.74, this decline would have led to an increase in output of 2.82 percent over the decade. Total output growth as a result of these two effects would thus have been 36.16 percent. These effects would have been more than offset by the negative effect of the constant of 45 percent (10 * 4.5). The equation thus predicts a decline in growth of 8.84 percent. In fact, noncomputer output fell by just 0.76 percent over the decade. Cumulatively, output growth was stronger by 0.85 percent a year or a total of around 8 percent *more* than predicted by the equation. In this specification, there is no additional role for trade to play in depressing output once this equation is used to predict noncomputer manufacturing output.

It is possible that this specification is not appropriate for capturing changes over a period as long as a decade. To capture the long-run behavior of output, a specification explaining the output *level* of noncomputer manufacturing may be more appropriate than its annual changes. Regression 6.2, estimated over 1960–2000, therefore explains the log of the quantity of noncomputer manufacturing output by the log of GDP and the log of lagged GDP in addition to the log of relative price of noncomputer output to the GDP deflator (*LRPNCMAN*).

Figure 6.5

Actual and predicted log of the output of noncomputer manufacturing in the United States (regression 6.2 results), 2001–18

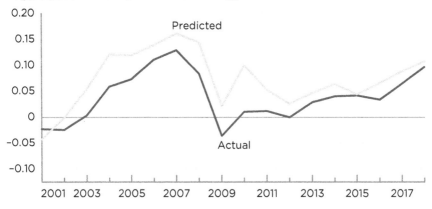

log(output of noncomputer manufacturing)

Source: Author's calculations.

Regression 6.2:

$$LQNCMAN_t = 1.54\ LQGDP_t - 1.15\ LQGDP_{t-1} - 1.55\ LRPNCMAN$$
$$\quad\quad\quad (0.30)\quad\quad\quad (0.29)\quad\quad\quad\quad (0.15)$$

41 observations, R-squared = 0.988, root mean square error = 0.0503.

This equation captures the long-run responsiveness of noncomputer manufacturing to GDP. Summing the impact over both the current and lagged periods indicates a long-run income elasticity of 0.39 (1.54 − 1.15). Unlike regression 6.1, regression 6.2 suggests that taking the relationships captured before 2000, noncomputer manufacturing output in 2002–18 was *lower* than expected (figure 6.5). The equation overpredicts the level of noncomputer manufacturing output by 8.92 percent in 2010 and by 1.03 percent in 2018. Assuming that the entire error over 2001–10 reflects the negative impact of trade would imply that trade could account for 8.92 percent (0.86 percent a year) of the annual output decline. Given the annual decline of 3.83 log points in the share of employment in noncomputer manufacturing, this suggests that trade accounted for 22.5 percent (0.86/3.83) of the decline in the labor share over the decade and productivity plus slow growth accounted for 77.5 percent.

Noncomputer manufacturing output grew at a much slower rate than GDP but somewhat faster than expected given the historic relationship between the two. It is possible that as trade is not explicitly modeled in the regression, the coefficients are picking up the historic impact of trade in previous decades. Even if they do so, however, if trade had a far greater negative impact on employment between 2000 and 2010, as some claim, the predicted residuals using these regressions should be significant, negative, and much larger than found here.

In sum, relatively rapid productivity growth played the most important role in the absolute decline in manufacturing employment between 2000 and 2010. It dominated the behavior of employment when the computer and electronics industry is included in manufacturing, and it accounted for just over half the decline in the employment share in noncomputer manufacturing. Slow GDP growth also played a major role in noncomputer employment, accounting for much of the remaining decline in the share. Based on regression 6.1 an additional shock due to trade accounted for none of the decline, whereas based on regression 6.2 it accounted for 22.5 percent of the declines. Averaging these results would place trade's contribution at just over 11 percent of the manufacturing job loss.

Long-Run Share of Manufacturing in GDP

The share of manufacturing in nominal GDP declined steadily between 1954 and 2019. For manufacturing as a whole the decline was associated with relatively rapid productivity growth and declining relative prices of manufacturing value added; the real output share of manufacturing remained basically constant over the period. Once the computer and electronics sector is excluded, a declining share of noncomputer output in real GDP rather than declining relative prices features more prominently in the explanation of the declining nominal share of noncomputer manufacturing in GDP. This result reflects inelastic income demand elasticity, which is especially apparent after 1970.

Equation 6.1 in section 1 decomposes changes in the MES into changes in manufacturing output growth relative to GDP and changes in labor productivity growth relative to aggregate productivity growth. It implies that if there were no difference between manufacturing and GDP output growth, relative productivity growth would account for all of the changes in the manufacturing labor share. This decomposition is helpful in understanding why relative productivity growth is so important in explaining the declining nominal share of manufacturing in GDP. Manufacturing's ratio to real US GDP was similar in 1948 and 2020 (figure 6.6); differences in output growth played very little role in the declining MES. The steady decline in the nominal share of manufacturing value added in GDP, especially since the mid-1960s, closely tracks the declining prices of manufacturing value added relative to the prices of GDP. This behavior is compat-

Figure 6.6

Ratios of manufacturing value added, quantities, and prices to GDP (log scale) in the United States, 1948–2018

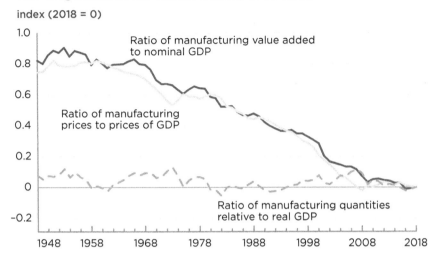

index (2018 = 0)

Ratio of manufacturing value added to nominal GDP

Ratio of manufacturing prices to prices of GDP

Ratio of manufacturing quantities relative to real GDP

Source: US Bureau of Economic Analysis, https://www.bea.gov/data/economic-accounts/industry.

ible with elasticities of close to 1 and 0 for income and prices, respectively. With these parameters, relative quantities do not change in response to price changes or GDP growth.

This combination is borne out by a simple regression analysis. Specifying the variables in logs and regressing the quantity of manufacturing output against real GDP and the deflators for manufacturing relative to the GDP deflator indicates long-run income and price elasticities of 1.07 and –0.128, respectively.[17]

Excluding Computers and Electronics

Like the manufacturing aggregate, the declining nominal share of noncomputer manufacturing was associated with a fairly constant real share and a trend decline in relative prices until the mid-1970s (figure 6.7). In some periods since the mid-1970s, such as 1980–88 and 2000–09, declining relative prices also contributed to the declining nominal share; in others, relative prices were fairly constant, and the declining nominal share reflected

---

17. The regression fitted between 1949 and 2018 with standard errors in parentheses is
$LQMAN = 1.071\ LQGDP_t - 0.0205\ LQGDP_{t-1} - 0.128\ LRPMAN$
   (0.015)   (0.009)   (0.019)
R-squared = 0.999, root mean square error = 0.036. Data are from national income accounts.

Figure 6.7

Ratios of noncomputer manufacturing value added, quantities, and prices to GDP (log scale) in the United States, 1948–2018

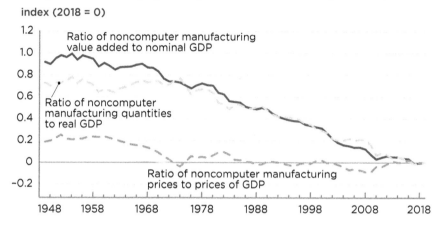

index (2018 = 0)

Source: US Bureau of Economic Analysis, https://www.bea.gov/data/economic-accounts/industry.

slower output growth in manufacturing. These results suggest that in contrast to the manufacturing aggregate, a driver of the declining nominal share of noncomputer manufacturing since the 1970s has been a low income elasticity of demand for noncomputer manufacturing output.[18] Indeed, a regression over 1949–2018 indicates an inelastic income elasticity for noncomputer manufacturing of 0.52 and a price elasticity of 1.84.

Explaining Absolute and Trend Declines

Two explanations can be offered for the absolute declines in US manufacturing employment between 2000 and 2010. If manufacturing output is treated as homogeneous and official aggregate data for manufacturing are used, the explanation is relatively more rapid productivity growth in manufacturing in an economy that grew significantly more slowly in 2000–10 than it had in the previous four decades. This explanation leaves no room for a large employment impact of trade. Over the long run, the trend decline in the MES can be almost fully explained by relatively rapid productivity growth, as the long-run income elasticity of demand for manufacturing output is near unity (1.05).

---

18. 1949–2018: $LQNCMAN = 0.516\ LQGDP_t - 0.152\ LQGDP_{t-1} - 1.835\ LRPNCMAN$
    (0.011)   (0.011)   (0.097)
R-squared = 0.989, root mean square error = 0.061.

Treating manufacturing as homogeneous overlooks important differences between industries. In particular, since the 1970s, the share of manufacturing output other than computers and electronics in real GDP has been declining, as demand has become less responsive to income growth and, with the notable exception of the 2000s, labor productivity growth in noncomputer manufacturing was not much higher than in the rest of the economy. Noncomputer output growth was also adversely affected by the stagnation of economic growth after 2000. As cyclical and income effects estimated using data before 2000 can account for the slow output growth with considerable accuracy thereafter, trade does not appear to have been a major factor in the employment decline even when considering only noncomputer manufacturing.

These different narratives are not mutually exclusive, but they suggest that caution is needed when making generalizations about the sources of job loss in manufacturing and the reasons for its declining share in nominal GDP. Rapid technological change in general, and automation in particular, has played an important role. But low income elasticities and slow growth need to be given more prominence in the explanation. In neither case is there much room for trade as an important part of the explanation. The experience since 2010 shows a break in the trend. Despite all the discussion about robots and automation and the presence of large trade deficits in manufacturing, manufacturing employment growth since the Great Recession was more robust than previous trends might have projected, precisely because productivity growth in manufacturing was negligible.

Studies of the Impact of Trade on Manufacturing Employment: A Survey

Three types of studies have been conducted to quantify the impact of trade on US manufacturing employment since the 1990s. The first is an accounting approach, which uses ex post data to assess the impact of trade and other factors. A second develops instrumental variables that help identify the causes of changes in trade flows, in order to estimate employment impact of trade across commuter zones or industries. A third uses general equilibrium models to simulate the economywide impacts of trade shocks on employment. This section describes the results of each approach.

Accounting Approaches

Michael Hicks and Srikant Devaraj (2017) use an accounting approach that attributes changes in manufacturing employment to productivity, trade, and demand growth. They use deflated measures to estimate employment changes associated with each of these components at the industry level and then aggregate these industry effects to obtain overall results for manufacturing. They conclude that between 2000 and 2010, changes in labor productivity accounted for 87.8 percent of the 5.64 million manufacturing job losses, changes associated with trade accounted for 13.4 percent of the decline, and changes associated with demand increased employment by 1.4 percent.[19] As they work with real output measures, their conclusions rest on the accuracy of the methods used to deflate the nominal changes discussed above as well as the implicit assumption that the components of the identity that defines employment demand can be used as exogenous changes.

Job Content of Trade Balances

In Lawrence and Edwards (2013), we estimate the manufacturing labor equivalence of US trade deficits and surpluses of the 19 industries that make up the manufacturing sector.[20] We use annual input-output tables to take account of the effects of changes in the trade balances of each industry on output in all manufacturing industries.[21] Instead of using real measures, we combine changes in industry nominal output with annual ratios of industry employment to value added to obtain estimates at the industry level of the job equivalence associated with trade balances. We aggregate the individual industry job estimates to obtain the employment equivalence of the overall manufacturing trade balance.[22] Implicitly, we are estimating the number of domestic manufacturing jobs that would be required to close the trade deficit in manufacturing at each point in time.

The Lawrence-Edwards approach has the advantage of not being sensitive to deflation methods.[23] We find that the full-time job equivalence of the manufacturing trade deficit was 1.65 million in 1990 and 3.3 million in 2000. This finding implies that had the United States maintained its spending levels, it would have needed 1.65 million more manufacturing

---

19. Their numbers do not add up to 100 percent because of rounding errors.

20. If both income and substitution elasticities are equal to 1, domestic expenditure shares will remain constant when the trade balance changes, as discussed in chapter 2. Under these assumptions, the contribution of the trade balance to the MES will be captured by the domestic employment equivalent of the trade balance. For support of this argument in the context of a well-specified model, see Uy, Yi, and Zhang (2013).

21. In a similar earlier study using input-output analysis, Baily and Lawrence (2004) find that on balance, trade accounted for only 314,000 of the 2.851 million decline in manufacturing employment between 2000 and 2003. They also find that the employment content of imports actually declined.

22. In Edwards and Lawrence (2013) we describe this methodology.

23. See the critiques of these methods by Houseman (2018) and Houseman et al. (2011).

workers in 1990 and 3.3 million in 2000 to be fully self-sufficient. We find that the full-time job equivalence of the deficit peaked at 3.7 million in 2006, falling to 2.3 million in 2009 and 2.8 million in 2010. Thus over the decade the deficit represented 500,000 fewer manufacturing jobs.

Two results of this analysis are of particular interest. First, the nominal trade deficit in manufactured goods in 2010 of $644 billion was more than twice the $256 billion deficit in 1998, but the number of manufacturing jobs required to substitute domestically manufactured goods for the trade deficit in manufacturing of the $644 billion deficit in 2010 was 2.77 million manufacturing jobs—very similar to the 2.5 million jobs required to produce the 1998 deficit domestically. This paradoxical finding reflects the growth of nominal output per worker over the period. Value added per FTE employee in manufacturing almost doubled over the period, increasing from $82,950 in 1998 to $160,110 in 2010. At 1990 levels of manufacturing value added per worker, the deficit in 2007 would have represented about 8 million jobs.

Second, in Lawrence and Edwards (2013) we add the manufacturing employment equivalence of the trade deficit to manufacturing employment. Figure 6.8 shows both the actual manufacturing employment and the series that includes the employment equivalence of the manufacturing trade deficit between 1990 and 2010. It shows that although manufacturing employment levels are higher in the adjusted series, the overall declines and timing of changes in manufacturing employment over the past decade in the two series are not very different. Both series indicate large and similar drops (on the order of 6 million jobs) in employment between 2000 and 2009, suggesting that recessions and nominal domestic productivity growth, which impact both series, rather than the job loss in the trade deficits can explain the employment declines over the decade. Baily and Bosworth (2014) reach a similar conclusion.

Robert Feenstra and Akira Sasahara (2018) use the World Input-Output Database's (WIOD) global input-output model to compute the employment impact of all US exports and imports between 1995 and 2011. They find that the growth in US merchandise exports over this period increased demand by 1.9 million jobs in manufacturing and that exports generated 3.7 million jobs in all industries. (In contrast, they find that US imports from China led to a reduction of 1.4 million jobs.) They estimate that the net effect of overall US trade with all economies in all sectors over the period led to a reduction in the demand for manufacturing workers of just 80,000. This result is roughly in line with estimates by Lawrence and Edwards (2013) of the changes between 1998 and 2010.

Figure 6.8
Actual manufacturing employment and counterfactual manufacturing employment without trade deficit in the United States, 1990–2010

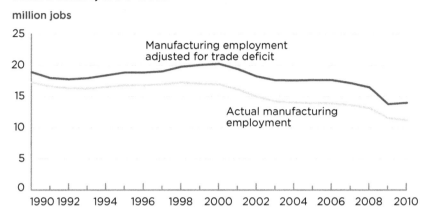

million jobs

Source: Lawrence and Edwards (2013, figure 4).

The analysis in chapter 3, which also uses the WIOD, can account for the 5.1 percent decline in the share of manufacturing in overall US employment between 1995 and 2011 in terms of the manufacturing value added in each of the components that determine the demand for manufacturing labor. It implies that 0.6 percentage point can be attributed to the decline in the trade balance in manufacturing value added, 3.9 percentage points to the decline in US spending on manufacturing value added, and 0.7 percentage point to the relatively more rapid increase in nominal value added per worker. The net trade balance in manufacturing value added is thus equal to 11.7 percent of the change in the labor share, and the overwhelming source of the decline is the fall in the share of domestic spending devoted to manufacturing value added. Trade accounted for around 11 percent of the decline. These results are consistent with the previous section's finding that demand is an important driver of manufacturing employment.

Problems with These Approaches

These approaches suggest that trade did not play a major role in manufacturing employment. But problems in the methods used could lead to both overstatement and understatement of the impacts of trade flows. In particular, the demand for manufacturing labor ultimately depends on the demand for manufacturing value added Y_m, which is equal to the manufacturing value added contained in US spending plus the output in the net trade balance: $Y_m = (C_m + I_m + G_m) + (X_m - M_m)$. Using the estimate of the labor content of the trade balance on manufacturing value added as the measure of the impact of trade requires assuming that the labor content of domestic absorption—$C_m + I_m + G_m$—remains constant when the manufacturing value added in the trade balance changes. (This could occur if both income and trade price elasticities are equal to 1.) If this assumption is not valid, the ex post accounting exercise is vulnerable to the impact of other variables that could change both the trade balance and spending. In the presence of unemployment, for example, an increase in exports as a result of foreign growth could set off multiplier effects and increase domestic spending. This spending might increase imports, so that the employment equivalence of the ex post trade balance would underestimate the full employment impact of trade.

More generally, trade flows are endogenous variables—outcomes rather than causes—and the association between trade flows and employment will be sensitive to the reason the trade flows are changing. Import growth, which enters negatively when an accounting approach is used, need not always cause job loss. An increase in domestic spending, for example, could generate more jobs at home and increase imports, so there need be no job loss. An increase in domestic production could similarly generate an increase in imported intermediate inputs without adversely affecting domestic employment. In the face of an increase in foreign supply, however, given domestic demand, imports could increase and domestic employment could decline. To deal with this issue, it is necessary to distinguish between shifts in demand and shifts in supply. Doing so requires instrumental variables that can identify separately causes that shift the supply and demand curves.

Studies Identifying the Causes of Endogeneity

Numerous studies use instrumental variables techniques to deal with this endogeneity. Pierce and Schott (2016) use the conditions under which China entered the World Trade Organization (WTO) in 2001 as an identifying strategy. By becoming a member of the WTO, China was granted permanent normal trade relations (NTR) by the United States, a status that implied a US commitment to grant China permanent most favored nation (MFN) treatment.[24]

---

24. Between 1979 and its accession to the WTO, China received conditional MFN treatment from the United States. That status was subject to annual review and could have been repealed and replaced with the US tariff schedule reflected in the Smoot-Hawley tariffs.

Justin Pierce and Peter Schott use the difference between the industry NTR rates applied to China in 2001 (which averaged 4 percent) and the alternative non-NTR rates, which data back to the 1930s and averaged 36 percent, which they call the NTR premium. This difference, they claim, is a good measure of the reduction in tariff uncertainty associated with WTO accession. They use the NTR premiums in each industry to explain the difference between each industry's employment growth after 2001, a cyclical peak, and employment growth after the previous cyclical peak in 1990. If an industry had an average NTR premium, they find that its employment growth in 2001–07 was 12–16 percentage points less than in the six-year period after the peak in 1990. Their methodology compares only differences in changes in employment between the two periods at the industry level; *it does not provide an aggregate estimate of the share of the overall manufacturing job loss attributable to trade.* Nevertheless, the authors claim that their evidence shows that US trade with China is "directly and indirectly associated with the large and long-lasting declines in US manufacturing employment after 2001" (p. 5). Their analysis uses no actual trade data, leaving gaps in the understanding of how China's WTO entry affected trade flows.

David Autor, David Dorn, and Gordon Hanson (ADH) (2013) use a different identification strategy. They exploit the fact that the industrial composition of local labor markets differs and these markets were therefore exposed differentially to Chinese competition. Rather than simply using Chinese exports to the United States (which could also reflect changes in US demand), they identify imports associated with increased Chinese supply capacity, by using an instrument derived from measuring Chinese industry-level exports to eight other high-income economies. For this instrument to be valid, demand shifts in these economies should not be correlated with those in the United States.

In the first of numerous papers that use this approach, ADH state that import competition from China explains one-quarter of the contemporaneous aggregate decline in US manufacturing employment between 1990 and 2007.[25] They estimate that the United States lost 548,000 manufacturing jobs to Chinese trade between 1990 and 2000 and 982,000 between 2000 and 2007. In later work, Autor, Dorn, and Hanson, together with Daron Acemoglu and Brendan Price (Acemoglu et al. 2016) use slightly different periods and take more explicit account of the associated shocks on

---

25. An early study by Bernard, Jensen, and Schott (2006) finds that import penetration from low-income countries accounted for 14 percent of the total decline of 675,000 US manufacturing workers between 1977 and 1997. They use plants and so may overestimate the net effects if workers move between them.

upstream and downstream industries using input-output tables for 1992. They also use multiplier analysis to estimate additional shocks that operate through expenditure effects as workers displaced by imports reduce the incomes of others. Combining estimates of the impact on industry value added with effects through input-output linkages, they estimate losses of 421,000 US manufacturing jobs between 1991 and 1999 and another 985,000 between 1999 and 2011. The estimate of 985,000 is equal to 17 percent of the 5.6 million decline in manufacturing jobs between 1999 and 2011. They also use input-output analysis to estimate jobs lost in nonmanufacturing industries. They conclude that between 1999 and 2011, 2.37 million manufacturing and nonmanufacturing jobs were lost—a headline number that has received considerable attention.[26]

Were these job losses permanent? The 1.475 million manufacturing jobs Acemoglu et al. (2016) estimate to have been lost to Chinese imports in 1991–2007 is similar to (and larger than) the 1.406 million they estimate to have been lost to Chinese imports in 1991–2011. Accepting these calculations implies that between 2007 and 2011, there were no additional net employment losses associated with imports from China.[27] Nicholas Bloom et al. (2019, 9) confirm and extend this result, finding "strong employment impacts from China from 2000 to 2007 but nothing from 2008 to 2015." Adam Jakubik and Victor Stolzenberg (2021) find that the negative effects identified in ADH are not present in 2008–14. These results suggest that the China shock may have run its course by 2008 and that once the United States adjusted by shutting down plants that competed with China (i.e., became fully specialized), it enjoyed the benefits from Chinese imports as a consumer and experienced few producer losses.[28]

The China shock was large, but it was not the only change in trade that affected employment. A full accounting should include the employment impact of exports as well as non-Chinese imports. Robert Feenstra, Mong Ma, and Yuan Xu (2019) conduct a comprehensive accounting, mirroring, where possible, the instruments used in the ADH approach. Among the

---

26. Jakubik and Stolzenburg (2021) find one-third fewer manufacturing job losses than ADH and quite different regional effects when using value added instead of gross trade flows to measure the China shock. Rothwell (2017) is also skeptical of the ADH study.

27. This result is not implausible, because the implicit labor content of US manufactured imports did not increase very much. Between 2007 and 2011, US manufactured imports from China increased 23.8 percent (from $315.3 billion to $389.9 billion), and US output per worker increased 18 percent (from $135,700 to $160,100). Between 2008 and 2019, nominal US manufactured imports from China increased by 35 percent and US nominal output in manufacturing per worker by 37 percent.

28. However, the initial shocks appear to have had long-lasting effects on local labor markets (Autor, Dorn, and Hanson 2021).

controls they use to distinguish foreign demand effects from those stemming from domestic US factors are exports of other high-income economies to foreign markets. They also use equations that predict US exports on the basis of foreign demand and the tariffs faced by US exporters and their competitors. They estimate these employment impacts at both the industry and local labor market levels. Their preferred specification in their industry analysis, which incorporates estimates of the impact of all imports and exports, indicates a net decline in manufacturing employment as a result of trade of just 117,000 jobs between 1999 and 2011. This figure represents only about 2 percent of the decline in manufacturing employment of 5.6 million over these years. They also estimate the net impacts in commuter zones for the same period, using a number of specifications, obtaining estimates of net manufacturing job loss of between 28,000 and 709,000. The largest of their estimates would equal 12.7 percent of the decline in manufacturing employment between 1999 and 2011.

Methodological Issues

A strength of the methodologies used by Pierce and Schott; Autor, Dorn, and Hanson; and Feenstra, Ma, and Xu lies in their use of instrumental variables to control for endogeneity. Pierce and Schott, for example, explain differences between industry response after 2001 and after 1990 by the NTR gap. ADH explain differences in employment before and after the shock by exposure to Chinese imports. A weakness in these approaches is that they generally use a difference-in-difference framework that isolates (cross-sectional) effects at the industry and/or local economy level but does not account for potential general equilibrium effects. Using this framework means that they do not account for effects that could spill over between zones or across industries or occupations or operate economywide.

Methods that evaluate relative differences in outcomes across regions, industries, or occupations in response to a particular shock also cannot reveal the net national response to shocks unless they can be benchmarked against an industry, region, or occupation in which the shock was absent. These methods fail to take account of general factors that may also have caused manufacturing job loss and would be captured by an intercept term.[29] As Marc-Andreas Muendler (2017, 17, footnote 10) notes, "It is indeed plausible that the China shock had a real impact on economy-

---

29. Muendler uses the example of a tide whose effect depends on boats' characteristics. Comparing the responses of the boats will provide estimates of relative effects but cannot give the absolute impact—that is, whether the tide lifted or lowered all the boats.

wide labor market outcomes, but neither the estimator [ADH] use nor the simple time trend (in their table 1) are suited to make the inference."[30]

As Kerwin-Kofi Charles, Erik Hurst, and Mariel Schwartz note (2019, 338), "Cross-area estimates only provide an accurate assessment of the effects of aggregate manufacturing decline on aggregate changes in employment rates and labor market conditions under a stringent set of conditions." This point is stressed in a number of other studies (Beraja, Hurst, and Ospina 2016; Nakamura and Steinsson 2014; and Esposito, Arkolakis, and Adao 2017). Cross-region estimates ignore the mobility of labor, capital, and goods across space; changes in national monetary, fiscal, and regulatory policy that affect all regions; and financial flows across regions through government transfers. All of these factors imply that the local employment elasticity to a local shock (like the decline in manufacturing labor demand) differs from the aggregate employment elasticity to the same aggregate shock. Given the analysis in the first section of this chapter—indicating, for example, that there were pervasive impacts of slow aggregate demand growth during the period of the China shocks—these assumptions seem untenable in this case. In addition, although the pace of migration between locations has slowed since the 1990s, the implicit assumption of total labor immobility is highly questionable.

General Equilibrium Studies

Lorenzo Caliendo, Maximiliano Dvorkin, and Fernando Parro (2019) develop a complex full general equilibrium simulation model with 22 sectors, 38 economies, and the 50 US states. The model is calibrated to take account of labor mobility frictions, geographic factors, input-output linkages, and international trade, in order to capture the dynamics of intersectoral trade, interregional trade, international trade, and labor market makers. It is used to simulate the impact of a China shock of the scale identified by ADH.

Caliendo, Dvorkin, and Parro (2019) estimate that the China shock resulted in a loss of 550,000 manufacturing jobs between 2000 and 2007 (16 percent of manufacturing jobs lost during this period)—just over half the job loss estimates of ADH (2013) of 982,000 for the same period and of 985,000 for a slightly different period (1999-2007) by Acemoglu et al. (2016). The substantial difference between these results and those of ADH (2013) could be interpreted to mean that general equilibrium effects may

---

30. See Adao, Kolesar, and Morales (2018) for a discussion of shift-share designs.

have offset a substantial share of the losses estimated by the ADH studies. Alternatively, it could be the result of the calibration of the parameters used by Caliendo, Dvorkin, and Parro (2019) in constructing their model.[31]

Broader Impacts of Trade on Employment

The discussion has emphasized results that explicitly estimate the impacts on manufacturing employment. Acemoglu et al. (2016) also provide estimates of the impact on total employment, which are more than twice as large. As noted, their estimate of 2.4 million jobs lost in both manufacturing and other sectors is the number that often grabs the headline in many accounts of their study (Lincicome 2020). However, there are reasons to be skeptical of such estimates.

Gene Grossman and Esteban Rossi-Hansberg (2008) explore the theory of trade in tasks. They show how cheaper imported inputs can act like a productivity improvement, allowing firms to reduce prices and increase output and employment. To the degree that imports from China were inputs that made the firms using them more competitive they may have increased rather than reduced employment.

Using a cross-regional reduced-form specification, Zhi Wang et al. (2018) incorporate this supply chain perspective, using intermediate input imports rather than total imports in computing the downstream impacts. They find that trading with China provides a boost to employment and real wages in the United States. "The most important factor is employment stimulation outside the manufacturing sector through the downstream channel" (abstract).

Pol Antràs, Teresa Fort, and Felix Tintelnot (2017) find that increases in Chinese import penetration were associated with declining firm-level employment in 1997–2007. In other firms in the same industry, however, increases in the value of imports from China that are directly imported by firms as intermediate inputs are associated with either increases or no change in employment.

A second effect operates through changes within firms. Offshoring and technological change may render some plants obsolete but not drive firms out of business. Even though they closed many of their plants, many firms continued to operate and expanded their nonmanufacturing activities in response to competition from China (Magyari 2017).

---

31. Adao, Arkolakis, and Esposito (2017) develop a methodology to capture the general equilibrium impact of trade shocks. Using it, they find small aggregate effects of trade shocks. Changing the costs associated with trade with China between 1997 and 2007 causes manufacturing employment to fall by just 1.2 percent.

According to Teresa Short, Justin Pierce, and Jeffrey Schott (2018), net firm deaths accounted for 25 percent of the overall decline in manufacturing employment between 1977 and 2012. They also report that although exposed firms shut down many of their manufacturing plants, they expanded their employment in service sector jobs, such as design and information technology. These firms employed slightly more workers in 2012 than they did in 1977.

Bloom et al. (2019) also explore how the China shock affected firm restructuring. They find that in areas of the United States with high human capital (primarily the West Coast and parts of the East Coast), manufacturing employment losses were smaller than elsewhere in the economy and came predominantly from plants switching to services. This finding is consistent with high-tech firms designing and marketing products in the United States but offshoring assembly production to China (the Apple model). In low human capital areas (such as much of the South and Midwest), plants closed and manufacturing job losses were great.[32] Bloom et al. also find that the negative effect of Chinese imports on manufacturing occurs mainly within large multinational firms that are simultaneously expanding employment in nonmanufacturing.[33]

These findings of downstream benefits have important policy implications, because they suggest that had the United States resorted to trade protection, or refused China's entry into the WTO, it might have lost fewer jobs directly to Chinese trade. But fewer jobs would have been gained elsewhere in the economy, and the benefits to US consumers would have been smaller.[34] Analysis by Gary Hufbauer and Sean Lowry (2012) of the employment and welfare implications of special safeguards through US tariffs on tires from China provides an example of the adverse impact of protection on employment that operates by raising import costs, as does the paper by Wang et al. (2018).

---

32. In a study of Danish firms' responses to import competition, Bernard, Smeets, and Warzynski (2017) argue that focusing only on manufacturing employment overstates the loss of manufacturing-related capabilities. They find that a "nonnegligible" part of the adjustment involved firms switching from manufacturing and either becoming wholesalers or retaining and expanding their R&D and technological capabilities.

33. See Bernard and Fort (2015) for a discussion of factoryless firms.

34. For an excellent review of the benefits of the China shock, see Lincicome (2020); also see Amiti et al. (2017).

Conclusion

Much of the political narrative has pointed to trade as the major reason for US manufacturing job loss. But when manufacturing is treated as a single aggregate, the manufacturing employment declines after 2000 are associated fully with relatively rapid productivity growth and slow overall growth in GDP. When the computer and electronics sector is excluded from manufacturing, relatively rapid productivity growth still accounts for about half of the employment decline between 2000 and 2010, and slower output growth caused by exceptionally slower GDP growth, including two recessions, accounts for most of the rest of the decline. International trade was possibly responsible for about 11 percent of the job loss.

Over the period 1948–2019, when manufacturing is treated as a single homogeneous sector, falling relative manufacturing prices as a result of faster productivity in the sector explain its declining share in both employment and nominal GDP. Without the electronics and computer industries, however, inelastic income demand plays a larger role in the declining share.

Studies of the impact of international trade shocks on the manufacturing employment loss after 2000 using three different methodologies confirm that trade may have contributed to but did not play a large role in aggregate job loss. Several studies convincingly indicate that trade did cause significant disruption to some workers and local communities, however. Trade also did not play a large role in the declining share of the United States in manufacturing employment over the long run. This trend dates back to long before trade was an important source of structural change in the United States.

7

Role of Manufacturing in the Rise and Fall of Inclusive US Growth

The declining manufacturing share in US employment and output since 1980 has played an important role in reducing US growth and making it less inclusive. This chapter shows how that decline reduced the employment and earnings opportunities for non-college-educated workers and how it helped boost the premium earned by workers with college degrees, thereby increasing wage inequality throughout the economy.

At the same time, it shows how changes within manufacturing changed the composition of employment within the industry, further reducing inclusion. The adoption of digital technologies increased automation and nontangible capital within the manufacturing sector, putting downward pressure on the earnings of less educated workers and reducing their opportunities to work in jobs that paid above-median wages. Technological change also reduced the share of labor compensation in manufacturing value added and thus the overall share of labor in earnings in the economy. Although manufacturing continued to provide workers (both with and without college degrees) premiums in wages and benefits after their other attributes (such as education, unionization, location, and gender) are taken into account, an ever smaller share of workers has been able to enjoy these benefits. Developments in manufacturing are not the only reasons for slower and less inclusive growth, but their impacts have been significant. Moreover, the small share of manufacturing in output and employment as of 2019 suggests that the sector can no longer provide the opportunities for growth and inclusion it once did.

This chapter is organized as follows. Section 1 documents the declining contributions of manufacturing in US output and employment growth. Section 2 profiles the development of employment and earnings. It highlights the reduced availability of manufacturing jobs that paid above median wages to non-college-educated men. Section 3 shows that the declining MES in the economy represented skill-biased *structural* change and estimates its role in the growing college premiums paid to men and women. Section 4 shows how within manufacturing the digital revolution led to skill-biased *technical* change that polarized wages and employment shares because of its adverse effects on non-college-educated workers with above median earnings. Section 5 shows that the declines in labor's income share in manufacturing reflected pervasive declines within industries rather than shifts in the composition of manufacturing toward industries with lower income shares. Section 6 shows how technological developments reduced labor's share in the income earned in manufacturing and contributed to growing US income inequality after 2000. Section 7 shows the growing role of intangibles such as intellectual property and software in the fixed assets of manufacturing, providing additional evidence of the skill-biased nature of technological change. Section 8 surveys the evidence showing that despite these developments, manufacturing continues to pay premium wages to workers with and without college degrees.

Contribution of Manufacturing to US Growth

Estimating the long-run contributions of manufacturing to GDP using long-run data for manufacturing output and real GDP is problematic when both are measured in chain-weighted constant dollars, because the industry shares in output are constantly changing and the data for individual industries do not add up to the total manufacturing output measure. It is possible, however, to provide a measure of the contributions of manufacturing to yearly growth since these data are not affected by changing weights. By averaging these estimates of annual contributions of industries to growth that are published in the industry accounts data produced by the US Bureau of Economic Analysis, estimates of decade contributions have been obtained.[1]

Annual US GDP growth rates were over 4 percent in the 1950s and 1960s; just over 3 percent in the 1970s, 1980s, and 1990s; and around 2 percent in the 2000s (table 7.1). On average, manufacturing output growth contributed 1.03 percentage points of the 4.24 percentage point annual growth in GDP in the 1950s—about 24.3 percent of all GDP growth. As the computer industry was small at that time, noncomputer and electronics

---

1. See US Bureau of Economic Analysis, https://apps.bea.gov/iTable/iTable.cfm?reqid = 150&step = 2&isuri = 1&categories = gdpxind.

Table 7.1

Contributions of manufacturing and nonmanufacturing to annual growth rates in the United States, by decade, 1950s–2010s

Item	1950–59	1960–69	1970–79	1980–89	1990–99	2000–09	2010–19
Percent GDP growth	4.24	4.53	3.24	3.13	3.23	1.93	2.25
Due to							
Manufacturing	1.03	1.37	0.63	0.48	0.59	0.24	0.23
Computers (NAICS 334)	0.01	0.12	0.17	0.27	0.40	0.26	0.08
Non-NAICS 334 manufacturing	1.02	1.25	0.45	0.21	0.19	-0.02	0.15
Nonmanufacturing	3.21	3.16	2.62	2.65	2.64	1.69	2.02
Percent contribution to growth							
Manufacturing	24	30	19	15	18	12	10
Non-NAICS 334 manufacturing	24	28	14	7	6	-1	7

Source: US Bureau of Economic Analysis.

manufacturing accounted for almost all this contribution. In the 1960s, manufacturing output growth added even more to GDP (1.37 percentage points), about 30.3 percent of the rapid overall annual GDP growth rate of 4.5 percent for the decade. Since the 1970s GDP growth has slowed, and the contribution of manufacturing to that growth declined significantly. In the 1980s, more than half of the recorded contribution of manufacturing to GDP of 0.48 percentage point annually came from the computer and electronics industry, and noncomputer manufacturing's contribution to growth shrank to just 0.21 percentage point—just 7 percent of the annual average growth of 3.13 percent. In the 1990s, computers and electronics dominated manufacturing's contribution of 18 percent of growth; noncomputer manufacturing contributed just 6 percent.

The contribution of manufacturing to growth declined substantially after 2000, even when the electronics sector is included. Noncomputer manufacturing made no contribution to growth in 2000–09. Between 2010 and 2019, aggregate GDP growth averaged just 2.25 percent year, with manufacturing contributing just 0.23 percentage point (10 percent of total growth) and noncomputer manufacturing contributing a mere 0.15 percentage point (7 percent of total growth). The decline in manufacturing's contribution to US growth of 0.80 percentage point between the 1950s and 2010–19 accounted for 40.2 percent of the overall decline in average GDP growth rates of 1.99 percentage points.

Manufacturing and Good Jobs in 1970

In 1970, US manufacturing still afforded many opportunities to acquire skills and earn incomes that could support middle-class lifestyles, especially for men without college education. Manufacturing played a particularly important role in providing such opportunities for Black men (Wilson 1996). Weekly earnings were also higher in manufacturing because the workweek was typically longer than in the rest of the economy and because in some industries, such as steel and autos, unions secured substantial wage premiums. In 1970, 72.0 percent of workers in manufacturing were men and 34.7 percent of working men (36.0 percent of men without a college degree) worked as manufacturing workers.[2] A smaller share of employed women worked in manufacturing, but the sector still accounted for 21.1 percent of all jobs held by women (23.2 percent among women without a college degree).

Manufacturing jobs were typically "good" jobs. In 1970, manufacturing jobs in the middle of the national wage distribution for men were

---

2. See Current Population Survey Data for Social, Economic and Health Research, http://cps.ipums.org/cps/.

Figure 7.1
Distribution of wages of men in the United States relative to median wage, 1970

percent of men in the labor force

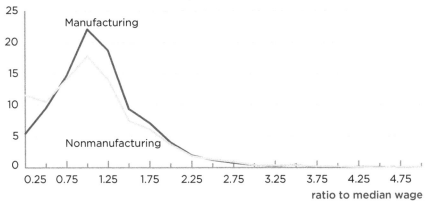

Source: Current Population Survey (Flood et al. 2021).

especially plentiful. The median wage earned by a man without a college degree in manufacturing was 8.4 percent higher than the median wage of a similar man in the economy as a whole, and the median wage of a college-educated man in manufacturing was 18.2 percent higher than that of a college-educated man in the economy as a whole. In 1970, half of men in manufacturing earned wages that paid 100–150 percent of the national median wage (figure 7.1). Jobs that paid men less than the median were less common in manufacturing than in nonmanufacturing.

Changes in Employment and Earnings: Role of Manufacturing

US employment increased by 61 million workers between 1970 and 2000, but employment in manufacturing fell. Manufacturing employment peaked in 1979, at 19.4 million workers, and fluctuated over the business cycles in the 1980s and 1990s, falling to 17.3 million in 2000. The declines were concentrated in steel, textiles, and apparel. They were associated with the emergence of competition from developing economies and Japan.

The variable most closely associated with increased wage inequality since 1980 is education.[3] According to data from the Current Population

---

3. Other determinants of earnings that may be associated with education (such as intelligence, experience, location, and race) are not accounted for. These results should therefore be interpreted only as changes in earnings that are correlated with a college education.

Figure 7.2

Ratio of mean wages of college-educated to non-college-educated workers in the United States, by gender, 1970–2019

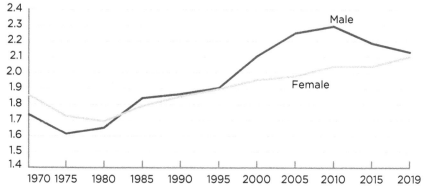

ratio of college-educated workers' wages to
non-college-educated workers' wages

Source: Current Population Survey (Flood et al. 2021).

Survey, in 1970, the median man with a college degree earned 57 percent more than the median man without a degree, and the median woman with a college degree earned 103 percent more than her non-college-educated counterpart.[4] College premiums declined in the 1970s, leading to talk of an "overeducated American" (Freeman 1976); they rose dramatically after 1980, for both women and men (figure 7.2).

For men, the college premium rose between 1975 and 2010, when it peaked, at 129 percent, before falling to 113 percent in 2019. For women, the premium rose continuously after 1980, rising steadily to 110 percent in 2019. Although much of the increased premiums resulted from changes within industries, as shown below, almost 20 percent can be explained by changes in employment between industries, in particular the declining share of overall employment in manufacturing, which skewed economy-wide demand toward college-educated workers. Given their dependence on jobs in manufacturing, the decline in the manufacturing employment share (MES) had especially adverse effects on non-college-educated men. Between 1970 and 2019, the share of such men who worked in manu-

---

4. This division of workers is crude and does not distinguish or weight workers with different years of education differently within each group. "College-educated workers" includes workers with graduate and professional degrees, and "non-college-educated" workers includes workers with less than high school, high school, and some college or vocational education. It is likely that the median college-educated man in this sample has only a college degree and the median non-college-educated man has a high school degree.

Figure 7.3
Shares of men and women with and without a college degree employed in manufacturing in the United States, 1970–2020

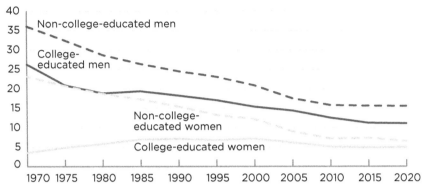

manufacturing employment share (percent)

Source: Current Population Survey (Flood et al. 2021).

facturing fell from 36.0 to 15.4 percent (Flood et al. 2021) (figure 7.3). Labor force participation by women increased from 43.4 percent in 1970 to 57.4 percent in 2019, but the role of manufacturing in providing jobs for women declined, and manufacturing employment became more male dominated.[5] In 2019, manufacturing employed just 6.3 percent of women who worked (7.2 percent among women without a college degree). In 2019, women without a college degree constituted 20.0 percent of manufacturing employment, down from 27.2 percent in 11970 (not shown in figure 7.3).

The US experience of declining female employment shares in manufacturing is not unusual. Joshua Greenstein and Bret Anderson (2017) associate the worldwide defeminization of manufacturing with the growing capital intensity of manufacturing, as part of the process of industrial upgrading of assembly work in which women tended to specialize, such as clothing and electronics, became increasingly automated.

Skill-Biased Structural Change

What Acemoglu and Autor (2011) call the "canonical approach" explains changes in the college premium in a closed economy by assuming that there are two types of workers (workers with and without college degrees) and that each type of worker performs a particular imperfectly substitut-

---

5. See Federal Reserve Bank of St. Louis, Federal Reserve Economic Data, https://fred.stlouisfed.org/series/LNS11300002.

able task.[6] If a single good is produced, the relative wages of college- and non-college-educated workers will result from the interaction of demand for each type of worker, which depends on their marginal productivities and the supply of each type of worker. Changes in relative wages are the result of changes in the demand for the two types of workers, resulting from technological change that alters their marginal products and changes in their relative supplies. When the supply of college-educated workers relative to non-college-educated workers keeps up with the demand that is determined by the bias in technological change in favor of skilled (or college-educated workers), the race ends in a tie and relative wages remain constant. If, in contrast, skill-biased change outpaces increases in the relative supply of college graduates, the skill premium will rise. This approach can be characterized as "the race between education and technology," the title of the pathbreaking study of relative wages in the 20th century by Claudia Goldin and Lawrence Katz (2008).

The responsiveness of relative wages to these changes in the demand for and/or supply of workers with and without college degrees can be captured by a parameter that reflects the ease with which the two types of workers can be substituted: the elasticity of substitution. Researchers have obtained a range of estimates for this measure. A widely used estimate is the 1.4 obtained by Katz and Kevin Murphy (1992). It implies that a 10 percent decline in the relative supply of college-educated workers (or a 10 percent increase in the relative demand for these workers) will increase the relative wages of college-educated workers by 7.1 percent (10/1.4).[7]

If there is only one industry or product, changes in the relative demand for workers of different types will reflect changes in the evolution of its technology. There is evidence that such change took place after 1980. If the college premium rises despite the growth in the relative supply of college-educated workers, it must be that the relative demand for such workers (as a result of skill-biased technological change) increased even more. The basic explanation for the growth in the college premium, therefore, is that the rise in educational attainment was slower than the increased demand

---

6. For a review of the evidence of the role trade played, see Cline (1999).

7. The basic equation in this model, derived from a constant elasticity of substitution production function, is

$$Ln\left(\frac{W_c}{W_{nct}}\right) = \left(\frac{1}{\sigma}\right)(D_t - \ln\left(\frac{C_t}{NC_t}\right))$$

where W_c = wage of college and W_{nc} = wages of non-college-educated workers, D_t is the demand for labor, and C and NC denote supplies of college- and non-college-educated workers.

for skilled workers. It is no surprise that one line of explanation for the rise in the college premium after 1980 applies the canonical approach as it emphasizes technological developments that might have caused such an increase, such as the increased adoption of information technology, which favored college-educated workers (Autor, Katz, and Krueger 1998), and/or the slower increases in the supply of college-educated workers that occurred at the same time [8]

A variant of the canonical model in which there is more than one industry is useful for estimating the impact of the decline in the MES on relative wages. If industries differ in the intensity with which they employ college- and non-college-educated labor, the relative demand for different types of workers will reflect both the technological changes within the industries (as in the canonical model) and changes in the industry shares in total employment. Under the assumption that there is no technological change within industries, this variant of the model can be used to estimate the impact of the declining MES on relative earnings throughout the economy.[9]

Francisco Buera, Joseph Kaboski, and Richard Rogerson (2015) develop a two-sector model that divides US goods and services into two categories based on their skill intensities. Controlling for within-sector technological change and relative factor supplies, they show how structural change across industries in both manufacturing and services in the United States between 1977 and 2005 that shifted toward larger shares of more skill-intensive sectors—what they call skill-biased structural change—can account for between a quarter and a third of the increase in the skill premium in overall compensation. (They obtain similar estimates for nine other OECD economies.)

The calculations below separate the US manufacturing sector from the rest of the economy and use a simpler approach by considering the impact of a changed MES under the assumption that other determinants of relative wages and factor use remain constant. It uses mean earnings data from the Current Population Survey to explain the impact of the declining MES on the relationship between the mean earnings of workers with different levels of education (table 7.2).

---

8. According to Autor, Goldin, and Katz (2020), the average annual increase in the relative supply of college graduates was 3.1 percent in 1939–79 and 2.1 percent in 1979–2017.

9. Even if technological change within sectors is not skill biased, the skill premium can change, because of changing sector shares. In this respect, the model resembles the Stolper-Samuelson (1941) theorem, which captures the way in which relative sector prices can affect relative factor prices.

Table 7.2

Hypothetical impact of no decline in the manufacturing employment share on the college wage premium of men in the United States, 1970 and 2019

Item	1970	2019
Measure		
Ratio of college- to non-college-educated workers among all male workers	0.155	0.536
Ratio of college- to non-college-educated workers among all male manufacturing workers	0.113	0.406
Ratio of college- to non-college-educated workers among all male nonmanufacturing workers	0.179	0.56
Manufacturing employment share	0.347	0.141
Mean ratio of wages of college-educated to non-college-educated men	1.734	2.131
Simulation		
1 Actual (L_c/L_{nc})		0.536
2 Hypothetical (L_c/L_{nc}) if manufacturing share = 35 percent		0.507
3 ln(1) – ln(2)		0.056
4 Change required in $\ln(W_c/W_{nc})$ with sigma = 1.4		0.040
5 Actual change in $\ln(W_c/W_{nc})$		0.206
6 Percent explained (4/5)*100		19.3

Source: Current Population Survey (Flood et al. 2021).

In 2019, the economywide ratio of college graduates to high school graduates for men was 0.536, which reflected a weighted average of the ratios of college to non-college-educated men in manufacturing and the rest of the economy: specifically, the employment of 14.1 percent of men in the manufacturing sector with a ratio of college-educated to non-college-educated men (C/NC) of 0.406 percent, and 85.9 percent of men in nonmanufacturing, with a (C/NC) ratio of 0.56. If the demand for US manufacturing value added in 2019 had been sufficient to provide employment for 34.7 percent of men (the male employment share in 1970) rather than the actual 14.1 percent, the ratio of college- to non-college-educated workers would have been 0.507. (0.347 * 40.6 + 0.653 * 56.0). In this scenario, there would initially have been an excess supply of college-educated workers and an excess demand for non-college-educated workers of 5.6 log points (log 53.6–log 50.7). If the elasticity of substitution (Ω) is 1.4, eliminating this excess supply of college-educated workers would have required a decline in the relative wages of college-educated to non-college-educated workers of 4.0 log points (5.6/1.4). In this counterfactual scenario, the college premium would have been lower by 19.3 percent. Thus, almost a fifth of the increase in college premium for men between 1970 and 2019 can be explained by the declining MES. This estimate is (roughly) in line with the impacts on the skill premium Buera, Kaboski, and Rogerson (2015) estimate for 1977–2005.

The same exercise using data for women indicates a decline of 3.1 log points (versus 4.0 for men). For women, the college premium was 12.4 log points. If the MES had remained at its 1970 level, it would have been 1.65 log points (instead of the actual 1.68 log points). The shift of shares between industries thus explains 24.9 percent of the rise in the premium. For men and women combined, raising the MES to its 1970 level would have reduced the relative wages of college graduates in 2019 by 4.3 log points.

For men, the college premium peaked at 2.29 in 2010 before declining by a total of 7.1 percent between 2010 and 2019. The share of manufacturing in male employment declined by 2.11 percent a year in 1970–2010 and by 0.55 percent in 2010–19, suggesting that most of the impact occurred between 1980 and 2010.[10]

In this exercise, which takes the skill-biased technological change that increased the within-industry ratios of the wages of college- to non-college-educated workers as given, declining employment opportunities in manufacturing depressed the relative wages of non-college-educated workers and contributed to increased wage inequality.[11] Between 1970 and 2019, the share of manufacturing in male employment in the United States fell from 34.7 percent to 14.1 percent, a decline of 90.4 log points. Had the MES remained at its 1970 level, the college premium would have risen by 19.3 percent less than it did. If this change had occurred through higher

---

10. Beaudry, Green, and Sand (2014) and Valletta (2018) interpret this slowing as indicating that the information technology revolution had matured and the trend of rising demand for college-educated workers slowed. In his comments on the Valletta paper, Autor (2018) argues that it reflects an acceleration in the relative supply of college graduates.

11. The International Monetary Fund (IMF 2018) points to evidence of increases in earnings disparities across all sectors, which it claims show that sectoral shifts did not play a major role in increased wage inequality across industrial countries. However, if labor is mobile across sectors, evidence of similar trends in relative wage changes across sectors does not rule out the possibility that changes in employment shares in sectors with different skill intensities may have led to relative wage changes in all sectors.

wages for non-college-educated men, in 2019 their mean earnings would have been $1,777 a year higher and the real growth in earnings (using the consumer price index) between 1970 and 2019 would have been 5.9 percent.

Skill-Biased Technological Change

Starting around 1980, the basis of employment growth changed, primarily because of technological change but also to some extent because of increased globalization. New digital technologies based on computers and semiconductors became increasingly important, as ever cheaper semiconductors were used to make smarter machines and many of the tasks performed using mainframe computers were taken over by desktop computers and other devices that used microprocessors (Berger and Frey 2016).

After 1980, the pace of computing power accelerated (Nordhaus 2007). Although the impact on productivity was not initially evident—and except in the decade after 1995 was very disappointing (Gordon 2012, Posen and Zettelmeyer 2019)—the effects of the new technologies on employment, wages, and the location of production were profound.

Technologies that drive innovation may have different implications for returns to different factors of production. Between 1940 and 1980, the maturing phase of the industrial technologies occurred in an age of mass production that entailed increased mechanization. Investments in capital tended to raise the productivity and wages of production workers with relatively low levels of education, who performed routinized tasks that were highly coordinated in large assembly operations. The manufacturing occupations in the middle of the wage distribution were plentiful and paid above-median wages.

Since 1980, advances in digital technologies have increased the earnings of workers with college (and postcollege) degrees by complementing their analytical skills. It also led to the substitution, with computers, of the more routine tasks that were performed by less educated workers in occupations such as production and clerical work (Autor and Dorn 2013, Reich 1991).[12] Because suppliers of services whose work can be less easily performed by machines or offshored were much less affected than other workers, the new technologies increased the value of education and human capital and made capital and less skilled labor less important as competitive inputs (Autor, Katz, and Krueger 1998).[13] Together with the increased

---

12. See Card and DiNardo (2002) for a skeptical view of skill-biased technological change.

13. Berger and Frey (2016) document a sharp change in the skill content of many new jobs after 1980. In the 1970s, they argue, mainframe computers complemented unskilled workers; after 1980, new job titles were concentrated in occupations and industries that required abstract skills, reflecting the greater availability of personal computers.

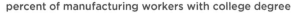

Figure 7.4
Share of manufacturing employees in the United States with a college degree, by gender, 1970–2019

percent of manufacturing workers with college degree

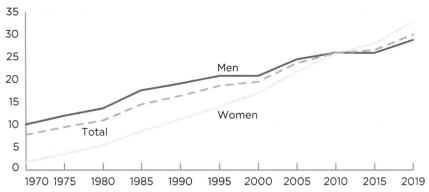

Source: Current Population Survey (Flood et al. 2021).

ability to offshore more routine assembly to economies in which labor was less expensive, the new technologies reduced the role of manufacturing in providing jobs and wages for mid-skilled production workers.[14] In addition, the relative price of computers declined after 1980, increasing the capital–labor ratio in production (Karabarbounis and Nieman 2014). As skilled labor and capital tend to be complementary (Griliches 1966), demand for and the relative wages of college-educated workers rose.[15]

Increase in Skill Intensity

Between 1970 and 2019, the share of men with a bachelor's degree employed in manufacturing increased from 10.2 to 28.9 percent; for women, it skyrocketed from 1.8 percent to 32.9 percent (figure 7.4). Manufacturing employment decreased by 46.0 percent over this period, but employment of college graduates in manufacturing increased by 106.8 percent.

Polarization of Earnings: The Declining Middle

The elegant "canonical" model described above is helpful in explaining the impact of changing MES on the skill premium. But it fails to capture other features in the labor market that have been especially evident in manu-

---

14. The impact of technological change was much smaller on workers in personal services, such as hairdressers, nurses, and janitors.

15. Perez-Laborda and Perez-Sebastian (2020) explore the roles of capital–skill complementarity and skill-biased technological change.

facturing and have exacerbated inequality and the meager growth in the wages and jobs of less skilled men, especially in mid-skill occupations, as Acemoglu and Autor (2011) note.

Between 1970 and 2015, the wage distribution of non-college-educated men shifted leftward while the wage distribution of college-educated men shifted rightward (figure 7.5). Larger shares of college-educated men were at the upper end of the distribution, and larger shares of non-college-educated men were at the lower end. Changes in the composition of employment within manufacturing therefore contributed to the polarization of earnings in the United States.

The simple model with two types of workers does a good job of explaining wage inequality until the mid-1990s. Although it fails to take account of other institutional factors, it nonetheless provides a powerful explanation of the increase in wage inequality until then. Wages at the top continued to increase after the mid-1990s, and wages at the bottom grew somewhat more rapidly than those in the middle. As a result, the ratio of wages at the 50th percentile to wages at both the 90th and 10th percentiles fell. As David Autor, Frank Levy, and Richard Murnane (2003) and Autor and Dorn (2013) argue, the simple (canonical) version of the skill-biased technological change explanation needs to be modified to account for this polarization of earnings growth, in which information technology complements high-education tasks, substitutes for tasks performed by workers in occupations that do not require a college education, and has no impact on providers of personal services that are relatively unaffected by either technological change or offshoring. In addition, there is evidence that offshoring contributed to polarization, as firms tend to offshore tasks performed by mid-income occupations (Oldenski 2014).

Declining Share of Labor Compensation

An important source of the contribution of manufacturing to relatively inclusive growth was the labor-intensive nature of its production technology. Value added for domestic products can be derived by subtracting intermediate inputs from gross output. In 1987, the ratio of labor compensation to gross value added was substantially higher for manufacturing (63.8) than for the rest of the economy excluding manufacturing (54.4).

The share of labor compensation in manufacturing declined steadily after 1987, falling to 46.7 percent in 2013 (figure 7.6). Over the same period, the share of labor compensation in the rest of the economy remained essentially constant (falling from 54.4 percent of value added to 53.3 percent). Between 1987 and 2013, in the economy as a whole, labor

Figure 7.5

Wage distribution of men employed in manufacturing in the United States, 1970 and 2015

percent of men in the labor force employed in manufacturing

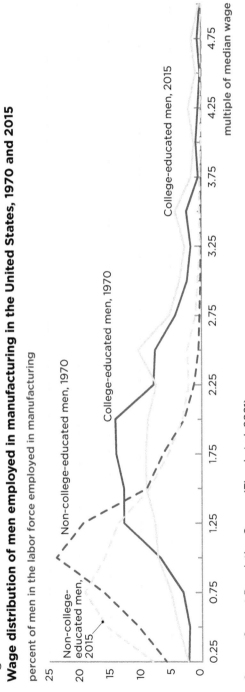

Source: Current Population Survey (Flood et al. 2021).

Figure 7.6

Shares of labor compensation in net value added in manufacturing, nonmanufacturing, and GDP in the United States, 1987–2019

labor compensation as percent of net value added

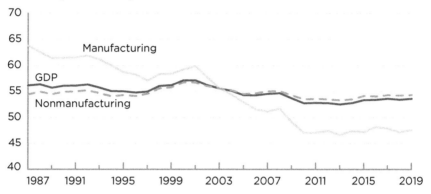

Source: US Bureau of Economic Analysis.

compensation declined from 56.1 percent to 52.5 percent of GDP, with the bulk of the change reflecting the impact of the declining share of labor compensation in manufacturing. After reaching troughs at the end of the Great Recession, the shares of labor compensation in net value added in both manufacturing and the rest of the economy rose slightly in 2013, but the manufacturing share remained below its 2008 level and the share in the rest of private industry returned to about the levels it had reached in 2005 and 1987. Thus, although an increased share of manufacturing in national production would have raised the share of labor compensation in 1987, as of 2019, the share of labor compensation in manufacturing was no longer higher than in the rest of the economy and an increased share of manufacturing would no longer increase the overall share of labor in compensation.

Roles of Compensation and Employment in the Declining Labor Payroll Share

Labor's aggregate manufacturing compensation reflects both the number of workers employed in the sector and average worker compensation. Compensation data suggest that most of the declining share in value added reflected declines in employment. The Employment Cost Index (ECI) is a useful index of labor compensation, because instead of simply monitoring aggregate compensation, which can be influenced by changes in the shares of workers with different attributes (education, gender, age), it tracks changes in the cost of employing workers with given attributes.[16]

The ECI for manufacturing closely tracks all civilian workers between 1987 and 2005. It shows that differences in compensation growth were not responsible for the declining share of manufacturing in overall labor compensation.[17] Although the nominal share of manufacturing value added in GDP declined from 18.1 percent in 1987 to 11.1 percent in 2019, the share of manufacturing gross operating surplus in national gross operating surplus only declined from 16.2 percent to 13.6 percent.

Within- and Between-Industry Changes in Labor's Compensation Share

Both the ratio of capital to labor services and the share of compensation in manufacturing value added reflect some combination of changes in industry shares in manufacturing value added and changes in capital and labor shares within industries. The National Bureau of Economic Research provides data on labor shares and output for 473 industries that allow for a decomposition of overall changes in labor shares into within- and between-industry shares. These calculations show that since 1980, the declines in labor shares within manufacturing can be ascribed to changes that occurred within the six-digit industries (table 7.3). The average manufacturing payroll share in value added declined from 41.1 percent in 1980 to 31.3 percent in 2000 and 27.3 percent in 2009. For both the full period (1980–2009) and the subperiod 2000–09, changes within industries were the dominant source of the declines, accounting for around 80 percent of the overall declines in the labor share in manufacturing value added in both periods. In 295 of 473 industries, accounting for 76 percent of value added in 2009, the within-industry labor share declined between 1980 and 2009. This outcome is consistent with the explanation that the declining labor share was pervasive across manufacturing, suggesting that widespread and common technological changes occurred within industries.

---

16. The current version of the ECI provides data back to the early 2000s. The previous version ended in 2005. The two versions were spliced to provide the combined series used in this analysis.

17. Between the first quarter of 2005 and the fourth quarter of 2009 (a period associated with the Great Recession), there was a decline in the relative ECI for manufacturing of 4.3 percentage points and only a small recovery, so that between the first quarter of 2005 and the first quarter of 2022, the decline is 4.1 percentage points. See US Bureau of Labor Statistics, https://beta.bls.gov/dataQuery/find?fq = survey:%5Bci%5D&s = popularity:D.

Table 7.3

Decomposition of changes in the payroll share in value added into between- and within-industry changes, United States, 1980–2009

Item	1980	2000	2009	Change in share 1980–2009[a]	Percent change	Change in share 2000–09[b]	Percent change
Payroll share in manufacturing value added	0.411	0.313	0.273	-0.139	100.0	-0.040	100.0
Due to:							
Changes in six-digit industry shares				-0.026	18.5	-0.010	26.2
Changes within six-digit industries				-0.114	81.5	-0.029	73.8

a. Total change in share is slightly greater than the difference between the payroll shares in 1980 and 2009 because of missing data in 1980 for three six-digit industries.

b. Changes do not sum to total change between 2000 and 2009 because of rounding errors.

Source: NBER–CES Manufacturing database, https://www.nber.org/research/data/nber-ces-manufacturing-industry-database.

Figure 7.7

Capital intensity of US manufacturing, 1987–2019

ratio of capital services to hours worked

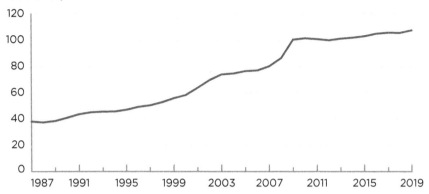

Source: Federal Reserve Bank of St. Louis, Federal Reserve Economic Data, https://fred.stlouisfed.org/.

Production also became more capital intensive. Direct measures of the capital-labor ratio in manufacturing and the capital–output ratio confirm that the former rose and the latter fell. The ratio of capital to labor services rose steadily after 1987; as labor is more easily shed than capital, during the Great Recession, the capital–labor ratio increased sharply (figure 7.7). After the Great Recession, the ratio appears to have stabilized, as the rise in labor services almost kept pace with the rise in capital services.

Manufacturing and Profit Shares

Between the early 1950s and the mid-1980s, the share of labor compensation in manufacturing gross product was about 70 percent (although it fluctuated over the business cycle). Beginning in the mid-1980s, manufacturing was transformed from a sector in which a large share of income was earned by labor into a sector in which labor's share was less than the average for the rest of the economy.

Until the early 2000s, the declining labor share within manufacturing was offset by increasing labor shares in other sectors, so that in the aggregate the share of labor compensation in US income was roughly constant. After 2000, labor's share in manufacturing continued to decline; together with declines in several other industries, the aggregate share of labor in the economy fell and the share of corporate profits reached the highest level since the 1920s.

The larger share of profits contributed to rising income inequality in the United States. The simplest explanation for the rising profit share would seem to be that manufacturing became more capital intensive. In fact, though, a particular type of technological change seems to be the cause (box 7.1).

There is also evidence that investment in manufacturing has been relatively weak and that the capital-output ratio in manufacturing has thus been declining. Figure 7.8 displays the capital-output ratio for manufacturing after 1983, which was driven by a decline in the net fixed capital stock in structures as well as relatively slow investment in the net fixed capital stock in equipment. The only major component of the capital–value added ratio that rose was investment in intellectual property products.

Changes in the Composition of Fixed Assets

The changed composition of fixed assets is also suggestive of a radical technological transformation. Valued at current costs, the manufacturing sector held 46.8 percent of its net fixed assets in equipment, 34.5 percent in structures, and 18.8 percent in intellectual property products in 1987 (figure 7.9). The decline in structures to 30.8 percent by 2019 and the dramatic decline in the structures–output ratio after 1983 reflect the closure of a large number of plants (Fort, Pierce, and Schott 2018). Despite all the talk of automation and robots, the share of manufacturing fixed assets in equipment shrank between 1987 and 2019, from 46.8 percent to 34.8 percent of the net stock of fixed assets.[18] The most striking change was the share of intellectual property products, which almost doubled, rising from 18.8 percent to 34.4 percent. Thus, not only did manufacturing become less intensive in labor, the capital that was substituted increasingly took the form of intellectual property products rather than plant or equipment.

Between 1987 and 2019, the ratio of net fixed assets in intellectual property products to value added in manufacturing increased by 130.4 percent in current-cost terms, and these assets' share of overall fixed assets increased by 83.1 percent. The pervasive increase is captured when manufacturing is disaggregated into data for the industries that make up the sector.

Table 7.4 ranks manufacturing industries by their shares of intellectual property products in their value added in 2019. The increasing role played by intellectual property assets is evident in the large increases in high-tech industries such as chemical products (which include pharmaceuticals), computers and electronics, and other transportation equipment (aircraft). In low-tech industries, such as textiles, food, primary metals, and printing, the shares and increases are much smaller. This change in the

---

18. See US Bureau of Economic Analysis, https://apps.bea.gov/iTable/?ReqID=10&step=2.

Box 7.1
What explains the declining labor share in manufacturing income?

The natural starting point for explaining changes in labor's share in income is the neoclassical theory of the functional distribution of income (Hicks 1932, Robinson 1932). This theory highlights the ease with which labor (L) and capital (K) can be substituted when their relative prices—w (wages) and r (rents [i.e., the cost of capital])—change. The responses of changes in relative supplies to changes in relative factors prices can be summarized with a single parameter: the elasticity of substitution (σ).

The magnitude of σ is crucial in determining how income shares respond to changes in relative factor prices or supplies. The logic is straightforward. By definition the ratio of capital to labor income is the product of the rents-wages ratio and the capital–labor ratio:

$$\frac{rK}{wL} = \frac{r}{w} \times \frac{K}{L} \, .$$

One would expect that $\frac{r}{w}$ and $\frac{K}{L}$ would move in opposite directions as factor prices or supplies change. More expensive capital, for example, encourages the use of a lower capital–labor ratio. As long as any substitution is possible, an increase in r/w will lead to a decline in K/L. Conversely, an increase in the relative supply of capital K/L, as occurred in manufacturing, tends to drive down its relative price (r/w). The degree of responsiveness of K/L to changes in r/w will determine whether the ratio of capital to labor income rises or falls. When $\sigma = 1$, any rise in the capital-labor ratio will be exactly offset by a proportional decline in the rents-wages ratio and factor shares in income will remain constant. When $\sigma > 1$, the factors are gross complements, and the relative increase in the supply of a factor will be larger than the fall in its relative return and its income share will rise.

Several studies claim that $\sigma > 1$ explains the declining share of labor income in industrial economies. Thomas Piketty and Gabriel Zucman (2013) ascribe the decline in the labor share to a rise in the capital-output ratio. Loukas Karabarbounis and Brent Neiman (2014) argue that a decline in the cost of capital as a result of falling equipment prices is the source of this increase. Michael Elsby, Bart Hobjin, and Aysegul Sahin (2013) argue that offshoring raised the capital intensity of US production. But these arguments are at odds with the large number of studies (e.g., Chirinko 2008) that find that $\sigma < 1$ in the United States, as Matthew Rognlie (2014) notes. If this is the case, an increase in capital intensity would increase rather than reduce labor's share in manufacturing.

Technological change that augments labor can produce the opposite result, however. Although the apparent increase in the capital–labor

box continues

Box 7.1 continued
What explains the declining labor share in manufacturing income?

ratio would increase labor's share if $\sigma < 1$, the effective capital–labor ratio could fall if such a change is sufficiently labor augmenting. In Lawrence (2015) I present evidence that this was the case in US manufacturing after 1980. The measured capital–labor ratio in manufacturing increased between 1980 and 2010 at an annual average rate of 3.5 log points, but the increases in net labor-augmenting technological change were so large that the effective capital–labor ratio fell. Thanks to technological change, even though employment declined, labor augmented by this technological change became more abundant, and given inelastic demand, its share in income fell.[1] Automation made workers more productive, increasing the effective supply of labor and driving down wage rates.

---

1. Oberfield and Raval (2014) provide additional evidence of labor-augmenting technical change in US manufacturing.

Figure 7.8

Ratio of real net stock of fixed assets to real value added in manufacturing in the United States, 1947–2019

index (2012 = 1)

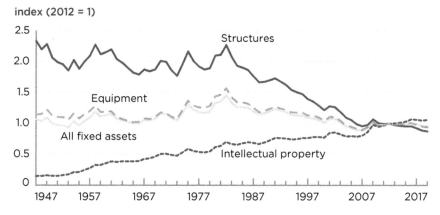

Source: US Bureau of Economic Analysis, Fixed Assets and Value Added by Industry.

Figure 7.9

Shares of assets in manufacturing in the United States of equipment, structures, and intellectual property, 1987–2019 (in current cost)

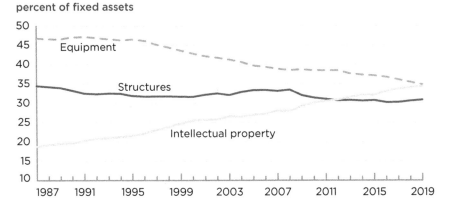

percent of fixed assets

Source: US Bureau of Economic Analysis, Fixed Assets, https://www.bea.gov/data/investment-fixed-assets.

Table 7.4

Intellectual property products as share of value added and net fixed assets, by sector in the United States, 1987 and 2019

Sector	Intellectual property products/value added	
	1987	*2019*
Private industry	0.11	0.19
Manufacturing	0.26	0.61
Chemical products	0.59	1.77
Computer and electronic products	0.38	0.88
Other transportation equipment	0.43	0.46
Motor vehicles, bodies and trailers, and parts	0.29	0.44
Electrical equipment, appliances, and components	0.28	0.42
Machinery	0.28	0.41
Miscellaneous manufacturing	0.38	0.41

table continues

Table 7.4 continued

Intellectual property products as share of value added and net fixed assets, by sector, 1987 and 2019

Sector	Intellectual property products/value added	
	1987	2019
Apparel and leather and allied products	0.04	0.35
Nonmetallic mineral products	0.21	0.35
Petroleum and coal products	0.66	0.31
Primary metals	0.16	0.26
Textile mills and textile product mills	0.04	0.20
Plastics and rubber products	0.15	0.20
Paper products	0.09	0.18
Fabricated metal products	0.09	0.15
Printing and related support activities	0.05	0.12
Food and beverage and tobacco products	0.09	0.12
Furniture and related products	0.04	0.11
Wood products	0.03	0.02
	Intellectual property products/net fixed assets	
Private industry	0.04	0.07
Manufacturing	0.19	0.34
Chemical products	0.32	0.64
Computer and electronic products	0.29	0.47
Other transportation equipment	0.42	0.37
Motor vehicles, bodies and trailers, and parts	0.30	0.25
Electrical equipment, appliances, and components	0.27	0.32
Machinery	0.23	0.27
Miscellaneous manufacturing	0.25	0.36
Apparel and leather and allied products	0.07	0.18

table continues

Table 7.4 continued
Intellectual property products as share of value added and net fixed assets, by sector, 1987 and 2019

Sector	Intellectual property products/net fixed assets	
	1987	*2019*
Nonmetallic mineral products	0.12	0.22
Petroleum and coal products	0.17	0.19
Primary metals	0.05	0.09
Textile mills and textile product mills	0.02	0.08
Plastics and rubber products	0.13	0.14
Paper products	0.05	0.08
Fabricated metal products	0.09	0.12
Printing and related support activities	0.05	0.11
Food and beverage and tobacco products	0.06	0.09
Furniture and related products	0.09	0.14
Wood products	0.02	0.02

Sources: Bureau of Economic Analysis. Data on value added are from https://apps.bea.gov/iTable/iTable.cfm?reqid=150&step=2&isuri=1&categories=gdpxind. Data on fixed assets are from https://apps.bea.gov/iTable/iTable.cfm?ReqID=10&step=2.

nature of capital helps explain why there was less manufacturing value added in investment (as captured in the negative coefficient in the investment regressions in chapter 4).

Premium Paid to Workers in Manufacturing

David Langdon and Rebecca Lehrman (2012) compare wage and compensation behavior in manufacturing with labor earnings in other sectors of the economy. They find that even after controlling for factors such as age, gender, race, marital status, education, location, and union membership, manufacturing workers received premium wage earnings in 2011. The compensation premium for workers with college degrees averaged 19 percent; the average for all workers in manufacturing was 15 percent. These premiums were even larger when healthcare and retirement benefits are taken into account.

These premiums could reflect the nature of manufacturing production, which takes place in large plants, making monitoring workers' effort and quality more difficult than in other sectors. These features could lead firms to pay workers premiums ("efficiency wages"), which raise the opportunity costs of job loss, in order to attract higher-quality workers (Stiglitz 1984); limit worker turnover (Krueger and Summers 1988); and improve self-monitoring of workers in large firms (Dickens and Katz 1986).

Manufacturing work is also characterized by upskilling in many jobs that requires on-the-job training. Premiums may compensate workers for their specialized technical skills (specific human capital) in ways that regressions that model general traits do not capture (Langdon and Lehrman 2012).

Langdon and Lehrman (2012) also provide evidence of the skill intensity of manufacturing by pointing out that the sector relies more heavily on workers in STEM (science, technology, engineering, and mathematics) than do nonmanufacturing sectors. In 2011, they note, nearly a third of college-educated workers in manufacturing had a job in STEM, compared with 10 percent of such workers in nonmanufacturing sectors. Combined with the fact that the highest premiums in the sector are earned by college-educated workers, this finding provides additional evidence of the increasing demand for skilled workers in manufacturing.

Marc Levinson (2017) suggests that the attractiveness of manufacturing jobs diminished because the sector no longer paid substantial premiums. Sree Ramaswamy et al. (2017) emphasize the difficulties manufacturing workers faced in 2000–10, when job losses were great. Lawrence Mishel (2018) explores the behavior of premiums between the 1980s and 2016. He finds evidence that premiums for working in manufacturing declined by 3.2 percent, because of increased outsourcing of manufacturing jobs to services firms, but emphasizes that premiums remained significant.

Conclusion

Changes in manufacturing contributed to the declining relative wages and employment prospects of workers without college education. The sector's contribution to GDP also declined. In the 1950s and 1960s, over a quarter of the more than 4 percent annual GDP growth in the United States originated in manufacturing. Between 2010 and 2019, GDP growth averaged barely 2 percent, and manufacturing contributed just 10 percent of it.

The declining share of employment in manufacturing led to skill-biased structural change that can explain 19.3 percent of the increase in the college premium for men in the whole economy and about a quarter of the increase in economywide college premium for women. In addition, widespread skill-biased technological change within industries reduced the share of non-college-educated workers employed in many manufacturing industries. Technological change also contributed to the polarization of the wage structure by reducing the share of jobs in the middle of the occupational wage distribution.

Manufacturing also became more capital intensive, and the nature of this capital changed. The share of structures shrank; the share of equipment remained roughly constant; and the share of intellectual property products soared, especially in technology-intensive industries such as chemicals, computers and electronics, and aircraft. This shift created fewer opportunities for workers in industries producing machinery and building factories. The jobs left in manufacturing continued to provide premium levels of compensation, however, especially to STEM college graduates—another indication of the sector's growing technological intensity.

In summary, the nature of manufacturing has radically changed. Even if policies were able to restore manufacturing's role in national employment and output, the sector would no longer provide the income escalator for large shares of men and women with limited education. As the discussion in part III will argue, given changes in production technology and the orientation of industrial policies toward advanced technologies, an expansion of modern manufacturing is more likely to raise the relative demand for more educated labor, capital, and intellectual property products, further depressing the relative earnings of the less educated.

8

Decline and Rise of Regional Inequality

The factors driving inequality in the US workforce have not simply widened differences between the incomes of well-educated and less educated workers. They have also produced dramatic geographic divisions, especially as superstar cities centered on high-tech and nonmanufacturing industries and populated by college-educated workers have thrived while many places that once depended heavily on manufacturing for their growth have stagnated, with devastating consequences for workers.

Since the 1980s, regional and income inequality have reinforced each other. By contrast, from the 1940s through the 1970s, economic growth in the poorest regions in the United States was more rapid than that in the richest regions, a relationship that persisted through the 1970s (Barro and Sala-i-Martin 1991, Ganong and Shoag 2017). After 1980, however, growth was more regionally divided, and convergence was much weaker. In the 1940s–1960s, population growth was more rapid in richer places; after 1980, there is some evidence of higher population growth in poor places (Ganong and Shoag 2017).

This chapter considers this growing divergence, contrasting its evolution with the convergence that marked the period between 1940 and the 1970s. It is organized as follows. The first section provides a general overview of how the evolution of technology can lead to periods of regional convergence and divergence. The second section considers the forces that drove convergence in the United States until the 1970s, emphasizing the role played by manufacturing. The third section describes the fairly resilient adjustments in manufacturing after the trade and technology shocks in the late 1970s and 1980s. The fourth section analyzes how technological and global forces have combined to create a far more polarized geography of growth since 1990. It highlights the declining role of worker mobility in response to negative local shocks, the negative social consequences of local manufacturing job loss, and the declining role of manufacturing in the growth of major US cities. Finally it considers if remote work could lead to regional growth that is less divergent.

Technological Change and Regional Convergence and Divergence

When developing new technologies, firms benefit from locating close to one another in innovative clusters populated by designers, scientists, engineers, and relatively skilled workers (Kemeny and Storper 2020, Eriksson et al. 2021).[1] In the early stages of a technology cycle, product and production process development are experimental. They require complementary innovations and adaptations by firms and their suppliers. These interactions are facilitated by coordination and communication, which are easier when firms and their suppliers are close by. There are also benefits of being close to affluent consumers, as their wants are likely to be emulated by others once they also become rich. Because of their higher levels of productivity and skills, innovation clusters can afford to pay higher wages and more for land (Moretti 2011). Their growth also attracts inward migration. Incomes and property values thus diverge regionally, as technology hubs reap increasing benefits of agglomeration and become generators of economic growth.

Once technologies mature, products become standardized and production processes become more routine and readily codified. Standardization allows firms to be more sensitive to costs in their location decisions. More tasks can be embodied in machines and performed by less skilled workers in plants that operate on a larger scale. In this phase, production moves out of expensive locations, and less developed locations can catch up by attracting investment and workers. This process is especially likely to occur if transport costs decline, making proximity to markets and suppliers less important. The result is greater equalization of regional incomes and productivity.[2] As international communications and transportation costs decline, and

---

1. Vernon (1966) applies a version of this theory in his explanation of international product cycles.

2. Eriksson et al. (2021) use the Vernon product cycle theory to show how, as large-scale production became more feasible and economic, industries that were later hit by the China shock in the 1990s and 2000s shifted from their initial location in the high-education, high-innovation, and high-wage economies of the Midwest and Northeast in the 1950s and 1960s to lower-wage regions with less educated workers in the Southeast.

foreign capabilities improve, this diffusion process can also take place internationally, allowing foreign economies to specialize in exports of the more standardized products (Vernon 1966) and more technologically advanced economies to specialize in products that are more technologically sophisticated. Box 8.1 describes how these forces operated in the most important region for US manufacturing: the Midwest.

Period of Convergence

The first four decades of the postwar period were marked by regional income equalization in the United States. Russ and Shambaugh (2019) report that the poorest counties in the 1960s were those that grew the most rapidly between 1960 and 1980. Barro and Sala-i-Martin (1991) estimate that between 1963 and 1986, gross state product per capita and productivity gaps between the richest and poorest US states closed at an annual rate of about 2 percent. Manufacturing made a disproportionate contribution to this intranational convergence. Barro and Sala-i-Martin find that regional disparities in manufacturing gross state product per worker declined by 4.6 percent a year—more than twice the convergence rates in any other sector.

These US data showing that manufacturing technologies can diffuse more easily than technologies in other sectors are consistent with international data and the work of Rodrik (2013). He finds that in contrast to other sectors, the closing of the productivity gap between manufacturing industries in economies that are lagging and those that are at the technological frontier occurs unconditionally (i.e., does not depend heavily on institutional factors).

With lower wages and taxes, cheaper land, more lenient regulations, and right-to-work laws, the southern states were particularly attractive as locations for manufacturing production. Amenities such as abundant housing, warm weather, and the ability to use air conditioning induced Americans to move south and west in increasing numbers.[3] These factors also attracted firms from other countries.

Between 1970 and 1990, the shares of US manufacturing employment rose from 26.7 percent to 30.1 percent in the South and from 13.1 percent to 17.6 percent in the West, according to the Current Population Survey. In an era of rising energy costs, the South's natural resource endowments and lax regulations also contributed to its competitive advantage in industries

---

3. Using data for 1947–92, Holmes (1998) finds that the average share of employment in manufacturing was a third higher in counties with right-to-work laws than in neighboring counties that had unions.

Box 8.1
The rise and fall of the Midwest

The evolution of the Midwest illustrates how manufacturing drove phases of regional development. In the first phase, the Midwest led US manufacturing industry. It attracted workers and its population grew. The combination of strong unions and dominant firms led to powerful oligopolies, high corporate profits, and wage premiums for workers.

In the second phase, the region's dominance declined, as domestic and international competitive pressures weakened the power of its oligopolies and led to the loss of technological advantage. The result was increased diffusion of capital and standardized production to lower-cost locations at home and abroad. According to Edward Glaeser (2012, 47):

> At the end of the 19th century, Detroit looked a lot like Silicon Valley in the 1960s and 1970s. The Motor City thrived as a hotbed of small innovators, many of whom focused on the new thing, the automobile. . . . The irony and ultimately the tragedy of Detroit is that its small, dynamic firms and independent suppliers gave rise to gigantic, wholly integrated car companies, which then became synonymous with stagnation.

Automobiles were not unique. As Richard Longworth (2008, 147) writes:

> In their youth, all Midwestern cities—Chicago most of all, but also Detroit, Cleveland, Milwaukee, Akron, Gary, St. Louis, Dayton, Flint, Toledo, Grand Rapids, Peoria—embodied American industrial dominance. . . . Chicago symbolized meatpacking, Detroit ruled the auto world, Gary made steel, Akron produced tires, Grand Rapids dominated furniture making, and Peoria grew rich on whiskey distilling.

By 1950, the manufacturing region bordering the Great Lakes had reached its peak, with firms such as General Motors and US Steel dominating their industries. The region accounted for more than half of all manufacturing jobs in the United States (Ohanian 2014). Dominant firms such as the Big Three in autos (General Motors, Chrysler, and Ford) faced little competition, reducing their incentives to innovate or improve productivity (Ohanian 2014).

Although its share of US manufacturing employment was already declining in the 1950s and 1960s, in 1970, the Midwest still employed almost a third of all US manufacturing workers. As shown in figure 8.1, the

box continues

Box 8.1 continued
The rise and fall of the Midwest

economies of the Midwest were driven by manufacturing production; 35 percent of workers held manufacturing jobs.[1]

The region continued to thrive, as the incomes earned in manufacturing generated demand for other local service providers. Median wages in Midwestern manufacturing in 1970 were 11 percent higher than the median US manufacturing wage and 42 percent higher than median manufacturing wage in the South. In 1970, 28 cities in the Midwest made the list of the top 100 most populous cities in the United States. They included Chicago (3.3 million), Detroit (1.5 million), Cleveland (750,000), Indianapolis (744,000), and Milwaukee (717,000).[2]

In 1970, the big auto and steel firms still dominated their industries, and their oligopoly position generated rents that they shared with their workers, who belonged to strong unions, most notably the United Auto Workers and the United Steel Workers. These unions raised costs and enforced work rules that impaired flexibility. Passage of the Taft-Hartley Act in 1947 (which restricted union actions and banned requiring all workers in a plant to be members of unions) encouraged companies to move their operations to right-to-work states in the South.

The competitive environment for the Rust Belt firms that had dominated manufacturing was radically transformed after 1980. In both steel and autos, Japan provided competitive pressures, and oil shocks shifted demand toward smaller, more fuel-efficient cars and away from the large, high-profit-margin cars and trucks the Big Three had specialized in. At the same time, nonunionized mini-mills—such as Nucor, located in North Carolina, which produced steel by recycling scrap metal—became increasingly important domestic competitors for conventional steel producers.[3]

These developments initiated an era that radically changed the role of manufacturing in Midwestern economies. Although it remained the

box continues

---

1. In contrast, manufacturing provided 25 percent of jobs in the South and 27 percent in the West (Flood et al. 2021).

2. For the list of the top 100 US cities in 1970 by population, see https://www.biggestuscities.com/1970.

3. Using an index of the degree of specialization, Holmes and Stevens (2004, 227–50) find that "as late as the 1950s manufacturing activity in the United States was heavily concentrated in the Northeast and Upper Midwest around the Great Lakes, in an area often called the manufacturing belt. But as of 2000 this area no longer specialized in manufacturing and in contrast certain areas of the South have become specialized in manufacturing, in effect fashioning a new manufacturing belt."

Box 8.1 continued
The rise and fall of the Midwest

US region most dependent on manufacturing (figure 8.1), by 2015, only 17 percent of Midwestern workers held a manufacturing job, and the median wage in manufacturing in the Midwest was just 7.5 percent higher than the median manufacturing wage in the South (Flood et al. 2021). By 2015, Detroit, Cleveland, and St. Louis had all lost about half of their 1970 populations. Of the 10 largest cities in the Midwest in 1970, only two—Indianapolis and Columbus, Ohio—experienced population growth.[4] Perhaps even worse were circumstances in many semirural towns whose economies had been dependent on one or two large manufacturing plants.[5]

---

4. Although by 2001 the manufacturing employment share was smaller, Schweitzer (2017) finds similarly large negative effects on the Midwestern economies of the manufacturing employment shocks between 1979 and 1983 and 2001 to 2010.

5. Goldstein (2017) provides a heart-wrenching description of the impact of the closure of a General Motors assembly plant that had been the mainstay of Janesville, Wisconsin.

such as petroleum refining and petrochemicals (Helper, Krueger, and Wial 2012). As the scale of industrial activity grew, unit transport costs within supply chains declined, partly as a result of the extension of transportation infrastructure, such as the interstate highway system. These factors fostered the dispersion of manufacturing activity and eventually a wider global unbundling of supply chains (Baldwin 2016). Firms at first moved the less skilled parts of their supply chains abroad; eventually, they moved skilled (or once skilled) activities.

The Interregnum

After 1979, there were substantial employment losses in some manufacturing industries and locations in response to the second oil shock (in 1979–80), two sharp recessions (in 1980 and 1982), and increasing competition from Japan and several emerging economies in Asia. These employment declines were concentrated in labor-intensive industries, such as clothing and textiles, and capital-intensive industries, such as machinery, steel, and automobiles. This period was an interregnum, because the adjustment to these shocks contained elements of both the mechanism of adjustment to adverse shocks that had been common in the phase of convergence (migration) and a new change: accelerated shifts toward increased demand for skilled workers as skill-biased technological change altered production methods within manufacturing firms and demand shifted from manufacturing to business services, information technology, and finance.

Migration to more prosperous locations was traditionally the glue that maintained incomes when workers were dislocated by regional shocks. Blanchard and Katz (1992) find that adverse demand shocks led to higher unemployment and lower wages in the short run; over the longer run, migration played the most important role, and unemployment and wage rates reverted to their previous levels. The long-run legacy of a negative shock was thus a smaller population and labor force, but the adverse shock did not have a permanently negative impact on local wages or per capita income.[4] Adjustment was completed within a decade and state unemployment rates in the 1970s and 1980s were essentially uncorrelated, supporting their finding that the impact on unemployment rates was relatively transitory. As more educated workers tend to be more mobile than less educated workers (Wozniak 2010), an adverse shock that leads to out-migration can also promote convergence if it disperses human capital to more promising lower-income locations.

Between 1977 and 1987, the US auto industry lost 500,000 job and steel lost 350,000 (Feyer, Sacerdote, and Stern 2007). Within five years, unemployment rates in the Rust Belt areas most affected had returned to the US average, and their per capita incomes had also recovered. Consistent with the Blanchard-Katz model, the adjustment took place "entirely through out-migration of people rather than in-migration of jobs or a change in labor force participation" (Feyer, Sacerdote, and Stern 2007, 42).

These responses did have some permanent effects. Out-migration, usually of younger workers, meant lower trajectories for regional employment growth and in some cases left cities with poorer public amenities, lower tax bases, and sometimes uninhabited buildings, contributing to the problems faced by cities such as Detroit, Flint, and Bethlehem.[5]

---

4. Bound and Holzer (2000) confirm that positive (negative) labor demand shocks are followed by labor in-migration (out-migration).

5. As Rust Belt cities shrank, the attractiveness of their restaurants, culture, and overall appearance declined as well (Feyer, Sacerdote, and Stern 2007). Allentown, 15 miles from Bethlehem, was made famous by Billy Joel's 1982 song "Allentown," which starts:
"Well, we're living here in Allentown
And they're closing all the factories down
Out in Bethlehem they're killing time
Filling out forms
Standing in line."

Studies of the trade shocks from increased competition from Japan and the Asian Tigers that took place in the late 1970s and early 1980s find that although these shocks were disruptive, they did not have permanent effects on unemployment rates. Charles, Hurst, and Schwartz (2019) find that local manufacturing employment declines during the 1980s had little effect on local employment rates in cities that were more diversified, more resilient, and better educated. After 2000, however, the impacts of shocks on labor force participation, employment, and wage rates were greater. The greater resilience to the earlier trade shocks can be explained by higher levels of education of the workers adversely affected. This allowed for innovation and workforce upgrading. Also significant was the fact that the industries that were affected were in earlier stages of their manufacturing product cycle. Another part of the process of renewal was the ability in the 1980s and early 1990s of local governments to attract leading foreign firms—including Toyota to Kentucky; Honda to Ohio; BMW to South Carolina; and Mercedes-Benz to Alabama—to set up assembly operations in the United States

Between the 1970s and the 1990s, employment in manufacturing at the national level remained fairly stable, but as shown in figure 8.1, the manufacturing employment share in the Northeast fell from 28.0 percent to 17.9 percent. Several Eastern states experienced very large declines in manufacturing employment over this period, including Pennsylvania (47 percent), New York (38 percent),[6] and New Jersey (16 percent). The losses were staggering: "In the 20-year period from 1967 to 1987, Philadelphia lost 64 percent of its manufacturing jobs, Chicago lost 60 percent, New York City 58 percent, and Detroit 51 percent" (Wilson 1996, Kindle edition, location 807).

Several of these cities were able to adapt, by shifting to more advanced manufacturing technologies, hiring more skilled workers, and specializing in other industries. In several cities with large manufacturing employment declines, employment in other sectors rose (Wilson 1996). During the 1980s, for example, New York City lost 135,000 jobs in industries in which workers averaged less than 12 years of education, but it gained almost 300,000 jobs in industries in which workers had 13 or more years of education. Philadelphia lost 55,000 jobs in low-education industries but gained 40,000 jobs for workers with high school plus at least some college. Baltimore and Boston also experienced substantial losses in industries employing low-education workers but experienced major gains in industries employing more educated workers (Wilson 1996).

---

6. New York's garment industry imploded in the late 1960s and 1970s, contributing to a loss of more than 300,000 manufacturing jobs between 1967 and 1977 (Glaeser 2012).

Figure 8.1

Regional manufacturing shares of employment in the United States, 1970–2019

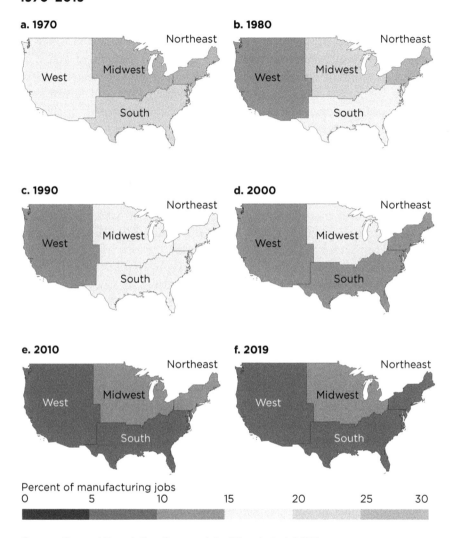

a. 1970

b. 1980

c. 1990

d. 2000

e. 2010

f. 2019

Percent of manufacturing jobs

0   5   10   15   20   25   30

Source: Current Population Survey data (Flood et al. 2021).

Period of Divergence

The dynamics of regional adjustments have changed since the era of convergence. The convergence rate among regional economies between 1990 and 2010 was less than half the 1.8 percent a year achieved earlier and "in the period leading up to the Great Recession (in 2008) there was virtually no convergence at all" (Ganong and Shoag 2017, 76). Blanchard and Katz (1992) had found no correlation in unemployment rates between the 1970s and the 1980s. For more recent periods, however, Russ and Shambaugh (2019) report stronger, statistically significant correlations in unemployment and wage rates in local economies over time. They find that poor areas experienced stagnant and high unemployment rates for long periods of time and that richer areas enjoyed persistently lower unemployment and rising incomes. This finding suggests a waning of migration as a source of convergence and weaker adjustment mechanisms to adverse shocks.

The share of manufacturing jobs in the United States requiring a college degree rose between 1970 and 2019 (figure 8.2). This shift had a profound impact on the location of production.

New technologies resulted in a new geography of jobs (Moretti 2013). Following the computer revolution, the creation of new jobs shifted toward cities with workers who had analytical skills. The divergence in the subsequent growth of US cities can in no small part be explained by the complementarities between new technologies and the increasing skill endowments of the cities that thrived.

After 1975, the share of adults with college degrees increased more in cities with higher initial schooling levels. Despite the increase in their relative supply, the wage premiums for college-educated workers in cities with already large shares of skilled workers rose especially rapidly (Berry and Glaeser 2005). As more highly educated workers are generally more mobile than other workers, the market for college graduates is basically national. Metropolitan areas like Washington, New York, Boston, Austin, Dallas, Raleigh-Durham, San Jose, San Francisco, and Seattle prospered, offering a growing number of high-paying jobs to college graduates in knowledge-intensive industries such as computers, telecommunications, software, finance, and life sciences.

These cities paid higher wages because their workers were more productive than workers in other cities. They enjoyed a virtuous cycle from agglomeration benefits that were generated by thick labor markets (markets with many employers and workers, allowing better matching of needs and greater specialization);[7] positive local spillovers of knowledge; greater availability

---

7. For evidence of the skill bias of this agglomeration, see Baum-Snow, Freedman, and Pavan (2018).

Figure 8.2

Share of manufacturing jobs in the United States requiring a college degree, by state, 1970–2019

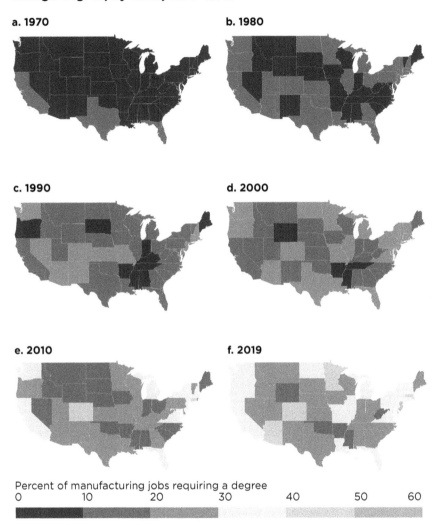

a. 1970

b. 1980

c. 1990

d. 2000

e. 2010

f. 2019

Percent of manufacturing jobs requiring a degree

| 0 | 10 | 20 | 30 | 40 | 50 | 60 |

Source: Current Population Survey data (Flood et al. 2021).

of specialized services, such as venture capital, legal services, and business consultants; and the benefits of being closer to wealthy customers (Moretti 2011). Many of these cities had important research universities (MIT, Harvard, Stanford, the University of Texas, Caltech, Duke, the University of North Carolina) and research institutes (the National Institutes of Health in Maryland). Their scale allowed them to offer more quality-of-life amenities, such as good schools, museums, parks, restaurants, and theaters, which made them attractive to their more educated populations.[8]

The migration of skilled workers to more skill-intensive places increased regional differentiation. Many educated workers left manufacturing cities. The shift in the economic paradigm away from the production of standardized industrial products hurt Rust Belt cities like Detroit, Flint, Cleveland, and Mobile, which found it difficult to develop new areas of specialization. This brain drain contributed to the processes of decline.[9]

Less educated US workers also found themselves in growing competition with imports from developing economies that were also taking advantage of the easier diffusion of standardized manufacturing technologies. Andrew Bernard, Bradford Jensen, and Peter Schott (2006) find that import penetration from low-income economies accounted for 14 percent of the decline of 675,000 manufacturing workers between 1977 and 1997.

These trends were exacerbated by the major national losses in manufacturing employment after 2000. The loss in manufacturing jobs between 2000 and 2010 ranged from 24.6 percent in the Midwest to 34.1 percent in the South (Flood et al. 2021). The regional pervasiveness of the losses lends support to the argument advanced in chapter 6 that weak national demand for manufactured products during this period was an important reason for this job loss.

As noted above, the decline in the share of mid-level jobs has been evident within manufacturing, as the share of workers earning at or above median wages has declined. It has also adversely affected service workers who perform routine clerical and secretarial tasks. Not all lower-

---

8. There is also evidence that growing up in these cities was conducive to greater intergenerational income mobility, which Chetty et al. (2014) ascribe to less residential segregation by race, less income inequality, better primary schools, greater social capital, and greater family stability.

9. The per capita incomes of 384 metropolitan areas were ranked in 1969 and 2019. Cities that had slipped in the rankings included many metropolitan areas that had had very large shares of employment in manufacturing in 1969. Flint (with an MES of 45 percent in 1969) fell from 84th to 302nd; Jackson, Mississippi (with an MES of 35 percent in 1969) fell from 91st to 338th; Kokomo, Indiana (with an MES of 51.7 percent in 1969), fell from 92nd to 298th (see US Bureau of Economic Analysis, https://apps.bea.gov/iTable/iTable.cfm?reqid = 99&step = 1#reqid = 99&step = 1&isuri = 1).

wage workers have been adversely affected, however. Opportunities have increased for personal service workers who perform tasks that require face-to-face contact or a range of differentiated responses to stimuli (examples include construction workers, mechanics, and nurses).

Reflecting these changes, income distribution in superstar cities is *U*-shaped, with larger numbers of very highly paid educated workers at the top, larger numbers of low-paid service workers at the bottom, and fewer workers in the middle of the occupation distribution (Autor 2019). At the same time, housing costs in high-income cities have increased because household incomes are high, as highly educated workers tend to marry each other, a process known as *assortative mating* (Becker 1981, Breen and Salazar 2011). Regulatory restrictions have also exacerbated the high cost of real estate in these cities (Glaeser 2012).[10]

Decline in Migration

Austin, Glaeser, and Summers (2018) confirm that the US workforce has become less mobile. They note that between 1950 and 1992, intercounty mobility never dropped below 6.0 percent a year; between 2008 and 2018, it never exceeded 3.9 percent a year. Supporting the idea that local economies are adjusting more slowly to adverse shocks, Dao Mai, Davide Furceri, and Prakash Loungani (2017) show that interstate migration because of labor market shocks declined after the 1990s.

Charles, Hurst, and Schwartz (2019) find that manufacturing declines had a larger effect on population changes in the 1980s than they did in the 2000s. In the 1980s, adverse shocks led workers to migrate and find jobs elsewhere; by the 2000s, the response of less skilled workers was to withdraw from the workforce. Over time, the incidence of nonemployment, i.e., working-age workers who are not in the labor force, has become concentrated in places that have had adverse shocks to employment regardless of their causes.

Benjamin Austin, Edward Glaeser, and Lawrence Summers (2018) report that a variety of shocks (related to industrial composition, trade, and base closings) led to higher "not-working rates" in local economies where the average not-working rate was higher to begin with. Partly as a result, national regional rates of nonemployment diverged as nonemployment became more regionally concentrated.[11] In addition, in contrast to the period

---

10. According to Ganong and Shoag (2017, 6), "In 1960 housing prices are 1 log point higher in a state with 1 log point higher income. By 2010 the slope doubles, with housing prices 2 log points higher in a state where income is 1 log point higher."

11. See Abraham and Kearney (2018) for a review of the causes of increased labor force nonparticipation.

before 1980, when migration tended to equalize incomes, unskilled workers are on balance migrating away from rather than toward wealthy places in recent years (Ganong and Shoag 2017). More recent evidence indicates that even educated workers are migrating from expensive large cities such as San Francisco, Washington, New York, and Los Angeles to cities such as Phoenix, Atlanta, Houston, and Tampa.[12]

Recent declines in mobility and increases in workforce nonparticipation are firmly established, but their causes are still being debated. One line of explanation emphasizes the decline in opportunities for mid-skilled employment in growing cities combined with much higher housing costs in these desirable locations. A second points to declining demand in the cities with high income growth for midlevel workers.

Another potential explanation for declining mobility could be increased government disability payments or transfers from other household members. Charles, Hurst, and Schwartz (2019) show that this explanation is not plausible, however, as only a small share of people who are not working receive disability payments. They also conclude that private firm transfers to workers they lay off are likely to be small.

Effects of Trade

Even if its contribution to aggregate net manufacturing job loss was not large (as argued in chapter 6), international trade placed additional pressures on manufacturing in many communities.

Import competition. Shushanik Hakobyan and John McLaren (2016) find that although imports did little to alter wages at the national level, those resulting from lower tariffs because of the North American Free Trade Agreement (NAFTA) reduced blue-collar wages for workers in the most affected industries and localities, including the wages of service workers that were not directly involved in trade. Avraham Ebenstein et al. (2014) find reductions in employment in industries that offshored to low-wage economies and reductions in earnings in both manufacturing and services in the occupations that were most affected by offshoring. Autor, Dorn, and Hanson (2013) and Pierce and Schott (2016) find large declines in manufacturing employment in some commuter zones and particular industries as a result of Chinese competition. The wages, employment, and labor force participation of less educated workers in these locations were also adversely impacted.

---

12. Emily Badger, Robert Gebeloff, and Josh Katz, "Coastal Cities Priced Out Low-Wage Workers. Now College Graduates Are Leaving, Too," *New York Times*, May 13, 2023, https://www.nytimes.com/interactive/2023/05/15/upshot/migrations-college-super-cities.html.

Technological upgrading. Nicholas Bloom, Mirko Draca, and John Van Reenen (2016) conclude that increased trade with developing economies causes faster technological upgrading. Their study of half a million firms in 12 industrial countries between 1996 and 2007 finds that agile firms responded to competition from Chinese imports by upgrading their technology—buying more computers, spending more on R&D, and improving their management policies. Firms with limited innovation and limited investment in information technology had a harder time reacting to Chinese imports and ended up laying off workers.

Bloom et al. (2019) show that the adjustments had a geographic dimension. They find that in high human capital areas (primarily the West Coast and parts of the East Coast), manufacturing employment losses in response to trade shocks were smaller and came predominantly from firms switching from production to supplying services. This finding is consistent with high-tech firms designing and marketing products in the United States but offshoring assembly production to China (the Apple model). In contrast, in low human capital areas (much of the South and Midwest), manufacturing saw large job losses driven by plant closures.

Trade versus other shocks. There is a debate in the literature over whether the local impact of the shocks to manufacturing employment resulting from international competition were like shocks to manufacturing from other factors, such as capital deepening, new management techniques, and changes in technology. Charles, Hurst, and Schwartz (2019) develop a variable that captures manufacturing shocks that are unrelated (orthogonal) to trade by extracting the China shock identified by Autor, Dorn, and Hanson (2013) from the variable they use to estimate responses to changes in manufacturing employment. They still find "large and persistent" effects on local employment rates, hours worked, and wages in regions where there were no manufacturing shocks from Chinese trade but there were manufacturing employment declines for other reasons. Once they control for initial industrial composition, the responses in the local economies with and without the China shock are virtually identical. This finding suggests that the reasons for these local responses lie less with trade per se and more with the variety of shocks that led to a weaker demand for manufacturing workers combined with the increased reluctance of workers to migrate.

Brian Asquith et al. (2019) draw a different conclusion. They find that the China shock affected employment mainly through plant closure, whereas the responses to more general adverse shocks to manufacturing took the form of layoffs and the suppression of new firm formation. Autor, Dorn, and Hanson (2015) also find that trade shocks are different. Although trade shocks tended to reduce employment of all types of workers in both manufacturing and nonmanufacturing, computerization shocks, for example, did not have large aggregate employment effects but instead led to occupational polarization.

Social Consequences of Deindustrialization

Many social maladies can be traced to declines in manufacturing employment opportunities. William Wilson (1996) finds abundant evidence of the devastating social impacts of manufacturing job loss in inner-city neighborhoods in the 1980s on Black families (box 8.2). More recent studies of the impacts of declining employment in manufacturing on local economies since 2000 find evidence of declines in marriage rates (Autor, Dorn, and Hanson 2018) and public spending (Feler and Senses 2017) and increases in household debt (Barrot et al. 2017); political polarization (Autor et al. 2020); more crime (Che, Xu, and Zhang 2018); opioid use (Charles, Hurst, and Schwartz 2019); and suicides and drug overdoses (Pierce and Schott 2017).[13]

Manufacturing's Declining Role in Major City Growth

Manufacturing is no longer a major driver of local growth and innovation in major cities. Robert Atkinson, Mark Muro, and Jacob Whiton (2019) identify the 20 cities with the largest shares of jobs in the most innovative industries, a group that includes both manufacturing and service sectors distinguished by measures such as their shares in innovative manufacturing and services industries. The MES in these innovative cities has been declining steadily and now averages only around 6 percent (figure 8.3), considerably lower than the national average, vividly illustrating a large share of employment in manufacturing is no longer associated with superstar status.

Can Remote Work Change the Story?

In the wake of the COVID pandemic, geographic agglomerations of highly skilled workers have become less important, as remote work has become common. Being able to work far from one's employer could allow towns and cities that can offer decent public amenities and a good quality of life to attract high-skilled workers. Attracting more highly skilled workers could raise opportunities and incomes for less skilled workers.

According to Enrico Moretti and Per Thulin (2013), the multipliers from high-tech workers in creating jobs for other workers are large, both because they need inputs from these workers and because their high

---

13. For a compelling analysis of the impact of poor economic performance on these pathologies, see Case and Deaton (2020).

Box 8.2
How did changes in manufacturing affect Black workers in the United States?

In his study of inner-city Chicago in the 1970s and 1980s, *When Work Disappears: The World of the New Urban Poor*, Harvard sociology professor William Julius Wilson (1996) documents the devastating social consequences of the declines in manufacturing employment opportunities for Black men.[1] He points to globalization as the reason for these declining employment opportunities. Mary Kate Batistich and Timothy Bond (2019) argue that competition from Japanese imports led to decreased manufacturing employment, labor force participation, and median earnings for Black people and increased receipt of public assistance.[2]

These manufacturing job losses for Blacks contrasted with increased manufacturing employment for whites. This compositional shift appears to have been caused by skill upgrading in the manufacturing sector. Losses were concentrated among Black high school dropouts, and gains occurred among college-educated whites, as manufacturing employment shifted toward professionals and college-educated production workers.

Overall, the responses to competition from Japan and the Asian Tigers in the 1970s and 1980s may have been less disruptive than the response to the China shock in the early 2000s (Charles, Hurst, and Schwartz 2019; Eriksson et al. 2021). But their impacts on Black inner-city employment and consequences for Black labor force participation, earnings opportunities, and social decay were harbingers of the kinds of problems caused by the loss of manufacturing jobs after 2000.

---

1. Bound and Holzer (1993) confirm that industrial shifts, particularly away from manufacturing, depressed wages and employment among Black and less skilled white men during the 1970s.

2. Acs and Danziger (1993, 627) find that "over the 1980s, a decade marked by a severe recession and then a prolonged recovery, both the falling mean and the rising low earnings rate for all three race/ethnic groups are primarily driven by structural changes. Shifting patterns of industrial employment explain a small portion of these trends for whites and Hispanics but a substantially larger portion for blacks."

---

incomes lead them to consume a wide range of professional and personal services that have to be supplied locally.[14] As a result of remote work, the 40-year era of regional divergence could be moderating and the economy could be on the threshold of the next phase of convergence. It is unlikely to be led by developments in manufacturing, however.

---

14. See also Goos, Konings, and Vandeweyer (2015).

Figure 8.3

Manufacturing employment share in metropolitan areas of the United States with the largest numbers of jobs in innovation industries, 1969–2019

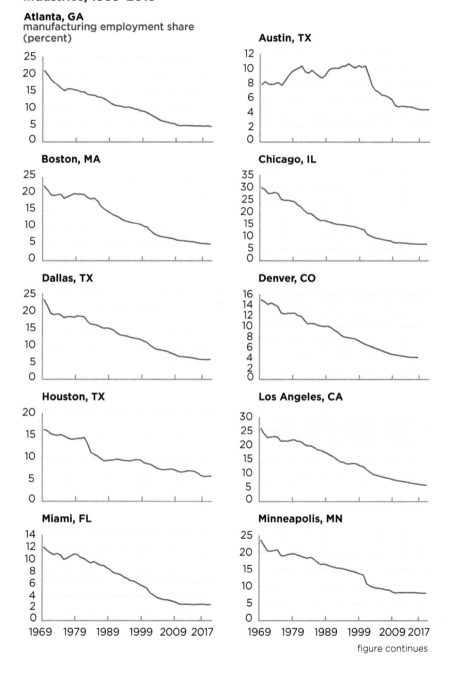

Figure 8.3 continued

Manufacturing employment share in metropolitan areas of the United States with the largest numbers of jobs in innovation industries, 1969–2019

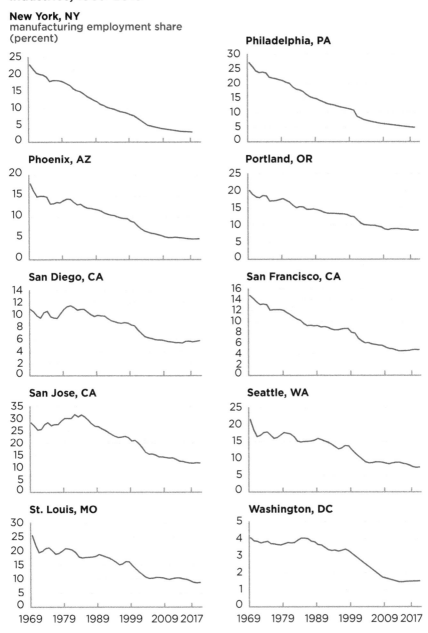

New York, NY
manufacturing employment share (percent)

Sources: Cities were identified by Atkinson, Muro, and Whiton (2019). Data are from the US Bureau of Economic Analysis.

Conclusion

This chapter traces some of the links between the changing role of manufacturing and the changes in the US experience of regional convergence. It emphasizes parallel developments between the experiences of people and the experiences of places.

In the first three decades of the postwar era, partly because of developments in manufacturing, middle-income jobs were plentiful, and the poorer parts of the United States enjoyed faster growth and income convergence, because manufacturing innovations were routinized and poorer places could attract workers without much education to work in factories. When local communities were hit with adverse shocks, their labor markets could restore their income and unemployment levels by reducing their workforces, as workers who were displaced migrated to places with better opportunities.

Starting in the late 1970s, manufacturing experienced a series of shocks, including soaring oil prices, two recessions, an influx of imports from Asia, and a strong dollar. Initially, the Mid-Atlantic lost large numbers of manufacturing jobs, but its labor market later recovered, as workers moved into manufacturing production that used more skill-intensive methods and service industries such as information technologies and finance. Mobile workers took advantage of new manufacturing opportunities created by foreign investment by moving to the South.

After strong growth and low unemployment in the 1990s, the combination of two recessions, relatively rapid productivity growth in manufacturing, and local shocks from imports and offshoring led to a major decline in manufacturing employment nationwide. Simultaneously, the digital revolution enhanced the geographic dispersion of growth, as college-educated workers dominated superstar cities, which reaped the economies of scale from agglomeration but were unable to provide displaced production workers with affordable housing and middle-income jobs. As a result, communities that once depended on manufacturing stagnated with non-college-educated manufacturing workers in many communities withdrawing from the labor force rather than migrating. At the same time, other industries that employed college graduates drove growth in the cities that prospered.

In his masterful book, Glaeser (2012) argues that the era of the industrial city is over and former manufacturing communities, large and small, that have been unable to reinvent themselves in the new era are in trouble. Glaeser describes New York's reinvention since 1970 from a city based on manufacturing of garments and other goods to a city based on finance, business services, and high technology. James and Deborah Fallows (2018) find numerous other examples of revitalizing towns and cities in their travels around the United States. As Lincicome (2020, 23) notes, "'Strong' localities, achieving high marks for growth, prosperity, and inclusion include not only well-known success stories such as Pittsburgh and cities close to Boston and Manhattan but also smaller places such as Beaumont, Texas; Waterloo, Iowa; and Bethlehem, Pennsylvania."[15]

These examples are exceptions, however. In general, the reduced resilience to shocks has led many communities to stagnate.

---

15. Lincicome cites Berube and Murray (2018), who find that 115 of the 185 US counties with the largest shares of manufacturing jobs in 1970 had transitioned successfully from manufacturing. Of the remaining 70, 40 exhibited strong or emerging economic performance between 2000 and 2016.

III

PROSPECTS AND POLICIES

Part III analyzes the widespread adoption of industrial policies that promote digital technologies, supply-chain resilience through reshoring and "friend-shoring," and policies to mitigate the impact of climate change. In several countries, these new policies represent a dramatic change in policies from reliance on free and open markets toward those based on a much greater role for government intervention. An important question in the context of this study is whether these policies fundamentally change the outlook for manufacturing employment and allow manufacturing to play a much greater role in helping countries achieve more inclusive growth.

The contents of this part are as follows: Chapter 9 provides a brief overview of the changed environment that has led to the new industrial policies being adopted. Chapter 10 analyzes the major initiatives of the Biden administration to promote manufacturing's role in its trade and industrial policies that aim at promoting infrastructure development, semiconductor technologies, securing supply chains, and decarbonizing the US economy. It emphasizes that, although these policies may advance critically important national goals, they are unlikely to have a major impact on the degree to which the United States deals with the problems of non-college-educated workers and depressed local economies. Chapter 11 therefore offers recommendations for additional policies to help people and places. Chapter 12 surveys industrial policies in advanced economies in Europe and Japan and compares them with those in the United States. Chapter 13 considers the implications of these policies and the technological changes associated with them for developing economies' growth prospects.

9

The Current Policy Context

Almost every country has adopted new policies toward manufacturing. This chapter briefly outlines the major reasons why. It first analyzes the geopolitical context, then considers national security concerns and the disruptive impact of the COVID-19 pandemic and trade wars on global supply chains, and concludes with a discussion of the need to deal with climate change.

Geopolitics

China and the West now view each other as rivals in trade, technology, military capabilities, and ideology. The global trading system has been transformed from being united under a multilateral organization for negotiating and enforcing rules into a clash of systems that have resulted from China's WTO accession in 2001 and its persistence in nonmarket practices. When China joined the WTO, it was recognized that the country retained many of the policies and institutions that were part of its communist history, but it was expected that after a transitional period China would converge toward the economic systems typical of most Western economies. But although China has engaged in extensive trade and investment opening, many features of its system have remained distinctive, with the state rather than market forces playing a prominent role in guiding resource allocation (Wu 2016). This has led to disputes over foreign investment, intellectual property rights, market access, and unfair trade practices and concerns about the ability of Chinese state-backed policies to compromise data security or enable surveillance.

For about a decade it appeared as if China was changing as expected and that its rise could be easily accommodated in the existing trading system. In addition, China's rapid growth made it attractive to foreigners as a market and the upgrading of its production capabilities as a location for production to service the local and global marketplace. However, the "Made in China 2025" program launched in 2015 aimed to encourage increased domestic content and use indigenous innovation to achieve global technological leadership. China laid out the market shares it desired in products such as new energy vehicles, high-tech shipping components, new and renewable energy equipment, industrial robots and high-performance medical devices, advanced tractors, mobile phone chips, and wide-body aircraft. Its announced intention was to transform China into a leader in high-tech manufacturing powered by robotics and artificial intelligence.

These shifts raised concerns about discriminatory treatment by foreign firms based in China and alarms in many Western countries about China's growing economic power. In clean energy China has achieved its goals.[1] As of 2020, more than 87 percent of the world's rare earth minerals, nearly 65 percent of cobalt, and nearly 58 percent of global lithium processed in China. In 2022 China spent $546 billion on investments that included solar and wind energy, electric vehicles, and batteries.[2] This spending was four times greater than US spending of $141 billion and far exceeded spending of $180 billion by the European Union.[3]

In 2021, China launched an industrial policy program that basically confirmed its support for the sectors that had been selected in the "Made in China 2025" program. It adopted a strategy characterized as promoting "dual circulation," which in part represented a response to the trade frictions that were sparked by the Trump administration. The strategy still provided a role for international trade and engagement (the first circula-

---

1. China's dominance in investment is not new: In 2010–19, it committed $758 billion; Europe $698 billion, led by Germany ($179 billion) and the United Kingdom ($122 billion); the United States $356 billion; and Japan $202 billion (see Sophia Wu, "These are the strategies behind China's ambitious clean energy transition," GreenBiz, November 3, 2021, https://www.greenbiz.com/article/these-are-strategies-behind-chinas-ambitious-clean-energy-transition. For the case of electric vehicles, see Michael Schuman, "The Electric-Car Lesson That China Is Serving up for America." *The Atlantic*, May 21, 2021, https://www.theatlantic.com/international/archive/2021/05/joe-biden-china-infrastructure/618921/.

2. "Global Low-Carbon Energy Technology Investment Surges Past $1 Trillion for the First Time," Bloomberg NEF, January 26, 2023, https://about.bnef.com/blog/global-low-carbon-energy-technology-investment-surges-past-1-trillion-for-the-first-time/.

3. Sara Schonhardt, "China Invests $546 Billion in Clean Energy, Far Surpassing the US," *E&E News*, January 30, 2023, https://www.scientificamerican.com/article/china-invests-546-billion-in-clean-energy-far-surpassing-the-u-s/.

tion) and involved increased trade and investment liberalization and joining large regional agreements such as the Regional Comprehensive Economic Partnership (RCEP) and the Comprehensive and Progressive Agreement for Trans-Pacific Partnership (CPTPP), but it also sought to make China less vulnerable to outside pressures by emphasizing technological self-sufficiency (the second circulation) especially in products like semiconductors and electric vehicles. In supporting this emphasis on "the second circulation," influential commentator Yu Yongding, president of the Chinese Society of World Economics, called for a shift from promoting services to returning to promoting manufacturing through creating a "relatively complete and independent industrial structure."[4]

China's growing industrial prowess enhanced its ability to use its economic position to project its power. It used import restrictions on countries such as Lithuania that it viewed as challenging its territorial claims on Taiwan, and Australia for being critical of its role in developing the virus that causes COVID-19, and has been willing to restrict its exports of key rare earths in response to Japan's detention of a Chinese fishing boat captain near disputed islands in the East China Sea. There has also been growing military rivalry in the South China Sea where China has asserted territorial claims and built new military installations. America has increased its naval presence to ensure its right to freedom of navigation. It is not surprising that Western countries have felt the need to respond to China's growth by enhancing their investments in new technologies.

Russia's invasion of Crimea also raised awareness of the potential vulnerability of depending on a potential adversary for vital inputs. Germany, in particular, depended on Russia for vital supplies of natural gas and was even in the process of implementing plans to build a second key pipeline when the war broke out. Its policies assumed that President Vladimir Putin was a reliable supplier, an assumption that was shattered, forcing a total rethinking of its energy position. The result has required a complete reorientation of its policies and demonstrated the need for prioritizing supply chain security over the cheapest supplier. The Ukraine war has also led to global price increases in key primary products such as grains and fertilizers that have impacted many importing countries. This has similarly demonstrated how geopolitical strife can have serious implications even for those not directly involved in conflicts.

---

4. Yu Yongding, "How to Realize the Transformation from 'International Circulation' to 'Dual Circulation'?" *Sina Finance*, August 18, 2020, http://finance.sina.com.cn/zl/china/2020-08-18/zl-iivhvpwy1713127.shtml.

National Security

Increasingly, technology has become a significant consideration for national security with advanced semiconductors playing an ever more important role. The pivotal role played by Taiwan Semiconductor Manufacturing Company Limited (TSMC), a company based in Taiwan just about 100 miles from the Chinese mainland in producing cutting-edge semiconductors, has further given rise to Western concerns about the supply chain vulnerabilities. As a result the Trump administration took steps to deny Chinese companies such as Huawei and ZTE access to the latest semiconductor chips and the Biden administration doubled down on policies restricting Chinese access not only to the latest chips but also to the technologies (such as lithography) and machinery required to produce the latest chips. As will be described in greater detail in chapters 10 and 12 the United States and European Union have vastly increased their financial support for research and development as well as the production of cutting-edge semiconductors. The United States and its allies have also sought to deny Chinese access to technologies with dual-use potential through more stringent controls on exports, and inward and outward foreign investment.

Supply Chain Security

Before 2017 firms concentrated their production activities in the least costly locations without much concern for their exposure to disruptions. But this created vulnerabilities when key chokepoints in their supply chains were disrupted, whether by tariffs, the trade war, shortages in chips and other key inputs as COVID shutdowns disrupted supply and consumer demand shifted from services to goods, or the use of trade sanctions for political purposes. Accordingly, the response has been policies that take supply chain resilience into account and emphasize domestic production (reshoring), diversification of suppliers, or only dealing with trusted foreign suppliers (friendshoring and derisking).

Climate Change

It has become increasingly difficult to deny the role of greenhouse gas emissions in causing global warming, which has led to extreme weather events. Progress in Paris in having countries adopt national determined mandates has led them to implement new policies for both mitigation and adaptation. This has spurred large amounts of investment in renewable energy technologies and production in solar, wind, and green hydrogen as well as carbon capture.

Conclusion

In sum, geopolitical rivalries are now intertwined with national security, technological development, insecure supply chains, and climate change. These are all cases that give rise to what are termed "market failures" and are unlikely to be adequately dealt with by private markets acting alone. It is not surprising therefore that new government policies are being adopted to deal with them. Many of these policies involve government measures to stimulate manufacturing, and for the central question of this book to be adequately answered, it is necessary to analyze these policies and ask whether they are likely to fundamentally change the role that manufacturing can play as a driver of inclusive growth.

10

Will the Biden Policies Lead to More Inclusive Growth for People and Places?

President Joseph R. Biden Jr. has made the goal of his economic policies to "build back better." He has emphasized helping workers without college degrees in order "to grow the economy from the bottom up and the middle out."[1] To do so the Biden-Harris Economic Blueprint gives the promotion of manufacturing through "making and building it in America" a central role.[2] However, although manufacturing employment recovered from its slump due to the COVID lockdowns, and reached 13.01 million in September 2023, this was only 1.7 percent above its level in January 2020, just before COVID emerged.[3] Moreover, according to the US Bureau of Labor Statistics' ten-year employment projections for 2032 forecast, that manufacturing employment would actually *decline* by 113,000 between 2022 and 2032.[4]

But private firms' announcements of investment intensions as tabulated by the White House[5] and a surge in manufacturing construction that

1. White House, The Biden-Harris Economic Blueprint, September 2022, p. 18, https://www.whitehouse.gov/wp-content/uploads/2022/09/Biden-Economic-Blueprint-Report-720PM-MASTER-DOC.pdf.

2. Ibid.

3. Federal Reserve Bank of St. Louis, Federal Reserve Economic Data, "All Employees, Manufacturing," https://fred.stlouisfed.org/series/MANEMP.

4. US Bureau of Labor Statistics, Employment Projections, https://www.bls.gov/emp/tables/employment-by-major-industry-sector.htm.

5. White House, Private Investments by State, https://www.whitehouse.gov/invest/.

started in 2023[6] raise the possibility that once they are fully implemented, the Biden programs could provide considerably more stimulus to manufacturing employment than the early data and projections suggest. Indeed, the analysis in this chapter will show that the Biden programs could increase the demand for manufacturing workers by over 8 percent, with a sizable number of states, some of which are key election battleground states, experiencing considerably larger percentage increases in demand. And since the tabulations of investment intentions are likely to grow over time, this would be a conservative estimate of the increase in demand, although this increased demand would also be offset by the dislocation of workers producing fossil-fuel-based manufacturing products such as chemicals and automobiles with internal combustion engines.

However, even if the programs are successful, they are unlikely to be a significant driver of more inclusive growth for people and places in the United States as a whole. Manufacturing has an important role to play in producing the hardware necessary for achieving the administration's goals with respect to infrastructure, the digital revolution, and the green transition and the more optimistic projections indicate the sector will make important contributions to the goals of these programs. Workers in manufacturing also earn premium wages based on their levels of education (Langdon and Lehrman 2012). But in 2022 only 8.1 percent of US full- and part-time jobs remained in manufacturing. Moreover, the bias toward hiring more skilled workers in high-tech manufacturing sectors is strong. This means that even if the high-end projections of the manufacturing employment demand prove accurate, the programs are unlikely to improve the opportunities of most workers without college degrees or to help most disadvantaged places. Indeed, in the aggregate the impact of these programs on manufacturing employment is likely to account for less than 1 percent of overall US employment (table 10.1).

This chapter addresses the effects of the Biden programs. The first section describes the three major domestic programs—the Bipartisan Infrastructure Law, the CHIPS and Science Act, and the Inflation Reduction Act of 2022 (IRA) in some detail—and reports the results of several early studies on their expected impacts on manufacturing employment. The second section provides larger estimates of the impacts of the programs on national and state employment, based on announcements of private sector investment intensions. This section also considers whether the programs are adequate for revitalizing disadvantaged communities and meeting the

---

6. Federal Reserve Bank of St. Louis, Federal Reserve Economic Data, "Total Construction Spending: Manufacturing in the United States," https://fred.stlouisfed.org/series/TLMFGCONS.

Table 10.1
Impact of announced Biden program investments on additional employment in 2025, by state

State	Manufacturing employment	Total employment	Additional employment	Percent increase in manufacturing employment	Percent increase in total employment
Arizona	191,537	3,235,617	157,238	82.1%	4.9%
West Virginia	46,867	716,184	24,709	52.7%	3.5%
Wyoming	9,874	293,005	4,493	45.5%	1.5%
Idaho	74,223	873,632	33,694	45.4%	3.9%
New Mexico	29,246	886,408	8,985	30.7%	1.0%
Nevada	66,045	1,542,578	15,724	23.8%	1.0%
New York	427,631	9,688,468	98,835	23.1%	1.0%
Texas	933,268	14,012,873	166,223	17.8%	1.2%
Georgia	424,304	5,033,591	74,126	17.5%	1.5%
Utah	151,684	1,775,773	24,709	16.3%	1.4%
Louisiana	135,282	2,019,083	20,216	14.9%	1.0%
Kansas	170,469	1,515,944	20,216	11.9%	1.3%

table continues

Table 10.1 continued

Impact of announced Biden program investments on additional employment in 2025, by state

State	Manufacturing employment	Total employment	Additional employment	Percent increase in manufacturing employment	Percent increase in total employment
Kentucky	254,769	2,080,741	29,201	11.5%	1.4%
Massachusetts	240,602	3,813,133	24,709	10.3%	0.6%
Ohio	692,343	5,683,355	69,634	10.1%	1.2%
Virginia	247,237	4,294,144	24,709	10.0%	0.6%
Tennessee	371,054	3,335,683	35,940	9.7%	1.1%
South Carolina	263,976	2,328,358	24,709	9.4%	1.1%
North Dakota	27,705	450,760	2,246	8.1%	0.5%
Michigan	616,276	4,494,627	49,418	8.0%	1.1%
Top 10 states	2,354,679	38,058,128	608,735	25.85%	1.60%
Next 10 states	3,019,713	30,015,828	300,998	9.97%	1.00%
Rest of states	7,513,809	89,536,503	200,946	2.67%	0.22%
Total	12,888,200	157,610,459	1,110,679	8.62%	0.70%

Note: Manufacturing employment baseline in 2022 for Wyoming was calculated averaging the manufacturing employment levels between 2018 and 2021.

Sources: US Bureau of Economic Analysis, Fixed Assets and Regional Data Employment by Industry; US Bureau of Labor Statistics, Employment Projections; and the White House, whitehouse.gov.

needs of displaced workers for adjustment assistance and skills acquisition. The third section assesses the claims that Biden's trade policies, which the administration has characterized as "worker-centric," are likely to enhance worker welfare. The final section concludes that even if the domestic programs have their intended impacts in increasing demand for manufacturing employment, they need to be supplemented with the more comprehensive policies that assist all displaced workers and left-behind places, described in chapter 11.

What Is in the Biden Programs?

The effects on US workers from Biden's programs will come primarily from the administration's three main domestic economic programs and trade policies. This section considers each in turn.

The Bipartisan Infrastructure Law

The Bipartisan Infrastructure Law (Infrastructure Investment and Jobs Act), enacted in 2021, seeks to "rebuild America's roads, bridges, and rails; expand access to clean drinking water; ensure every American has access to high-speed Internet; tackle the climate crisis; advance environmental justice; and invest in communities that have too often been left behind."[7] It includes the Build America, Buy America program, which establishes a domestic procurement preference for all federal financial assistance in the program. The program requires all iron, steel, manufactured products, and construction materials used in the act's infrastructure projects to be produced in the United States. It also provides funds for adopting electric school buses and building charging stations for electric vehicles (EVs). The legislation will invest $7.5 billion to build out a national network of EV chargers in the United States. This is a critical step in the president's strategy to fight the climate crisis, and it will create good US manufacturing jobs.[8]

The program increases infrastructure spending by $550 billion over five years. According to a simulation by Suarez-Cuesta, Latorre, and Lawrence (2022), the bill will add 565,000–640,000 jobs, the majority in construction.[9] The new construction jobs will increase construction employment by

---

7. White House, Fact Sheet: The Bipartisan Infrastructure Deal, Briefing Room Statement, November 6, 2021, https://www.whitehouse.gov/briefing-room/statements-releases/2021/11/06/fact-sheet-the-bipartisan-infrastructure-deal/.

8. Ibid.

9. The estimates depend on whether the additional spending is financed through domestic saving or foreign borrowing.

6.9 percent over its 2022 level.[10] As the federal government will pay union wage rates in the projects it funds, the program will create relatively high-paying jobs for the mostly male workers who work in the sector, many of whom do not have college degrees.[11] Suarez-Cuesta, Latorre, and Lawrence estimate that the program will raise wages in the economy by about 3.4 percent and reduce income inequality marginally, by raising labor's share of total income from 54.4 percent to between 55.3 and 55.5 percent after it is fully implemented. Although the program will affect a relatively small share of the US labor market, it provides a significant medium-term boost to construction employment and enhances inclusive growth, both by providing additional employment opportunities and by improving both the physical and virtual access of communities in outlying areas to other markets and people, which should enhance economic development in these places.

The CHIPS and Science Act

The CHIPS and Science Act, enacted in 2022, appropriates $24 billion for tax credits for firms building semiconductor plants and $52.7 billion for other semiconductor projects, including $39 billion for programs that promote US-based semiconductor production.[12] The Department of Commerce will also allocate $2 billion for producing legacy chips used in automobiles and defense systems in the United States and $13.2 billion for semiconductor research and development (R&D) development (Badlam et al. 2022). The act also includes funding for a new directorate at the National Science Foundation to strengthen the commercialization of research and technology in a wide range of other cutting-edge technologies, in order to help ensure that "what is invented in America is made in America."[13] The act authorizes but does not appropriate an additional $179 billion for R&D on a wide range of advanced technologies.

---

10. Suarez-Cuesta, Latorre, and Lawrence (2022) estimate that construction employment will increase by 538,000. Aggregate construction employment in 2022 was 7.75 million (Federal Reserve Bank of St. Louis, Federal Reserve Economic Data, https://fred.stlouisfed.org/series/USCONS).

11. As in manufacturing, a large share of construction jobs are held by workers without college degrees, especially among men. Charles, Hurst, and Notowidigdo (2016) note that the housing bubble masked the decline in manufacturing employment.

12. For an analysis of how the Department of Commerce should allocate these funds, see Hunt (2022b).

13. White House, Fact Sheet: CHIPS and Science Act, Briefing Room Statement, August 9, 2022, https://www.whitehouse.gov/briefing-room/statements-releases/2022/08/09/fact-sheet-chips-and-science-act-will-lower-costs-create-jobs-strengthen-supply-chains-and-counter-china/.

The ultimate impact of the CHIPS program is hard to estimate, because the amount of US employment and spending it will generate will depend on (1) how the private sector responds to the tax incentives, (2) the criteria the Department of Commerce uses to allocate funds under its grant program, (3) whether state and local governments provide additional funds to supplement the programs,[14] and (4) whether Congress appropriates the additional R&D funds (a prospect that appears unlikely in the short run).

According to a 2021 study commissioned by the Semiconductor Industry Association and conducted by global advisory firm Oxford Economics, the US semiconductor industry employed 277,000 domestic workers in 2020 (185,000 in semiconductor manufacturing, and 92,000 in firms that design semiconductors but do not produce them). The study reports that 56 percent of the semiconductor workforce had at least a college degree, 9 percent an associate degree, and 36 percent a high school degree or less. Excluding design, more than 60 percent of workers in semiconductor manufacturing did not have a college degree.

Written just before passage of the CHIPS Act, the study estimated that a $50 billion federal investment program would stimulate the building of 10 new fabrication plants and result in an annual increase of 185,000 temporary jobs during the build-out phase (2021–26). In the long run, employment of semiconductor industry workers would increase by 42,000, increasing the size of the semiconductor workforce to 319,000. A similar study by Will Hunt (2022a) estimates that the CHIPS Act will lead to the construction of eight new plants and the hiring of 27,000 new workers in the long run.

Even if the act increases employment of more non-college-educated workers within manufacturing, it is likely to increase relative demand for college workers in the economy as a whole. Both studies suggest that most of the new permanent employees will have at least a college degree and could make employment in the industry even more skill intensive.[15] Hunt, for example, estimates that employment of skilled engineers and software

---

14. The CHIPS program will assess companies' proposals for grants and loans partly on the basis of support from state and local governments (Tyson and Mendonca 2023). Eligibility will also be contingent on the provision of affordable childcare services to employees. For a critical response to this provision, see Michelle Bezark, "Perspective: Addressing the Child Care Crisis Will Take More than the CHIPS Act," *Washington Post*, March 15, 2023 (https://www.washingtonpost.com/made-by-history/2023/03/14/chips-act-child-care/).

15. Hatton et al. (2023) estimate that 230,000 new workers would be required to double the US global share of semiconductors (from 12 to 24 percent). They estimate how many workers already have the skills and could use them in new jobs, how many would need to be trained, and which areas would suffer shortages of workers and where they would come from.

developers will have to grow by 19 percent and that of low-skilled technical workers by 11 percent. He argues that the number of skilled workers required exceeds the availability of such workers in the United States and therefore requires an increase in immigration.[16]

These studies estimate that a program of magnitude similar to the $52 billion in the CHIPS Act would create 27,000–42,000 permanent manufacturing jobs. If these jobs mirror the skill proportions of the existing semiconductor workforce, using the 42,000 estimates would mean an additional 23,500 jobs for workers with college degrees and 18,500 jobs for non-college-educated workers.

This bias toward increasing demand for more educated workers will be even stronger if the $179 billion for the additional relative programs authorized by the CHIPS Act is appropriated. These programs call for the "R&D, and commercialization of leading-edge technologies, such as quantum computing, AI, robotics, clean energy, and nanotechnology, and a bigger, more science, technology, engineering, and math (STEM) workforce."

Although it may well enhance US competitiveness, productivity, and supply chain resilience, the CHIPS Act is thus likely to marginally increase rather than reduce inequality in US wages along the lines of skill.

The Inflation Reduction Act

The Inflation Reduction Act of 2022 (IRA) will expand US renewable energy manufacturing capacity and production and secure domestic supply chains for critical materials that serve as inputs for clean energy technology production. It incentivizes investment in and production of clean energy, transport, and manufacturing. It also stimulates demand through incentives to purchase EVs for which final assembly takes place in North America and to use batteries in which the minerals are either mined or refined in the United States or a country with which the United States has a free trade agreement. The act includes additional incentives for the purchase of energy-efficient appliances, solar panels, efficient insulation and heating, and home batteries.

---

16. A Brookings Institution study (Muro, Parillo, and Ross 2023) provides a contrary view. It claims that 60 percent of the permanent long-run jobs in manufacturing semiconductors in 2021 did not require a college degree. It used the US Bureau of Labor Statistics' definition for semiconductor employment, which is less comprehensive than the definition in the semiconductor industry study (Semiconductor Industry Association and Oxford Economics 2021), which includes workers involved in semiconductor design firms that do no fabrication.

The use of credit subsidies, rather than taxes on emission, increases the political acceptability of the IRA.[17] However, as the credits depend on private responses rather than public outlays and are not capped, it is more difficult to predict both the climate and budgetary impacts of the act.

The IRA seeks to achieve multiple objectives. Clean energy technologies that meet minimal eligibility requirements receive a base-level production tax credit. Projects meeting labor requirements, such as paying prevailing wages and providing apprenticeship programs, receive a tax credit that is five times higher than the base rate. Additional increases to the base credit are available for projects that meet domestic content requirements, projects located in "energy communities" (defined as communities currently dependent on fossil fuel mining and energy production based on fossil fuels), and projects in low-income communities. These complex eligibility requirements for IRA subsidies reflect the approach President Biden has adopted in all of these programs.

Seeking multiple goals through these programs could make them more expensive—and thus less effective in achieving their core objectives.[18] Using trade protection through local content to increase domestic manufacturing, even when national security is not at risk, will raise the prices of EVs and the steel and aluminum required to build the wind turbines and solar panels that are vital for the Biden climate policies.[19] Setting complicated conditions to qualify for climate and chips subsidies also requires time-consuming regulatory approvals, which will constrain implementation and reduce the program's cost effectiveness.

Given the complexity of the IRA, it is not surprising that studies come to very different conclusions about its likely effects and costs. According to Meghan Mahajan et al. (2022), by 2030 the program will reduce US emissions to 37–43 percent below 2005 levels, while John Bistline et al. (2022) estimate reductions of 32–42 percent—significant progress toward achieving the US goal of reducing emissions by 50–52 percent below 2005 levels. The US Energy Information Administration (US EIA 2021) estimates much lower reductions, of 27–34 percent below 2005 levels by 2030.

---

17. One exception in the IRA was the introduction of a methane waste emissions charge for oil and gas facilities reporting annual methane emissions of more than 25,000 metric tons of CO_2 equivalent gas. This charge is the first federal fee on any kind of greenhouse gas emissions (Westmore and Leandro 2023).

18. For an argument that paying prevailing wages has a relatively small impact on the cost and speed of deployment of utility-scale solar photovoltaics and wind power, see Mayfield and Jenkins (2021).

19. The implementing regulations reduced discrimination against foreign vehicles by exempting autos that are leased. See Bown (2023).

Roughly two-thirds of the baseline spending is allocated to provisions for which the potential federal credit/incentive is uncapped. The Congressional Budget Office (CBO) estimates that these incentives will cost $271 billion and the full program $392 billion.[20] Bistline et al. (2022) estimate the uncapped costs at $780 billion—more than three times the CBO levels—which would put the costs of the entire program at $900 billion. Goldman Sachs estimates an even higher cost ($1.2 trillion).[21]

Effects of the Domestic Biden Programs

The Biden programs have been presented as helping American workers without college degrees and workers in places that have been left behind. How successful are they likely to be in achieving these goals?

Employment Effects: Will the Biden Programs Lead to a "Manufacturing Renaissance"?

The promotion of manufacturing employment is central to the Biden programs. The sector is not only important for the role it plays in achieving the goals for semiconductors and clean energy; it is also viewed as key to revitalizing the middle class and the many towns, especially in the Rust Belt (defined here as Illinois, Indiana, Michigan, Ohio, Pennsylvania, and Wisconsin) that have been hard hit by deindustrialization.

This view is supported by a 2022 study by the McKinsey Global Institute (Carr et al. 2022). *Delivering the US Manufacturing Renaissance* argues that a reindustrialization program could increase US employment by creating 1.5 million "direct and indirect" jobs and increase US GDP by 15 percent. In August 2022, the administration claimed that its policies had achieved "massive gains for American manufacturing" and that since President Biden had assumed office manufacturing employment had grown "faster than under any other president."[22] Between January 2021 and August 2022, it pointed out, manufacturing employment increased by 668,000 jobs. But this characterization is heavily influenced by the COVID shutdowns. By August 2023, manufacturing employment was only 195,000 more than

---

20. Congressional Budget Office and Joint Committee on Taxation, Summary Estimated Budgetary Effects of Public Law 117–169, to Provide for Reconciliation Pursuant to Title II of S. Con. Res. 14, September 7, 2022.

21. Editorial Board, "The Real Cost of the Inflation Reduction Act Subsidies: $1.2 Trillion," *Wall Street Journal*, March 24, 2023, https://www.wsj.com/articles/inflation-reduction-act-subsidies-cost-goldman-sachs-report-5623cd29.

22. White House, The Biden-Harris Economic Blueprint.

in January 2020 when COVID struck the United States.[23] By comparison, overall, US employment increased by 4.44 million over the same period. Manufacturing thus accounted only for 4.6 percent of the employment increase over the period.[24]

Early studies of the impact of the Biden programs on manufacturing indicated that their impact on manufacturing employment was likely to be fairly modest over the long run. The study of the Infrastructure Act by Suarez-Cuesta, Latorre, and Lawrence (2022) projected a long-run total increase in manufacturing employment of up to 200,000. The study of the CHIPS Act by the Semiconductor Industry Association and Oxford Economics (2021) projected a 42,000 increase in the employment of semi-conductor industry workers. Using an Energy Policy Simulator developed by Energy Innovation: Policy and Technology LLC, Mahajan et al. (2022) concluded that the IRA could employ up to 404,000 additional workers in manufacturing. These initial studies imply an increase of around 655,000, equal to 5 percent of manufacturing employment in August 2023 and 0.41 percent of total US employment in 2023.[25]

Every year, the US Bureau of Labor Statistics (BLS) releases projections of US employment over the decade to come. It uses a comprehensive measure of the US labor force that includes not only nonfarm wage and salary workers but also people who work in agriculture or are self-employed. In September 2023, it issued a report that projected that US employment would increase by 4.665 million jobs between 2022 and 2032 while manufacturing employment would decline by 113,500 jobs over the 2022–32 decade.[26] As a result, by their comprehensive measure, the manufacturing employment share of total employment in the United States would *fall* to 7.5 percent, down from 7.8 percent in 2022. This analysis presumably took account of the anticipated impact of the Biden programs passed a year earlier. Together with the studies cited above, the BLS projections suggest that the claim that manufacturing employment was poised to flourish as a result of the programs did not seem warranted.

Notwithstanding these studies, it became increasingly common to read about an imminent manufacturing renaissance. At about the same

---

23. Federal Reserve Bank of St. Louis, Federal Reserve Economic Data, "All Employees, Manufacturing," https://fred.stlouisfed.org/series/MANEMP.

24. Federal Reserve Bank of St. Louis, Federal Reserve Economic Data, "All Employees, Total Nonfarm," https://fred.stlouisfed.org/series/PAYEMS.

25. Total employment is obtained by adding nonfarm employment to agricultural employment in the Federal Reserve Economic Data.

26. US Bureau of Labor Statistics, Employment Projections 2022–2032, https://www.bls.gov/news.release/ecopro.nr0.htm.

time BLS issued its outlook, in a column titled "The American Renaissance Is Already at Hand," *New York Times* columnist David Brooks wrote about "a torrid manufacturing boom."[27] His colleague, Nobel Prize–winning economist Paul Krugman, suggested that the new industrial policy had already generated a huge wave of private investment in manufacturing, even though very little federal money had yet been distributed.[28]

The more pessimistic estimates may have failed to take account of the possibilities of a much larger impact from the private sector in response not only to federal subsidies but also to the tax breaks in the CHIPS Act, the additional subsidies provided by state and local governments, and changed views about the desirability of reshoring production in light of the instability that had been revealed in global supply chains. A more optimistic view also seemed to be supported by the rapid acceleration in manufacturing construction spending, which soared from $108.8 billion a year in June 2022 to $195.8 billion a year in June 2023.[29] The White House has presented evidence in support of this view and has kept a running total as manufacturing firms announce their plans for new investments in clean energy, EVs, and semiconductors. As of August 15, 2023, it reported that since President Biden assumed office, these announced investments totaled $503 billion.[30]

The White House released details of these investments by state.[31] They can be used to roughly estimate the number of additional manufacturing jobs that these investments could generate. Because it will take some time for the investments to reach fruition, it seems appropriate to estimate the additional employment that will occur in 2025.

The most recent data for the net capital stock in manufacturing available at the time of writing are for 2021, when it was valued at $4.776 trillion.[32] The estimate assumes that absent these investments, the capital

---

27. David Brooks, "The American Renaissance Is Already at Hand," *New York Times*, September 7, 2023, https://www.nytimes.com/2023/09/07/opinion/economy-china-america-decline.html?searchResultPosition=1.

28. Paul Krugman, "Biden and America's Green Push," *New York Times*, August 17, 2023, https://www.nytimes.com/2023/08/17/opinion/biden-green-ira-industrial-trade.html?action=click&module=RelatedLinks&pgtype=Article.

29. See Federal Reserve Bank of St. Louis, Federal Reserve Economic Data, "Total Construction Spending: Manufacturing in the United States," https://fred.stlouisfed.org/series/TLMFGCONS.

30. The *Financial Times* undertook a similar exercise. It reached optimistic conclusions about the prospects of US manufacturing growth.

31. White House, "Private Investments by State," https://www.whitehouse.gov/invest/.

32. Bureau of Economic Analysis, Table 3.1ESI. Current-Cost Net Stock of Private Fixed Assets by Industry, https://apps.bea.gov (accessed on September 21, 2023).

stock would grow at the same 5.1 percent annual rate it averaged between 2016 and 2021, reaching $5.832 trillion in 2025. The announced investments would increase the stock by 8.62 percent in 2025.

These estimates also assume that the capital-labor ratio in manufacturing remains unchanged and that manufacturing employment in 2025 would thus also be higher by 8.62 percent.[33] Using data for manufacturing employment from mid-2023, they assume that manufacturing employment grows at the same annual rate as projected by BLS for all employment over the decade from 2022 to 2032 (0.3 percent). This assumption leads to an estimate of the total baseline number of manufacturing jobs in 2025 of 12.878 million and an additional increased demand for 1.111 million more workers due to the Biden announcements. Without taking account of jobs that could be displaced, for example, by closure of fossil-fuel-based mines and power plants, and assuming these are all manufacturing jobs, this would imply an upper-bound increase in the share of manufacturing employment in total employment from 8.2 to 8.9 percent.[34]

The US Bureau of Economic Analysis (BEA) reports total and manufacturing employment by state for 2022. These are also estimated for 2025 assuming growth of 0.3 percent annually. The estimated demand for 1.11 million jobs is allocated to each state in proportion to the investments announced for that state.[35] Table 10.1 ranks the states based on the percentage increase in their manufacturing job demand associated with the announced investments.[36]

Several states are projected to experience very substantial increases in demand for manufacturing employment. The top seven are Arizona (82.1 percent increase), West Virginia (52.7 percent), Wyoming (45.5 percent),

33. An alternative but more complicated approach would be to apply a traditional (Solow) growth model assuming a constant capital-output ratio and estimate employment with assumptions about labor productivity growth.

34. As some of the investments could increase employment in other sectors, such as utilities and services, and some of the planned investments may not be implemented, this estimate probably errs on the upside of the actual increase in manufacturing.

35. The BEA reports only full- and part-time employment rates. Those rates were converted to a persons working measure by using the national ratio of full- and part-time employment to the number of persons engaged in production for 2021 available in BEA National Income Accounts, Tables 6.4D and 6.8D, http://apps.bea.gov/iTable. Employment growth is assumed to match the growth in nonfarm employment until mid-2023 and then to grow by 0.3 percent a year until 2025. The same conversion factor and growth assumptions were used to adjust the state employment and manufacturing data available at https://apps.bea.gov/iTable.

36. Alaska, Hawaii, and Washington, DC were not included in the analysis because comprehensive data for them were not available.

Idaho (45.4 percent), New Mexico (30.7 percent) Nevada (23.8 percent), and New York (23.1 percent). The average projected increase in manufacturing employment demand is 25.85 percent for the top 10 beneficiary states and 9.97 percent for the next 10. Forty percent of US states in the sample are projected to see increases in manufacturing employment demand of at least 8 percent.

In a few states the effect on overall employment could be significant. The largest aggregate impacts include (4.9 percent in Arizona, 3.9 percent in Idaho, and 3.5 percent in West Virginia). But the increase is at or below 1.5 percent of total employment in the remaining states and on average, the impact on the overall economy is equal to only 0.7 percent of employment.

The programs are not going to provide a disproportionate boost to manufacturing employment demand in depressed states. Regressing the percentage change in employment due to announced investments on the state's unemployment rates in 2022 shows that, on average, having a 1 percentage point higher unemployment rate is associated with a 0.12 percentage point increase in employment added due to announced investments in the state, which is not statistically different from zero. This indicates that the policies are not especially targeted to the states that have higher unemployment rates.

The use of the term *renaissance* to describe the impacts on manufacturing denotes a rebirth. But a rebirth would mean that the new additions to manufacturing employment would be concentrated in the Rust Belt, once the American industrial heartland. They are not. The Rust Belt states with the greatest percentage estimated increases in manufacturing employment demand are Ohio (ranked 15th) and Michigan (ranked 20th). In 2025, without the Biden programs, manufacturing employment in all Rust Belt states would be 71.1 percent of their 2000 level (3.49 million versus 4.91 million). With the programs, assuming these states are not negatively impacted by any displacement of manufacturing jobs due to the IRA, manufacturing employment demand would rise to 74.49 percent of the 2000 manufacturing employment level, and overall employment in Ohio and Michigan could increase by 1.23 and 1.10 percent, respectively. While there will be some impressive growth in manufacturing employment in some states, it will not occur in the states where large declines in manufacturing employment occurred over the past two decades.

This exercise reveals that even large percentage increases in manufacturing employment are too small to affect the overall US labor market.

These estimates do not taken account of the jobs that could be lost from decarbonization.[37] The White House has decomposed the announced

---

37. For an analysis, see Hanson (2023) and Lawrence (2024).

investments in major categories.[38] It is likely that a quarter of the cumulated investments announced in September 2023 will be in electric vehicles and batteries. As the discussion in box 10.1 suggests, these investments could be associated with job losses in the assembly of vehicles with combustion engines and their parts; the production of clean power similarly could lead to job losses in petroleum refining; and the jobs in clean energy manufacturing to job displacement of workers in fossil fuel-based manufacturing jobs. In addition the investments in clean power could show up as jobs in the utilities sector rather than manufacturing.

All told, as a strategy for boosting manufacturing in numerous states the Biden programs look likely to succeed, but as a strategy for "building the economy from the bottom up and the middle out" it is totally inadequate.

Impact on Places

The Biden administration has made special efforts to help depressed communities in all three of these programs. The Bipartisan Infrastructure Law provides $65 billion to ensure that everyone in the United States has access to affordable high-speed internet. This provision is important to the estimated 30 million Americans who live in rural and other communities that do not have broadband services that provide internet at minimally acceptable speeds.[39] Poorer Americans will also benefit disproportionately from improved public transit, the cleanup of Superfund and brownfield sites, and improvements in providing clean water and eliminating lead service lines.

The location of innovative manufacturing (and service) industries in the United States that are being targeted by most of the programs is concentrated geographically; an open competition for grants would therefore probably give the grants to places that already have these industries. Superstar cities dominate employment in R&D-intensive industries. Between 2005 and 2017, five cities—Boston, San Diego, San Francisco, San Jose, and Seattle, which together accounted for just 5.8 percent of the US population—accounted for 90 percent of the country's "innovation sector employment growth," increasing their share of such employment from 17.6 percent in 2005 to 22.5 percent in 2017 (Atkinson, Muro, and Whiton 2019). As of 2017, a third of the country's innovation jobs were in just 16 of the country's more than 3,000 counties, and more than half were concentrated in 41 counties (Atkinson, Muro, and Whiton 2019). In 2016, 7 of the 10 highest-

---

38. White House, "President Joe Biden: Investing in America," https://www.whitehouse.gov/invest/.

39. White House Fact Sheet: The Bipartisan Infrastructure Deal.

Box 10.1

How will the switch to electric vehicles affect employment in the automotive sector?

Internal combustion engine (ICE) autos and battery-based electric vehicles (EVs) have fundamental differences that affect their production and the number and types of workers needed to build them. Conventional gas and diesel vehicles have complex engines with pistons, drive trains, and gear transmissions that are produced in multiple plants by highly specialized components producers. In contrast, EVs have a motor with far fewer parts and a power train that generates variable speeds without the need for gears. ICEs have around 1,400 parts, EVs about 200 (Casper and Sundin 2021). The most complicated assembly work in EVs involves building the battery pack from thousands of battery cells.

The switch from ICE vehicles to EVs could reduce total employment in car manufacturing but increase demand for higher-skilled labor. It would reduce the need for mechanical machining and increase the need for testing and assembly (Casper and Sundin 2021).[1]

A paper by the United Auto Workers quotes Ford and Volkswagen executives as saying that EVs will reduce labor hours by 30 percent.[2] The jobs that now involve engineering and assembling parts such as pistons, gears, and drive trains for ICE vehicles will be supplanted by jobs that involve assembling battery packs and electric motors.

In 2022, 1.013 million workers were employed in US automobile production,[3] of whom 460,000 worked in assembly and 552,800 in manufacturing components, including 55,400 workers who produced gasoline engines and parts and 74,900 who produced power train components.[4] The switch to EVs could reduce the demand for workers

box continues

---

1. For media coverage of this issue, see Mike Colias, "Gas Engines, and the People Behind Them, Are Cast Aside for Electric Vehicles," *Wall Street Journal*, July 23, 2021, https://www.wsj.com/articles/gas-engines-cast-aside-electric-vehicles-job-losses-detroit-11627046285; Tom Krisher and John Seewer, "Autoworkers Face Uncertain Future in an Era of Electric Cars," AP News, February 11, 2021, https://apnews.com/article/technology-ohio-coronavirus-pandemic-toledo-34c63cb0747518d58b4a29de3797f2be; Michael Sheetz, "Electric Vehicles Could Cost the Auto Industry Millions of Jobs, a Top Analyst Says," CNBC, March 15, 2019, https://www.cnbc.com/2019/03/15/morgan-stanley-electric-vehicles-will-cost-millions-of-auto-jobs.html.

2. "Autoworkers Face Uncertain Future in an Era of Electric Cars," *Autoblog*, February 13, 2021, https://www.autoblog.com/2021/ 02/13/uaw-uncertain-future-evs/.

3. US Bureau of Labor Statistics, "Automotive Industry: Employment, Earnings, and Hours," https://www.bls.gov/iag/tgs/iagauto.htm.

4. According to statistics from the Bureau of Labor Statistics, in 2021, 54,000 workers produced motor vehicle gasoline engines and parts (NAICS 33631), out of total employment in motor vehicle parts of 539,000 (NAICS 3363); another 73,000 workers produced power train components (NAICS 33635).

Box 10.1 continued
How will the switch to electric vehicles affect employment in the automotive sector?

in the automobile industry by 268,000 (26.5 percent).[5] As some workers could be retrained as battery workers, this figure represents an upper bound of the number of workers displaced. However, all of the Big Three plan to produce their batteries in a joint venture with a Korean firm.[6] Production and sourcing decisions could be highly disruptive if automakers buy batteries from nonunion firms or firms located outside the United States or produce them internally rather than buying them from US ICE parts suppliers. If other EV makers adopt Tesla's production methods, these changes will be skill biased, with demand for software engineers rising and demand for mechanical engineers falling. There are also likely to be changes in the way vehicles are sold (fewer showrooms) and less need for services such as oil changes.

The competitive dynamics of the transition to EVs is also likely to alter the shares of the market held by firms selling in both the United States and Europe, a process that could lead to additional job churning and loss. If producers such as Tesla, BYD, and numerous other Chinese firms expand their global market shares but market demand for cars in the United States and the European Union does not expand, employment in firms that historically produced ICEs is likely to fall.[7] Such changes could lead to plant closures. As a result, the switch to EVs would not only affect aggregate auto employment, it would also likely affect market shares and the location of production.

New jobs will also be created. Vehicle electrification is expected to generate demand for labor in three main areas: the design and development of EV models; the production of batteries that power them; and the manufacture, installation, and maintenance of charging infrastructure. The shift to this technology will cause major disruptions, however, and many lower-skilled workers could suffer from it.

---

5. "Autoworkers Face Uncertain Future in an Era of Electric Cars," *Autoblog*, February 13, 2021, https://www.autoblog.com/2021/ 02/13/uaw-uncertain-future-evs/.

6. David Ferris, "How Korea Underpins America's EV Dreams," EnergyWire, June 6, 2022, https://www.eenews.net/articles/how-korea-underpins-americas-ev-dreams/.

7. In principle, the IRA provides its full subsidies of $7,500 only to firms that have their final assembly in North America and use batteries with components made in the United States or a country with which the United States has a free trade agreement. The ruling by the Treasury Department that these requirements do not apply to cars that are leased could offset this advantage, however.

earning Metropolitan Statistical Areas (MSAs) were in states that were in the top 10 in terms of per capita public R&D (Gruber and Johnson 2019, 141) and none of the top 10—or even the top 20—highest-paying MSAs was in a state that was in the bottom half of public spending on R&D per capita.

In both the United States and the United Kingdom, central government spending on R&D is highly concentrated geographically. In the United States, Maryland, Virginia, and the District of Columbia were among the top five recipients of federal R&D funding per worker in 2020.[40]

R&D spending in the United Kingdom also disproportionally benefits economically stronger regions (Stansbury, Turner, and Balls 2023). The Golden Triangle (Oxford, Cambridge, and London) accounted for 41 percent of public sector spending on R&D in the United Kingdom according to data developed by the Centre for Cities.[41] Given the fixed costs of building research facilities, attracting the best researchers, and building reputations for success, new money typically follows old, even in open competitions.

To counteract the concentration of R&D, the CHIPS Act instructs the Department of Commerce to spend $10 billion over five years to establish 20 regional R&D technology and innovation hubs in areas that are not currently leading technology centers. This figure represents about a seventh of the funds appropriated for programs and subsidies in the act; if the full $278 billion that has been authorized for R&D is spent, this part of the program will account for just 3.6 percent of the total. These programs will help diversify US R&D geographically to some degree, but the relationship between research and innovation is complex. These hubs can contribute significantly to local growth directly through increased R&D spending and to the diversification of R&D opportunities, but it is less certain that they will stimulate additional local growth beyond their direct effects. The UK evidence provided by the Centre for Cities suggests that diversification of R&D requires other conditions, such as the presence of innovative firms, to be met.

The IRA is supposed to devote 40 percent of its expenditures to depressed communities.[42] It provides special bonus incentives in the form of tax credits for investment and clean energy production in "energy com-

---

40. National Science Board, "Federal R&D Obligations per Employed Worker," https://ncses.nsf.gov/indicators/states/indicator/federal-rd-obligations-per-employed-worker.

41. Kathrin Enenkel, "How Will More R&D Spending Level up the UK?," Centre for Cities blog, September 14, 2023, https://www.centreforcities.org/blog/how-will-an-more-rd-spending-level-up-the-uk/.

42. See the memo on the Justice40 Initiative, https://www.whitehouse.gov/wp-content/uploads/2023/01/M-23-09_Signed_CEQ_CPO.pdf.

munities." Daniel Raimi and Sophie Pesek (2022, abstract) make a convincing case that the credits are poorly targeted, however, and that the law is "unlikely to steer investment specifically toward communities that will be most heavily affected by the fossil fuel transition."[43] In addition, it is questionable whether the optimal adjustment response of most of these communities is to continue to produce energy (albeit renewable). Many of these communities' opportunities probably lie elsewhere, but the act does not provide enough funds for community adjustment outside the energy area. Some workers who are dislocated might do better by moving away, but the act does not provide them with assistance to do so.[44]

Impact on Worker Adjustment

According to National Security Advisor Jake Sullivan, "As [President Biden has] often said, when he hears 'climate,' he thinks 'jobs.' He believes that building a 21st-century clean-energy economy is one of the most significant growth opportunities of the twenty-first century—but that to harness that opportunity, America needs a deliberate, hands-on investment strategy to pull forward innovation, drive down costs, and create good jobs."[45]

Studies confirm the president's view that the net employment impact of the green transition in the United States as well as in most US states is likely to be positive. Detailed simulations by the Princeton Net-Zero for America Project (Larson et al. 2020) predict a net increase in the number of energy supply jobs in the United States of 0.3–0.6 percent of the labor force by 2030 and 0.5–2.5 percent by 2050. Accentuating the *net* positive

---

43. According to Raimi and Pesek (2022, 1), "Communities can qualify if they have brownfield sites, above average unemployment rates and certain threshold levels of tax revenues from fossil fuels. Although the law is likely to channel additional resources to certain regions with high levels of dependence on fossil fuels for jobs and tax revenue, such as Alaska, Pennsylvania, West Virginia, Wyoming, and parts of Ohio and the Gulf Coast, it excludes other regions with high levels of dependence, such as North Dakota, Oklahoma, Utah, and west Texas. In addition, the IRA appears to include large swathes of states where fossil fuel extraction, processing, and use do not play a major role in the economy, such as California, Maine, Michigan, Oregon, and Washington State."

44. By contrast, earlier programs by the Economic Development Administration under the American Rescue Plan were less constrained and allowed for better tailoring of the programs to community and worker needs. The funds allocated to these programs were only about $3 billion for the whole country, however. See https://www.eda.gov/funding/programs/american-rescue-plan/good-jobs-challenge and https://www.eda.gov/funding/programs/american-rescue-plan/build-back-better.

45. White House, Remarks by National Security Advisor Jake Sullivan on Renewing American Economic Leadership, April 27, 2023, https://www.whitehouse.gov/briefing-room/speeches-remarks/2023/04/27/remarks-by-national-security-advisor-jake-sullivan-on-renewing-american-economic-leadership-at-the-brookings-institution/.

impacts, however, overlooks the fact that as noted some jobs will be lost. Many mines, power plants, fossil fuel producers, and segments of the auto industry that produce parts such as transmissions and combustion engines will have to close (exceptions include companies able to capture their carbon emissions and take advantage of the incentives the IRA offers for production of renewable energy) (Popp et al. 2022). These activities are often highly concentrated geographically, because they were located where energy or oil was cheap and available. Job growth related to renewables could lie elsewhere.

Gordon Hanson has studied the impact on communities of the disruptive shock of the expansion of US trade with China (Autor, Dorn, and Hanson 2013). In Hanson (2023) he points out that the characteristics of the oil-, gas-, coal-, and energy-intensive manufacturing industries, which pay relatively high wages to workers without college degrees, are very similar to those of communities that depended on manufacturing. According to Hanson (2023, 157), "Without improving how local economies respond to job loss, we risk miring more communities in distress." The Biden programs generally do not provide general adjustment assistance for workers who are dislocated by them, even though the impacts of climate policies could be highly disruptive (box 10.1).

Impact on Skills Acquisition

All of the Biden programs fund some worker training, but skills experts have criticized them as inadequate. According to Megan Evans of the National Skills Coalition:

> Despite public commitments from Democrats that job-creating investments in infrastructure and energy would be paired with enough funding for the workforce training that is essential to filling these new jobs, the IRA contains none of the $40 billion for workforce that skills advocates had been pursuing. There is also no funding for strategies the National Skills Coalition network identified as critical for supporting infrastructure and energy job creation, including expanding federal financing for high-quality, short-term programs at community and technical colleges; investing in partnerships between industry, educators, and other workforce experts; and supporting worker access to and success in training for jobs for which businesses are and will be hiring.[46]

---

46. Megan Evans, "Inflation Reduction Act: Limited Funding for Workforce, but Not Enough," National Skills Coalition blog, August 19, 2022, https://nationalskillscoalition. org/blog/news/inflation-reduction-act-limited-funding-for-workforce-but-not-enough/.

The CHIPS Act, for example, favors much more generous provision of immigration visas in principle as a complement for training but firms complain these have not been increased for decades.[47]

All of the bills recognize the importance of human capital, and each provides some support for skills development, primarily through tax credits to employers and funds for local governments (Tyson and Mendonca 2023). But none provides sufficient adjustment assistance for workers and communities that could be hurt by the impact of climate policies on old jobs or enough funding to all workers to find and train for the new jobs that will be needed. These tasks have been left mainly to state and local governments.

Are Biden's Trade Policies "Worker-Centric"?

To promote American production, President Biden strengthened the "Buy American" provisions in his infrastructure bill by raising the required US content to qualify for federal purchases from 55 percent in 2021 to 75 percent by 2029. He also established a "Made in America" office within the Office of Management and Budget, tasked with creating a stronger domestic manufacturing base. He provided over $70 billion dollars in tax breaks and other programs for new US semiconductor plants and semiconductor R&D that will take place in the United States. The IRA grants generous uncapped incentives for spending on US-based investment and production of renewables and carbon capture. It grants additional credits if spending on renewables uses US content. As mentioned earlier, it also rewards qualified consumers who purchase EVs whose final assembly takes place in North America and whose batteries contain minerals and parts made in America or a country with which the United States has a trade agreement.

Several of the president's trade policies also favor some US manufacturing industries, albeit sometimes at the expense of others that use imported inputs. His trade policies generally mirror the protectionist approaches of the Trump administration.[48] President Biden renewed the Trump safeguard tariff protection on US solar panels, for example (although he later

---

47. The number of H-1B visas for skilled workers (65,000 plus 20,000 for workers with master's degrees) has not increased since 2006. The annual allotment for fiscal 2022, which ended in September 2022, was filled by February (American Immigration Council, "The H-1B Visa Program and Its Impact on the US Economy," https://www. americanimmigrationcouncil.org/research/h1b-visa-program-fact-sheet).

48. For a full account, see Chad P. Bown and Melina Kolb, Trump's Trade War Timeline: An Up-to-Date Guide, Peterson Institute for International Economics, https://www.piie. com/blogs/trade-and-investment-policy-watch/trumps-trade-war-timeline-date-guide.

suspended it, to support his climate policies).[49] He maintained the Trump tariffs on steel, aluminum, and a wide range of Chinese goods. He even added duties to Chinese products that Trump had excluded.[50]

US Trade Representative Katherine Tai claims these trade policies are "worker-centric."[51] It is hard to concur with that claim. A worker-centric policy would provide good jobs and raise workers' living standards. By raising input costs, Trump's tariffs reduced US employment by increasing costs in downstream industries and inducing retaliation by trade partners (Flaaen and Pierce 2019). As American consumers ultimately have paid most of the tariffs, the policies also raise prices and reduce worker buying power.[52]

A worker-centric trade policy would defend US workers hurt by unfair foreign trade practices. By refusing to appoint new judges to the World Trade Organization (WTO) Appellate Body or provide guidance for its reform, the United States crippled the WTO dispute settlement system. Although the system has flaws, it has offered important ways to challenge unfair trade practices. Currently, countries that win cases at the initial panel stage of a dispute cannot obtain a final judgment.[53]

A worker-centric policy would promote US exports that pay blue-collar workers premium wages and level the playing field for US exporters (Riker 2010). Other countries continue to lower export barriers to each other in agreements such as the Regional Comprehensive Economic Partnership (RCEP), a free trade agreement among 15 Asia-Pacific countries, and the Comprehensive and Progressive Trans-Pacific Partnership (CPTPP). In contrast, the Biden administration has excluded market access negotiations in its major trade initiative, the Indo-Pacific Economic Framework.

---

49. On June 2022, President Biden declared an emergency and temporarily waived tariffs, including countervailing and antidumping duties on solar panels from Southeast Asian countries. See Bown and Kolb, Trump's Trade War Timeline.

50. See Bown and Kolb, Trump's Trade War Timeline.

51. "Our agenda begins with a commitment to putting workers at the center of our trade policy" (Testimony of US Trade Representative Ambassador Katherine Tai on US Trade Policy Agenda Hearing, Senate Finance Committee, March 31, 2022).

52. See Foy (2019) and National Bureau of Economic Research, US Consumers Have Borne the Brunt of the Current Trade War, NBER Digest no. 5, https://www.nber.org/digest/may19/us-consumers-have-borne-brunt-current-trade-war.

53. See Chad P. Bown, Testimony before the European Parliament Committee on International Trade Hearing on 'Can We Save the WTO Appellate Body?' December 3, 2019, https://www.piie.com/sites/default/files/documents/bown20191203.pdf.

A worker-centric policy would help workers displaced by trade adjust through training and other benefits. The Trade Adjustment Assistance program has helped 100,000 workers a year get this assistance, but unfortunately it applies only to workers affected by trade when it should help all workers dislocated by a variety of factors.[54] In mid-2022, the administration allowed the program to lapse.[55] The move was surprising for an administration whose narrative about previous trade policies is that they failed to help workers who were hurt.[56]

Conclusion

The Biden administration has given the restoration of manufacturing jobs a key role in its plans to aid blue-collar workers and left behind places. But several studies suggest that prospects for increasing the share of manufacturing significantly over the next decade are not promising. The more optimistic announcements of private sector investment intentions suggest that the investment plans announced by the White House as of September 2023 could create 1.1 million new manufacturing jobs. This estimate could exaggerate the impact of the programs if firms fail to follow through on their announcements, and it does not account for the jobs that could be displaced by decarbonization policies. Even if implemented, these investments would have a relatively small impact on total US employment and thus not significantly impact the overall welfare of non-college-educated workers. They would, however, potentially boost manufacturing employment in several states.

The infrastructure program creates a large number of construction jobs in the short run and should boost growth in far-flung communities by improving their infrastructure, but its impact on long-run manufacturing employment will be limited. In the long run, the CHIPS Act is biased toward the employment of college-educated workers. The funds it allocates to create technology hubs could help some communities, but they

---

54. For a report of the program for 2021, see US Department of Labor (2021).

55. See US Department of Labor, Employment and Training Administration, "Trade Adjustment Assistance for Workers," https://www.dol.gov/agencies/eta/tradeact (accessed July 2023).

56. See, for example, the speech by National Security Advisor Jake Sullivan in which he points to the failure of domestic economic policies to adequately help workers hit by trade, especially the "China shock" (White House, Remarks by National Security Advisor Jake Sullivan on Renewing American Economic Leadership at the Brookings Institution, April 27, 2023, https://www.whitehouse.gov/briefing-room/speeches-remarks/2023/04/27/remarks-by-national-security-advisor-jake-sullivan-on-renewing-american-economic-leadership-at-the-brookings-institution.

are unlikely to turn many of the places that are given these awards into superstar locations. The optimistic forecasts of the jobs and opportunities that the IRA will create also overlook the act's negative impact on production workers dependent on fossil fuels.[57]

Biden's trade policies are unlikely to boost the employment prospects and welfare of many American workers, despite claims that they will be worker-centric. In addition, major economywide programs to help the adjustment of workers who are dislocated, workers who need skills, and places that need development assistance are all conspicuous by their absence.

The Biden programs exemplify the unfortunate tendency to try to sell programs with worthwhile goals as policies that will "revitalize the middle class." Policies that seek to enhance national security, accelerate innovation, achieve green growth, and build more resilient international supply chains are valuable in their own right and should aim to achieve their goals as efficiently as possible. They should not be diverted or diluted to achieve objectives that are worthy but are far better accomplished through dedicated, stand-alone policies that are adequately financed and have the primary purpose of aiding non-college-educated workers and communities that need help.

---

57. For an extensive discussion of the labor market adjustment challenges of climate change policies in the United States and the European Union, see Lawrence (2024).

11

Toward Programs that Help All People and Communities in Need in the United States

The basic goals of President Joseph R. Biden Jr.'s policies are sound. Infrastructure, technological development, national security, and climate change are classic examples of public goods that will not be dealt with in an optimal fashion by a free market acting without government intervention. Government policies to correct market failures are therefore warranted.

The difficult question is how such failures should be corrected. Jan Tinbergen (1956), winner of the first Nobel Prize in economics, showed that policymakers need at least as many policy instruments as they have goals. His insight implies that if instead of prioritizing single goals, programs are made conditional on achieving additional goals, they are unlikely to achieve their goals efficiently.

For example, the incentives for producing renewable energy in the US Inflation Reduction Act (IRA) are higher if producers pay union wages, use US materials, and locate in "energy communities," and the program allocates funds to help displaced workers train for jobs in the production of renewable energy. It would be far more effective if the objectives reflected in these other measures were achieved through dedicated economywide programs devoted to achieving the additional goals.

This chapter therefore examines broader policies designed to provide more targeted adjustment assistance to US workers and depressed communities regardless of the reasons for their circumstances.

Helping People

The diffusion of new technologies and international competition can be highly disruptive and costly for workers displaced if they lack the skills needed to take advantage of new opportunities or live in places where such opportunities do not exist.

Getting laid off can be demoralizing and very costly for workers. Steven Davis and Till Von Wachter (2011) look at earnings 20 years after a mass layoff in the United States. They find that, in present value terms, men with three or more years of tenure lose the equivalent of 1.4 years of their predisplacement earnings when the unemployment rate is 6 percent or less and twice as much when unemployment is above 8 percent.[1] As the discussion of the conversion to electric vehicles makes clear (see box 10.1), policies such as decarbonization are likely to cause substantial numbers of workers to lose their jobs through no fault of their own. This section outlines some measures that could help workers who lose their jobs and new entrants find jobs that improve their long-term earnings prospects.[2]

Taxes and Transfers

The straightforward and often most efficient way to deal with inequitable outcomes is to use direct taxes and transfers. Two approaches to these policies are usefully distinguished. The first is targeted tax and transfer programs that raise taxes on upper-income individuals and transfer these resources to the people most in need. These programs provide money only to poor people and are therefore less costly than programs that provide broader benefits.

An alternative is to raise revenues and provide more broadly based transfers to everyone (this approach could be implemented in a moderately progressive way by phasing out grants to people with very high incomes). This approach is more expensive than the first and thus sometimes considered economically inefficient, but it is more politically robust. Examples include Social Security, Medicare, and child tax credits that provide fixed amounts of money to everyone with children of a certain age.

Some countries are considering a more radical version of this approach that involves provision of a universal minimum basic income. These programs—which Canada, Finland, and the Netherlands have piloted—appear effective in reducing or eliminating poverty. Unlike welfare payments only to the poor, they should garner political support from the middle class.

---

1. For others estimates of the costs of displacement, see Topel (1990) and Ruhm (1991).

2. For discussion of policies to help workers, see Hanson (2021) and Rodrik (2022).

Their downside, according to their critics, is that they reduce the incentive of people with low incomes to work. This concern may not be valid. Indeed, such benefits may actually increase labor force participation by making child care affordable, allowing mothers to join the labor force. The high rates of labor force participation in Scandinavian countries suggest that similar programs may encourage work. Universal grants also avoid the problem endemic to targeted programs that are reduced above certain income levels, implying very high marginal tax rates for people contemplating working. A more significant weakness in the approach is that for many people work is more than a job. Instead, it helps define who they are. Programs that allocate generous benefits to people on the condition that they work may be more effective than a cash grant that does not provide people with a similar sense of purpose and contributing to others.

Unemployment insurance is the first line of defense, but the tax system can help cushion the blow to people left behind by economic disruption whatever its source. Low earners in the United States with children are eligible for the earned income tax credit. It could be expanded to include childless workers.

The Biden administration expanded the child tax credit in the American Rescue Plan. This expansion reduced child poverty. Expansions of both the earned income tax credit and the child tax credit would help people who face economic disruption. Basing the level of federal support for universal income and other policies on location could provide more support for depressed areas, as discussed below.

Compensating Wage Losses

Another way to cushion the blow of structural adjustment is through wage-loss insurance, an idea originally proposed in Lawrence and Litan (1986). A wage insurance program would supplement the wages of displaced workers who find new jobs that pay less than they previously earned.[3] This approach would compensate workers for the loss of earnings associated with the erosion of job-specific human capital and enhance their incentive to remain active in the labor market and to accept another job sooner. It could be introduced as part of a revamped and expanded labor market adjustment program.

---

3. A limited version of this program was implemented for older workers as part of Trade Adjustment Assistance. Brainard, Litan, and Warren (2005) estimate that a wage insurance program that replaces 50 percent of earnings losses for workers over 45 (up to a maximum of $10,000 a year) for up to two years would cost roughly $3.5 billion a year and require an annual insurance premium of roughly $25 per worker.

Adjustment Policies

The United States has generally taken a passive approach to dealing (or not dealing) with most displaced workers, relying primarily on unemployment insurance and actions taken by workers themselves to find training and new jobs rather extensive programs to assist them. This approach has depended on the labor market being flexible and on workers being willing to move to where new jobs become available.

Labor mobility has declined, especially since the 1990s. Rather than moving to new jobs, a growing share of prime-age workers, especially men, has dropped out of the labor force or taken disability benefits (Austin, Glaeser, and Summers 2018). As a result, workers who do not even attempt to look for work have become much more common, especially in left-behind places.

Instead of increasing efforts to deal with this problem, the United States has continued to devote a very small share of federal spending on active labor market programs that assist worker adjustment.[4] At 0.1 percent of GDP, US spending is far lower than the average of 0.5 percent of GDP spent by other OECD countries (Council of Economic Advisers 2016). In fiscal 2021, for example, the Department of Labor allocated just $3.6 billion to employment and training.[5]

Other advanced economies are far more active in supporting their unemployed workers, "facilitating matches between workers and firms, helping workers in their job searches, and sometimes creating jobs when these are not available in the private sector" (Bown and Freund 2019, 2). Labor force participation has been far more robust in these countries than in the United States. According to Chad P. Bown and Caroline Freund, who survey the evidence from other countries, policies such as job placement services, training, and wage subsidies have generally been successful in providing assistance; direct job creation by governments appears to have been less successful in providing permanent employment.

The United States has identified trade as a source of structural change that merits a special program; its Trade Adjustment Assistance program assists workers who can prove they lost their job as a result of trade. People who qualify are given extended unemployment benefits, training, job search assistance, and relocation allowances; on a limited basis, reemployed older workers also receive wage loss compensation.

---

4. For a more extensive discussion of US adjustment assistance, see Lawrence (2014).

5. US Department of Labor, "Budget of the United States Government Fiscal Year 2021," https://www.dol.gov/sites/dolgov/files/ETA/budget/pdfs/21ETA_Appx.pdf.

Trade Adjustment Assistance typically provided assistance to around 100,000 a year. The Biden administration allowed the program to lapse and has not fought for its renewal. Admittedly, the evidence on its effectiveness is mixed. Both Mathematica Policy Research and Social Policy Research (2012) and Marcal (2001) reach negative conclusions about its efficacy. Benjamin Hyman (2018) is more positive. He finds that the program raised earnings and labor force participation rates over a 10-year period, especially in regions where disruption was high.

The rationale for a special program for workers displaced by trade is, however, weak; similar workers who lose their jobs for other reasons beyond their control are equally deserving of assistance. The United States should create a new, much more generous general adjustment assistance program that offers a menu of services and consolidates its efforts to help all dislocated US workers, regardless of the reasons for their displacement.[6] The United States has had some small programs that are more general in nature. But they have generally been severely underfunded. One of the largest general programs, which was under the Workforce Innovation and Opportunity Act (WIOA), spent just $1.044 billion in 2021 to provide services to 598,960 workers ($1,744 per served participant). The cost per participant is so low that these programs are unlikely to meet the needs of most participants.[7]

Despite the adverse consequences of not having such programs for workers who need them, obtaining support for them in the United States has been very difficult politically. This weakness has resulted in efforts to implement special adjustment programs in the context of other programs for which there is more political support, but it has resulted in programs that do not fill the needs of all who are dislocated.

Equipping Workers to Find New Jobs

The skill bias that characterizes new technologies increases the importance of technical education. Computer literacy should be taught in high school, and access to and financing for postsecondary institutions, such as community colleges, and short courses that provide skills to workers without college education need to be increased.

A key to greater inclusion is equipping the labor force to take advantage of opportunities to obtain middle-class jobs as digital and other tech-

---

6. In its budget proposals for fiscal 2014, the Obama administration proposed just such a change, in the form of a Universal Displaced Worker (UDW) Program that would integrate the Trade Adjustment Assistance and Dislocated Worker programs into an expanded whole, delivered through the nationwide American Job Center network. The policy was never adopted.

7. See WIOA Annual Reports, https://rsa.ed.gov/wioa-resources/wioa-annual-reports.

nologies are increasingly diffused throughout the economy. The starting point is recognition that almost 63 percent of Americans do not have a college degree[8] but nearly two-thirds of jobs created between 2010 and 2015 required medium or advanced levels of digital skills.[9] Many of the needed skills can be acquired through training, including on-the-job training, rather than by obtaining a college degree.

Peter Blair et al. (2020) argue that as many as 30 million American workers are qualified to move into new jobs that pay on average 70 percent more than their current ones. McKinsey has developed a "job progression tool" that allows job coaches and career navigators to consider how promising employment options can advance economic opportunities.[10]

Many large technology firms also provide training and certification. Google has developed inexpensive programs that allow workers to identify opportunities and take low-cost or free courses that equip them with digital skills in occupations such as IT support, data analytics, website design, and project management. It provides career certificates that allow people who pass these courses to show prospective or current employers that they have mastered these skills. Amazon has committed to providing free cloud-computing skills to 29 million people worldwide by 2025.[11] IBM, Microsoft, and Amazon have extensive training programs that develop and certify IT skills.

Some state governments have joined in the effort to remove unnecessary obstacles to people without college education in obtaining jobs where formal degrees are not really required. The governors of Pennsylvania, Maryland, and Utah eliminated the requirement of a four-year college degree for most jobs in state government.[12] In Pennsylvania, the state gov-

---

8. College Transitions, "The Percentage of Americans with College Degrees in 2023," August 12, 2023, https://www.collegetransitions.com/blog/percentage-of-americans-with-college-degrees.

9. Burning Glass Technologies and Capital One, *Crunched by the Numbers: The Digital Skills Gap in the Workforce*, March 2015, https://www.voced.edu.au/content/ngv%3A69272. See also Markle Foundation, "Rework America," https://www.markle.org/rework-america/.

10. The tool (https://www.mckinsey.com/featured-insights/sustainable-inclusive-growth/future-of-america/job-progression-tool) is based on data on 4 million job transitions.

11. "Amazon to Help 29 Million People around the World Grow Their Tech Skills with Free Cloud Computing Skills Training by 2025," https://www.aboutamazon.com/news/workplace/amazon-to-help-29-million-people-around-the-world-grow-their-tech-skills-with-free-cloud-computing-skills-training-by-2025.

12. Editorial Board, "See Workers as Workers, Not as a College Credential," *New York Times*, January 28, 2023, https://www.nytimes.com/2023/01/28/opinion/jobs-college-degree-requirement.html.

ernment opened 92 percent of state government jobs to anyone with relevant work experience and skills-based training, regardless of educational attainment.[13]

The federal government has also acted. In 2021, the Office of Management and Budget (OMB) issued a reminder to agencies of the "long-standing requirement to limit the use of educational requirements in favor of stated skills when acquiring information technology (IT) services. Agencies are encouraged to apply this same general principle when acquiring other types of services that do not require licenses and can be procured using performance-based contracting principles."[14]

Increasing Demand for Non-College-Educated Workers

To make growth more inclusive, the private sector must change its perceptions, hiring habits, and career development programs. Practices often change when an economy faces shortages of workers. During World War II, for example, factories hired women when skills shortages emerged after millions of men joined the military, and the Navy allowed Black men to enlist. Advances in hiring minorities occurred when unemployment reached exceptionally low rates during the 1960s. The very low rates of unemployment in the 1960s disproportionately benefited low-skilled workers (Okun 1973). Stephanie Aaronson et al. (2019) find similar results when the unemployment rate fell below 4 percent in the final years of the Trump expansion just before the COVID pandemic.[15]

Highly stimulative fiscal policies adopted to spur recovery from the slump caused by the pandemic created shortages of workers, which led firms to loosen hiring requirements and adjust conditions of work. "Up and down the wage scale," reports the *New York Times*, "companies are becoming more willing to pay a little more, to train workers, to take chances on people without traditional qualifications, and to show greater flexibility in where and how people work."[16] David Autor, Arindrajit Dube, and

---

13. Ibid.

14. See OMB memorandum at https://www.whitehouse.gov/wp-content/uploads/2021/01/Limiting-Use-of-Educational-Requirements-in-Federal-Service-Contracts.pdf.

15. Aaronson et al. (2019, abstract) find "suggestive evidence that when the labor market is already strong, a further increment of strengthening provides some extra benefit to some disadvantaged groups, relative to earlier in the labor market cycle. In addition, we provide some evidence suggesting that these gains are persistent, at least for a while, for some groups, particularly blacks and women."

16. Neil Irwin, "Workers Are Gaining Leverage Over Employers Right before Our Eyes," *New York Times*, July 20, 2021, https://www.nytimes.com/2021/06/05/upshot/jobs-rising-wages.html.

Annie McGrew (2023) confirm the benefits of a tight labor market in their study of low unemployment following the COVID pandemic. They find that rapid relative wage growth at the bottom of the distribution reduced the college wage premium and counteracted approximately a quarter of the four-decade increase in aggregate 90–10 log wage inequality. They also find that the pandemic reduced employer market power and spurred rapid relative wage growth among young non-college-educated workers, who disproportionately moved from lower-paying to higher-paying and potentially more-productive jobs. Even more effective than changing mindsets, therefore, is changing the balance of power in favor of employees.

Sectoral Programs

Sectoral programs also seem promising. Lawrence Katz et al. (2022) survey evidence from randomized evaluations of sectoral employment programs that forge relationships with employers and combine training in soft skills (such as those involving direct customer contact) and occupational skills. They find that these programs, typically led by community organizations, can generate "substantial and persistent" earnings gains (12–34 percent) by moving participants into higher-paying jobs. These programs train job seekers for employment in specific industries and occupational clusters that are believed to have strong current local labor demand and opportunities for longer-term career advancement. Targeted sectors typically include health care, IT, and manufacturing. A goal is to open the doors for individuals with noncollege backgrounds to assist them in attaining high-wage jobs in the targeted sectors.

Concluding Comments

In sum, labor market policies should cushion losses and assist displaced and new entrants in finding and training for new jobs throughout the economy. The connections between workers and employers need to be improved by breaking down barriers to hiring workers where a college degree is not needed and by developing sector-based collaborative policies at the community level to provide jobs in sectors that offer prospects for long-run career advancement.

Helping Places

Many of the towns and cities where non-college-educated workers live are experiencing hard times, reducing their employment opportunities and local government fiscal revenues. As the circumstances in which poor communities find themselves are often very different, a one-size-fits-all approach is unlikely to be appropriate in all circumstances. Accordingly, this discussion presents a variety of approaches that might be adopted, in combination or individually. The choices need to be tailored to the challenges and the potential strengths of each town or city.[17]

Six options are considered:

- A broad program offering tax base insurance
- Policies that encourage out-migration
- The use of federal grants for economic development
- Programs that fund research and development
- Programs that help distressed people in distressed places
- Programs that attract remote workers

Tax Base Insurance

Local governments that are constrained to balance their budgets can be forced to deal with short-term revenue shocks by cutting spending or increasing taxes. A prime example is communities that depend on fossil fuel production for their revenues (Morris, Kaufman, and Doshi 2019). These fiscal reactions can exacerbate shocks, creating the risk of a downward spiral, as cutbacks in services induce more and more residents to leave.

Some cities and states have rainy day funds to tide them over tough times. It would be more efficient if they pooled their risks and developed a program that insures their tax base. Such a pool could be created privately or through the federal government.

In Deep and Lawrence (2008) we propose an affordable instrument that could mitigate the impact of tax revenue shocks on communities by allowing them to pool their risks and buy tax base insurance. Such a program would pay for unexpected losses in community taxes that could result from any of a host of shocks, such as plant closures, crop failures, or declines in capital gains taxes collected. (Revenue losses from tax cuts would, of course, be excluded.) Additional revenue sharing and economic stabilization through fiscal policies might still be needed for major economywide shocks, such as a nationwide recession. The programs Deep and Lawrence propose would be triggered by shocks that are primarily local. Having a program in place would predetermine eligibility, define causes, and the value of compensation. It would be dependable because it would establish a property right that communities have already paid for.

---

17. For a discussion of place-based policies, see World Bank (2009), OECD (2011), Neumark and Simpson (2014), and Rodrik and Stantcheva (2021).

Out-migration

Traditionally, out-migration was a major mechanism for adjustment. Since the 1990s, poorer workers have not been migrating to promising places, often because housing costs in such places are high (Ganong and Shoag 2017). Generally, only highly paid educated workers migrate to these cities, deepening geographic differences in income.

Federal government policies could help workers relocate by giving them mobility subsidies and more portable benefits for unemployment and health. Providing such benefits to workers displaced from coal-based communities, for example, could have helped ease their adjustment. Relaxing zoning restrictions in superstar cities could provide more affordable housing, although doing so is difficult, because owners of high-priced homes generally oppose new building that could bring down the value of their properties. Rationalizing obsolete occupational licensing systems throughout the economy could also help improve labor mobility. Regional and sectoral mobility could also be promoted by providing subsidies covering the cost of occupational licensing for workers who lose their jobs.

Out-migration policies would do little to help people left behind in depressed places other than reducing the number of unemployed looking for work, however. And if the most enterprising residents migrate, such policies could worsen the plight of the places they leave behind. For this reason, policies to assist left-behind places and people are also required.

Federal Grants

Since 1965, policies for regional development have been administered through the Economic Development Administration (EDA) of the Department of Commerce. Its record in targeting communities in need has been poor. Consider this description from Daniel Gallagher and Amy Glasmeier (2020, 14):

> The programmatic history of EDA presents a cautionary tale of the prospects and pitfalls associated with policy interventions that are pulled in opposing directions....From the start, tasked with improving the conditions of distressed locations, EDA assumed the responsibility to legitimize the overall effort without the resources needed to accomplish the task given the initial designation criteria [which were] so all encompassing that almost any place in the country qualified as a distressed county.

At first, the EDA gave priority to areas with the worst economic conditions, as measured by high or sudden unemployment, persistent unemployment, substantial population decline, and/or low median family incomes; it also prioritized Indian reservations. In the late 1960s, EDA staff began to question this "worst first" approach, because of its limited effectiveness. They judged that small rural communities that qualified for assistance lacked initiative and resources and demonstrated limited potential for economic development. As Gallagher and Glasmeier (2020, 14) note:

> Over time, political pressures led to the shift from an almost exclusive rural focus to incorporating distressed urban centers as well as providing relief to areas affected by natural disasters. Owing to an expansion in its already vague eligibility criteria, approximately half of all US counties were eligible for EDA assistance by the mid-1970s and the largest recipients of EDA funds over its history have been the nation's major urban areas of Los Angeles, New York and Chicago.

The political dynamics of these programs foreshadows the problems in the IRA's special programs for energy communities. Determining the optimal mix between grants that are narrowly directed to particular purposes and allowing for local initiative is not easy. The CHIPS and Science Act seeks to promote regional R&D hubs, and the IRA seeks to achieve climate justice. The administration wants "40 percent of the overall benefits of certain federal investments [to] flow to disadvantaged communities that are marginalized, underserved, and overburdened by pollution."[18]

Another problem with these programs is that the beneficiaries may be people who move to the area to take advantage of the programs rather than the original residents the program was supposed to help. The Tennessee Valley Authority program, launched in 1933 by President Franklin Delano Roosevelt, made massive investments in electricity and transportation. The program was very successful in creating manufacturing jobs, which grew rapidly. But the major beneficiaries of the higher wages and employment were new migrants from the rest of the South; the program did not raise local wages in any significant way (Kline and Moretti 2011).

As with economic development in general, a top-down policy is unlikely to be appropriate for communities. It may be more important to establish private-public partnerships with feedback mechanisms that are designed to respond to new developments and the appearance of binding constraints to growth than to assume that a program can be implemented in a top-down approach that lays out all the steps to be taken in advance.[19]

---

18. The White House, Justice 40: A Whole of Government Approach, https://www.whitehouse.gov/environmentaljustice/justice40/.

19. See Hausman, Rodrik, and Velasco (2006) for a discussion of binding constraints to growth in a development context.

As James and Deborah Fallows (2018) show, community involvement and public-private partnerships play a key role in successful towns.[20] What is striking from their descriptions of successful towns is how varied the approaches have been. Leaving room for local discretion and involvement would thus seem to make sense.

Once the federal government is involved, doing so is not easy. According to Beverly Moss Spatt (2016), a New York City Planning Commissioner from 1966 to 1970, "the [Model Cities] program [of the 1960s] was plagued by vague, often confusing, guidelines, as well as by the competing visions among the black middle class, business interests, and city officials."

The Opportunity Zones program of the Trump administration went to the other extreme, placing almost no constraints on the tax breaks it granted for investments in designated areas. As a result, investors who created few jobs or benefits for current residents—including by investing in storage units and luxury condominiums—were able to take advantage of the program.[21]

The Empowerment Zones and Enterprise Communities program of the Clinton administration appears to have been more successful in finding a happy medium between central and local direction. Beneficiaries were selected based on the quality of a comprehensive, bottom-up strategic plan that included input from all community stakeholders and described a community vision for economic revitalization and job creation. An evaluation of the New York version of the program found a 15 percent gain in employment and an 8 percent increase in hourly wages paid to residents (Busso, Gregory, and Kline 2010). Among the reasons for the program's success was that it targeted workers who already lived and worked in the neighborhood and insisted on local investors matching federal subsidies, so that they had skin in the game.

Another approach would be to link firms, educational and training institutions, and nonprofit organizations. Federal programs could provide incentives for collaboration between local firms and training institutions and between local and state governments, specialized services, and technical assistance in sectoral programs. As noted above, Katz et al. (2022) find that such programs have been successful.

Timothy Bartik (2020) argues that the federal government could help distressed areas by providing economic development grants. These grants should be used flexibly, depending on local needs, which could include

---

20. For stories of the varied ways towns have succeeded, see Fallows and Fallows (2018).

21. According to an evaluation by the Tax Foundation, it is unclear whether opportunity zone tax preferences used to attract investment will actually benefit distressed communities (Eastman and Kaeding 2019).

infrastructure spending, public sector jobs, and employer subsidies for job creation or hiring or manufacturing services. He adds that in addition to ensuring that beneficiaries are current residents, place-based policies should target higher-multiplier industries (i.e., industries whose spending spreads both upstream and downstream) and should avoid favoring large firms. Bartik believes that the evidence indicates that programs providing consulting help to small firms are particularly promising.

Bartik also suggests that helping distressed places with only one program is problematic, because a single program does not allow for the synergy that can emerge from multiple programs. For example, a wage subsidy to encourage the hiring of disadvantaged workers will create more jobs and have smaller displacement effects if it is combined with customized business services that promote local job creation in businesses that buy inputs and services from other local industries (Moretti 2010).

Research and Development

The CHIPS and Science Act approach is a less grand version of the approach envisaged by Jonathan Gruber and Simon Johnson (2019), who propose using "breakthrough" science spending to build technology hubs that allow promising US cities to overcome the barriers that prevent them from emulating superstar cities. The act follows more closely the proposals of Atkinson, Muro, and Whiton (2019), who would designate "heartland metro areas" that would participate in a 10-year program that would provide them with structured benefits entailing major R&D grants ($700 million for 10 years) as well as workforce development funding and regulatory support. The goal of these ideas is to turn selected second-tier cities into self-generating growth centers. Communities would compete for the grants. The cooperation necessary to compete, proponents argue, would make these cities more likely to succeed by reflecting local needs.

Conceptually, programs that emphasize R&D are problematic, because they use a single instrument to try to achieve two goals, violating the Tinbergen principle of one goal/one instrument.[22] Correcting the market failure of too little R&D and overcoming the regional polarization of growth are two distinct goals; a single instrument—regional R&D spending—is unlikely to achieve both optimally. The United States might become a weaker innovator by diffusing the focus of its competitive R&D efforts regionally. Proponents of this approach claim that it would strengthen political support for R&D, but experience suggests that political forces can also lead

---

22. Rodrik (2022) decries some novel proposals for using federal R&D to create good jobs through federal worker–friendly technological development and local worker–friendly industrial policies.

these efforts to be diffused too broadly to make an important difference to any particular left-behind place.[23] Excessive diffusion seems to characterize the IRA, as energy communities singled out for special help covered large shares of the US landmass (Raimi and Pesek 2022).

The track record of place-oriented programs is not good. An official evaluation of the National Science Foundation's place-based program operating in 2019 found that "no state that has participated in the program has permanently 'graduated' from it."[24] The program began in 6 well-chosen states but expanded to 29. Although proponents of these proposals make compelling arguments about the potential role of government to facilitate innovation, their plans for simultaneously seeking regional inclusion raise numerous questions that are familiar in debates about the wisdom of the government picking winners and losers.

Kathrin Enenkel explores the relationship between R&D spending and local growth in the United Kingdom.[25] She finds that whether a city's university is strong in research and innovation does not inevitably dictate how successful its wider economy is and that places with more innovative businesses perform better than those with innovative universities. In addition, innovation output—measured by patents and trademarks registered—does not always lead to more growth. In general, places with access to a larger pool of skilled workers and stronger job density perform better than those with a smaller pool and lower density. Therefore, she concludes, before weaker places receive increased public R&D investment, they may require other complementary interventions, such as investment in skills or public infrastructure.

One can ask how successful selection committees would have been had these programs existed in the 1980s, before some of today's superstar cities flourished. It is hard to assert that the promise of these cities was apparent before they took off or that they were spurred by "a big push" rather than a cumulative and incremental process whose logic is easy to see in retrospect but hard to have predicted. Federal spending has historically played a role in stimulating local growth in some areas, which then enjoyed sustained growth through agglomeration (Washington, DC is the prime example).

---

23. Edward Glaeser, "'Jump-Starting America' Review: Investing in the Brain," *Wall Street Journal*, May 8, 2019, https://www.wsj.com/articles/jump-starting-america-review-investing-in-the-brain-11557355297.

24. Ibid.

25. Kathrin Enenkel, "How Will More R&D Spending Level up the UK?" Centre for Cities blog, September 14, 2020, https://www.centreforcities.org/blog/how-will-an-more-rd-spending-level-up-the-uk/.

But the purpose of that spending was not regional economic development but meeting technological and other goals that turned out to have cumulative positive agglomeration effects.

Moretti (2013) describes how entrepreneurs such as D.W. Griffith (the movie *Birth of a Nation*), Bill Gates (Microsoft), Walter Gilbert (Biogen), and William Shockley (Fairchild Semiconductor) saw opportunity and provided the initial boost that sparked a cumulative virtuous cycle that resulted in the movie industry centering in Hollywood, software in Seattle, bioscience in Boston, and information technology in Silicon Valley. None was spawned by a deliberate geographically based big push from the public sector.[26] Moreover, even assuming the new hubs launched by the CHIPS and Science Act are successful, they are unlikely to significantly affect the geographical dispersion of growth in the United States.

Helping Distressed People in Distressed Places

Policies that subsidize the employment of people who reside in places with high unemployment and nonemployment rates should be seriously considered as a way to stimulate employment and earnings. This approach would help the people in poor places rather than concentrating help on just a few hubs with ambitious developmental goals, as in the R&D approach.

Austin, Glaeser, and Summers (2018) find that increases in labor demand appear to have greater impacts on employment in areas where not working has been historically high. They suggest that pro-employment policies, such as ramped-up earned income tax credits, that target regions with more elastic employment responses could plausibly reduce suffering and materially improve economic performance.

Traditionally, unemployment insurance has been extended beyond the time allowed by states only when warranted by national conditions. This program could be reformed to be more generous and long-lasting for depressed regions. To make sure that it is the current residents who benefit, these benefits should be granted only to people already living in these places.

Attracting New Workers through Remote Work

The COVID lockdowns increased remote work. Firms and workers learned about the benefits and costs of such practices. Could the importance of

---

26. See Bresnahan et al. (2001) for an analysis reaching similar conclusions on how innovation agglomeration started in Silicon Valley and several other international locations.

the geographic agglomerations of highly skilled workers in superstar cities diminish as remote work becomes more acceptable?

If more high-income employees work from home, lower-income service workers living in outlying areas could benefit, as long as they are not priced out by rising housing costs in the new digital hubs. High-tech workers create large numbers of jobs for other workers (Moretti 2010), including jobs for people who work with or for them(e.g., lawyers, financial specialists, consultants) and people who provide them with personal services (e.g., hairdressers, baristas, waiters, personal trainers). Towns and cities that can offer decent public amenities, cheaper housing, and a better quality of life could become more attractive to high-skilled workers, raising opportunities and incomes for middle-income and less skilled service workers.

In the postpandemic workplace, employees are dispersed, in some cases living far from their offices.[27] The *Wall Street Journal* and Realtor.com have developed an Emerging Housing Markets Index that is based on indicators such as housing supply and demand, housing price trends, relative costs of living, amenities, commuting times, taxes, wages, unemployment, and number of foreign-born residents. In July 2021, it reported that many Americans were rethinking whether they wanted to return to commuting—or even live near their office at all.[28] In their sample of the 300 most populous US areas, smaller and more rural housing markets with average populations of 300,000 emerged as the hottest new places to live and own a home.[29]

The 40-year era of regional divergence in both the United States and the European Union could be closing.[30] Construction of the interstate highway system facilitated the wider diffusion of manufacturing activity in the 1950s; the combination of vastly improved communications software and broadband that form the information superhighway could similarly lead to a greater diffusion of workers today. If this argument is correct,

---

27. Nicole Friedman, "Montana Boomtown Jumps to No. 1 on WSJ/Realtor.com Housing Market Index," *Wall Street Journal*, July 20, 2021, https://www.wsj.com/articles/montana-boomtown-jumps-to-no-1-on-wsj-realtor-com-housing-market-index-11626773400.

28. David Ewalt and Alana Beyer, "See the Full Rankings for WSJ/Realtor.com's Emerging Housing Markets Index," *Wall Street Journal*, July 20, 2021, https://www.wsj.com/real-estate/see-the-full-rankings-for-wsj-realtor-coms-summer-emerging-housing-markets-index-45a2cd20.

29. Ibid.

30. Europe's experience has been similar to that of the United States: "EU–wide convergence of regional incomes since 1996 has benefited from convergence of incomes between countries, while within-country income disparities remain substantial and have even widened slightly over time. Metropolitan regions—and even more so capital regions—have grown faster than average, thereby contributing to regional convergence across EU countries but also to within-country disparities" (National Bank of Belgium 2020, abstract).

outlying areas might do better by investing in communications technologies and better amenities in order to attract high-income earners (who would increase their tax base) rather than trying to attract firms to become the next innovation or production hub.

What emerges from this brief consideration of approaches to local development is that a single approach or particular combination of policy measures is unlikely to work in all places.[31] A more fruitful approach is to identify the constraints to growth for a particular place at a particular point in time. Anna Stansbury, Dan Turner, and Ed Balls (2023) provide an example of this type of identification analysis for regional economies in the United Kingdom. They argue that the most important constraints in weak regions of the United Kingdom are deficiencies in the availability of STEM workers and transportation infrastructure and that the regional concentration of R&D spending and high real estate prices in London are major constraints on migration. Their approach, which systematically considers a variety of hypotheses to determine those that are holding growth back, should be used to prioritize among the plausible options for US regional development discussed in this chapter.

Conclusion

As the role of manufacturing in the economy has declined and manufacturing production has become more skill intensive, it has become harder and harder for workers without college education to earn middle-class incomes. The United States continues to underinvest in labor market policies that would benefit these workers.

President Biden recognizes the problems facing workers without college education and would like to solve them. But he has mostly addressed them indirectly, in the context of his other initiatives, rather than implementing a general labor market adjustment program on a scale similar to that of the infrastructure bill, the CHIPS and Science Act, or the IRA.

A standalone program would bolster US policies to aid workers who lose their jobs through no fault of their own. It would provide unemployed workers with a menu of services, including financial support, training, job search assistance, relocation allowance, and grants for sectoral employment programs that forge relationships with employers and combine training in soft skills (work readiness) and occupational skills. Workers who find low-wage jobs would be assisted through an expanded earned income tax credit; workers who find jobs that pay wages lower than they

---

31. For a systematic approach to diagnosing binding constraints to development, see Hausmann, Rodrik, and Velasco (2006).

previously earned would benefit from wage-loss insurance, which would make up some of the difference between their earnings in a new job and their earnings in their previous job.

The United States should also increase its programs to assist depressed towns and cities. No single approach would work for all, and striking the right balance between bottom-up approaches led by local communities and stakeholders and top-down approaches that can provide resources, expertise, and discipline on how assistance is best used is tricky. There are also problems in a federal system in defining eligibility in the face of political pressures that tend to spread assistance too widely. Nonetheless, more generous narrowly targeted versions of programs such as the earned income tax credit and unemployment assistance for places with unusually high unemployment as well as the provision of a range of services that can aid economic development should be seriously considered. These efforts could involve the provision of customized business services, infrastructure such as broadband, and the development of land for commercial services. The creation of a self-financing system for tax base insurance could also help communities prevent shocks that lead to downward spirals as amenities decay. In addition to creating a more attractive environment for firms and business recruitment, communities should also consider adopting programs that attract remote workers.

12

Will Industrial Policies in Other Developed Economies Enhance Inclusion?

Nearly all developed economies share the goals of promoting digital technologies and the green transition and making their international supply chains more resilient. These policies are also often motivated by domestic political concerns that seek to make growth more inclusive by providing jobs to less skilled workers and accelerating growth in depressed regions. Encouraging tech-driven growth could increase the demand for skilled workers to the detriment of workers with fewer skills, however. And the digital and green transitions are likely to reinforce each other, increasing the demand for skilled workers (Vandeplas et al. 2022).

Europe

The European Union has embarked on industrial policy strategies to increase the share in GDP of value added in manufacturing. As early as November 2008, at the peak of the financial and economic crisis, the European Commission proposed a program to support Europe's competitiveness in key industrial sectors through research and innovation and public-private partnerships.

One initiative, Horizon Europe, has had several iterations. Its most recent version allocates €95 billion to be spent between 2021 and 2027. It aims to improve European manufacturing enterprises' "technological capability in adapting to environmental pressures" and "adequately respond to increasing global consumer demand for greener, more customized and higher-quality products."[1] It also seeks to prevent further manufacturing employment losses, especially of highly skilled workers and to increase the share of EU manufacturing in value added from 16 to 20 percent (Filos 2015).[2]

In 2022, the European Union proposed additional measures to strengthen its technology sector.[3] To address the global semiconductor shortage (which affected its automotive industry, healthcare industry, industrial automation, and defense), its version of the US CHIPS and Science Act would increase public and private investment in semiconductor production by €43 billion by 2030, including €2.65 billion of public funds for the Horizon Europe program. In 2022, Europe produced 10 percent of the world's microchips. The European Chips Act would increase European production capacity to 20 percent of the global market by 2030, reducing Europe's reliance on global markets for semiconductors.

To avoid falling behind the United States and China, the Europeans have sought to implement a new policy of "open strategic autonomy," in which the European Union reduces its technological dependence and regains leadership in important areas (Molthof, Zandee, and Cretti 2021).[4] In July 2021, the European Commission adopted its flagship climate initiative (Fit for 55), which aims to reduce carbon emissions by 2030 by 55 percent from 1990 levels (40 percent from 2019 levels). To achieve this goal, the European Union is adopting directives and policies that include €1 trillion for investments in clean energy, sustainable industry, buildings and renovations, sustainable mobility, and a cap-and-trade program.[5] In addition, it allocated €750 billion (€360 billion in loans and €390 billion in

---

1. European Commission, Horizon 2020, https://ec.europa.eu/programmes/horizon2020/what-horizon-2020#Article.

2. Ibid.

3. European Commission, European Chips Act, May 12, 2022, https://ec.europa.eu/info/strategy/priorities-2019-2024/europe-fit-digital-age/european-chips-act_en.

4. See also "A European Sovereignty Fund for an Industry 'Made in Europe,'" blog of Commissioner Thierry Breton, European Commission, September 15, 2022, https://ec.europa.eu/commission/presscorner/detail/en/STATEMENT_22_5543.

5. The financing of the EU Green Deal program includes over €1 trillion, €528 billion of which comes from the EU budget and the remainder from the InvestEU program, which combines €279 billion from the public and private sectors and €114 billion from national cofinancing. The European Innovation Council has also set aside €300 million to invest in market-creating innovations that contribute to the goals of the EU Green Deal. Part of this funding is for a "just transition mechanism," which will focus exclusively on regions and sectors most affected by the transition. It draws on the EU budget and the InvestEU program to generate €100 billion of funding. See Anne Lapierre and Katie McDougall, "The EU Green Deal Explained," April 2021, https://www.nortonrosefulbright.com/en/knowledge/publications/c50c4cd9/the-eu-green-deal-explained.

grants) in NextGenerationEU funds to support decarbonization and digitalization processes and a European Climate Law that proposes that all EU policies contribute to the EU Green Deal objective. The European Union has also created a €72.2 billion Social Climate Fund that will support vulnerable households, transportation users, and microenterprises affected by the introduction of emissions trading for fuels used in road transport and buildings.[6]

The European Union also aims to reduce its dependence on imports from unreliable countries in order to enhance its strategic autonomy. This position was reflected in European Commission President Ursula von der Leyen's 2022 State of the Union address, in which she declared, "I will push to create a new European Sovereignty Fund. Let's make sure that the future of industry is made in Europe."[7]

The European Sovereignty Fund includes money granted under the European Chips Act, which requires modifying state aid rules to allow governments to increase their funding; developing the capacity to produce batteries that reach 70 percent of expected demand by 2025 and 90 percent in 2030; and enhancing European production of green hydrogen, solar panels, and mining of critical raw minerals. The European Commission proposal emphasizes the development of rare earth activities on EU soil so that European extraction can meet 10 percent of annual consumption, 40 percent of annual processing, and 15 percent for annual recycling, all by 2030. In addition, no more than 65 percent of the annual consumption of each strategic raw material should be sourced or processed from a single country outside the European Union.[8]

Individual European countries also have their own industrial programs. In 2011, Germany came up with the term *Industry 4.0* to describe the process by which the government encourages people, machines, and industrial processes to network so that production equipment can communicate directly to provide performance data, call for repairs, or order new mate-

---

6. European Commission, "Member States Commit to Action for a Fair Transition towards Climate Neutrality," June 16, 2022, https://ec.europa.eu/social/main.jsp?langId=en&catId=89&newsId=10297.

7. "A European Sovereignty Fund for an Industry 'Made in Europe,'" blog of Commissioner Thierry Breton, European Commission, September 15, 2022, https://ec.europa.eu/commission/presscorner/detail/en/STATEMENT_22_5543.

8. Cecilia Malmstrom, "Will the Scramble for Rare Earths Produce a Transatlantic Trade Accord?" PIIE RealTime Economics blog, April 6, 2023, https://www.piie.com/blogs/realtime-economics/will-scramble-rare-earths-produce-transatlantic-trade-accord.

rials.[9] In 2018, it initiated a seven-year €3.5 billion "Made in Germany" program for artificial intelligence,[10] most of which was to be devoted to research designed to retain Germany's technological competitiveness. In 2020, it published a High-Tech Strategy 2025 and later a National Industrial Strategy 2030 that aimed to improve the conditions for entrepreneurial activity (through measures such as competitive taxation, reducing red tape, modernizing competition law, and expanding infrastructure); strengthen new technologies; and allow government ownership if necessary to maintain the technological sovereignty of the German economy.[11]

France has developed an "industries of the future strategy." Eighteen strategic sector committees engage representatives of the state, companies, and employees in dialogue. Together they implement joint projects for each sector in five areas: sector digitization, sector research and innovation, promotion of employment and skills training, the conquering of international markets, and support for small and medium-sized enterprises.[12]

Italy's version of the Industry 4.0 strategy focuses on R&D funding for advanced manufacturing, public guarantee schemes for investments in advanced manufacturing, and workforce training. The strategy sets targets for infrastructure development (100 percent of Italian firms having access to 30 Mbps internet), the number of students attending vocational schools for manufacturing, and R&D expenditure as a share of GDP.[13]

The United Kingdom's innovation agency, Innovate UK, has an annual budget of around £500 million, a quarter of which it invests in its manufacturing and materials program. Funding is allocated to innovation centers, such as the graphene and formulation centers. The agency holds sector-

9. See Klaus Lüber, Smart factories in German industry, November 3, 2024, https://www.deutschland.de/en/topic/business/artificial-intelligence-industry-40-smart-factories. The term Industry 4.0 was later given a broader meaning by Klaus Schwab (2016), managing director of the World Economic Forum, who used it to refer to the Fourth Industrial Revolution, which includes developments in fields based on digital technologies such as artificial intelligence, robotics, the Internet of Things, autonomous vehicles, 3-D printing, nanotechnology, biotechnology, materials science, energy storage, and quantum computing.

10. German Federal Government, 2018, Artificial Intelligence Strategy, https://www.ki-strategie-deutschland.de/home.html?file=files/downloads/Nationale_KI-Strategie_engl.pdf.

11. For a discussion of this strategy, see American-German Institute, "The German Industry Strategy 2030: Inconsistent and Dangerous!" 2019, https://americangerman.institute/2019/05/the-german-industry-strategy-2030-inconsistent-and-dangerous.

12. République française, Conseil national de l'industrie, "Les CSF: Remettre les filières au cœur de la politique industrielle française," https://www.conseil-national-industrie.gouv.fr/csf-remettre-filieres-au-coeur-de-la-politique-industrielle-francaise.

13. Ministero dello Sviluppo Economico, "Italy's Plan Industria 4.0," http://www.mise.gov.it/images/stories/documenti/2017_01_16-Industria_40_English.pdf.

specific competitions for grants to technologies such as additive manufacturing and autonomous vehicles.

Japan

Like other advanced economies, Japan promotes digital technologies, reshoring, and green energy. Its Fifth Science and Technology Basic Plan, launched in 2016, had among its objectives improving competitiveness in manufacturing and value-added creation in information and communications technology and the Internet of Things.[14] The plan set goals to be achieved by 2020. They included increasing the number of researchers at universities and research institutes by 20 percent, doubling the number of license agreements on patents and the number of initial public offerings launched by venture capital firms, and raising the share of GDP spent on R&D to 4 percent.

In 2020, Japan supplemented these policies by launching a special COVID stimulus plan valued at $2.3 billion. Among other measures, it sought to encourage Japanese multinationals in China to reshore their production back to Japan or divert it to other countries in the Association of Southeast Asian Nations (ASEAN).[15]

In 2023, Japan signed an agreement with the United States to strengthen the supply chains for critical minerals. The two countries pledged not to impose restrictions on each other's mineral exports.[16]

Japan has adopted commitments to reduce greenhouse gas (GHG) emissions by 26 percent from 2013 levels by 2030 and to achieve net-zero GHG emissions by 2050. Despite the Fukushima Daiichi nuclear plant accident, nuclear power will play a large role in its greening.

Japan is also deploying an array of other policy tools to achieve these goals, including grants, tax incentives, regulatory reform, and international cooperation. It is also promoting R&D in new technologies through a Green Innovation Fund, which will spend ¥2 trillion over 10 years and is expected to stimulate ¥15 trillion in private R&D and investment (METI 2021).

---

14. Council for Science, Technology and Innovation Cabinet Office, Government of Japan, *Report on the 5th Science and Technology Basic Plan*, December 18, 2015, https://www8.cao.go.jp/cstp/kihonkeikaku/5basicplan_en.pdf.

15. Ben Dooley and Makiko Inoue, "Japan Is Paying Firms to Make Things at Home. But China's Pull Is Still Strong," *New York Times*, September 26, 2020, https://www.nytimes.com/2020/09/26/business/japan-onshoring.html.

16. US Trade Representative, "Agreement between the Government of the United States of America and the Government of Japan on Strengthening Critical Minerals Supply Chains," October 7, 2019, https://ustr.gov/sites/default/files/2023-03/US%20Japan%20Critical%20Minerals%20Agreement%202023%2003%2028.pdf.

Implications

Many of these industrial and trade policies assume that improved technological know-how will enhance national competitiveness, stimulate economic growth, raise living standards, provide climate benefits, and strengthen national security. The policies are often accompanied by objectives that include increasing the share of manufacturing in value-added output and encouraging domestic reshoring of production.

As in the United States, these policies are motivated partly by domestic political concerns that relate to social rather than technological goals. They are promoted as measures that will provide jobs, especially for the workers who have been displaced by the decline of manufacturing employment; accelerate growth in regions that have been depressed; and alleviate some of the political pressures that have led to populist movements.

As in the United States, however, the impact of the new industrial policies could well be counterproductive. By emphasizing high-tech activities, they could further shift the composition of the manufacturing sector's employment toward more jobs for high-level occupations that require college-educated workers and fewer jobs in mid-level occupations that do not require college degrees. They could also increase the concentration of innovative manufacturing industries in the cities that are already technological superstars and do little to improve the prospects of places that have been left behind. In industries such as energy, mining, and automobiles, which have been important providers of relatively well-paid jobs for non-college-educated workers, the impacts of new environmental policies are likely to be highly disruptive.

Many industrial policies are designed to make manufacturing more productive by employing robotics, computer-aided design (CAD), advanced manufacturing (3D printing), and more efficient supply chains that follow Industry 4.0 approaches that link producers with each other and with consumers. These innovations are likely to reduce the labor and capital required to produce and deliver final goods. By making goods cheaper, the productivity improvements generated by these policies could initially increase demand, especially if the goods produced are novel (like electric vehicles). But higher demand for manufactured goods does not necessarily imply higher employment in the sector in the long run because, as was seen in part I of this book, demand for manufactures is both price and income inelastic. This means that as manufacturing technology reduces the prices of goods and income grows, larger shares of spending will be devoted to services. As a result, the share of workers who produce manufactured goods will inevitably decline.

Trade Protection and Improved Competitiveness

The forces that operate through domestic demand also imply that neither trade protection nor improved competitiveness is likely to provide long-term increases in the manufacturing employment share. If a country uses higher tariffs or preferential procurement to replace manufactured imports with domestic products (through reshoring, for example) employment could initially increase in favored industries, albeit at the cost of reduced gains from trade. But given the interdependence that has been created by global supply chains, higher costs for industrial inputs could reduce overall competitiveness and manufacturing employment by raising the costs facing downstream producers (Hufbauer and Lowry 2012). In addition, once the transition to import substitution is completed, additional income and manufacturing productivity growth are likely to result in higher spending on services and smaller shares of employment in manufacturing.

Implications of Skill-Biased Technological Change in Europe

According to a study of European economies by the European Commission, "between 2015 and 2025, opportunities will grow for highly skilled people (+21 percent), stagnate for medium-skill levels, and decline for the low skilled (–17 percent). Depending on the country and occupation, 25–45 percent of jobs will be subject to automation."[17] These projections underscore that digital technologies are likely to continue to complement skilled manufacturing workers and substitute for unskilled workers. Even if trade and industrial policies increase production, therefore, it is unlikely that the same kinds of workers who were displaced would be employed. But could the application of digital technologies in manufacturing increase the demand for less skilled workers in other parts of the European economy?

Terry Gregory, Anna Salamons, and Ulrich Zierahn (2019) develop a model that allows them to examine the impact of technological progress on the overall demand for labor in manufacturing when such progress is biased against routine labor. Using data from 27 European countries between 1999 and 2010, they find that although the direct impact of automation that substituted for routine workers resulted in substantial labor displacement, this effect was outweighed by the combination of increased product demand from the sectors experiencing the productivity improvements and spillovers in increased demand for the output of the nontraded sector. All told, therefore, in line with the predictions of Autor and Dorn

---

17. European Commission, Skills for Industry, https://ec.europa.eu/growth/industry/policy/skills_fi.

(2013), automation increased the demand for routine labor in these economies.

Gregory, Salamons, and Zierahn (2019) emphasize that the distribution of income in manufacturing can affect both the size and location of these positive spending spillovers into services. This spending will be larger if the benefits accrue to workers with higher propensities to spend than to owners with higher propensities to save. The national benefits from spending on nontraded (local) services will be larger if manufacturing capital is owned domestically than if it is owned by foreigners. In the aggregate then, skilled and unskilled labor can be complements rather than substitutes, and skilled workers can create higher income for unskilled workers not only by hiring them or working with them in a way that makes them more productive but also by buying their services.

Implications of the Green Transition in Europe

All in all, the green transition and the European Green Deal are set to reshape the geography of jobs and wealth across EU regions. The winners likely will consist of already prosperous urban regions, which will experience significant increases in capital investments and inflows of skilled workers from other regions. The losers will consist of the already weaker regional economies and development-trapped societies, which will suffer from outflows of capital and talent.[18]

Jan-Philipp Sasse and Evelina Trutnevyte (2023) conclude that the benefits of low-carbon scenarios occur mostly in regions of Northern Europe and that vulnerabilities exist mostly in regions of Southern and Southeastern Europe. Regions with the highest composite benefit indices are located primarily in the Baltics, Germany, Ireland, Scandinavia, and Scotland. These benefits reflect new investment and employment gains, decreased electricity prices, lower greenhouse gas and particulate matter emissions, and reduced land use. Regions with the highest composite vulnerability indices are located mostly in the Balkans, southern Italy, Portugal, Poland, and Spain.

Although there are some differences between the United States and Europe in the shares of employment accounted for by particular fossil

---

18. Europe's within-country experiences have been similar to that of the United States. According to the National Bank of Belgium (2020, 30), "EU-wide convergence of regional incomes since 1996 has benefited from convergence of incomes between countries, while within-country income disparities remain substantial and have even widened slightly over time. Metropolitan regions—and even more so capital regions—have grown faster than average, thereby contributing to regional convergence across EU countries but also to within-country disparities."

fuel-based industries, the problems faced on both sides of the Atlantic are similar.[19] The most vulnerable jobs are highly concentrated in relatively few communities, and the worker skills and education levels in industries that produce fossil fuels are not a very close match for those that are demanded for green jobs. These differences suggest that unless policies can mitigate the impact of the achievement of net-zero emissions, the less skilled workers and communities that currently produce fossil fuels will find the transition costly and painful.

The European Union has strengthened its climate policies through the European Green Deal. To ensure that no one is left behind under this fourth pillar, it has established the Just Transition Mechanism, which provides targeted support to help mobilize around €55 billion between 2021 and 2027 to alleviate the socioeconomic impact of the transition in regions in which CO_2-intensive industries are currently located and thus most affected by the transition. In contrast to the United States, the European Union starts from a base in which it already spends a significant share of its budget on cohesion policies that help members undertake local economic and social initiatives.[20] Thus, even if the Just Transition Fund had not been created, regions that have low per capita incomes and are depressed or relatively poor would have received disproportionate technical and financial assistance both from Brussels and from their national governments. These funds amounted to €532.6 billion between 2014 and 2020.[21]

The European Commission designed the Just Transition Fund to alleviate the impacts of the transition in the most affected territories. It does so by promoting balanced socioeconomic development based on investments in sectors that offer opportunities for affected workers and jobseekers. The two main priorities of the fund are to diversify local economies (so that they do not depend anymore on a single polluting sector) and to reskill and upskill workers and jobseekers.[22] Unlike the United States, the European Union helps workers and communities adjust by acquiring new skills and investments wherever they are expected to be most viable rather than only in green energy.

---

19. For a more complete comparison, see Lawrence (2024).

20. The major elements in the program are a European regional development fund, a cohesion fund, a European social fund, and a youth employment initiative.

21. European Commission, 2014-2020 Cohesion Policy Overview, https://cohesiondata. ec.europa.eu/cohesion_overview/14-20.

22. European Commission, "The Just Transition Mechanism: Making Sure No One Is Left Behind," https://commission.europa.eu/strategy-and-policy/priorities-2019-2024/ european-green-deal/finance-and-green-deal/just-transition-mechanism_en.

The contrast between the United States and European Union is note-worthy. Europe commits major resources to assist workers and communities; the federal government in the United States provides nominal assistance. According to Bartik (2020, 101), assembling data from numerous sources for years around 2015, the US federal government spent only $10.1 billion in 2019 dollars on tax incentives and programs on place-based jobs programs (and US states around $50 billion).[23]

Are There Political Payoffs to Industrial Policies? Evidence from Europe

Some observers claim that more place-based policies could reduce growing populism, which is fanned in part by regional economic divergences. According to Clara Hendrikson, Mark Muro, and William Galston (2018, 32):

> Economic divergence...creates demand for the very political leadership and policies likely to intensify the plight of left-behind communities. This dangerous feedback loop plagues liberal democracies across the West today and intervening to disrupt this cycle is the challenge of our time. As one *Economist* article on the dangers of regionally imbalanced economic growth warns, "if economists cannot provide answers, populist insurgents will."[24]

But the European experience should give pause to the view that economic policies can provide the solution to populist pressures. The idea that economic grants will bolster support for the European project reflects the supposition that populism and emergent nationalism are being driven by economic considerations rather than concerns about threats to local identities, religious and cultural norms, and antagonism toward the elitism perceived in European governance by many working-class Europeans.

Between 2014 and 2020, for example, Poland was by far the largest recipient of such funds, receiving more than €60 billion—three times as much as Italy, the second-largest recipient. Despite this largesse, after 2015, the attitude toward the European Union of the authoritarian Law and

---

23. For a more complete analysis of labor and capital market adjustment in the US and EU in response to climate change policies, see Lawrence (2024).

24. According to *The Economist*, "In many rich economies prosperous areas already support poor ones. Subsidies—health and pension payments, as well as industrial and agricultural protections—provide a cushion against regional decline. But they are not a basis for long-run economic recovery and have not been enough to stem the growth of populist political movements" ("Place-Based Economic Policies as a Response to Populism," *The Economist*, December 15, 2016, https://www.economist.com/finance-and-economics/2016/12/15/place-based-economic-policies-as-a-response-to-populism).

Justice Party under President Andrzej Duda was hostile, partly because of concerns among conservative Polish voters about European liberal social attitudes, including on abortion and LGBTQ rights.

The situation is similar in France, where the biggest recipient of EU cohesion funds in mainland France is Nord-Pas-de-Calais, once a major producer of coal, steel, and textiles. In the National Assembly, it is represented by Marine Le Pen, the head of the right-wing National Rally party (formerly the National Front). Thus some of the biggest recipients of funding are now hotbeds of discontent, brimming with voters unsettled by the cultural and political pressures that have accompanied European integration and threatening the bloc's cohesion.[25] The political disruptions due to climate change policies could exacerbate these tensions.[26]

Conclusion

Industrial policies are back in vogue throughout the developed world. The United States, Europe, and Japan have all adopted policies that seek to achieve goals that free markets would not automatically realize. These goals include enhancing R&D spending to improve technological capacity, especially in semiconductors; increasing national security goals by imposing controls on inward and outward foreign investment and trade; establishing more secure international supply chains; and decarbonizing their economies. To help attain these objectives, countries have taken steps to encourage domestic production and in some cases the reshoring of production.

These policies may achieve some of these goals, but they are also bound to affect the distribution of income among people and places and not necessarily in a way that makes growth more inclusive. Indeed, although they are often promoted as measures that will help less skilled workers and left-behind places, whatever manufacturing they do stimulate is more likely to be biased towards helping more skilled workers and places that are already benefiting from growth based on innovation.

Although the policy goals may be similar, there are some striking differences in the approaches being adopted, because of differences in conceptions about the appropriate role for government and differences in political forces at play. Climate policies provide a telling example. Both the United

25. Laurence Norman and Drew Hinshaw, "The EU Spent a Bundle to Unify the Continent. It's Not Working," *Wall Street Journal*, April 8, 2018, https://www.wsj.com/articles/the-eu-spent-a-bundle-to-unify-the-continent-its-not-working-1533743729.

26. See Sarah Marsh, Kate Abnett, and Gloria Dickie, "'Greenlash' fuels fears for Europe's environmental ambitions," Reuters, August 10, 2023, www.reuters.com/sustainability/greenlash-fuels-fears-europes-environmental-ambitions-2023-08-10/.

States and the European Union have announced the goal of achieving net-zero emissions by 2050. The European Union has implemented an emissions trading system that raises the costs of production that uses fossil fuels.[27] Partisan politics have prevented the United States from implementing such a system at the federal level. Instead, subsidies for renewable energy investment and production have been more politically palatable.

Policymakers in both the United States and the European Union have acknowledged the need to accompany their actions to decarbonize their economies with policies that achieve "climate justice" and "leave no one behind." The resources and policies implemented by the federal government in the United States are unlikely to achieve these goals. Aid is available to too many communities, and the focus on trying to remedy the dislocation of workers and communities through green jobs is too narrow. Additional measures are needed to help communities and workers take advantage of opportunities, regardless of whether they involve green energy.

In Europe the resources devoted to the Just Transition Fund complement the generous programs already in place to promote structural change and aim at helping workers take advantage of opportunities beyond green energy. Although there are some noteworthy examples of success, such as the programs for coal workers in the Ruhr (Arora and Schroeder 2022), implementing successful place-based policies remains challenging even in the European Union.

---

27. For more discussion of climate policies and their labor market impacts in Europe, see Lawrence (2024).

13

Can Developing Economies Thrive in the New Environment?

Many if not most developing economies seek to promote manufacturing to achieve economic growth. Despite premature deindustrialization, countries still in the earlier stages of economic development—on the upward slope of the manufacturing employment share (MES) curve (analyzed in part I of this book)—should still be able to grow by producing manufactured goods for their domestic markets and export markets. Manufacturing is likely to provide fewer employment opportunities than it used to, however.

This chapter considers some of the challenges and opportunities these major developments pose for manufacturing growth in developing economies: digital technologies, developments in the trading system, effects of geopolitics, and the green transition.

Digitally Driven Opportunities for Growth

Digital technologies can help raise living standards in poor countries. The use of mobile devices allows people in poor countries to obtain a vast amount of information and knowledge. The ability at little or no cost to acquire educational resources, participate in online courses, learn new skills, and become informed about the latest global trends and best practices can foster innovation, improve decision making, and enhance productivity.

Mobile phones, for example, allow countries to establish communications networks that have enhanced the efficiency of finance through mobile banking and payments mechanisms. The M-Pesa payments system in East Africa and others like it have fostered financial inclusion, saving banks the resources required to build brick and mortar branches and saving people the time and money required to obtain banking services and helping them avoid the security dangers of carrying cash. Mobile phones can also be used to improve the performance of farmers and fisherfolk by giving them access to prices and potential buyers in real time (Jensen 2007).

Blockchain technology offers opportunities to protect contracting and property rights by storing data in a transparent digital ledger that cannot be altered. National identity and credit cards in India have facilitated the distribution of government assistance directly into individual bank accounts of poor families, reducing inefficiency and corruption.

These technologies also open up new opportunities for a wide range of entrepreneurial endeavors. E-commerce allows firms to expand their customer base and individuals and firms to market and sell their services. Digital technologies allow firms to use scarce capital more efficiently. They allow car owners to become taxi drivers by joining firms like Uber and homeowners to sell hospitality services through firms like Airbnb. The cloud facilitates the sharing of hardware, such as servers and software, and data, saving upfront costs for liquidity-constrained firms. The ability to track goods through the internet can reduce waste and facilitate transportation.

Digital technologies can also play an important role in developing economies' infrastructure. Smart grid systems can improve energy distribution and efficiency. The Internet of Things can enhance the efficiency of transportation and product distribution. Digital platforms can also improve distribution systems in commerce. E-commerce giants like Amazon and Alibaba host millions of third-party sellers, and millions of small and medium-sized enterprises use Facebook for marketing.

As in advanced economies, however, technologies that improve productivity in manufacturing relative to services can reduce manufacturing employment, potentially accelerating deindustrialization (as shown in chapter 4). China's emphasis on technology in its industrial policies, for example, is increasing demand for more educated and skilled Chinese workers, increasing wage inequality, and potentially undermining President Xi Jinping's goals of shared prosperity.

It is also far easier for developing economies to import technologies embodied in machines than technologies that require skilled people with tacit knowledge for their implementation. As described by Jonathan Haskel and Stian Westlake (2017), new digital technologies have changed the nature of fixed assets from equipment to intangible capital (such as R&D, software, and branding), some of which is likely to be more difficult for poorer countries to adopt if they lack the people or skills needed to do so. Indeed, there is evidence that even in industrial economies, this form of capital tends to be highly concentrated in a few firms and not easily diffused (Claes and Demertzis 2021). Nonetheless, all told, the potential role of these technologies in stimulating growth points to the growing importance for developing economies of policies that encourage investments in broadband connectivity and integrate digital skills in their education systems.

New Challenges and Opportunities for Trade

The spread of digital technologies could both restrict and promote manufacturing production and trade. On the one hand, as developed economies improve and diffuse robotics and advanced manufacturing (3D printing), the demand for labor-intensive tasks and products produced in developing economies could fall.[1] This decline could reduce their opportunities for growth led by the export of manufactured goods.

On the other hand, 3D printing could give developing economies access to specialized inputs that could be combined with more labor-intensive tasks, making them more competitive, as Caroline Freund and colleagues note, using the example of hearing aids.[2] Artificial intelligence could replace some routine activities undertaken by developing economies, but it could also give these countries access to capabilities they currently lack.[3]

Even if they make export-led growth through manufacturing more difficult, information technologies could lead to more export-led growth by making services more tradable. Richard Baldwin (2019) argues that new technologies facilitating remote work, such as conferencing software, could expand the production and export of services by developing economies. This "globotization" of services could take advantage of low labor costs in developing economies in combination with cheap and effective communications technologies. Instant translation technologies could make cross-border cross-language interactions easier. These changed opportunities could allow better-educated workers in developing economies to export services

---

1. Paul Bairoch (1993) describes the negative impact of the original Industrial Revolution on manufacturing in the developing world.

2. Caroline Freund, Alen Mulabdic, and Michele Ruta, "Myth Busting: Why 3-D Printing May Actually Be Good for Trade," World Bank blog, November 18, 2019, https://blogs.worldbank.org/trade/myth-busting-why-3-d-printing-might-actually-be-good-trade.

3. There is evidence that ChatGPT compresses the productivity distribution by benefiting low-ability workers more than those with high abilities. See Noy and Zhang (2023). See also the comments by David Autor quoted in an NPR episode of *Planet Money*, https://www.npr.org/sections/money/2023/05/09/1174933574/what-if-ai-could-rebuild-the-middle-class.

such as software, coding, data processing, accounting services, marketing services, and call centers as long as regulations in developed economies permit such transactions.

Geopolitics

Geopolitical tensions have heightened insecurity about global supply chains, changing perceptions of the dangers of excessive dependence on a single supplier for vital inputs. Both China and the United States have tried to use their dominance of particular goods and technologies to gain political advantage. The United States cut off the sale of key semiconductors to Huawei and ZTE as part of the trade war with China started by former president Donald Trump, and President Joseph R. Biden Jr. has doubled down in preventing Chinese access to machines that are vital for the production of advanced semiconductors. China has used denial of its exports of rare earths to counter actions by its adversaries and sanctions on trade to silence critics such as Lithuania and Australia. Numerous industries were caught in the crossfire when the United States imposed tariffs on steel and aluminum and other countries retaliated on US exports. Russia's invasion of Ukraine and the war that has ensued brought home to Germany the dangers of excessive reliance on Russian natural gas.

Even setting aside geopolitics, the shortages created by the economic distortions from shutdowns in response to the COVID epidemic heightened awareness of the importance of "derisking" trade. As countries encourage reshoring, the opportunities for developing economies to participate in global supply chains could be shrinking.

As with digital technologies, these developments can also provide new opportunities. Rather than bring production home to developed economies, where labor costs tend to be high, firms can diversify their supply chains away from excessive dependence on China toward other developing economies. The "China plus one" strategies multinational companies are adopting are providing new opportunities for developing economies such as India, Vietnam, Cambodia, and Mexico to attract foreign investors. Rather than deglobalizing, the world could move toward globalization that is more dispersed.

The Green Transition

Without developing-economy participation, efforts to limit global warming will fail. But the mounting pressures on developing economies to undertake mitigation policies have raised concerns about the constraints climate mitigation will place on their economic growth. The fact that climate change is a problem that has been overwhelmingly caused by advanced economies has given rise to understandable demands for compensation by developing economies in order to pay for the costs they are now being required to bear.

As countries turn away from producing and consuming fossil fuels, trade in oil, coal, and natural gas seems bound to decline. Countries that export these products or the manufactured goods (such as steel, aluminum, fertilizers, and cement) that embody them in their production will suffer. In addition, making investments in renewable energy requires forgoing other investments, which could mean slower growth.

But the shift toward renewables also has the potential to generate new sources of green growth that could be produced by developing economies and exported, either as raw materials or as goods with additional domestic value added. Renewable energy is less easily transportable than oil; places with access to water, wind, sun, and thermal power may therefore become more competitive locations for producers of energy-intensive products. New places, many in developing economies, could become more attractive locations for the production of solar panels, wind turbines, hydroelectric generators, and electric vehicles as well as energy-intensive products like steel, fertilizers, and plastics (Hausmann and Ahuja 2023). In addition, unexploited copper, nickel, and zinc deposits in many developing economies are vital for electrification, and raw materials such as lithium and cobalt are needed for batteries. Refining and battery assembly could move closer to where they are mined.

Developing economies also have abundant biomass resources, including plants specifically grown for this purpose and agricultural waste. For example, the large shrub called jatropha can be grown in arid and marginal lands, making it suitable for biofuel production without competing with food crops. Forest residues and jatropha can be used to produce fuel, allowing for the continued operation of combustion engines and machines that require them. Biomass products such as pellets and briquettes, which can be used for heating, cooking, and generating electricity, can be produced and exported.

Conclusion

Even in a world dominated by automation, technological and geopolitical rivalry, supply chain insecurity, and the challenge of climate change, globalization is not dead. These factors do change the nature of global trade, however.

Digital technologies favor trade in services more than trade in goods, geopolitical rivalries could encourage diversification and friendshoring more than reshoring, and the green transition could promote rather than constrain growth by providing many developing economies with new opportunities for specialization. Although countries need to shift their policies to take advantage of new opportunities, the prospects for manufacturing export-led growth in developing economies may not be as bleak as some might suppose.

References

Aaronson, Stephanie, Mary C. Daly, William Wascher, and David W. Wilcox. 2019. Okun Revisited: Who Benefits Most from a Strong Economy? *Brookings Papers on Economic Activity* (Spring). Washington: Brookings Institution. Available at https://www.brookings.edu/bpea-articles/okun-revisited-who-benefits-most-from-a-strong-economy/.

Abraham, Katharine, and Melissa Kearney. 2018. *Explaining the Decline in the US Employment-to-Population Ratio: A Review of the Evidence*. NBER Working Paper 24333. Cambridge, MA: National Bureau of Economic Research.

Acemoglu, Daron, and David H. Autor. 2011. Skills, Tasks and Technologies: Implications for Employment and Earnings. In *Handbook of Labor Economics*, vol. 4B, ed. Orley Ashenfelter and David E. Card, 1043–171. Amsterdam: Elsevier.

Acemoglu, Daron, David Autor, David Dorn, Gordon H. Hanson, and Brendan Price. 2016. Import Competition and the Great US Employment Sag of the 2000s. *Journal of Labor Economics* 34, no. S1: S141–98.

Acs, Gregory, and Sheldon Danziger. 1993. Educational Attainment, Industrial Structure, and Male Earnings through the 1980s. *Journal of Human Resources* (Summer): 618.

Adao, Rodrigo, Michal Kolesar, and Eduardo Morales. 2018. *Shift-Share Designs: Theory and Inference*. NBER Working Paper 24944. Cambridge, MA: National Bureau of Economic Research.

Amirapu, Amrit, and Arvind Subramanian. 2015. *Manufacturing or Services? An Indian Illustration of a Development Dilemma*. Working Paper 409. Washington: Center for Global Development.

Amiti, Mary, Mi Dai, Robert Feenstra, and John Romalis. 2017. *How Did China's WTO Entry Benefit U.S. Consumers?* Discussion Paper 12076. London: Centre for Economic Policy Research.

Anand, Rahul, Saurabh Mishra, and Shanaka J. Peiris. 2013. *Inclusive Growth: Measurement and Determinants*. IMF Working Paper 135. Washington: International Monetary Fund.

Antràs, Pol, Teresa C. Fort, and Felix Tintelnot. 2017. The Margins of Global Sourcing: Theory and Evidence from US Firms. *American Economic Review* 107, no. 9: 2514–64.

Arora, Anmol, and Heike Schroeder. 2022. How to avoid unjust energy transitions: insights from the Ruhr region. *Energy, Sustainability and Society* 12, no. 19. Available at https://doi.org/10.1186/s13705-022-00345-5.

Arrow, Kenneth J. 1962. The Economic Implications of Learning by Doing. *Review of Economic Studies* 29, no. 3: 155–73.

Asquith, Brian, Sanjana Goswami, David Neumark, and Antonio Rodriguez-Lopez. 2019. US Job Flows and the China Shock. *Journal of International Economics* 118: 123–37. Available at https://www.sciencedirect.com/science/article/abs/pii/S0022199619300169.

Atkinson, Robert D., Mark Muro, and Jacob Whiton. 2019. *The Case for Growth Centers: How to Spread Tech Innovation across America*. Washington: Brookings Institution.

Austin, Benjamin, Edward Glaeser, and Lawrence Summers. 2018. Jobs for the Heartland: Place-Based Policies in 21st Century America. *Brookings Papers on Economic Activity* (Spring): 151–232.

Autor, David. 2018. Comment on Chapter 9: "Recent Flattening in the Higher Education Wage Premium: Polarization, Skill Downgrading, or Both?" by Robert G. Valletta. In *Education, Skills, and Technical Change: Implications for Future US GDP Growth*, ed., Charles R. Hulten and Valerie A. Ramey, 342–54. Cambridge, MA: National Bureau of Economic Research.

Autor, David. 2019. Work of the Past, Work of the Future. *AEA Papers and Proceedings* 109: 1–32. Available at https://www.aeaweb.org/articles?id=10.1257/pandp.20191110.

Autor, David, and David Dorn. 2013. The Growth of Low Skill Service Jobs and the Polarization of the US Labor Market. *American Economic Review* 103, no. 5: 1553–97.

Autor, David, David Dorn, and Gordon Hanson. 2013. The China Syndrome: Local Labor Market Effects of Import Competition in the United States. *American Economic Review* 103, no. 6: 2121–68.

Autor, David, David Dorn, and Gordon Hanson. 2015. Untangling Trade and Technology: Evidence from Local Labour Market. *Economic Journal* 125, no. 584: 621–46.

Autor, David, David Dorn, and Gordon Hanson. 2018. *When Work Disappears: Manufacturing Decline and the Falling Marriage-Market Value of Young Men*. NBER Working Paper 23173. Cambridge, MA: National Bureau of Economic Research.

Autor, David, David Dorn, and Gordon Hanson. 2021. On the Persistence of the China Shock. *Brookings Papers on Economic Activity* (Fall). Washington: Brookings Institution. Available at https://www.brookings.edu/bpea-articles/on-the-persistence-of-the-china-shock/.

Autor, David, Arindrajit Dube, and Annie McGrew. 2023. *The Unexpected Compression: Competition at Work in the Low Wage Labor Market*. NBER Working Paper 31010. Cambridge, MA: National Bureau of Economic Research.

Autor, David, Claudia Goldin, and Lawrence F. Katz. 2020. Extending the Race between Education and Technology. *AEA Papers and Proceedings* 110: 347–51.

Autor, David H., Lawrence F. Katz, and Alan B. Krueger. 1998. Computing Inequality: Have Computers Changed the Labor Market? *Quarterly Journal of Economics* 113, no. 4: 1169–213.

Autor, David, Frank Levy, and Richard J. Murnane. 2003. The Skill Content of Recent Technological Change: An Empirical Exploration. *Quarterly Journal of Economics* 118, no. 4: 1279–33.

Autor, David, David Dorn, Gordon Hanson, and Kaveh Majlesi. 2020. Importing Political Polarization? The Electoral Consequences of Rising Trade Exposure. *American Economic Review* 110, no. 10: 3139–83.

Badlam, Justin, Stephen Clark, Suhrid Gajendragadkar, Adi Kumar, Sara O'Rourke, and Dale Swartz. 2022. *The CHIPS and Science Act: Here's What's in It*. McKinsey & Company, October 4. Available at https://www.mckinsey.com/industries/public-and-social-sector/our-insights/the-chips-and-science-act-heres-whats-in-it.

Bah, El-hadj M. 2011. Structural Transformation Paths across Countries. *Emerging Markets Finance and Trade*. African Development Bank, May.

Baily, Martin N., and Barry P. Bosworth. 2014. US Manufacturing: Understanding Its Past and Its Potential Future. *Journal of Economic Perspectives* 28: 3–26.

Baily, Martin, and Robert Z. Lawrence. 2004. What Happened to the Great US Jobs Machine? The Role of Trade and Electronic Offshoring. *Brookings Papers on Economic Activity*, no. 2: 211–70. Washington: Brookings Institution.

Bairoch, Paul. 1993. *Economics and World History, Myths and Paradoxes*. Chicago: University of Chicago Press.

Baldwin, Richard. 2006. Globalisation: The Great Unbundling(s). *Economic Council of Finland* 20: 5–47.

Baldwin, Richard. 2016. *The Great Convergence: Information Technology and the New Globalization*. Cambridge, MA: Harvard University Press.

Baldwin, Richard. 2019. *The Globotics Upheaval: Globalization, Robotization and the Future of Work*. Oxford: Oxford University Press.

Barro, Robert J., and Xavier Sala-i-Martin. 1991. Convergence across States and Regions. *Brookings Papers on Economic Activity*, no. 1: 107–82. Washington: Brookings Institution.

Barrot, Jean-Noël, Erik Loualiche, Matthew Plosser, and Julien Sauvagnat. 2017. *Import Competition and Household Debt*. Staff Report 821. Federal Reserve Bank of New York.

Bartik, Timothy J. 2020. Using Place-Based Jobs Policies to Help Distressed Communities. *Journal of Economic Perspectives* 34, no. 3: 99–127.

Batistich, Mary Kate, and Timothy N. Bond. 2019. *Stalled Racial Progress and Japanese Trade in the 1970s and 1980s*. IZA Discussion Paper 12133. Bonn: Institute of Labor Economics.

Baumol, William. 1967. Macroeconomics of Unbalanced Growth: The Anatomy of Urban Crisis. *American Economic Review* 57, no. 3: 415–26.

Baumol, William, and William G. Bowen. 1965. On the Performing Arts: The Anatomy of Their Economic Problems. *American Economic Review* 55, no. 2: 495–502.

Baumol, William, Sue Anne Batey Blackman, and Edward N. Wolff. 1985. Unbalanced Growth Revisited: Asymptotic Stagnancy and New Evidence. *American Economic Review* 75, no. 4: 806–17. Available at https://www.jstor.org/stable/1821357.

Baum-Snow, Nathaniel, Matthew Freedman, and Ronni Pavan. 2018. Why Has Urban Inequality Increased? *American Economic Journal: Applied Economics* 10, no. 4: 1–42.

Beaudry, Paul, David A. Green, and Benjamin M. Sand. 2014. The Declining Fortunes of the Young since 2000. *American Economic Review* 104, no. 5: 381–86.

Becker, Gary. 1981. *Treatise on the Family*. Cambridge, MA: Harvard University Press.

Beraja, Martin, Erik Hurst, and Juan Ospina. 2016. *The Aggregate Implications of Regional Business Cycles*. NBER Working Paper 21956. Cambridge, MA: National Bureau of Economic Research.

Berger, Thor, and Carl Benedikt Frey. 2016. Did the Computer Revolution Shift the Fortunes of US Cities? Technology Shocks and the Geography of New Jobs. *Regional Science and Urban Economics* 57: 38–45.

Bernard, Andrew B., and Teresa C. Fort. 2015. Factoryless Goods Producers in the US. *American Economic Review* 105, no. 5: 518–23.

Bernard, Andrew B., J. Bradford Jensen, and Peter K. Schott. 2006. Survival of the Best Fit: Exposure to Low-Wage Countries and the (Uneven) Growth of US Manufacturing Plants. *Journal of International Economics* 68, no. 1: 219 –37.

Bernard, Andrew B., Valerie Smeets, and Frederic Warzynski. 2017. Rethinking Deindustrialization. *Economic Policy* 32, no. 89: 5–38. Available at https://doi.org/10.1093/epolic/eiw016.

Berry, Christopher, and Edward Glaeser. 2005. The Divergence of Human Capital Levels across Cities. *Papers in Regional Science* 84, no. 3.

Berube, Alan, and Cecile Murray. 2018. *Renewing America's Economic Promise through Older Industrial Cities*. Washington: Brookings Institution. Available at https://www.brookings.edu/research/older-industrial-cities/#01073.

Bistline, John, Neil Mehrotra, and Catherine Wolfram. 2023. Economic Implications of the Climate Provisions of the Inflation Reduction Act. Draft presented at spring 2023 meeting of the *Brookings Papers on Economic Activity*.

Bistline, John, Nikit Abhyankar, Geoffrey Blanford, Leon Clarke, Rachel Fakhry, Haewon McJeon, John Reilly, et al. 2022. Actions for Reducing US Emissions at Least 50% by 2030. *Science* 376: 922–24. Available at https://doi.org/10.1126/science.abn0661.

Blair, Peter Q., Tomas G. Castagnino, Erica L. Groshen, Papia Debroy, Byron Auguste, Shad Ahmed, Fernando Garcia Diaz, and Cristian Bonavida. 2020. *Searching for STARs: Work Experience as a Job Market Signal for Workers without Bachelor's Degrees*. NBER Working Paper 26844. Cambridge, MA: National Bureau of Economic Research.

Blanchard, Olivier Jean, and Lawrence Katz. 1992. Regional Evolutions. *Brookings Papers on Economic Activity*, no. 1: 1–75.

Blau, Francine D., and Lawrence M. Kahn. 2017. The Gender Wage Gap: Extent, Trends and Explanations. *Journal of Economic Literature* 55, no. 3: 789–865.

Bloom, Nicholas, Mirko Draca, and John Van Reenen. 2016. Trade Induced Technical Change: The Impact of Chinese Imports on Innovation, IT, and Productivity. *Review of Economic Studies* 83, no. 1: 87–117.

Bloom, Nicholas, Andre Kurmann, Kyle Handley, and Philip Luck. 2019. The Impact of Chinese Trade on U.S. Employment: The Good, the Bad, and the Apocryphal. *2019 Meeting Papers* 1433. Society for Economic Dynamics. Available at https://ideas.repec.org/p/red/sed019/1433.html.

Boppart, Timo. 2014. Structural Change and the Kaldor Facts in a Growth Model with Relative Price Effects and Non-Gorman Preferences. *Econometrica* 82, no. 6: 2167–96.

Bound, John, and Harry J. Holzer. 1993. Industrial Shifts, Skills Levels, and the Labor Market for White and Black Males. *Review of Economics and Statistics* 75, no. 3: 387–96.

Bound, John, and Harry J. Holzer. 2000. Demand Shifts, Population Adjustments, and Labor Market Outcomes during the 1980s. *Journal of Labor Economics* 18, no. 1: 20–54.

Bound, John, and George Johnson. 1992. Changes in the Structure of Wages in the 1980s: An Evaluation of Alternative Explanations. *American Economic Review* 82, no. 3: 371–92.

Bown, Chad P. 2023. *How the United States Solved South Korea's Problems with Electric Vehicle Subsidies under the Inflation Reduction Act.* PIIE Working Paper 23-6. Washington: Peterson Institute for International Economics. Available at https://www.piie.com/sites/default/files/2023-07/wp23-6.pdf.

Bown, Chad, and Caroline Freund. 2019. *Active Labor Market Policies: Lessons from other Countries for the United States.* PIIE Working Paper 19-2. Washington: Peterson Institute for International Economics. Available at https://www.piie.com/publications/working-papers/active-labor-market-policies-lessons-other-countries-united-states.

Brainard, Lael, Robert Litan, and Nicholas Warren. 2005. A Fairer Deal for America's Workers in a New Era of Offshoring. In *Offshoring White-Collar Work: The Issues and Implications*, ed. Lael Brainard and Susan M. Collins. Washington: Brookings Trade Forum.

Breen, Richard, and Leire Salazar. 2011. Educational Assortative Mating and Earnings Inequality in the United States. *American Journal of Sociology* 117, no. 3: 808–43.

Bresnahan, Timothy, Alfonso Gambardella, Anna Lee Saxenian, and Scott Wallsten. 2001. *"Old Economy" Inputs for "New Economy" Outcomes: Cluster Formation in the New Silicon Valley.* SIEPR Discussion Paper 00-43S. Stanford, CA: Stanford Institute for Policy Research.

Broz, J. Lawrence, Jeffry Frieden, and Stephen Weymouth. 2021. Populism in Place: The Economic Geography of the Globalization Backlash. *International Organization.* Available at https://www.cambridge.org/core/journals/international-organization/article/abs/populism-in-place-the-economic-geography-of-the-globalization-backlash/98ED873D925E0590CB9A78AEC68BB439.

Buera, Francisco J., and Joseph P. Kaboski. 2009. Can Traditional Theories of Structural Change Fit the Data? *Journal of the European Economic Association* 7: 469–77.

Buera, Francisco J., Joseph P. Kaboski, and Richard Rogerson. 2015. *Skill Biased Structural Change.* NBER Working Paper 21165. Cambridge, MA: National Bureau of Economic Research.

Busso, Matias, Jesse Gregory, and Patrick M. Kline. 2010. *Assessing the Incidence and Efficiency of a Prominent Place Based Policy.* NBER Working Paper 16096. Cambridge, MA: National Bureau of Economic Research.

Byrne, David M., and Carol Corrado. 2017. *ICT Prices and ICT Services: What Do They Tell Us about Productivity and Technology?* Finance and Economics Discussion Series 2017-015. Washington: Board of Governors of the Federal Reserve System. Available at https://doi.org/10.17016/FEDS.2017.015.

Byrne, David M., Stephen D. Oliner, and Daniel E. Sichel. 2017. *How Fast Are Semiconductor Prices Falling?* Finance and Economics Discussion Series 2017-005. Washington: Board of Governors of the Federal Reserve System.

Caliendo, Lorenzo, Maximiliano Dvorkin, and Fernando Parro. 2019. Trade and Labor Market Dynamics: General Equilibrium Analysis of the China Trade Shock. *Econometrica* 87, no. 3: 741–835.

Card, David E., and John DiNardo. 2002. *Skill Biased Technological Change and Rising Wage Inequality: Some Problems and Puzzles.* NBER Working Paper 8769. Cambridge, MA: National Bureau of Economic Research. Available at https://ssrn.com/abstract=299813.

Carr, Tyler, Eric Chewning, Mike Doheny, Anu Madgavkar, Asutosh Padhi, and Andrew Tingley. 2022. *Delivering the US manufacturing renaissance.* McKinsey & Company, August 29.

Case, Anne, and Angus Deaton. 2020. *Deaths of Despair and the Future of Capitalism.* Princeton, NJ: Princeton University Press.

Casper, R., and E. Sundin. 2021. Electrification in the automotive industry: Effects in remanufacturing. *Journal of Remanufacturing* 11: 121–136.

Charles, Kerwin-Kofi, Erik Hurst, and Matthew J. Notowidigdo. 2016. The Masking of the Decline in Manufacturing Employment by the Housing Bubble. *Journal of Economic Perspectives* 30, no. 2: 179–200.

Charles, Kerwin-Kofi, Erik Hurst, and Mariel Schwartz. 2019. The Transformation of Manufacturing and the Decline in US Employment. *NBER Macroeconomics Annual 2018*, vol. 33, ed. Martin Eichenbaum and Jonathan A. Parker. Chicago: University of Chicago Press for the National Bureau of Economic Research.

Che, Yi, Xun Xu, and Yan Zhang. 2018. Chinese Import Competition, Crime, and Government Transfers in US. *Journal of Comparative Economics* 46: 544–67.

Chetty, Raj, Nathaniel Hendren, Patrick Kline, and Emmanuel Saez. 2014. Where Is the Land of Opportunity? The Geography of Intergenerational Mobility in United States. *Quarterly Journal of Economics* 129, no. 4: 1553–623. Available at https://academic.oup.com/qje/article/129/4/1553/1853754.

Chirinko, Robert S. 2008. *The Long and Short of It.* CESifo Working Paper Series 2234. Available at https://ssrn.com/abstract=1098827.

Claes, Grégory, and Maria Demertzis. 2021. *The Productivity Paradox: Policy Lessons from MICROPROD.* Policy Contributions 01/21. Brussels: Bruegel.

Clark, Colin. 1957. *The Conditions of Economic Progress.* London: Macmillan.

Cline, William R. 1999. *Trade and Income Distribution: The Debate and New Evidence.* PIIE Policy Brief PB99-07. Washington: Peterson Institute for International Economics. Available at https://www.piie.com/publications/policy-briefs/trade-and-income-distribution-debate-and-new-evidence.

Colantone, Italo, and Piero Stanig. 2018. The Trade Origins of Economic Nationalism: Import Competition and Voting Behavior. *American Journal of Political Science* 62, no. 4: 936–53.

Comin, Diego A., Danial Lashkari, and Martí Mestieri. 2021. Structural Change with Long-Run Income and Price Effects. *Econometrica* 89, no. 1: 311–74.

Conference Board. 2016. Conference Board Total Economy Database (TED). New York.

Corden, W. M. 1984. Booming Sector and Dutch Disease Economics: Survey and Consolidation. *Oxford Economic Papers*, New Series 36, no. 3: 359–80.

Coricelli, Fabrizio, and Farshad R. Ravasan. 2017. *Structural Change and the China Syndrome: Baumol versus Trade Effects*. CEPR Discussion Paper DP12069. London: Centre for Economic Policy Research.

Council of Economic Advisers. 2016. *Active Labor Market Policies: Theory and Evidence for What Works*. Issues Brief, August. Washington. Available at https://obamawhitehouse.archives.gov/sites/default/files/page/files/20161220_active_labor_market_policies_issue_brief_cea.pdf.

Dabla-Norris, Era, Alun Thomas, Rodrigo Garcia-Verdu, and Yingyuan Chen. 2013. *Benchmarking Structural Transformation across the World*. IMF Working Paper WP/13/176. Washington: International Monetary Fund.

Dadush, Uri. 2015. *Is Manufacturing Still a Key to Growth?* Research Papers & Policy Papers 1507. Rabat, Morocco: Policy Center for the New South. Available at https://ideas.repec.org/p/ocp/rpaper/pp-15-07.html.

Dasgupta, Sukti, and Ajit Singh. 2006. *Manufacturing, Services and Premature Deindustrialization in Developing Countries: A Kaldorian Analysis*. Research Paper 2006/049. Helsinki: UNU-WIDER, United Nations University.

Davis, Steven, and Till Von Wachter. 2011. Recessions and the Costs of Job Loss. *Brookings Papers on Economic Activity* (Fall): 1–72. Washington: Brookings Institution. Available at https://www.brookings.edu/wp-content/uploads/2011/09/2011b_bpea_davis.pdf.

De Bolle, Monica, and Jeromin Zettelmeyer. 2019. *Measuring the Rise of Economic Nationalism*. PIIE Working Paper 19-15. Washington: Peterson Institute for International Economics. Available at https://www.piie.com/publications/working-papers/measuring-rise-economic-nationalism.

Deep, Akash, and Robert Z. Lawrence. 2008. *Stabilizing State and Local Budgets: A Proposal for Tax-Based Insurance*. Discussion Paper 2008-01, Hamilton Project. Washington: Brookings Institution.

Dew-Becker, I., and R. J. Gordon. 2005. Where Did the Productivity Growth Go? Inflation Dynamics and the Distribution of Income. *Brookings Papers on Economic Activity*, no. 2: 67–150. Washington: Brookings Institution.

Dey, Matthew, Susan N. Houseman, and Anne E. Polivka. 2012. Manufacturers' Outsourcing to Staffing Services. *Industrial and Labor Relations Review* 65, no. 3: 533–59.

Diamond, Rebecca, and Enrico Moretti. 2021. *Where Is Standard of Living Highest? Local Prices and the Geography of Consumption*. NBER Working Paper 29533. Cambridge, MA: National Bureau of Economic Research. Available at https://www.nber.org/papers/w29533.

Diao, Xinshen, Margaret McMillan, and Dani Rodrik. 2017. The Recent Growth Boom in Developing Economies: A Structural-Change Perspective. Available at https://drodrik.scholar.harvard.edu/files/dani-rodrik/files/recent_growth_boom_in_ldcs.pdf.

Dickens, William T., and Lawrence F. Katz. 1986. *Interindustry Wage Differences and Industry Characteristics*. NBER Working Paper 2014. Cambridge, MA: National Bureau of Economic Research.

Dimova, Dilyana. 2019. *The Structural Determinants of the Labor Share in Europe.* IMF Working Paper 2019/067. Washington: International Monetary Fund. Available at https://www.imf.org/en/Publications/WP/Issues/2019/03/22/The-Structural-Determinants-of-the-Labor-Share-in-Europe-46668.

Dollar, David, and Aart Kraay. 2002. Growth Is Good for the Poor. *Journal of Economic Growth* 7, no. 3: 195–225. Available at http://www.jstor.org/stable/40216063.

Duarte, Margarida. 2020. Manufacturing Consumption, Relative Prices, and Productivity. *Journal of Macroeconomics* 65. Available at https://www.sciencedirect.com/science/article/abs/pii/S0164070420301580.

Duarte, Margarida, and Diego Restuccia. 2010. The Role of the Structural Transformation in Aggregate Productivity. *Quarterly Journal of Economics* 125, no. 1: 129–73.

Duff-Brown, Beth. 2018. *The Fog of Development: Evaluating the Millennium Villages Project.* Stanford University, April 20. Available at https://fsi.stanford.edu/news/fog-development-evaluating-millennium-villages-project.

Eastman, Scott, and Nicole Kaeding. 2019. *Opportunity Zones: What We Know and What We Don't.* Tax Foundation, January 8. Available at https://taxfoundation.org/opportunity-zones-what-we-know-and-what-we-dont/.

Eaton, Jonathan., and Samuel. Kortum. 2002. Technology, Geography and Trade. *Econometrica* 70, no. 5: 1741–79.

Eatwell, Roger, and Matthew Goodwin. 2018. *National Populism: The Revolt against Liberal Democracy.* London: Pelican Books.

Ebenstein, Avraham, Ann Harrison, Margaret McMillan, and Shannon Phillips. 2014. Estimating the Impact of Trade and Offshoring on American Workers Using the Current Population Surveys. *Review of Economics and Statistics* 96, no. 3: 581–95.

Eberstadt, Nicholas. 2016. *Men without Work: America's Invisible Crisis.* West Conshohocken, PA: Templeton Press.

Edwards, Lawrence, and Robert Z. Lawrence. 2013. *Rising Tide: Is Growth in Emerging Economies Good for the United States?* Washington: Peterson Institute for International Economics. Available at https://www.piie.com/bookstore/rising-tide-growth-emerging-economies-good-united-states.

Elsby, Michael W. L., Bart Hobjin, and Aysegul Sahin. 2013. The Decline of the US Labor Share. *Brookings Papers on Economic Activity* (Fall). Washington: Brookings Institution.

Engel, Ernst. 1895. Die Productions- und Consumptionsverhaeltnisse des Koenigsreichs Sachsen. In *Zeitschrift des Statistischen Buereaus des Koeniglich Saechsischen Ministeriums des Inneren,* no. 8 und 9.

Eriksson, Katherine, Katheryn Russ, Jay Shambaugh, and Minfei Xu. 2021. Trade Shocks and the Shifting Landscape of US Manufacturing. *Journal of International Money and Finance* 111. Available at https://www.sciencedirect.com/science/article/abs/pii/S0261560620302102.

Esposito, Federico, Costas Arkolakis, and Rodrigo Adao. 2017. *Endogenous Labor Supply and the Gains from International Trade.* Meeting Paper 1044. Society for Economic Dynamics.

Fallows, James, and Deborah Fallows. 2018. *Our Towns: A 100,000 Mile Journey into the Heart of America.* New York: Knopf Doubleday Publishing Group.

Feenstra, Robert C., and Akira Sasahara. 2018. The China Shock. Exports and US Employment: A Global Input-Output Analysis. *Review of International Economics* 26, no. 5: 1053–83.

Feenstra, Robert C., Mong Ma, and Yuan Xu. 2019. US Exports and Employment. *Journal of International Economics* 120: 46–58.

Feler, Leo, and Mine Z. Senses. 2017. Trade Shocks and the Provision of Local Public Goods. *American Economic Journal: Economic Policy* 9, no. 4: 101–43.

Felipe, Jesus, and Aashish Mehta. 2016. Deindustrialization? A Global Perspective. *Economics Letters* 149: 148–51.

Felipe, Jesus, Aashish Mehta, and Changyong Rhee. 2019. Manufacturing Matters but It's the Jobs That Count. *Cambridge Journal of Economics* 43, no. 1: 139–68.

Feyer, James, Bruce Sacerdote, and Ariel Dora Stern. 2007. *Did the Rust Belt Become Shiny? A Study of Cities and Counties That Lost Steel and Auto Jobs in the 1980s.* Brookings-Wharton Papers on Urban Affairs 41–102.

Filos, Erastos. 2015. Four Years of 'Factories of the Future' in Europe: Achievements and Outlook. *International Journal of Computer Integrated Manufacturing* 30, no. 1. Available at https://www.tandfonline.com/doi/abs/10.1080/0951192X.2015.1044759.

Flaaen, Aaron, and Justin Pierce. 2019. Disentangling the Effects of the 2018-2019 Tariffs on a Globally Connected U.S. Manufacturing Sector. *Finance and Economics Discussion Series* 2019-086. Washington: Board of Governors of the Federal Reserve System. Available at https://doi.org/10.17016/FEDS.2019.086.

Flood, Sarah, Miriam King, Renae Rodgers, Steven Ruggles, J. Robert Warren, and Michael Westberry. 2021. Integrated Public Use Microdata Series, Current Population Survey: Version 9.0 [dataset]. Minneapolis, MN: IPUMS. Available at https://doi.org/10.18128/D030.V9.0.

Foellmi, Reto, and Josef Zweimüller. 2008. Structural Change, Engel's Consumption Cycles and Kaldor's Facts of Economic Growth. *Journal of Monetary Economics* 55, no. 7: 1317–28.

Foroohar, Rana. 2022. After Neoliberalism: All Economics Is Local. *Foreign Affairs*, October 28. Available at https://www.foreignaffairs.com/united-states/after-neoliberalism-all-economics-is-local-rana-foroohar.

Fort, Teresa C. 2017. Technology and Production Fragmentation: Domestic versus Foreign Sourcing. *Review of Economic Studies* 84, no. 2: 650–87.

Fort, Teresa C., Justin R. Pierce, and Peter K. Schott. 2018. New Perspectives on the Decline of US Manufacturing Employment. *Journal of Economic Perspectives* 32, no. 2: 47–72.

Foy, Morgan. 2019. *U.S. Consumers Have Borne the Brunt of the Current Trade War.* NBER Digest no. 5 (May). Available at https://www.nber.org/digest/may19/us-consumers-have-borne-brunt-current-trade-war.

Freeman, Richard. 1976. *The Overeducated American.* Cambridge, MA: Academic Press.

Gallagher, Daniel, and Amy Glasmeier. 2020. *Just Institutions for Deep Decarbonization? Essential Lessons from 20th Century Regional Economic and Industrial Transitions in the United States.* MIT CEEPR Working Paper. The Roosevelt Project Special Series. Cambridge, MA: MIT Center for Energy and Environmental Policy Research.

Ganong, Peter, and Daniel Shoag. 2017. Why Has Regional Income Convergence in the US Declined? *Journal of Urban Economics* 102: 76–90.

Gardiner, Ben, Ron Martin, Peter Sunley, and Peter Tyler. 2013. Spatially Unbalanced Growth in the British Economy. *Journal of Economic Geography* 13, no. 6: 889–928. Available at https://doi.org/10.1093/jeg/lbt003.

Gerschenkron, Alexander. 1951. Economic Backwardness in Historical Perspective. Reprinted as chapter 1 in *Economic Backwardness in Historical Perspective*. Cambridge, MA: Harvard University Press, 1962.

Ghani, Ejaz, and Stephen D. O'Connell. 2014. *Can Service Be a Growth Escalator in Low-Income Countries?* Policy Research Working Paper 6971. Washington: World Bank Group.

Glaeser, Edward. 2012. *Triumph of the City*. New York: Penguin Publishing Group.

Goldberg, Pinelopi, and Tristan Reed. 2023. Is the Global Economy Deglobalizing? And if so, why? And what is next? *Brookings Papers on Economic Activity* (Spring). Washington: Brookings Institution.

Goldin, Claudia, and Lawrence F. Katz. 2008. *The Race Between Education and Technology*. Cambridge, MA: Belknap.

Goldstein, Amy. 2017. *Janesville: An American Story*. New York: Simon and Schuster.

Goos, M., J. Konings, and M. Vandeweyer. 2015. *Employment Growth in Europe: The Roles of Innovation, Local Job Multipliers and Institutions*. TKI Discussion Paper 15-10. Utrecht University School of Economics.

Gordon, Robert J. 2012. *Is US Economic Growth Over? Faltering Innovation Confronts Six Headwinds*. NBER Working Paper 18315. Cambridge, MA: National Bureau of Economic Research.

Grabow, Colin. 2022. Protectionist Buy America Requirements Undermine Biden Administration's Infrastructure Goals. Cato at Liberty blog, February 23. Cato Institute. Available at https://www.cato.org/blog/protectionist-buy-america-requirements-undermine-biden-administrations-infrastructure-goals.

Greenstein, Joshua, and Bret Anderson. 2017. Premature Deindustrialization and the Defeminization of Labor. *Journal of Economic Issues* L1, no. 2: 446–57.

Gregory, Terry, Anna Salamons, and Ulrich Zierahn. 2019. *Racing with or against the Machine? Evidence from Europe*. IZA DP 12063. Bonn: Institute of Labor Economics. Available at https://www.iza.org/publications/dp/12063/racing-with-or-against-the-machine-evidence-from-europe.

Griliches, Zvi. 1966. Capital-Skill Complementarity. *Review of Economics and Statistics* 51, no. 4: 465–68.

Groshen, Erica L., John Paul MacDuffie, Susan Helper, and Charles Carson. 2019. *Is a Driverless Future Also Jobless?* Policy Brief. Kalamazoo, MI: W.E. Upjohn Institute for Employment Research.

Grossman, Gene M., and Esteban Rossi-Hansberg. 2008. Trading Tasks: A Simple Theory of Offshoring. *American Economic Review* 98, no. 5: 1978–97.

Gruber, Jonathan, and Simon Johnson. 2019. *Jump-Starting America: How Breakthrough Science Can Revive Economic Growth and the American Dream*. New York: Public Affairs Press.

Guvenen, Fatih, Greg Kaplan, Jae Song, and Justin Weidner. 2017. *Lifetime Incomes in the United States over Six Decades*. NBER Working Paper 23371. Cambridge, MA: National Bureau of Economic Research.

Gyourko, Joseph, Christopher Mayer, and Todd Sinai. 2013. Superstar Cities. *American Economic Journal: Economic Policy* 5, no. 4: 167–99.

Hakobyan, Shushanik, and John McLaren. 2016. Looking for Local Labor Market Effects of NAFTA. *Review of Economics and Statistics* 98, no. 4: 728–41.

Hanson, Gordon H. 2021. Can Trade Work for Workers? The Right Way to Redress Harms and Redistribute Gains. *Foreign Affairs* (May/June). Available at https://www.foreignaffairs.com/articles/united-states/2021-04-20/can-trade-work-workers.

Hanson, Gordon. 2023. *Local Labor Market Impacts of the Energy Transition: Prospects and Policies*. NBER Working Paper 30871. Cambridge, MA: National Bureau of Economic Research. Available at https://doi.org/10.3386/w30871.

Hanson, Gordon H., and Raymond Robertson. 2010. China and the Manufacturing Exports of Other Developing Countries. In *China's Growing Role in World Trade*, ed. Robert Feenstra and Shang-Jin Wei Wei. Chicago: University of Chicago Press for the National Bureau of Economic Research.

Haraguchi, Nobuya, Charles Fang Chin Cheng, and Eveline Smeets. 2017. The Importance of Manufacturing in Economic Development: Has It Changed? *World Development* 93, no. C: 293–315.

Haskel, Jonathan, and Stian Westlake. 2017. *Capitalism without Capital: The Rise of the Intangible Economy*. Princeton, NJ: Princeton University Press.

Hatton, Tim, Echo Liu, Bledi Taska, and Rucha Vankudre. 2023. *Rebuilding Our Semiconductor Workforce: Making the Most of the CHIPS Act*. Lightcast. Available at https://lightcast.io/resources/research/rebuilding-our-semiconductor-workforce.

Hausmann, Ricardo, and Ketan Ahuja. 2023. A More Globally Minded European Green Industrial Policy. Chapter 8 in *Sparking Europe's New Industrial Revolution: A Policy for Net Zero Growth and Resilience*, ed. Reinhilde Veugelers and Simone Tagliapietra. Bruegel Blueprint 33. Brussels: Bruegel. Available at https://www.bruegel.org/sites/default/files/2023-07/Bruegel%20Blueprint%2033_chapter%208.pdf.

Hausmann, Ricardo, Dani Rodrik, and Andrés Velasco. 2006. Getting the Diagnosis Right. *Finance and Development* 43, no. 1. Available at https://www.imf.org/external/pubs/ft/fandd/2006/03/hausmann.htm.

Helper, Susan, Timothy Krueger, and Howard Wial. 2012. *Locating American Manufacturing: Trends in the Geography of Production*. Washington: Brookings Institution. Available at https://www.nist.gov/system/files/documents/2017/05/09/Brookings_locating_american_manufacturing_report.pdf.

Hendrickson, Clara, Mark Muro, and William A. Galston. 2018. *Countering the Geography of Discontent: Strategies for Left-Behind Places*. Washington: Brookings Institution.

Herrendorf, Berthold, Richard Rogerson, and Ákos Valentinyi. 2013. Two Perspectives on Preferences and Structural Transformation. *American Economic Review* 103, no. 7: 2752–89.

Herrendorf, Berthold, Richard Rogerson, and Ákos Valentinyi. 2014. Growth and Structural Transformation. In *Handbook of Economic Growth*, vol. 2B, 855–941. Amsterdam: Elsevier B.V.

Hicks, John R. 1932. *The Theory of Wages*. London: MacMillan.

Hicks, Michael, and Srikant Devaraj. 2017. *The Myth and the Reality of Manufacturing in America*. Muncie, IN: Center for Business and Economic Research, Ball State University.

Hirschman, Albert O. 1958. *The Strategy of Economic Development*. New Haven, CT: Yale University Press.

Hochschild, Arlie Russell. 2016. *Strangers in Their Own Land*. New York: New Press.

Holmes, Thomas J. 1998. The Effect of State Policies on the Location of Manufacturing: Evidence from State Borders. *Journal of Political Economy* 106, no. 4: 667–705.

Holmes, Thomas J., and John J. Stevens. 2004. Geographic Concentration and Establishment Size: Analysis in an Alternative Economic Geography Model. *Journal of Economic Geography* 4, no. 3: 227–50.

Houseman, Susan N. 2018. *Understanding the Decline of US Manufacturing Employment*. Upjohn Institute Working Paper 18-287. Kalamazoo, MI: W.E. Upjohn Institute for Employment Research. Available at https://doi.org/10.17848/wp18-287.

Houseman, Susan N., Timothy J. Bartik, and Timothy Sturgeon. 2015. Measuring Manufacturing: How the Computer and Semiconductor Industries Affect the Numbers and Perceptions. In *Measuring Globalization: Better Trade Statistics for Better Policy*, Volume 1. Biases to Price, Output, and Productivity Statistics from Trade, ed. Susan N. Houseman and Michael Mandel. Kalamazoo, MI: W.E. Upjohn Institute for Employment Research. Available at https://doi.org/10.17848/9780880994903.vol1ch5.

Houseman, Susan, Christopher Kurz, Paul Lengermann, and Benjamin Mandel. 2011. Offshoring Bias in US Manufacturing. *Journal of Economic Perspectives* 25, no. 2: 111–32.

Hufbauer, Gary, and Sean Lowry. 2012. *US Tire Tariffs: Saving Few Jobs at High Cost*. PIIE Policy Brief PB12-9. Washington: Peterson Institute for International Economics. Available at https://www.piie.com/publications/policy-briefs/us-tire-tariffs-saving-few-jobs-high-cost.

Hunt, Will. 2022a. *Reshoring Chipmaking Capacity Requires High-Skilled Foreign Talent: Estimating the Labor Demand Generated by CHIPS Act Incentives*. Washington: Center for Security and Emerging Technology, Georgetown University. Available at https://cset.georgetown.edu/publication/reshoring-chipmaking-capacity-requires-high-skilled-foreign-talent/.

Hunt, Will. 2022b. *Sustaining US Competitiveness in Semiconductor Manufacturing*. Washington: Center for Security and Emerging Technology, Georgetown University. Available at https://cset.georgetown.edu/publication/sustaining-u-s-competitive-ness-in-semiconductor-manufacturing/.

Hyman, Benjamin. 2018. *Can Displaced Labor Be Retrained? Evidence from Quasi-Random Assignment to Trade Adjustment Assistance*. Federal Reserve Bank of New York. Available at http://dx.doi.org/10.2139/ssrn.3155386.

Inglehart, Ronald F., and Pippa Norris. 2016. *Trump, Brexit, and the Rise of Populism: Economic Have-Nots and Cultural Backlash*. HKS Working Paper RWP16-026. Cambridge, MA: Harvard Kennedy School.

IMF (International Monetary Fund). 2018. Manufacturing Jobs: Implications for Productivity and Inequality. *World Economic Outlook*. Washington.

Jakubik, Adam, and Victor Stolzenburg. 2021. The 'China Shock' Revisited: Insights from Value Added Trade Flows. *Journal of Economic Geography* 21, no. 1: 67–95.

Jensen, Robert. 2007. The digital provide: Information (technology), market performance, and welfare in the South Indian fisheries sector. *Quarterly Journal of Economics* 122, no. 3: 879–924.

Johnson, Harry G. 1976. Notes on the Classical Transfer Problem. *The Manchester School* 44, no. 3: 211–19.

Johnson, Marianne. 2002. More Native than the French: American Physiocrats and Their Political Economy. *History of Economic Ideas* 10, no. 1: 15–31.

Jorgenson, Dale W. 2001. Information Technology and the US Economy. *American Economic Review* 91, no. 1: 1–32.

Jorgenson, Dale W., and Marcel P. Timmer. 2011. Structural Change in Advanced Nations: A New Set of Stylised Facts. *Scandinavian Journal of Economics* 113, no. 1: 1–29. Available at doi:10.1111/j.1467-9442.2010.01637.

Judis, John. 2016. *The Populist Explosion: How the Great Recession Transformed American and European Politics.* New York: Columbia Global Reports.

Kaldor, N. 1966. *Causes of the Slow Rate of Economic Growth of the United Kingdom: An Inaugural Lecture.* Cambridge: Cambridge University Press.

Karabarbounis, Loukas, and Brent Neiman. 2014. The Global Decline of the Labor Share. *Quarterly Journal of Economics* 129, no. 1: 61–103.

Katz, Lawrence F., and Kevin M. Murphy. 1992. Changes in Relative Wages, 1963–1987: Supply and Demand Factors. *Quarterly Journal of Economics* 107, no. 1: 35–78.

Katz, Lawrence F., Jonathan Roth, Richard Hendra, and Kelsey Schaberg. 2022. Why Do Sectoral Employment Programs Work? Lessons from WorkAdvance. *Journal of Labor Economics* 40: S249–91. Available at https://www.journals.uchicago.edu/doi/10.1086/717932.

Kemeny, Thomas, and Michael Storper. 2020. *Superstar Cities and Left-Behind Places: Disruptive Innovation, Labor Demand, and Interregional Inequality.* Working Paper 41. London: International Inequalities Institute, London School of Economics and Political Science.

Kline, Patrick, and Enrico Moretti. 2011. Local Economic Development, Agglomeration Economies and the Big Push: 100 Years of Evidence from the Tennessee Valley Authority. *Quarterly Journal of Economics* 129, no. 1: 275–331.

Kongsamut, Piyabha, Sergio Rebelo, and Danyang Xie. 2001. Beyond Balanced Growth. *Review of Economic Studies* 68: 869–82.

Krueger, Alan B., and Lawrence H. Summers. 1988. Efficiency Wages and the Inter-Industry Wage Structure. *Econometrica* 56, no. 2: 259–93.

Kuznets, Simon. 1965. *Modern Economic Growth: Rate, Structure and Spread.* New Haven, CT: Yale University Press.

Langdon, David, and Rebecca Lehrman. 2012. *The Benefits of Manufacturing Jobs.* Washington: US Department of Commerce.

Larson, E., C. Greig, J. Jenkins, E. Mayfield, A. Pascale, C. Zhang, J. Drossman, R. Williams, S. Pacala, R. Socolow, EJ Baik, R. Birdsey, R. Duke, R. Jones, B. Haley, E. Leslie, K. Paustian, and A. Swan. 2020. *Net-Zero America: Potential Pathways, Infrastructure, and Impacts.* Interim Report (December 15). Princeton University.

Lawrence, Robert Z. 1983. Is Trade Deindustrializing America? A Medium-Term Perspective. *Brookings Papers on Economic Activity*, no. 1: 129–71.

Lawrence, Robert Z. 2008. *Blue Collar Blues: Is Trade to Blame for Rising US Income Inequality?* Policy Analyses in International Economics 85. Washington: Peterson Institute for International Economics. Available at https://www.piie.com/bookstore/blue-collar-blues-trade-blame-rising-us-income-inequality.

Lawrence, Robert Z. 2014. Adjustment Challenges. In *Bridging the Pacific: Toward Free Trade and Investment between China and the United States*, ed. Fred C. Bergsten, Gary Clyde Hufbauer, Sean Miner, and Tyler Moran. Washington: Peterson Institute for International Economics. Available at https://www.piie.com/bookstore/bridging-pacific-toward-free-trade-and-investment-between-china-and-united-states.

Lawrence, Robert Z. 2015. *Recent Declines in Labor's Share in US Income: A Neoclassical Account*. NBER Working Paper 21296. Cambridge, MA: National Bureau of Economic Research. Available at https://www.nber.org/papers/w21296.

Lawrence, Robert Z. 2016. Does Productivity Still Determine Worker Compensation? Domestic and International Evidence. In *The US Labor Market: Questions and Challenges for Public Policy*, ed. Michael R. Strain. Washington: American Enterprise Institute.

Lawrence, Robert Z. 2017. *Recent US Manufacturing Employment: The Exception That Proves the Rule*. PIIE Working Paper 17-12. Washington: Peterson Institute for International Economics. Available at https://www.piie.com/publications/working-papers/recent-us-manufacturing-employment-exception-proves-rule.

Lawrence, Robert Z. 2019. *China, Like the US, Faces Challenges in Achieving Inclusive Growth through Manufacturing*. PIIE Policy Brief 19-11. Washington: Peterson Institute for International Economics. Available at https://www.piie.com/publications/policy-briefs/china-us-faces-challenges-achieving-inclusive-growth-through.

Lawrence, Robert Z. 2024. Climate Action: Implications for Factor Market Reallocation. In *The Green Frontier: Assessing the Economic Implications of Climate Action*, ed. Jean Pisani-Ferry and Adam S. Posen. Washington: Peterson Institute for International Economics. Available at https://www.piie.com/bookstore/2024/green-frontier-assessing-economic-implications-climate-action.

Lawrence, Robert Z., and Robert Litan. 1986. *Saving Free Trade: A Pragmatic Approach* Washington: Brookings Institution.

Lawrence, Robert Z., and Lawrence Edwards. 2013. *US Employment Deindustrialization: Insights from History and the International Experience*. PIIE Policy Brief 13-27. Washington: Peterson Institute for International Economics. Available at https://www.piie.com/publications/policy-briefs/us-employment-deindustrialization-insights-history-and-international.

Leamer, Edward. 1987. Paths of Development in the Three-Factor, *n*-Good General Equilibrium Model. *Journal of Political Economy* 95, no. 5: 961–99.

Lebergott, Stanley. 1966. Labor Force and Employment, 1800-1960. In *Output, Employment, and Productivity in the United States after 1800*, ed. Dorothy S. Brady. Cambridge, MA: National Bureau of Economic Research.

Levinson, Marc. 2017. *Job Creation in the Manufacturing Revival*. Washington: Congressional Research Service.

Lewis, W. Arthur. 1954. Economic Development with Unlimited Supplies of Labor. *The Manchester School* 22, no. 2: 139–91. Available at https://doi.org/10.1111/j.1467-9957.1954.tb00021.x.

Lincicome, Scott. 2020. *Testing the "China Shock": Was Normalizing Trade with China a Mistake?* Policy Analysis 895. Washington: Cato Institute.

Lincicome, Scott, and Huan Zhu. 2021. *Questioning Industrial Policy: Why Government Manufacturing Plans Are Ineffective and Unnecessary.* Working Paper. Washington: Cato Institute. Available at https://www.cato.org/working-paper/questioning-industrial-policy-why-government-manufacturing-plans-are-ineffective.

Longworth, Richard. 2008. *Caught in the Middle: America's Heartland in the Age of Globalism.* New York: Bloomsbury USA.

Maddison, Angus. 1980. Phases of Capitalist Developments. In *Economic Growth and Resources,* ed. R. C. O. Matthews. International Economic Association Series. London: Palgrave Macmillan. Available at https://doi.org/10.1007/978-1-349-04063-6_1.

Magyari, Ildikó. 2017. *Firm Reorganization, Chinese Imports, and US Manufacturing Employment.* Working Paper 17-58. Washington: Center for Economic Studies, US Census Bureau.

Mahajan, Meghan, Olivia Ashmoore, Jeffrey Rissman, Robbie Orvis, and Anand Gopal. 2022. *Updated Inflation Reduction Act Modeling Using the Energy Policy Simulator.* San Francisco: Energy Innovation: Policy and Technology LLC. Available at https://energyinnovation.org/wp-content/uploads/2022/08/Updated-Inflation-Reduction-Act-Modeling-Using-the-Energy-Policy-Simulator.pdf.

Mai, Dao, Davide Furceri, and Prakash Loungani. 2017. Regional Labor Market Adjustment in the United States: Trend and Cycle. *Review of Economics and Statistics* 99, no. 2: 243-57.

Marcal, Leah H. 2001. Does Trade Adjustment Assistance Help Trade-Displaced Workers? *Contemporary Economic Policy* 19, no. 1: 59-72.

Marin, Giovanni, and Francesco Vona. 2019. Climate policies and skills-biased employment dynamics: Evidence from EU countries. *Journal of Environmental Economics and Management* 98: 102253. Available at https://doi.org/10.1016/j.jeem.2019.102253.

Martin, Will, and Devashish Mitra. 2001. Productivity Growth and Convergence in Agriculture versus Manufacturing. *Economic Development and Cultural Change* 49, no. 2: 403-22. Available at https://www.journals.uchicago.edu/doi/10.1086/452509.

Mathematica Policy Research and Social Policy Research. 2012. *Estimated Impacts for Participants in the Trade Adjustment Assistance (TAA) Program under the 2002 Amendments.* Final report prepared as part of the evaluation of the Trade Adjustment Assistance Program. Washington.

Matsuyama, Kiminori. 1992. Agricultural Productivity, Comparative Advantage, and Economic Growth. *Journal of Economic Theory* 58, no. 2: 317-34. Available at https://www.sciencedirect.com/science/article/abs/pii/002205319290057O.

Matsuyama, Kiminori. 2009. Structural Change in an Interdependent World: A Global View of Manufacturing Decline. *Journal of the European Economic Association* 7, no. 2-3: 478-86.

Matsuyama, Kiminori. 2019. Engel's Law in the Global Economy: Demand-Induced Patterns of Structural Change, Innovation and Trade. *Econometrica* 87, no. 2: 497-528.

Mayfield, Erin, and Jesse Jenkins. 2021. Influence of High Road Labor Policies and Practices on Renewable Energy Costs, Decarbonization Pathways, and Labor Outcomes. *Environmental Research Letters* 16, no. 12. Available at https://doi.org/10.1088/1748-9326/ac34ba.

McMillan, Margaret, Dani Rodrik, and Inigo Verduzo-Gallo. 2014. Globalization, Structural Change and Productivity Growth, with an Update on Africa. *World Development* 63: 11–32. Available at https://drodrik.scholar.harvard.edu/files/dani-rodrik/files/globalization_structural_change_productivity_growth_with_africa_update.pdf.

METI (Ministry of Economy, Trade, and Investment). 2021. *Overview of Japan's Green Growth Strategy through Achieving Carbon Neutrality in 2050*. Tokyo.

Mishel, Lawrence. 2018. *Yes, manufacturing still provides a pay advantage, but staffing firm outsourcing is eroding it*. Policy Report. Washington: Economic Policy Institute. Available at https://www.epi.org/publication/manufacturing-still-provides-a-pay-advantage-but-outsourcing-is-eroding-it/.

Molthof, Luuk, Dick Zandee, and Giulia Cretti. 2021. *Unpacking Open Strategic Autonomy: From Concept to Practice*. Clingendael Report. The Hague: Netherlands Institute of International Relations. Available at https://www.clingendael.org/sites/default/files/2021-11/Unpacking_open_strategic_autonomy.pdf.

Moretti, Enrico. 2010. Local Multipliers. *American Economic Review* 100, no. 2: 373–77.

Moretti, Enrico. 2011. Local Labor Markets. In *Handbook of Labor Economics*, Volume 4b, ed. David Card and Orley Ashenfelter. Elsevier.

Moretti, Enrico. 2013. *The New Geography of Jobs*. New York: Houghton Mifflin Harcourt.

Moretti, Enrico, and Per Thulin. 2013. Local Multipliers and Human Capital in the United States and Sweden. *Industrial and Corporate Change* 22, no. 1: 339–62.

Morris, Adele C., Noah Kaufman, and Siddhi Doshi. 2019. *The Risk of Fiscal Collapse in Coal-Reliant Communities*. New York: Columbia SIPA and Brookings.

Muendler, Marc-Andreas. 2017. *Trade, Technology, and Prosperity: An Account of Evidence from a Labor-Market Perspective*. WTO Staff Working Paper ERSD-2017-15. Geneva: Economic Research and Statistics Division, World Trade Organization.

Munk, Nina. 2013. *The Idealist: Jeffrey Sachs and the Quest to End Poverty*. New York: Doubleday.

Muro, Mark, Jacob Whiton, and Robert Maxim. 2019. *What Jobs Are Affected by AI? Better-Paid, Better-Educated Workers Face the Most Exposure*. Washington: Metropolitan Policy Program, Brookings Institution. Available at https://www.brookings.edu/wp-content/uploads/2019/11/2019.11.20_BrookingsMetro_What-jobs-are-affected-by-AI_Report_Muro-Whiton-Maxim.pdf.

Muro, Mark, Lavea Brachman, and Yang You. 2023. *With High-Tech Manufacturing Plants Promising Good Jobs in Ohio, Workforce Developers Race to Get Ready*. Washington: Brookings Institution. Available at https://www.brookings.edu/research/with-high-tech-manufacturing-plants-promising-good-jobs-in-ohio-workforce-developers-race-to-get-ready/.

Muro, Mark, Joseph Parillo, and Martha Ross. 2023. *What State and Local Leaders Need to Know about Biden's Semiconductor Subsidies*. Washington: Brookings Institution. Available at https://www.brookings.edu/blog/the-avenue/2023/03/02/what-state-and-local-leaders-need-to-know-about-bidens-semiconductor-subsidies/.

Murray, Charles. 2012. *Coming Apart: The State of White America 1960–2010*. New York: Crown Forum.

Nager, Adams. 2017. *Trade versus Productivity: What Caused Manufacturing's Decline and How to Revive It.* Washington: Information Technology and Innovation Foundation. Available at https://www2.itif.org/2017-trade-vs-productivity.pdf.

Nakamura, Emi, and Jon Steinsson. 2014. Fiscal Stimulus in a Monetary Union: Evidence from US Regions. *American Economic Review* 104, no. 3: 753–92.

National Bank of Belgium. 2020. Does the EU Convergence Machine Still Work? *Economic Review* (June).

Neumark, David, and Helen Simpson. 2014. *Place-Based Policies.* NBER Working Paper 20049 Revised. Cambridge, MA: National Bureau of Economic Research.

Ngai, L. Rachel, and Christopher A. Pissarides. 2007. Structural Change in a Multi-Sector Model of Growth. *American Economic Review* 97: 429–43.

Noland, Marcus. 2019. *Protectionism under Trump: The China Shock, Intolerance, and the First White President.* PIIE Working Paper 19-10. Washington: Peterson Institute for International Economics. Available at https://www.piie.com/publications/working-papers/protectionism-under-trump-china-shock-intolerance-and-first-white.

Nordhaus, William. 2005. *The Sources of the Productivity Rebound and the Manufacturing Employment Puzzle.* NBER Working Paper 11354. Cambridge, MA: National Bureau of Economic Research.

Nordhaus, William. 2007. Two Centuries of Productivity Growth in Computing. *Journal of Economic History* 67, no. 1: 128–59.

Nordhaus, William. 2008. Baumol's Diseases: A Macroeconomic Perspective. *Contributions in Macroeconomics* 8, no. 1.

Noy, Shakked, and Whitney Zhang. 2023. Experimental Evidence on the Productivity Effects of Generative Artificial Intelligence. Unpublished working paper. MIT Department of Economics. Available at https://economics.mit.edu/sites/default/files/inline-files/Noy_Zhang_1.pdf?utm_source=npr_newsletter&utm_medium=email&utm_content=20230508&utm_term=8392792&utm_campaign=money&utm_id=27864752&orgid=&utm_att1=.

Oberfield, Ezra, and Devesh Raval. 2014. *Micro Data and Macro Technology.* NBER Working Paper 20452. Cambridge, MA: National Bureau of Economic Research.

OECD (Organization for Economic Cooperation and Development). 2011. *OECD Regional Outlook 2011: Building Resilient Regions for Stronger Recovery.* Paris.

Ohanian, Lee E. 2014. *Competition and the Decline of the Rust Belt.* Federal Reserve Bank of Minneapolis. Available at https://www.minneapolisfed.org/article/2014/competition-and-the-decline-of-the-rust-belt.

Okun, Arthur. 1973. Upward Mobility in a High-Pressure Economy. *Brookings Papers on Economic Activity*, no. 1: 207–62. Washington: Brookings Institution.

Oldenski, Lindsay. 2014. Offshoring and the Polarization of the US Labor Market. *Industrial and Labor Relations Review* 67, no. 3 (suppl.): 734–61.

Perez-Laborda, Alejandro, and Fidel Perez-Sebastian. 2020. Capital-Skill Complementarity and Biased Technical Change across US Sectors. *Journal of Macroeconomics* 66: 1–18. Available at https://www.sciencedirect.com/science/article/abs/pii/S0164070420301804.

Pierce, Justin R., and Peter K. Schott. 2016. The Surprisingly Swift Decline of US Manufacturing Employment. *American Economic Review* 106: 1632–62.

Pierce, Justin R., and Peter K. Schott. 2017. *Trade Liberalization and Mortality: Evidence from US Counties.* NBER Working Paper 22849. Cambridge, MA: National Bureau of Economic Research.

Piketty, Thomas. 2014. *Capital in the Twenty-First Century.* Cambridge, MA: Belknap.

Piketty, Thomas, and Emmanuel Saez. 2003. Income Inequality in the United States, 1913–1998. *Quarterly Journal of Economics* 118, no. 1: 1–41. Available at https://eml.berkeley.edu/~saez/pikettyqje.pdf.

Piketty, Thomas, and Gabriel Zucman. 2013. *Capital Is Back: Wealth-Income Ratios in Rich Countries 1700–2010.* CEPR Discussion Paper 9588. Washington: Center for Economic Policy Research.

Popp, David, Francesco Vona, Giovanni Marin, and Ziqiao Chen. 2020. *The Employment Impact of Green Fiscal Push: Evidence from the American Recovery Act.* NBER Working Paper 27321. Cambridge, MA: National Bureau of Economic Research. Available at https://doi.org/10.3386/w27321.

Popp, David, Francesco Vona, Myriam Gregoire-Zawilski, and Giovanni Marin. 2022. *The Next Wave of Energy Innovation: Which Technologies? Which Skills?* NBER Working Paper 30343. Cambridge, MA: National Bureau of Economic Research.

Posen, Adam S. 2021. America's Self-Defeating Economic Retreat. *Foreign Affairs* (May/June).

Posen, Adam S., and Jeromin Zettelmeyer. 2019. *Facing Up to Lower Productivity Growth.* Washington: Peterson Institute for International Economics. Available at https://www.piie.com/bookstore/facing-low-productivity-growth.

Raimi, Daniel, and Sophie Pesek. 2022. *What Is an "Energy Community"? Alternative Approaches for Geographically Targeted Energy Policy.* Issue Brief 22-12. Washington: Resources for the Future. Available at https://www.rff.org/publications/reports/what-is-an-energy-community-alternative-approaches-for-geographically-targeted-energy-policy/.

Ramaswamy, Sree, James Manyika, Gary Pinkus, Katy George, Jonathan Law, Tony Gambell, and Andrea Serafino. 2017. *Making It in America: Revitalizing US Manufacturing.* McKinsey Global Institute, November.

Ravallion, Martin, and Shaohua Chen. 2003. Measuring Pro-Poor Growth. *Economics Letters* 78, no. 1: 93–99. Available at https://doi.org/10.1016/s0165-1765(02)00205-7.

Reich, Robert. 1991. *The Work of Nations: Preparing Ourselves for 21st Century Capitalism.* New York: Alfred A. Knopf.

Riker, David. 2010. *Do Jobs in Export Industries Still Pay More? And Why?* Manufacturing and Services Economics Briefs. Washington: International Trade Administration, US Department of Commerce. Available at https://legacy.trade.gov/mas/ian/build/groups/public/@tg_ian/documents/webcontent/tg_ian_003208.pdf.

Rodrik, Dani. 2013. Unconditional Convergence in Manufacturing. *Quarterly Journal of Economics* 128, no. 1: 165–204.

Rodrik, Dani. 2016. Premature Deindustrialization. *Journal of Economic Growth* 21: 1–33.

Rodrik, Dani. 2018. *New Technologies, Global Value Chains and the Developing Countries.* Background paper. Pathways for Prosperity Commission. Available at https://drodrik.scholar.harvard.edu/files/dani-rodrik/files/new_technologies_global_value_chains_developing_economies.pdf.

Rodrik, Dani. 2022. *An Industrial Policy for Good Jobs*. Washington: The Hamilton Project, Brookings Institution.

Rodrik, Dani, and Stefanie Stantcheva. 2021. Fixing Capitalism's Good Jobs Problem. *Oxford Review of Economic Policy* 37, no. 4: 824–37.

Rogerson, Richard. 2008. Structural Transformation and the Deterioration of European Labor Market Outcomes. *Journal of Political Economy* 1, no. 16: 235–59.

Rognlie, Matthew. 2015. Deciphering the Fall and Rise in the Net Capital Share. *Brookings Papers on Economic Activity* (Spring). Washington: Brookings Institution.

Rosés, Joan R., and Nikolaus Wolf. 2018. The Return of Regional Inequality: Europe from 1900 to Today. VoxEU, March 18. Available at https://voxeu.org/article/return-regional-inequality-europe-1900-today.

Rothwell, Jonathan. 2017. Cutting the Losses: Reassessing the Costs of Import Competition to Workers and Communities. Draft Working Paper. Gallup Inc.

Rowthorn, Robert, and Ramana Ramaswamy. 1999. *Growth, Trade, and Deindustrialization*. IMF Staff Paper 64, no. 1: 18–41. Washington: International Monetary Fund.

Ruggles, Steven, Sarah Flood, Ronald Goeken, Megan Schouweiler, and Matthew Sobek. 2022. IPUMS USA: Version 12.0 [dataset]. Minneapolis, MN: IPUMS. Available at https://doi.org/10.18128/D010.V12.0.

Ruhm, Christopher J. 1991. Are Workers Permanently Scarred by Job Displacements? *American Economic Review* 81: 319–32.

Russ, Katheryn, and Jay C. Shambaugh. 2019. Education and Unequal Regional Labor Market Outcomes: The Persistence of Regional Shocks and Employment Responses to Trade Shocks. Paper prepared for the Federal Reserve Bank of Boston Conference Session: Rethinking Regional Responses to Economic Shocks, October 4–5, Boston. Photocopy.

Saez, Emmanuel, and Thomas Piketty. 2003. Income Inequality in the United States, 1913–1998. *Quarterly Journal of Economics* 118, no. 1: 1–39.

Sasse, Jan-Philipp, and Evelina Trutnevyte. 2023. A low-carbon electricity sector in Europe risks sustaining regional inequalities in benefits and vulnerabilities. *Nature Communications* 14, no. 2205. Available at https://doi.org/10.1038/s41467-023-37946-3.

Schwab, Klaus. 2016. *The Fourth Industrial Revolution*. World Economic Forum. New York: Crown Business.

Schweitzer, Mark E. 2017. *Manufacturing Employment Losses and the Economic Performance of the Industrial Heartland*. Working Paper 17-12. Federal Reserve Bank of Cleveland. Available at https://doi.org/10.26509/frbc-wp-201712.

Semiconductor Industry Association and Oxford Economics. 2021. *Chipping In: The Positive Impact of the Semiconductor Industry on the American Workforce and How Federal Industry Incentives Will Increase Domestic Jobs*. Available at https://www.semiconductors.org/wp-content/uploads/2021/05/SIA-Impact_May2021-FINAL-May-19-2021_2.pdf.

Short, Teresa, Justin Pierce, and Jeffrey Schott. 2018. New Perspectives on the Decline of Manufacturing Employment. *Journal of Economic Perspectives* 32, no. 2: 47–72.

Spatt, Beverly Moss. 2016. Making Sense of Model Cities. Urban Omnibus, November 1. Available at https://urbanomnibus.net/2016/11/making-sense-of-model-cities/.

Spence, Michael, and Sandile Hlatshwayo. 2011. *The Evolving Structure of the American Employment Challenge*. Working Paper. New York: Council on Foreign Relations.

Sposi, Michael. 2018. Evolving Comparative Advantage, Sectoral Linkages, and Structural Change. *Journal of Monetary Economics* 103: 75–87. Available at https://doi.org/10.1016/j.jmoneco.2018.08.003.

Stansbury, Anna, Dan Turner, and Ed Balls. 2023. *Tackling the UK's Regional Economic Inequality: Binding Constraints and Avenues for Policy Intervention*. MIT Sloan Working Paper 6836-23. Cambridge, MA: MIT Sloan School of Management.

Stolper, Wolfgang F., and Paul A. Samuelson. 1941. Protection and Real Wages. *Review of Economic Studies* 9, no. 1: 58–73.

Stiglitz, Joseph E. 1984. *Theories of Wage Rigidity*. NBER Working Paper 1442. Cambridge, MA: National Bureau of Economic Research.

Stiglitz, Joseph E., and Dani Rodrik. 2024. *Rethinking global governance: Cooperation in a world of power*. Working Paper (March). Columbia University and Harvard University.

Suarez-Cuesta, David, Maria C. Latorre, and Robert Z. Lawrence. 2022. Macroeconomic, sectoral and distributional effects of the Infrastructure Investment and Jobs Act in the United States. Paper presented at the 25th Annual Conference on Global Economic Analysis. Global Trade Analysis Project (GTAP). Purdue University, West Lafayette, IN. Available at https://www.gtap.agecon.purdue.edu/resources/res_display.asp?RecordID=6542.

Święcki, Tomasz. 2017. Determinants of Structural Change. *Review of Economic Dynamics* 24: 95–131.

Timmer, Marcel P., Gaaitzen de Vries, and Klaas de Vries. 2015. Patterns of Structural Change in Developing Countries. In *Handbook of Industry and Development*, ed. J. Weiss and M. Tribe, 65–83. London: Routledge.

Timmer, Marcel P., Erik Dietzenbacher, Bart Los, Robert Stehrer, and Gaaitzen J. de Vries. 2015. An Illustrated User Guide to the World Input–Output Database: The Case of Global Automotive Production. *Review of International Economics* 23: 575–60. Available at https://onlinelibrary.wiley.com/doi/10.1111/roie.12178.

Tinbergen, Jan. 1956. *Economic Policy: Principles and Design*. New York: North-Holland. Available at http://hdl.handle.net/1765/16740.

Topel, Robert. 1990. Specific Capital and Unemployment: Measuring the Costs and Consequences of Job Loss. In *Carnegie-Rochester Conference Series on Public Policy* 33: 181–214.

Tyson, Laura, and Lenny Mendonca. 2023. *America's New Era of Industrial Policy*. Project Syndicate, January 2. Available at https://www.project-syndicate-org.ezp-prod1.hul.harvard.edu/commentary/biden-industrial-policy-renewables-semiconductors-good-jobs-by-laura-tyson-and-lenny-mendonca-2023-01.

US Department of Labor. 2021. *Trade Adjustment Assistance for Workers Program: FY 2021 Annual Report*. Washington: Employment and Training Administration. Available at https://www.dol.gov/sites/dolgov/files/ETA/tradeact/pdfs/AnnualReport21.pdf.

US EIA (Energy Information Administration). 2021. *AEO2023 Issues in Focus: Inflation Reduction Act Cases in the AEO2023*. Washington. Available at https://www.eia.gov/outlooks/aeo/IIF_IRA/pdf/IRA_IIF.pdf.

Uy, Timothy, Kei-Mu Yi, and Jing Zhang. 2013. Structural Change in an Open Economy. *Journal of Monetary Economics* 60, no. 6: 667–82. Available at https://www.sciencedirect.com/science/article/abs/pii/S030439321300086X.

Valletta, Robert B. 2018. Recent Flattening in the Higher Education Wage Premium: Polarization, Skill Downgrading, or Both? In *Education, Skills, and Technical Change: Implications for Future US GDP Growth*, 313–42. Cambridge, MA: National Bureau of Economic Research.

Vandeplas, Anneleen, Istvan Vanyolos, Mauro Vigani, and Lukas Vogel. 2022. *The Possible Implications of the Green Transition for the EU Labour Market*. European Commission Discussion Paper 176. Available at https://doi.org/10.2765/583043.

Vernon, Raymond. 1966. International Investment and International Trade in the Product Cycle. *Quarterly Journal of Economics* 80, no. 2: 190–207.

Wang, Zhi, Shang-Jin Wei, Xinding Yu, and Kunfu Zhu. 2018. *Re-Examining the Effects of Trading with China on Local Labor Markets: A Supply Chain Perspective*. NBER Working Paper 24886. Cambridge, MA: National Bureau of Economic Research.

Westmore, B., and A. Leandro. 2023. *Selected Policy Challenges for the American Middle Class*. OECD Economics Department Working Paper 1748. Paris: OECD Publishing. Available at https://doi.org/10.1787/1b864f22-en.

White House. 2021. *Building Resilient Supply Chains, Revitalizing American Manufacturing and Fostering Broad Based Growth*. 100-Day Reviews under Executive Order 14017, June. Washington.

Wilson, William Julius. 1996. *When Work Disappears: The World of the New Urban Poor*. New York: Alfred A. Knopf.

World Bank. 2009. *World Development Report 2009: Reshaping Economic Geography*. Washington. Available at https://openknowledge.worldbank.org/handle/10986/5991.

World Bank Commission on Growth and Development. 2008. *Growth Report: Strategies for Sustained Growth and Inclusive Development*. Washington: World Bank. Available at https://openknowledge.worldbank.org/bitstream/handle/10986/6507/449860PUB0Box3101OFFICIAL0USE0ONLY1.pdf.

Wozniak, Abigail. 2010. Are College Graduates More Responsive to Distant Labor Market Opportunities? *Journal of Human Resources* 45, no. 4: 944–70.

Wu, Mark. 2016. The "China, Inc." Challenge to Global Trade Governance. *Harvard International Law Journal* 261.

Yi, Kei-Mu, and Jing Zhang. 2010. *Structural Change in an Open Economy*. Working Paper 60. Research Seminar in International Economics. University of Michigan.

Index

earned income tax credit, expanding to include childless workers, 257

earnings
changes in correlated with a college education, 177n3
data, converting into 2019 dollars, 136n5
of men without college degrees, 136, 142
polarization of, 185–86

Eastern states, declines in manufacturing employment, 208

ECI. *See* Employment Cost Index (ECI)

economic development, structural change and, 13–33

Economic Development Administration (EDA), of the Department of Commerce, 264–65

economic development grants, providing, 266–67

economic divergence, creating demand for political leadership and policies, 282

economic growth, 16–17, 18, 141

economic power, alarms about China's, 226

economies
implementing industrial policies, 70
increasing shares in foreign markets, 42
with larger trade surpluses, 66
not experiencing a decline in MVA spending, 62–63
with positive changes in net MVA exports, 66
results for top 10 and bottom 10, 60–61, 67
top 10 ranked by net trade balances, 54

EDA. *See* Economic Development Administration (EDA)

educated workers, 207, 212, 214, 238

education, associated with increased wage inequality, 177–78

"efficiency wages," firms paying workers premiums as, 198

Egypt, 38f

elasticity of demand, inversely related to foreign market share, 42

elasticity of substitution, effect on wages of workers, 29n13

electric vehicles (EVs). *See* EVs (electric vehicles)

elitism, perceived by many working-class Europeans, 282

Emerging Housing Markets Index, 270

emerging-market economies, not likely to reproduce the manufacturing employment experience of today's industrial economies, 88

empirical support, for the model of structural change, 29–32

employees, 262, 270

employment
broader impacts of trade on, 170–71
changes associated with levels and changes in trade balance in manufacturing, 51
declining share in value added reflected declines in, 188
declining share of in manufacturing, 198
need to maintain high levels of without inflation, 9
reallocation of during economic growth, 16–17
role in the declining labor payroll share, 188–89
understanding the behavior of in a sector, 29

Employment Cost Index (ECI), 188–89, 189n16, 189n17

employment declines, 161, 172, 206

employment dummy, taking account of productivity, 125

employment effects, of the Biden programs, 240–45

employment equation results, not pointing to a major role for trade, 126

employment expansion at home, at the expense of manufacturing jobs abroad, 41

employment response, to additional increases in productivity dissipating, 36

employment shares
in agriculture declining as MES rises, 43
for net importers in an open economy, 110f
typical evolution of as economies develop, 2

employment stimulation, outside the manufacturing sector, 170
Empowerment Zones, of the Clinton administration, 266
endogeneity, studies identifying causes of, 165–71
"energy communities," projects located in, 239
Energy Policy Simulator, 241
Enterprise Communities program, of the Clinton administration, 266
entrepreneurial endeavors, technologies opening up, 286
entrepreneurs, sparking a cumulative virtuous cycle, 269
equations, 120, 168
Ethiopia, 38*f*
EU Green Deal program, financing of, 274*n*5
Europe
assisting workers and communities, 282
including many economies that have passed their peaks, 18
manufacturing real output share, 21*f*
manufacturing share of employment, 93*f*
regressions, 124, 125*n*15
relationship of manufacturing employment share with per capita GDP, 19*f*
within-country experiences similar to that of the United States, 280*n*18
European Chips Act, 274, 275
European Climate Law, 275
European Commission, designed the Just Transition Fund, 281
European Green Deal, 280, 281
European Innovation Council, 274*n*5
European Sovereignty Fund, creating a new, 275
European Union, 273–76, 281, 284
EVs (electric vehicles), 235, 238, 246–47*b*. *See also* automobiles
export barriers, 252
export-led growth, prospects for in developing economies, 290
exports, employment impact of, 167
ex post trade balance, 165

farmers, mobile phones improving the performance of, 286
federal government policies, helping workers relocate, 264
federal grants, 237, 264–67
federal spending, stimulating local growth, 268
federal system, problems in defining eligibility in the face of political pressures, 272
Fifth Science and Technology Basic Plan, in Japan, 277
final demand, categories of, 29
final demand substitution elasticities, model findings on, 30
firms
developing new technologies, 202
diversifying supply chains, 288
expanding employment in service sector jobs, 171
improving self-monitoring of workers in, 198
second effect operating through changes within, 170
switching from manufacturing, 171*n*32
fiscal policies, stimulative created shortages of workers, 261
Fit for 55, climate initiative of the European Commission, 274–75
fixed assets, 192–97, 194*f*
fixed capital, of manufacturing consisting of intellectual property assets, 5
foreign demand, 36, 168
foreign economies, specializing in exports, 203
foreign manufacturing demand, 43
foreign manufacturing producers, 41
fossil fuel-based industries, shares of employment accounted for, 280–81
fossil fuel-based manufacturing jobs, displacement of workers in, 245
fossil fuel production, communities depending on, 263
France, 39*f*, 276
free market policies, MES declining in economies adopting, 9
FTE employment, in US manufacturing, 152

H-1B visas, for skilled workers, 251n47
Hamilton, Alexander, champion of manufacturing, 13
"heartland metro areas," designating, 267
high human capital areas, manufacturing employment losses as smaller, 215
high-income employees, working from home, 270
highly skilled workers, 216, 279
high-tech activities, shifting composition of, 278
high-tech firms, 171, 215
high-tech industries, large increases in, 192
High-Tech Strategy 2025, in Germany, 276
high-tech workers, creating jobs for other workers, 216–17, 270
Hong Kong, 37, 38f
Horizon Europe initiative, iterations of, 273–74
household income, annual growth in real in the US, 134f
housing costs, in high-income cities increased, 213
human capital, importance of, 251
hump-shaped MES curve
    capturing with statistical significant coefficients, 19
    changing income elasticities helping explain, 23
    countries following as they develop, 8
    as evident in both deficit and surplus economies, 37
    explaining in a closed economy, 20–26
    impact of being on the downward slope of, 70
    as more robust in an open economy, 44
    present when countries run large trade deficits, 35
hump-shaped profile, 26, 35, 44

IBM, training programs, 260
import barriers, effects of reducing, 90
import competition
    from China, 166
    effects of, 214
imported inputs, 148n11, 170

import penetration, 166n25, 212
import restrictions, 227
inclusive growth, 131, 132, 133–42
income disparities, within EU countries, 270n30
income effects, 23–24, 31
income elasticities, 23, 23n11, 30
income elasticity, 23, 27, 113
income equalization, across regions of the US, 140
income growth, 23, 27, 133–34
income inequality, 131, 139, 201, 236
incomes, 142
individual wage data, 134
Indo-Pacific Economic Framework, 252
industrial and trade policies, 8, 278
industrial city, era of as over, 220
industrial countries, shallow bell shape for manufacturing employment, 16n5
industrialization, employment share of services larger, 15–16
"industrial losers," European, 6n5
industrial policies, 199, 226, 273–384
industrial programs, of individual European countries, 275
industrial prowess, of China, 227
Industry 4.0, linking producers with each other and with consumers, 278
industry analysis, incorporating estimates of the impact of all imports and exports, 168
industry nominal output, 162
industry NTR rates applied to China in 2001, 166
industry shares, in output as constantly changing, 174
inelastic demand, 25, 30
inelastic income demand elasticity, apparent after 1970, 158
inequality, contributed to workers' weak real earnings growth from 1970 to 2011, 136
Inflation Reduction Act of 2022 (IRA)
    expanding US renewable energy manufacturing capacity, 238–40
    granting generous uncapped incentives, 251
    incentives for producing renewable energy in, 255

negative impact on production workers dependent on fossil fuels, 254

seeking to achieve climate justice, 265

seeking to achieve multiple objectives, 239

supposed to devote 40 percent of its expenditures to depressed communities, 248–49

information superhighway, leading to a greater diffusion of workers today, 270

information technology, 181, 183n10, 287

infrastructure, digital technologies playing an important role in developing, 286

infrastructure development, Italian strategy setting targets for, 276

infrastructure program, creating a large number of construction jobs, 253

infrastructure spending, 235

inner-city neighborhoods, social impacts of manufacturing job loss, 216

Innovate UK, funding innovation centers, 276

innovation, 184, 268, 278

innovation clusters, 202

innovation industries, metropolitan areas of the US with jobs in (1959–2010), 218–19f

innovation jobs, in just 16 of the country's more than 3,000 counties, 245

"innovation sector employment growth," five cities accounting for, 245

innovative manufacturing industries, increasing the concentration of in cities, 278

input-output analysis, estimating jobs lost in nonmanufacturing industries, 167

input prices, overstating, 148n11

instrumental variables, 161, 165

intangible capital, 116

intangibles, role of, 174

intellectual property, 91, 118f, 194f, 195f

intellectual property products, 116, 192, 195–97t, 199

internal combustion engine (ICE) autos, 246b. See also automobiles

international capital flows, 45–46

International Monetary Fund (IMF), pointing to increases in earnings disparities, 183n11

international trade, responsibility job loss, 172

Internet of Things, 7, 277, 286

interstate highway system, completion of, 206

interstate migration, 213

interventionist industrial policies, MES declining in economies adopting, 9

inverted U curve, relating the MES to income, 6

inverted-U relationship, between the MES and GDP per capita as evident globally, 17

inverted U-shaped path, of the MES curve of late developers, 99

InvestEU program, 274n5

investment

adding as a variable to the standard regression, 125–26

as an additional potential cause for premature deindustrialization, 126

becoming less manufacturing intensive, 113

changes in the level and composition of, 91

evidence of changes in, 116–18

in GDP, effects of a reduction in the share of, 115

as an important contributor to downward shifts, 125–26

large share of in Asian economies as closely related to rapid growth, 55

less responsive demand for as income grows reducing spending on manufacturing, 127

in manufacturing as relatively weak, 192

simulation of the effect of changes in, 113–15

investment spending, 55, 59b

Ireland, 66, 116n8

Italy, 39f, 276

Japan

detention of a Chinese fishing boat captain, 227

manufacturing share of employment, 39f

now on the downward-sloping part of the MES curve, 2
promoting digital technologies, reshoring, and green energy, 277
responses to competition from, 217b
jatropha shrub, suitable for biofuel production, 289
job content, of trade balances, 162–64
job placement services, training, as successful in other countries, 258
"job progression tool," 260
jobs
  creation of shifted toward cities, 141
  manufacturing and good in 1970, 176–77
  manufacturing providing relatively high-paying, 4
  permanence of losses, 167
  requiring on-the-job training, 198
  sharp change in the skill content of new after 1980, 184n13
job seekers, moving into higher-paying jobs, 262
Just Transition Fund, 284
Just Transition Mechanism, 281

Kenya, 38f

labor, augmented by technological change, 194b
labor compensation
  between 1947 and 1970 increased at an annual rate of 2.6 percent, 133
  versus capital income, 139–40
  declining share of, 186–91
  in net value added in manufacturing, nonmanufacturing, and GDP in the US, 188f
  in net value added rose slightly in 2013, 188
  share of in domestic income in the United States (1929-2019), 140f
  in US income as roughly constant, 191
labor content, of the trade balance on manufacturing value added, 165
labor demand, increases in, 269
labor equivalence, calculating, 111t
labor force participation, increasing by making child care affordable, 257
labor income, robust growth of, 133

labor-intensive infrastructure, including spending on, 9
labor-intensive tasks, performing, 5
labor market, benefits of a tight, 262
labor mobility, declined since the 1990s, 258
labor productivity, 100, 147n6, 154f, 162
labor productivity growth
  in manufacturing, 32, 103, 150
  not much higher than in the rest of the economy, 161
labor-saving technologies, 7
labor share, 189, 191, 193b
late developers, 99, 100
Latin America
  low peaks occurring at low-income levels, 18
  manufacturing real output share, 21f
  manufacturing share of employment, 93f
  manufacturing trade balance fell in the 2000s, 112
  regressions, 124
  relationship of manufacturing employment share with per capita GDP, 19f
Law and Justice Party, in Poland, 282–83
"learning by doing," fewer dynamic benefits from, 88
least squares specification, 47
"leave no one behind," policies achieving, 284
legacy chips, producing, 236
Le Pen, Marine, 283
less educated workers, 7–8, 173, 212
less skilled workers, 213
literature
  on premature deindustrialization, 126
  on shifts in the MES curve, 89–91
lithium and cobalt, needed for batteries, 289
local communities, shocks to as more persistent since the 1990s, 141
local economies, 213, 281
local governments, attracting leading foreign firms, 208
local labor markets, industrial composition of, 166
local responses, lying with the variety of shocks, 215
local spillovers, of knowledge, 210

experiencing relatively rapid productivity growth between 2000 and 2010, 154
explaining output demand for, 155–58
output measure for, 149
ratio of productivity to productivity in GDP, 154
noncomputer manufacturing output between 1987 and 2000, 152
grew at a much slower rate than GDP but somewhat faster than expected, 157–58
growth as higher than might have been expected, 155–56
low income elasticity of demand for, 160
ratio to FTE employment in noncomputer manufacturing, 153
stagnated between 2000 and 2010, 152
noncomputer manufacturing value added, ratios of to GDP in the United States (1948–2018), 160f
noncomputer output, 156, 161
nonemployment, incidence of, 213
nonmanufacturing activities, expanding in response to competition from China, 170
Nord-Pas-de-Calais, biggest recipient of EU cohesion funds, 283
North American Free Trade Agreement (NAFTA), 214
Northern England, voted for Brexit, 6
NTR premiums, in each industry, 166
Nucor, produced steel by recycling, 205b

OECD/WTO project, on TiVA linking input-output matrices of economies, 53
offshoring
contributing to polarization, 186
effects of, 214
not driving firms out of business, 170
occurring within multinational firms and sometimes at arm's length, 5
raised the capital intensity of US production, 193b
oil-, gas-, coal-, and energy-intensive manufacturing industries, characteristics of, 250
oil shocks, shifted demand toward smaller, more fuel-efficient cars, 205b

oligopolies, domestic and international competitive pressures weakened the power of, 204b
online data package, for this volume, 14n1
open economy, 35–50, 36n1, 108f
"open strategic autonomy," Europeans new policy of, 274
Opportunity Zones program, of the Trump administration, 266
ordinary least squares regressions, 128
organization, of this book, 8–9
Organization for Economic Cooperation and Development (OECD), 52, 131
out-migration, 207, 264
output demand, for noncomputer manufacturing output, 155
output growth, 152, 153, 153n14, 158
output per worker, 32, 153
output variables, 125
outsourcing of services, by manufacturing firms, 148n10

parameters, used in simulations, 115t
peak GDP per capita, fell in the 1960s to the 2000s, 99
peak manufacturing employment share (MES), 96, 99
people, helping in the United States, 256–62
per capita and productivity gaps, between the richest and poorest US states, 140
per capita incomes, 16, 53
Personal Consumption Expenditures (PCE) deflator, 134n2
personal service workers, 185n14, 213
petroleum refining, job losses in, 245
place-based policies, 267, 282, 284
place-oriented programs, track record of, 268
places
helping, 262–71
impact on, 245–49
plants, closure of a large number of, 192
Poland, largest recipient of economic grants from the EU, 282
polarization, of wages, 138–39
policies
affecting the distribution of income, 283

for developing economies, 287
generating larger trade surpluses, 52
increasing the share of manufacturing, 278
providing more targeted adjustment assistance, 255
subsidizing employment of people residing in places with high unemployment and nonemployment rates, 269
policy context, current, 225–29
policymakers, 88, 255
political disruptions, 283
political narrative, pointing to trade, 172
political parties, representing labor, 4
poor areas, unemployment rates for long periods of time, 210
poor communities, 262, 263, 269
poorer areas, of the United States enjoyed faster growth and income convergence, 220
poorer workers, have not been migrating to promising places since the 1990s, 264
poorest counties, in the 1960s, 203
poorest regions in the United States, economic growth in, 201
population growth, in richer versus poorer places, 201
populism, globalization and manufacturing important role in, 6n6
populist insurgents, providing answers if economists cannot, 282
positive productivity shock, effect of, 103f
premature deindustrialization
in Africa and Latin America, 108
leftward shift in the curve, 92
occurring in developed economies, 126
posing serious problems for developing economies, 87–89
possible in Asia that was not apparent, 99
regression analysis of, 119–26
weaker investment shares playing a role in, 116
premium, paid to workers in manufacturing, 197–98
price changes, generating structural change, 25
price effects, 25–29, 31

price takers, small economies as in world markets, 67
prime-age workers, growing share of dropped out of the labor force, 258
Princeton Net-Zero for America Project, 249
private firms, 231
private-public partnerships, with feedback mechanisms, 265
private sector, response to federal subsidies and to tax breaks in the CHIPS Act, 242
production
became more capital intensive, 191
labor-intensive nature of technology, 186
moving out of expensive locations, 202
productivity
affecting the amount of labor required, 41–42
association with manufacturing trade surpluses, 60
higher demanding fewer workers, 25
higher in manufacturing raising income, 29
as an important part of the explanation for large negative dummies, 125
increase in leading to fewer manufacturing workers being needed, 43
productivity gap, closing, 203
productivity growth
in agriculture, 33
as a driver of spending on services, 26
effects of faster in manufacturing, 44
faster in computers and electronics, 143
interaction with demand generating structural change, 27
in manufacturing, 27, 100, 125
sector rankings in the closed economy model, 31
sectors with slow as increasingly expensive, 25
in services as slowest, 26
slow between 2010 and 2018, 152
as strong in the "progressive" sector, 25
productivity improvements, 278, 279

productivity shocks, positive and negative, 103*f*
pro-employment policies, targeting regions, 269
programs, helping people and communities in need in the United States, 255–72
public transit, poorer Americans benefiting disproportionately from, 245
Putin, Vladimir, 227

R&D. *See* research and development (R&D)
rapid growth, of China, 226
rapid productivity growth, 146, 147*n*7, 154, 158
rare earths
    China willing to restrict its exports of, 227
    development of on EU soil, 275
real annual median earnings, of men and women in the United States, 137*f*
real GDP, average growth in the United States (1950s–2010s), 145*f*
real output growth rate, in the manufacturing sector, 147
real wages, 135*f*, 138*f*
recessions, 144, 155, 163, 206
Regional Comprehensive Economic Partnership (RCEP), 227, 252
regional divergence, 217, 270
regional economic divergences, populism fanned by, 282
regional effects, 5, 109
regional income equalization, in the United States, 203
regional inequality, decline and rise of, 201–221
regression analysis, 47–50, 119–26
regression results, 22*t*, 48–49*t*, 105–106*t*, 120–26
regressions
    in all groupings, 92
    confirmation results of, 60–61
    grouped by level of development and region, 18
    as statistical descriptions of ex post associations, 120
    tracking the share of capital formation over time, 116

reindustrialization program, increasing US employment, 240
relative backwardness, advantages of, 100
relative manufacturing productivity, 62*f*, 120, 125
relative price competitiveness variable, 47*n*8
remote work, 202, 216–17, 269–71, 287
renaissance, denoting a rebirth, 244
renewable energy, 228, 289
renewables, shift toward, 289
research and development (R&D), 3, 248, 267–69, 277
research institutes, such as the National Institutes of Health in Maryland, 212
research universities, cities with important, 212
Ricardian framework, with only one factor of production, 41*n*3
Ricardian model, 40–43
rich countries, increasingly filled with desperate immigrants, 6
richer areas, enjoying lower unemployment and rising incomes, 210
right-wing parties, in Europe, 6
Roosevelt, Franklin Delano, 265
Russia, invasion of Ukraine, 227, 288
Rust Belt
    appearance declined as well, 207*n*5
    found it difficult to develop new areas of specialization, 212
    with the greatest percentage of estimated increases, 244
    resulting from technological change, 5
    revitalizing towns in, 240
    unemployment rates in, 207

Scandinavian countries, labor force participation in, 257
"the second circulation," emphasis on, 227
second oil shock, in 1979–80, 206
second-tier cities, turning selected into self-generating growth centers, 267
sectoral employment, 15
sectoral employment programs, 262
sectoral employment shares, 14*f*, 16, 17*f*
sectoral programs, as promising, 262
sectoral shares of employment, 28*f*

sectoral shifts, not playing a major role in increased wage inequality, 183*n*11
sector income elasticities, 23, 31
sector output shares, changes in, 32
sector productivity growth, 14, 35
sector product prices, 25
sectors, methods of categorizing, 29
self-financing system, for tax base insurance, 272
semiconductor employment, definition for, 238*n*16
semiconductor industry, domestic workers employed in 2020, 237
Semiconductor Industry Association, 237
semiconductor production, promoting US-based, 236
semiconductor research and development (R&D), funding for, 236
semiconductors, 3, 148
service employment, compared to the share of manufacturing employment, 16*n*5
services
  dominance of over manufacturing in the share of employment, 16
  employment growth faster and larger in than in manufacturing, 15
  employment in growing more rapidly than employment in manufacturing, 21
  employment path, 107
  positive spending spillovers into, 280
  relative price of rising, 26
  upward shift in the curve tracking the share of employment in, 101
  US economy now dominated by, 13
  value of final sales of reflecting the use of manufactured goods, 52
services sector
  characterizing as static, 26*n*12
  described, 16*n*6
service workers, adverse effects on, 212
share of manufacturing, in real output following a pattern, 14
shocks. *See also* adverse shocks; China shock; manufacturing shocks; oil shocks; tax revenue shocks; technology shocks; trade shocks
  migration as the response to prior to the 1970s, 220

reduced resilience to leading many communities to stagnate, 221
unexpected losses in community taxes resulting from, 263
variety of led to higher "not-working rates" in local economies, 213
shortages, created by economic distortions, 288
Silicon Valley, innovation agglomeration started in, 269*n*26
Singapore, 2, 38*f*, 66
skill bias, characterizing new technologies, 259
skill-biased structural change, 174, 179–84
skill-biased technological change, 5, 184–86, 199, 207
skilled and unskilled labor, as complements, 280
skilled workers, 116, 207, 212, 273, 280
skill endowments, of new technologies, 141
skill intensity, increase in, 185
skill-intensive technologies, countries seeking mastery of, 7
skill premium, 180, 181*n*9, 183
skills, acquiring through training, 9, 250–51, 260
smart grid systems, improving energy distribution and efficiency, 286
Social Climate Fund, of the EU, 275
social consequences
  of declines in manufacturing employment, 217*b*
  of deindustrialization, 216–17
Social Security data, estimating real earnings over 31 working years, 138
social welfare spending, cutbacks in widening political polarization, 6
solar panels, enhancing European production of, 275
the South, natural resource endowments and lax regulations, 203, 206
South China Sea, military rivalry in, 227
southern states, particularly attractive as locations for manufacturing production, 203
South Korea
  on the downward-sloping part of the MES curve, 2
  experienced large declines in MESs, 66

manufacturing share of employment, 39f

sector-biased productivity growth and nonhomothetic preferences as more important than trade, 50n10

special adjustment programs, implementing in the context of other programs, 259

spillovers, 25, 29

"stagnant" sector, identified as services, 25

state and local governments, providing additional funds, 237

state governments, joined in the effort to remove unnecessary obstacles, 260

states, projected to experience substantial increases in demand for manufacturing employment, 243–44

static sector (services), as a demand taker, 26

steel industry, lost 350,000 jobs between 1977 and 1987, 207

STEM, 198, 199, 271

Stolper-Samuelson (1941) theorem, 181n9

structural change
driven by forces that are common and pervasive, 13
exerting a powerful impact, 15
income or relative price effects explaining, 30
skill-biased, 179–84
sources of, 31
typical pattern of, 15–20

structural forces, decline in the share of manufacturing jobs, 1

structural shifts, variables explaining, 99–118

substitution
with computers for routine tasks, 184
elasticity, 25, 30
elasticity of, 180, 183, 193b
production function, 180n7

Sullivan, Jake (National Security Advisor), 253n56

superstar cities
attracting more high-skilled workers, 141
dominating employment in R&D-intensive industries, 245

income distribution in as U-shaped, 213
reaped economies of scale from agglomeration, 220
relaxing zoning restrictions in, 264
thriving in jobs requiring college degrees, 6

supply chains, 170, 206, 228

surplus economies
decline in the MES in, 63
versus deficit economies, 55–60
expenditure on and employment in services declining, 46
manufacturing employment as income rises will be hump-shaped, 42
manufacturing employment moving along a higher curve, 107
share of manufacturing employment (1960–2010), 39f

Sweden, manufacturing share of employment, 39f

Taft-Hartley Act in 1947, 205b

Tai, Katherine (US Trade Representative), 252

Taiwan, manufacturing share of employment, 39f

Taiwan Semiconductor Manufacturing Company Limited (TSMC), pivotal role played by, 228

Tanzania, manufacturing share of employment, 38f

tariffs, on tires, 171

tariff uncertainty, 166

tax and transfer programs, in the US, 256

tax base insurance, broad program offering, 263

tax credits, for firms building semiconductor plants, 236

tax incentives, how the private responds to, 237

tax revenue shocks, 263

technical skills, premiums compensating workers for, 198

technological advantage, loss of, 204b

technological capability, improving European manufacturing enterprises, 273–74

technological change
altering marginal products and changes in relative supplies, 180

not playing a large point in aggregate job loss, 172
not playing a role in the declining MOS curve, 124
versus other shocks to manufacturing employment, 215–16
outlook for as not entirely bleak, 7
parameters used to simulate, 109t
role in depressing employment, 143
role in the declining MES, 148
role of in the share of MVA production in GDP, 54
as a source of premature deindustrialization, 89–90
as a source of structural change meriting a special program, 258
yielding estimates of statistically significant hump-shaped MES curves in all groupings, 47
Trade Adjustment Assistance program, 253, 258, 259
trade and domestic demand, as sources of declining manufacturing labor demand, 44
trade and investment shocks, negative effects on output and employment, 127
trade balance(s)
changes in relating to manufacturing employment share, 66–69
declines in the manufacturing employment share (MES) with larger, 51–70
defined, 45
as an endogenous variable, 112
exploring changes in, 108
at the global level as positive and statistically significant, 47
impact on manufacturing employment shares, 108f
job content of, 162–64
trade balance and incomes, measured in nominal terms, 109
trade balance in manufacturing, 54, 63
trade barriers, reducing, 6
trade deficits and surpluses, manufacturing labor equivalence of US, 162
trade effects, 36, 124
trade flows, 146, 164–65

Trade in Value Added (TiVA), 53, 53n1, 54, 113
trade performance, 103–112
trade policies, Biden's, 251–53, 254
trade protection, improved competitiveness and, 279
trade shocks, 170n31, 208, 215–16
trade surplus economies, 63
trade surpluses, 35, 60, 61
trade variables, inclusion of, 91
trading, with China, 170
transfer problem, simplest version of, 45
transfers, providing more broadly based, 256
translation technologies, making cross-border cross-language interactions easier, 287
transportation infrastructure, 206, 271
trend decline, in the MES, 160
Trump, Donald, 6, 288
Trump administration, denying Chinese companies access to the latest semiconductor chips, 228
Trump safeguard tariff protection on US solar panels, renewed by Biden, 251–52
Trump's tariffs, reduced US employment, 252
2000, decade after characterized by two sharp recessions, 155

Ukraine, Russia's invasion of, 288
Ukraine war, 7, 227
unconditional convergence, 100
unemployed workers, providing with a menu of services, 271–72
unemployment, conditions of high and low in particular locations, 142
unemployment and wage rates, correlations in in local economies over time, 210
unemployment insurance, 257, 269
unemployment rates, impact on as relatively transitory, 207
unions, 4, 176, 205b
union wage rates, 236
United Auto Workers, 205b
United Kingdom
central government spending on R&D is highly concentrated geographically, 248

identification analysis for regional economies in, 271
innovation agency, Innovate UK, 276
manufacturing share of employment, 39f
R&D spending and local growth in, 268

United States
average growth in real GDP by decade (1950s–2010s), 145f
average trade deficit in MVA equal to 1.2 percent of GDP, 59b
as a case study of the historical relationship between manufacturing and inclusive growth, 8
central government spending on R&D is highly concentrated geographically, 248
continuing to underinvest in labor market policies, 271
crippled the WTO dispute settlement system, 252
detrimental effects on opportunities for less educated workers, 89
implemented subsidies for renewable energy investment and production, 284
manufacturing played a historic role in growth and income distribution in, 1
regional convergence and divergence, 140–41
rise and fall of inclusive growth in, 133–42
role of manufacturing employment in generating inclusive growth in, 131
sectoral employment shares in (1810–2020), 14f
sought to deny Chinese access to technologies with dual-use potential, 228
sources of demand for manufacturing, 59–60b
trade war with China started by Donald Trump, 288

United Steel Workers, 205b
Universal Displaced Worker (UDW) Program, 259n6
universal minimum basic income, 256–57

unskilled workers, migrating away from, 214
US Bureau of Economic Analysis (BEA), 243
US Bureau of Labor Statistics (BLS), 241
US Energy Information Administration, estimating IRA emissions reductions, 239–40
utility function, Stone-Geary function as, 23n10

value added
in manufacturing, 30, 54
per FTE employee in manufacturing, 163
per worker, increases in relative, 67
in producing goods and services, 29–30
using rather than gross trade and final expenditure data, 52–53

variables
explaining structural shifts, 99–118
interpreting the regression results after adding, 120–26
linking trade balance in manufacturing value added, 53–61
vehicle electrification, expected to generate demand for labor, 247b
Vernon product cycle theory, 202n2
Vietnam, replacing China in global supply chains, 7
von der Leyen, Ursula, 275
vulnerabilities, of low-carbon scenarios, 280

wage distribution, of men employed in manufacturing in the United States (1970 and 2015), 187f
wage earnings, time series data, 134n2
wage inequality, 177–78, 186
wage insurance program, 257n3
wage losses, compensation in the US, 257
wage-loss insurance, 9, 257, 272
wage premiums, for college-educated workers, 210
wages
polarization of, 138–39
responsibilities of, 180
wage subsidies, 258
Wales, voted for Brexit, 6

www.ingramcontent.com/pod-product-compliance
Ingram Content Group UK Ltd.
Pitfield, Milton Keynes, MK11 3LW, UK
UKHW020443150225
454998UK00004B/6